CW00832947

Wordsworth's reading 1770-1799 lists all of the authors and (where possible) books known to have been read by William Wordsworth from his childhood until his move to Dove Cottage in 1799 at the age of twenty-nine. This information is presented in an easy-to-use form - in alphabetical order by author - and includes dates of reading and full discussions of the evidence. It draws on analyses of Wordsworth's manuscripts contained in current and forthcoming scholarly editions of his works, and incorporates a great deal of original research into the poet's intellectual development, including studies of the libraries of John Wordsworth Sr (the poet's father), Hawkshead Grammar School, Racedown Lodge, and the Bristol Library Society. Where possible, surviving copies of Wordsworth's books are examined and described. This is the most complete study of Wordsworth's reading to date, and will be an essential reference tool for all scholars and students of his work.

Wordsworth's reading 1770-1799

Wordsworth's reading 1770-1799

DUNCAN WU

Postdoctoral Fellow of the British Academy
St Catherine's College, Oxford

To Constance Parrish,
with much love

Duncan

16. 6. 94

CAMBRIDGE
UNIVERSITY PRESS

Published by the Press Syndicate of the University of Cambridge
The Pitt Building, Trumpington Street, Cambridge CB2 1RP
40 West 20th Street, New York, NY 10011-4211, USA
10 Stamford Road, Oakleigh, Victoria 3166, Australia

First published 1993

Printed and bound in Great Britain by
Woolnough Bookbinding Ltd, Irthlingborough, Northamptonshire

A catalogue record for this book is available from the British Library

Library of Congress cataloguing in publication data

Wu, Duncan.
Wordsworth's reading, 1770-1799 / by Duncan Wu.
p.   cm.
Includes bibliographical references and index.
ISBN 0-521-41600-0 (hardback)
1. Wordsworth, William, 1770-1850 - Books and reading.
2. Wordsworth, William, 1770-1850 - Library - Catalogs.
3. Books and reading - England - History - 18th century. I. Title.
PR5892.B6W8 1993
821'.7 - dc20 92-17220 CIP

ISBN 0 521 41600 0 hardback

Contents

Preface

This book grew out of the desire to offer a corrective to the various misleading remarks made both by Wordsworth's contemporaries and by the poet himself about his reading. I was inspired also by the growing tendency in recent years to discuss his work in terms of external influences, particularly literary, philosophical, and political ones. The resulting volume aims to place within easy reach of the critic and scholar all the hard evidence for Wordsworth's reading up to 1799. I believe it to be the most complete record to have been made available up to now.

But it contains not merely the scholarly information available on the subject; there are occasions when the scholarly evidence, such as it is, is inextricably intertwined with critical conjecture or speculation. In these cases I have done my best to combine open-mindedness with rigour. Where I have reservations about the likelihood of a reading suggested by a critic or scholar, I have generally included it, and have expressed reservations in the entry. I have been as inclusive as I can in dealing with suggestions made by others.

That said, I am only too keenly aware that certainty is seldom possible in the subjects with which this book is concerned. My primary aim has been to present what I have learned during my years of research. For instance, I do not know whether Wordsworth actually did read the works of Marco Girolamo Vida in 1797-8 (note 248), but the evidence points that way, and I felt bound to present it to the reader.

My claim is not that Wordsworth read each of the books listed from cover to cover, but that he had access to them for a time, and sampled their contents. Many appear thanks to allusions, echoes, and other borrowings detectable in works by Wordsworth. That is not to say that I claim to present all literary borrowings in Wordsworth's poetry before 1800. However, as a co-editor of the forthcoming Longman *Selections from Wordsworth*, a work that aims to present as full an account as possible of his borrowings, I have had access to much new material concerning these, some of which appears below.

Allusions are not, admittedly, a consistently reliable form of evidence for readings. It does not follow that because Wordsworth alludes to a poem in a particular year, he also read it in that year. Authors such as Milton, Shakespeare and Spenser were often read long before they were mentioned, and quoted from memory. The situation is further complicated by the fact that Wordsworth had an extremely retentive memory for lesser-known writers; Hazlitt recalls that in 1803 he quoted St Pierre's *Paul et Virginie* (Howe xvii 115-16). I see little option but to record the borrowing or reference, so that this knowledge is at least made generally available.

This study takes 1799 as its terminal date, partly so that it may serve as a companion to Mark L. Reed's *Wordsworth: The Chronology of the Early Years 1770-1799* (1967). December 1799 also marks a natural break in Wordsworth's life. In that month he and Dorothy moved into Dove Cottage. With the *Two-Part Prelude* behind him, he was on the way (so he thought) to composing *The Recluse*. It was a new era: his domestic and artistic life changed, as did the range of books available to him. It made sense to break this study at the moment when Wordsworth gave up a nomadic existence for a settled one.

While researching this book I reconstructed the catalogues of libraries Wordsworth is known to have used, but lack of space has compelled me to issue two of them separately. Readers may find it helpful to consult these in conjunction with this volume; citations for 'The Hawkshead School Library in 1788: A Catalogue', and 'The Wordsworth Family Library at Cockermouth: Towards a Reconstruction', are given on page xvi. No attempt has been made here to document Wordsworth's readings of his own manuscripts or published works - properly the subject of another, quite different book. I have permitted myself the sole exception of *Lyrical Ballads* (1798), since it was co-authored by Coleridge.

A project such as this will never be complete, for our scholarly and critical understanding of this great poet is constantly growing. This volume aims, nevertheless, to provide the fullest account possible of the scholarship concerning Wordsworth's reading. I hope that its publication will stimulate further research, and that one day it will be possible to publish an updated, and even fuller account.

Acknowledgements

For permission to publish manuscripts and related materials, I am indebted to the Wordsworth Trust, Grasmere; the British Library; the Bristol Record Office; R. D. L. Brownson and the Hawkshead School Foundation; the Master, Fellows, and Scholars of St John's College, Cambridge; and the Pinney Family and the University of Bristol Archives.

I am grateful also to those librarians and archivists who have helped during my researches: George Mabey and Nicholas Lee, University of Bristol archive; Christopher Robinson, Keeper of the Theatre Collection, University of Bristol; Geoffrey Langley, Reference Librarian at the Bristol Central Library; Jim Grisenthwaite and the staff of the Record Office, Kendal; D. M. Bowcock and the staff of the Record Office, Carlisle; Clive Hirst, Alison Northover, and the staff of the Bodleian Library; Malcolm Underwood, archivist at St John's College, Cambridge; John West of the Hawkshead Grammar School Library; J. S. Williams, City Archivist, Bristol Record Office; and the staff of the Birkbeck College Library and Archive, London. Jeff Cowton of the Wordsworth Library, Grasmere, deserves particular thanks for his patience, dependability, and resourcefulness.

Scholars and friends have assisted me in numerous ways and it is a pleasure here to express my gratitude to them. The Wordsworth Summer Conference and Winter School in Grasmere, organized by Richard and Sylvia Wordsworth on behalf of The Wordsworth Trust, has enabled me to discuss Wordsworth's reading with many distinguished scholars and critics. Paul F. Betz, Richard W. Clancey, and Nicholas Roe provided me with a good deal of material, and offered advice and encouragement at every stage. Leslie F. Chard, II, made a number of suggestions, including crucial advice for the organization of this work, and Dr Robert S. Woof provided vital corrections and additional material. Mark L. Reed and Jared Curtis have been especially helpful in their responses to queries pertaining to books and manuscripts. I am particularly indebted to W. J. B. Owen, who read several versions of the list, provided corrections, new material, and much moral support. For generous aid of many kinds I wish to thank: James A. Butler, Stephen Gill, C. D. Landon, H. J. Jackson, Molly Lefebure, D. F. McKenzie, Richard Parish, Stephen M. Parrish, Don Poduska, Ian Reid, Richard S. Tomlinson, Nicola Trott, Mary Wedd, Pamela Woof, and Jonathan Wordsworth. Thanks are due to the anonymous readers of the Cambridge University Press for their advice and suggestions, and to my editor, Kevin Taylor, for his belief in this work, and the will to see it into print.

My greatest debt is to the British Academy: this book would have been neither completed nor published were it not for the postdoctoral Fellowship which I hold in their name at St Catherine's College, Oxford. I wish to acknowledge the work of those scholars currently in the field, and to record my continuing appreciation of the labours of John Livingston Lowes, George Whalley, Chester L. Shaver, and John Finch.

This book is dedicated to my parents.

DUNCAN WU
Oxford, 1992

Abbreviations

Album	*Poems and Extracts Chosen by William Wordsworth for an Album Presented to Lady Mary Lowther, Christmas, 1819* (1905)
Averill	*Wordsworth and the Poetry of Human Suffering*, by James H. Averill (1980)
Betz	'The Elegiac Mode in the Poetry of William Wordsworth', by Paul F. Betz (Ph.D. thesis, 1965)
Bicknell	*The Picturesque Scenery of the Lake District*, by Peter Bicknell (1990)
BLS	*A Catalogue of the Books Belonging to the Bristol Library Society*, by Revd. Thomas Johnes (1798)
BNYPL	*Bulletin of the New York Public Library*
BRH	*Bulletin of Research in the Humanities*
BWS	*Bicentenary Wordsworth Studies*, ed. Jonathan Wordsworth (1970)
Butcher	*The Poetics of Aristotle*, ed. and tr. S. H. Butcher (1911)
Butler *ELN*	Review of Chester L. and Alice C. Shaver, *Wordsworth's Library* (1979), by James A. Butler, *ELN* 18 (1981) 301-4
Butler *JEGP*	'Wordsworth, Cottle, and the *Lyrical Ballads*: Five Letters, 1797-1800', by James A. Butler, *JEGP* 75 (1976) 139-53
Butler *WC*	'Wordsworth in Philadelphia Area Libraries, 1787-1850', by James A. Butler, *WC* 4 (1973) 41-64
C	Samuel Taylor Coleridge
CC	*Collected Coleridge Series*, Bollingen Series 75
CC *Biographia*	*Biographia Literaria*, ed. James Engell and Walter Jackson Bate (2 vols., 1983)
CC *Essays*	*Essays on his Times*, ed. David Erdman (3 vols., 1978)
CC *Friend*	*The Friend*, ed. Barbara Rooke (2 vols., 1969)
CC *Lectures 1795*	*Lectures 1795 On Politics and Religion*, ed. Lewis Patton and Peter Mann (1971)
CC *Literature*	*Lectures 1808-1819 On Literature*, ed. R. A. Foakes (2 vols., 1987)
CC *Marginalia*	*The Marginalia*, ed. George Whalley and H. J. Jackson (5 vols., 1980-)
CC *Watchman*	*The Watchman*, ed. Lewis Patton (1970)
Chandler	*Wordsworth's Second Nature: A Study of the Poetry and Politics*, by James K. Chandler (1984)
Chard	*Dissenting Republican: Wordsworth's Early Life and Thought in Their Political Context*, by Leslie F. Chard, II (1972)
Chard *BNYPL*	'Joseph Johnson: Father of the Book Trade', by Leslie F. Chard, II, *BNYPL* 79 (1975) 51-82
CLB	*Charles Lamb Bulletin*
Coffman	*Coleridge's Library: A Bibliography of Books Owned or Read by Samuel Taylor Coleridge*, by Ralph J. Coffman (1987)
Cornell *B*	*The Borderers*, ed. Robert Osborn (1982)

Cornell *DS*	*Descriptive Sketches*, ed. Eric Birdsall (1984)
Cornell *EW*	*An Evening Walk*, ed. James Averill (1984)
Cornell *13-Book Prelude*	*The Thirteen-Book Prelude*, ed. Mark L. Reed (2 vols., 1991)
Cornell *14-Book Prelude*	*The Fourteen-Book Prelude*, ed. W. J. B. Owen (1985)
Cornell *PB*	*Peter Bell*, ed. John E. Jordan (1985)
Cornell *Poems 1800-1807*	*Poems in Two Volumes, and Other Poems, 1800-1807*, ed. Jared Curtis (1985)
Cornell *Poems 1807-1820*	*Shorter Poems, 1807-1820*, ed. Carl H. Ketcham (1989)
Cornell *Prelude 1798-9*	*The Prelude 1798-1799*, ed. Stephen Parrish (1977)
Cornell *RC*	*The Ruined Cottage and The Pedlar*, ed. James Butler (1979)
Cornell *SP*	*The Salisbury Plain Poems*, ed. Stephen Gill (1975)
Curry	*New Letters of Robert Southey*, ed. Kenneth Curry (2 vols., 1965)
D.C.MS	Dove Cottage MS, at the Wordsworth Library, Grasmere
Dendurent	'The Coleridge Collection in Victoria University Library, Toronto', by H. O. Dendurent, *WC* 5 (1974) 225-86
DW	Dorothy Wordsworth
DWJ	*Journals of Dorothy Wordsworth*, ed. Ernest De Selincourt (2 vols., 1951)
EHC	*The Poetical Works of Samuel Taylor Coleridge*, ed. E. H. Coleridge (2 vols., 1912)
ELN	*English Language Notes*
Erdman	*Commerce des Lumières: John Oswald and the British in Paris, 1790-1793*, by David V. Erdman (1986)
Erdman *BNYPL*	'Immoral Acts of a Library Cormorant: the Extent of Coleridge's Contributions to the *Critical Review*', by David V. Erdman, *BNYPL* 63 (1959) 433-54, 515-30, 575-87
EY	*Letters of William and Dorothy Wordsworth: The Early Years, 1787-1805*, ed. Ernest De Selincourt, rev. Chester L. Shaver (1967)
Fink	*The Early Wordsworthian Milieu*, by Zera S. Fink (1967)
Gilchrist and Murray	*The Press in the French Revolution*, by J. Gilchrist and W. J. Murray (1971)
Gill	*William Wordsworth: A Life*, by Stephen Gill (1989)
Gill Diary	Diary of Joseph Gill, caretaker at Racedown, in Papers of the Pinney family, on deposit in the Bristol University Library
Grasmere Journals	*The Grasmere Journals*, ed. Pamela Woof (1991)
Graver	'Wordsworth's Translations from Latin Poetry', by Bruce Edward Graver (Ph.D. thesis, 1983)
Griggs	*The Letters of Samuel Taylor Coleridge*, ed. E. L. Griggs (6 vols., 1956-71)
Grosart	*The Prose Works of William Wordsworth*, ed. Revd. Alexander B. Grosart (3 vols., 1876)
Healey	*The Cornell Wordsworth Collection*, by George Healey (1957)
Howe	*The Works of William Hazlitt*, ed. P. P. Howe (21 vols., 1930-4)

Hunt	'Wordsworth's Marginalia in Dove Cottage, to 1800: A Study of his Relationship to Charlotte Smith and Milton', by Bishop C. Hunt, Jr (B.Litt. thesis, 1965)
Jacobus	*Tradition and Experiment in Wordsworth's Lyrical Ballads, 1798*, by Mary Jacobus (1976)
JEGP	*Journal of English and Germanic Philology*
JW Sr	John Wordsworth Sr (Wordsworth's father)
Landon	'A Survey of an Early Manuscript of Wordsworth, Dove Cottage, MS 4, Dating from his School Days, and of Other Related Manuscripts, Together with an Edition of Selected Pieces', by C. D. Landon (Ph.D. thesis, 1962)
Landon (1970)	'Some Sidelights on *The Prelude*', by C. D. Landon, *BWS* 359-76
Legouis	*The Early Life of William Wordsworth: 1770-1798*, by Emile Legouis, tr. J. W. Matthews (1921)
Lienemann	*Die Belesenheit von William Wordsworth*, by Kurt Lienemann (1908)
Lonsdale	*The Poems of Thomas Gray, William Collins, Oliver Goldsmith*, ed. Roger Lonsdale (1969)
Love Letters	*The Love Letters of William and Mary Wordsworth*, ed. Beth Darlington (1981)
Lowes	*The Road to Xanadu*, by John Livingstone Lowes (2nd edn, 1930)
Lucas	*The Letters of Charles Lamb and Mary Lamb 1796-1843*, ed. E. V. Lucas (3 vols., 1935)
LY	*The Letters of William and Dorothy Wordsworth: The Later Years*, ed. Ernest De Selincourt, *i: 1821-8*, rev. Alan G. Hill (1978); *ii: 1829-34*, rev. Alan G. Hill (1982); *iii: 1835-9*, rev. Alan G. Hill (1982); *iv: 1840-53*, rev. by Alan G. Hill (1988)
Lyon	*The Excursion: A Study*, by Judson Stanley Lyon (1950)
Marrs	*The Letters of Charles and Mary Anne Lamb 1796-1817*, ed. Edwin J. Marrs (3 vols., 1975-8)
Mason *LB*	*Lyrical Ballads*, ed. Michael Mason (1992)
Masson	*The Collected Writings of Thomas De Quincey*, ed. David Masson (14 vols., 1889-90)
Memoirs	*Memoirs of William Wordsworth*, by Christopher Wordsworth (2 vols., 1851)
MH	*The Music of Humanity: A Critical Study of Wordsworth's 'Ruined Cottage'*, by Jonathan Wordsworth (1968)
MLN	*Modern Language Notes*
Moorman	*William Wordsworth: A Biography; The Early Years*, by Mary Moorman (1957)
Morley	*Henry Crabb Robinson on Books and Their Writers*, ed. Edith J. Morley (3 vols., 1938)
Muirhead	'A Day with Wordsworth', by James Patrick Muirhead, *Blackwood's Magazine* 221 (1927) 728-43

MY	*The Letters of William and Dorothy Wordsworth: The Middle Years*, ed. Ernest De Selincourt, *i: 1806-11*, rev. Mary Moorman (1969); *ii: 1812-20*, rev. Mary Moorman and Alan G. Hill (1970)
N&Q	*Notes and Queries*
Nethercot	*The Road to Tryermaine*, by A. H. Nethercot (1939)
Newlyn	*Coleridge, Wordsworth, and the Language of Allusion*, by Lucy Newlyn (1986)
Notebooks	*The Notebooks of Samuel Taylor Coleridge*, ed. Kathleen Coburn (1957-)
Owen LB	*Wordsworth & Coleridge: Lyrical Ballads 1798* ed. W. J. B. Owen (2nd edn, 1969)
Park	*Sales Catalogues of Libraries of Eminent Persons: Poets and Men of Letters* Vol. 9: *Wordsworth, Southey, Moore, Barton, Haydon*, ed. Roy Park (1974)
Parrish	*The Art of the Lyrical Ballads*, by Stephen Maxfield Parrish (1973)
Patton	*The Amherst Wordsworth Collection*, by Cornelius Howard Patton (1936)
PMLA	*Publications of the Modern Language Association of America*
Potts	*Wordsworth's Prelude: A Study of Its Literary Form*, by Abbie Findlay Potts (1953)
Prose Works	*The Prose Works of William Wordsworth*, ed. W. J. B. Owen and Jane Worthington Smyser (3 vols., 1974)
PW	*The Poetical Works of William Wordsworth*, ed. Ernest De Selincourt and Helen Darbishire (5 vols., 1940-9)
Recollections	*Early Recollections, Chiefly Relating to the Late Samuel Taylor Coleridge, During his Long Residence in Bristol*, by Joseph Cottle (2 vols., 1837)
Reed i	*Wordsworth: The Chronology of the Early Years, 1770-1799*, by Mark L. Reed (1967)
Reed ii	*Wordsworth: The Chronology of the Middle Years, 1800-1815*, by Mark L. Reed (1975)
Reed PBSA	'Wordsworth on Wordsworth and Much Else: New Conversational Memoranda', by Mark L. Reed, *Papers of the Bibliographical Society of America* 81 (1987) 451-8
RES	*Review of English Studies*
Robberds	*A Memoir of the Life and Writings of the Late William Taylor of Norwich*, compiled and ed. J. W. Robberds (2 vols., 1843)
Roe	*Wordsworth and Coleridge: The Radical Years*, by Nicholas Roe (1988)
RW	Richard Wordsworth
Sadler	*Diary, Reminiscences and Correspondence of Henry Crabb Robinson*, ed. Thomas Sadler (3 vols., 1869)

List of abbreviations

Sadleir	*Archdeacon Francis Wrangham 1769-1842*, by Michael Sadleir, Supplement 12 to *The Library* (1937)
Sandford	*Thomas Poole and his Friends*, by Mrs Henry Sandford (2 vols., 1888)
Schneider	*Wordsworth's Cambridge Education*, by Ben Ross Schneider (1957)
Shaver	*Wordsworth's Library: A Catalogue*, by Chester L. and Alice C. Shaver (1979)
Sheats	*The Making of Wordsworth's Poetry, 1785-1798*, by Paul Sheats (1973)
SIB	*Studies in Bibliography*
Simmons	*Southey*, by Jack Simmons (1945)
Stein	*Wordsworth's Art of Allusion*, by Edwin Stein (1988)
Table Talk of Rogers	*Recollections of the Table-Talk of Samuel Rogers*, ed. Revd. Alexander Dyce (1856)
TLS	*Times Literary Supplement*
Trott	'Wordsworth's Revisionary Reading', by Nicola Trott (D.Phil. thesis, 1990)
TWT	*Wordsworth's Hawkshead*, by T. W. Thompson, ed. Robert Woof (1970)
W	William Wordsworth
WC	*The Wordsworth Circle*
Whalley	'The Bristol Library Borrowings of Southey and Coleridge, 1793-8', by George Whalley, *The Library* 4 (1949) 114-32
Woof Ph.D.	'The Literary Relations of Wordsworth and Coleridge, 1795-1803: Five Studies', by Robert S. Woof (Ph.D. thesis, 1959)
Woof *SIB*	'Wordsworth's Poetry and Stuart's Newspapers: 1797-1803', by Robert Woof, *SIB* 15 (1962) 149-89
Woof *BWS*	'Wordsworth and Coleridge: Some Early Matters', by Robert Woof, *BWS* 76-91
Wrangham	*The English Portion of the Library of the Ven. Francis Wrangham, M.A., F.R.S., Archdeacon of Cleveland*, by Francis Wrangham (1826)
Wu D.Phil.	'A Chronological Annotated Edition of Wordsworth's Poetry and Prose 1785-1790', by Duncan Wu (D.Phil. thesis, 1990)
Wu *CWAAS*	'The Hawkshead School Library in 1788: A Catalogue', by Duncan Wu, *Transactions of the Cumberland and Westmorland Antiquarian and Archaeological Society* 91 (1991) 173-97
Wu *Library*	'The Wordsworth Family Library at Cockermouth: Towards a Reconstruction', by Duncan Wu, *The Library* 14 (1992) 127-35

Dates of readings

The most problematic part of this list has been assigning dates of reading. For some entries a particular dating is demanded by the evidence, but the majority are difficult to place with certainty and the datings offered here should be regarded only as a general guide. Nor should they be taken to imply that Wordsworth read a particular book at that moment, straight through. Like most of us, he did not always finish a book he started, nor did he always read it in one sitting. Readings may have spanned months, even years. Wordsworth's copies of Gilpin's *Observations on the Lakes* and *Observations on the Highlands* followed him from London to Racedown, on to Alfoxden, and finally back to London again, and it is impossible to know how many times he reread them (if at all). It is my task not to catalogue those books in Wordsworth's possession but to list his readings, so that Gilpin's *Observations* are not entered in each section during the years they are known to have followed him around the world, but appear only when the evidence points towards a reading.

A note on texts

Wherever possible, poetry, manuscript material, and Fenwick Notes by Wordsworth are quoted from the texts and transcriptions provided by the Cornell Wordsworth Series. Otherwise, poetry and Fenwick Notes are quoted from *PW*. Prose is taken from *Prose Works*.

In the case of poems composed 1785-90, some of which remain unpublished, I quote directly from the manuscripts concerned; references to *The Vale of Esthwaite* provide the corresponding line numbers in De Selincourt's text (*PW* i 270-83). For example, '*D.C.MS 3* 6v; De Selincourt 67-8' = lines quoted from *D.C.MS 3*, 6 verso, corresponding with *Vale of Esthwaite* 67-8 in *PW*.

In the citations the place of publication may be assumed to be London unless otherwise stated; all italics are mine unless otherwise stated, and all material within square brackets is editorial.

In the list, dates within square brackets are those of the first edition; the fact that they are within square brackets indicates that we do not know whether Wordsworth used that edition or not. Dates within round brackets are those of the edition Wordsworth is believed to have read, as in *The Dramatick Works of Philip Massinger ... with notes critical and explanatory by John Monck Mason* (4 vols., 1779). *Common Sense* [1776] is the title of a work read by Wordsworth, followed by the date of its first publication; we do not know whether he read that edition or not.

Wordsworth's reading 1770-1799

1. Addison, Joseph, *Cato*
Suggested date of reading: by 1791
References: Cornell *DS* 40
In *Descriptive Sketches* W alludes to Syphax's description of an African who 'Blesses his stars, and thinks it luxury' (*Cato* I iv 71).

2. Aikin, John and Anna Laetitia Aikin, *Miscellaneous Pieces in Prose* (1773)
Suggested date of reading: by spring 1787
References: see note
Miscellaneous Pieces contains a Gothic prose fragment called *Sir Bertrand* from which W borrowed several details for one of the central episodes in *The Vale of Esthwaite*, composed during the spring and summer of 1787 (lines 210-21 in De Selincourt's text). The episode begins:

> I the while
> Look'd through the tall and sable isle
> Of Firs that too a mansion led
> With many a turret on it's head (*D.C.MS 3* 18r; De Selincourt 210-13)

Although W may be thinking of the castellated and partly ruined Calgarth Hall on the eastern shore of Windermere, the description probably borrows from *Sir Bertrand*: 'by momentary glimpse of moon-light he had a full view of a large antique mansion, with turrets at the corners' (*Miscellaneous Pieces* 129).

3. Akenside, Mark
(i) *The Poems of Mark Akenside* [1772]
Suggested date of reading: 1779-87; by spring 1785
References: see note
W's earliest surviving poem, *Lines Written as a School Exercise* (1785), contains a reference to 'fair majestic truth' (line 12). Akenside's invocations at the beginning of *The Pleasures of Imagination* include one to 'The guide, the guardian of their lovely sports, / Majestic Truth' (i 22-3). Borrowings from this and other poems by Akenside can be found throughout W's juvenile verse; for instance, Landon 225 finds a borrowing from Akenside's *Ode to Lyric Poetry* in W's *Anacreon Imitated* (1786); see also Landon 232. This indicates that W was reading Akenside's *Poems* by the mid-1780s.

(ii) *The Pleasures of the Imagination*
Suggested date of reading: 1793-4; spring 1794
References: see note
In the 1794 *Evening Walk*, W describes being 'guided by some hand unseen' (line 33), echoing Akenside's *The Pleasures of the Imagination* (1770):

> I wander'd through your calm recesses, led
> In silence by *some powerful hand unseen*. (iv 44-5)

Sheats 101 proposes a possible allusion in *Descriptive Sketches*, and Jump, '"That Other Eye": Wordsworth's 1794 Revisions of *An Evening Walk*', *WC* 17 (1986) 156-63, states the case for a 1793-4 reading.

1

(iii) *The Pleasures of Imagination* **with an essay by Mrs Barbauld (1794)**
Suggested date of reading: 18 Aug. 1795 onwards
References: EY 151
In her letter of 2 and 3 Sept. 1795, DW told Mrs John Marshall how William Rawson, the Halifax merchant and husband of her distant 'Aunt' Threlkeld, bought this book for her, together with a copy of Rogers' *The Pleasures of Memory* (*EY* 151). Although the Rogers survives at the Wordsworth Library, the whereabouts of the Akenside is unknown; it is not bound up with the Rogers, as claimed by Pamela Woof (*Grasmere Journals* 176). The Rogers contains a presentation inscription: 'D Wordsworth / The Gift of M^r. W^m. Rawson / August 18.th 1795'. This gives us a date for these gifts, and indicates that W would have had copies of Akenside and Rogers within easy reach from that time onwards.

(iv) *Works*
Suggested date of reading: 1798
References: Jacobus 51-8, 111-12
Jacobus argues that the ideas in Akenside were 'peculiarly relevant to the Wordsworth of 1798' (p. 53). In particular, she points out similarities between *The Pleasures of the Imagination* and *Tintern Abbey* (pp. 111-12). This is supported by Owen, who finds that W's phrase, 'The guide, the guardian of my heart' (*Tintern Abbey* 111), echoes Akenside's invocation at the beginning of *The Pleasures of Imagination* to 'The guide, the guardian of their lovely sports, / Majestic Truth' (i 22-3). This invocation was evidently a favourite of W's, since it is echoed also at *Thirteen-Book Prelude* v 377; see also note 3 (i).

4. Allott, Robert, *England's Parnassus* **(1600)**
Suggested date of reading: 1790
References: Cornell Library Journal 1 (1966) 28-39; Shaver 7
Curtis, 'Wordsworth and Earlier English Poetry', *Cornell Library Journal* 1 (1966) 28-39, p. 34, finds that a copy of *England's Parnassus* (1600), now at the Folger Shakespeare Library, Washington, D.C., contains W's signature, dated 1790. Clancey, who inspected the volume in autumn 1989, tells me that the signature 'has a very sharp "Wm" and then follows in somewhat weaker script "Wordsworth 1790"... This volume is a newly bound book with the binder's identification and nineteenth-century date on a pasted slip in the back cover. It contains Wordsworth's signature on the title-page and, as nearly as I could determine, not another mark in the entire volume' (letter to me). *England's Parnassus* is a dictionary of over 2,000 poetical quotations grouped under subject headings. The poets most frequently represented are Spenser, Drayton, William Warner, Lodge, Daniel, Sir John Harington, Joshua Sylvester, Shakespeare, Chapman, Sidney, Marlowe, and Jonson.

5. Anacreon
(i) *Odes*
Suggested date of reading: by 7 Aug. 1786
References: PW i 366; Reed i 17; Shaver 8
The MS draft of W's imitation of Anacreon is dated 'Hawkshead August 7th 1786' (*D.C.MS 4* ff.1-2; see *PW* i 261-2). Besides displaying his competence as a translator, W successfully adapts the poem to his own time. It was a bold stroke, though not a wholly original one; William Combe had attempted the same thing in his *Poetical Epistle to Sir Joshua Reynolds*

(1777), which begins as an adaptation of Anacreon where, as in W, the 'best of painters' is Reynolds. I find no positive evidence, however, that W read Combe.

(ii) *Ode XXVIII* tr. James Sterling

Suggested date of reading: by 7 Aug. 1786
References: see note

When imitating Anacreon in Aug. 1786 W used Sterling's translation as a crib. The original Greek text is addressed to the 'best of painters', who is instructed how to paint the poet's mistress. At one point, directions are given for the portrayal of her eyebrows: 'neither divide, nor mingle, for me, the eyebrows; but let the portrait have them as she has - imperceptibly uniting'. W renders this:

> *Nicely bend* the living line
> Black and delicately fine
> As you paint her *sable brows*
> Arch'd like two ætherial bows.   (lines 17-20)

The words in italics have no equivalent in the Greek original, and derive from Sterling's translation:

> With Care the *sable Brows* extend,
> And in two Arches *nicely bend* ...   (lines 15-16)

I have found other borrowings; see Wu D.Phil. 34-6.

   Sterling's translation was first published in *The Guardian* 168 (23 Sept. 1713), edited by Richard Steele, and reprinted in John Addison's *The Works of Anacreon* (1735), pp. 99-103, and Francis Fawkes' *The Works of Anacreon, Sappho, Bion, Moschus and Musæus* (1760), pp. 69-72. It did not appear in Sterling's *Poetical Works* (Dublin, 1734), nor in his *Loves of Hero and Leander from the Greek of Musæus* (Dublin, 1728) - both of which do however contain other translations by Sterling from Anacreon, pp. 39-62.

6. Analytical Review

(i)

Suggested date of reading: by Nov. 1791
References: Chard *BNYPL* 66-7

It was during the first five months of 1791, when W was in London, that he probably met Samuel Nicholson, a Unitarian and member of the radical Society for Constitutional Information.[1] Nicholson apparently introduced him to Joseph Johnson, who had co-founded the *Analytical* with Thomas Christie in May 1788, and who was to publish *An Evening Walk* and *Descriptive Sketches* two years later.[2] Given W's presence in London in 1791, and acquaintance with Johnson, it is likely that he knew of, and read, the *Analytical* at that time. If he did not read it then, he would have done so soon after.

---

   [1] Although Reed supposes this acquaintance to have taken place during 1792-3 (Reed i 138), most scholars and biographers seem now to follow Chard in dating it 1791 (Chard 55-6; see also Roe 24 and Gill 54-5).
   [2] As implied by Roe 27: '[Nicholson] was almost certainly acquainted with the liberal publisher and unitarian Joseph Johnson, which might account for Johnson's publication of "An Evening Walk" and "Descriptive Sketches" in 1793'.

3

The *Analytical* was a distinguished periodical and continued to publish for the next eleven years; according to Chard, it was

> never particularly strident and certainly not radical. It gave very qualified praise to the works of Paine, for example, and refused to endorse the more extreme ideas that certain radicals were then enunciating. But it was more militant and progressive than Johnson's earlier periodicals; above all, it was more varied in its contents. Particularly worth noting is the presence in it of analyses and translations of numerous literary and philosophical works then appearing in Germany. (Chard *BNYPL* 67)

(ii) March 1793
Suggested date of reading: c. April 1793
References: Reed i 141
W must have read the generally favourable review of *An Evening Walk* and *Descriptive Sketches* in the *Analytical* for March 1793, reprinted Cornell *DS* 299, Cornell *EW* 303.

(iii) June 1792
Suggested date of reading: Sept. 1798
References: *Prose Works* i 97; *EY* 246n
Shaver points out that 'Some time between 23 and 27 Sept [1798] W borrowed from Remnant a copy of the *Analytical Review* which he wished to show to Klopstock because it contained some specimens of a blank verse translation of his *Messiah*' (*EY* 246n). In the issue for June 1792, a review of Richard Cumberland's *Calvary* (1792) 'concludes (pp. 130-8) with specimens of a translation, presumably by the reviewer ("R.R."), in Miltonic blank verse, corresponding to *Der Messias* (1748) ii 427-736 and iv 110-71' (*Prose Works* i 97).

When W first read the translation is another matter. A probable explanation is as follows: in the first half of Sept., immediately before embarking on his 1798 German tour, he stopped off in London and met his old friend Joseph Johnson at least three times (Reed i 247). At one of these meetings he told Johnson of his impending visit to Klopstock, and Johnson showed him the translation of Klopstock's *Messias* in his own periodical, the *Analytical*. Thus, when the subject of translations came up in Hamburg, W knew where to find one. William Remnant, Johnson's agent in Hamburg, would have had back numbers of the *Analytical* at hand.

(iv) Dec. 1798
Suggested date of reading: 1799
References: Reed i 261-2
W would probably have sought out the review of *Lyrical Ballads* that appeared in the journal published by his friend, Joseph Johnson.

7. Anderson, Robert, *The Works of the British Poets. With Prefaces, Biographical and Critical, by Robert Anderson* (13 vols., London and Edinburgh, 1792-5)
Suggested date of reading: 16 July 1797 onwards
References: Reed ii 202-3 and n; Shaver 8-9
C had acquired his set of Anderson's *British Poets* by April 1796 (*Notebooks* i 84); this is now at the Folger Shakespeare Library (Coffman A56), and is described CC *Marginalia* i 37. It would have been available to W from the time he moved into Alfoxden, 16 July 1797 (Reed i 201).

W acquired his own set only in 1800, when one was presented to him by his brother John.[1] This is now at the Wordsworth Library. Vol. 1 bears the title-page inscription, 'Wm Wordsworth from his dear Brother John'.

8. 'annals of the department'

Suggested date of reading: 1791-2
References: *EY* 77
W's letter to Mathews of 19 May 1792 mentions that

> in London you have perhaps a better opportunity of being informed of the general concerns of france, than in a petty provincial town in the heart of the kingd[om] itself. The annals of the department are all with which I have a better opportunity of being acquainted than you, provided you feel sufficient interest in informing yourself.
>
> (*EY* 77)

W was evidently reading his local newspaper, the 'annals of the department', during his stay in France, 1791-2. In fact, 1792 saw an explosion in regional newspaper production in France; Kennedy points out that

> A *Journal du département de Loir-et-Cher* was launched about March 2 [1792] with the backing of the Blois society and apparently lasted a few weeks. About the same date, three clubbists of Nantes established the *Courrier du département de la Loire-Inférieure* and put out at least seventeen numbers.[2]

It is difficult to say with certainty which of these W meant by the phrase, 'annals of the department'. The *Journal du département de Loir-et-Cher* seems the most likely, for it would have been newly available when W wrote to Mathews. W may also have known the regional *Annales Orléanoises*, published in eight volumes, 15 Dec. 1789-31 Dec. 1791, 'trois fois par semaine'.[3]

9. *Annual Anthology* (Bristol, 1799)

Suggested date of reading: Aug. 1799; by 2 Sept. 1799
References: Butler *JEGP* 149-50
On 27 July 1799 W thanked Cottle for the book parcel sent earlier that month, and looked forward to the next: 'We shall be very glad to receive your volume of original Poetry' (Butler *JEGP* 149). The 'volume of original Poetry' was *The Annual Anthology* ed. Southey, published by Cottle. W received a copy in Aug., and discussed it in his letter to Cottle of 2 Sept.: 'Your poem of the Killcrop we liked better than any ... The poem we liked next was Charles Lloyds verses to a young man' (Butler *JEGP* 150). I suspect that W is being charitable; Cottle's *The Killcrop*[4] is characterized by its hysterical, ham Gothicism.

---

[1] See Cornell *Poems 1807-1820* 527.

[2] *The Jacobin Clubs in the French Revolution: The Middle Years* (Princeton, 1988), p. 193.

[3] See André Martin and Gérard Walter, *Catalogue de l'histoire de la Révolution Française*, Vol. 5: *Ecrits de la période révolutionnaire: journaux et almanachs* (Paris, 1943), p. 115.

[4] The poem was published anonymously, and was formerly attributed to Southey; it appears, for instance, in the Galignani edition of his works (Paris, 1829), pp. 715-17.

The idea of the *Annual Anthology* was suggested by William Taylor in his letter to Southey of 26 Sept. 1798:

> I wonder some one of our poets does not undertake what the French and Germans so long supported in great popularity - an Almanack of the Muses - an annual Anthology of minor poems - too unimportant to subsist apart, and too neat to be sacrificed with the ephemeral victims of oblivion. Schiller is the editor of one, and Voss of another such poetical calendar in Germany; their names operate as a pledge that no sheer trash shall be admitted. (Robberds i 228)

Taylor was the anonymous author of *A Topographical Ode*, with which the anthology opens. Southey refers to the 'Almanack of the Muses' in his 'Advertisement' to the volume, and although his name does not appear on the title-page as a pledge that no 'sheer trash' be included, most of its readers were aware of its editor's identity. The volume contains poems by Coleridge, Lloyd, Southey, Davy, Lamb, Lovell, Beddoes, Dyer, and Amos Cottle.

10. *Annual Register* 26 (1783)
Suggested date of reading: between 1783 and 1787; by 1787
References: LY ii 691
In Feb. 1834, W remembered having first read Crabbe in the *Annual Register* during the 1780s; there he also read Beattie's 'Illustrations on Sublimity'. See notes 21 (i) and 68.

11. *The Arabian Nights*, also known as *The Thousand and One Nights*
Suggested date of reading: before 1779; 1779-87
References: Thirteen-Book Prelude v 482-500
In the *Prelude* W recalls that, as a boy, he owned a 'yellow canvass-cover'd' copy of *The Arabian Nights*, and that when he arrived at Hawkshead he saved up for another in which 'there were four large Volumes, laden all / With kindred matter' (*Thirteen-Book Prelude* v 482-91). This was probably *Arabian Nights Entertainments: consisting of One Thousand and One Stories... Translated into French from the Arabian MSS. by M. Galland of the Royal Academy; and now done into English from the last Paris Edition*, a four-volume set published first in Manchester, 1777, and frequently thereafter.

12. Ardabîlî, Ahmad, *A Series of Poems, Containing the Plaints, Consolations and Delights of Achmed Ardebeili, a Persian Exile. With Notes Historical and Explanatory, by Charles Fox* (Bristol, 1797)
Suggested date of reading: June 1797 onwards
References: Reed i 275; Griggs i 325; N&Q NS 37 (1990) 412
On 8 June 1797 C told Cottle that W 'has received Fox's Achmed - he returns you his acknowledgements & presents his kindliest respects to you' (Griggs i 325); C probably brought the volume on his visit to Racedown. Its influence on W is discussed in my article, 'Wordsworth's Reading of Ahmad Ardabîlî', *N&Q* NS 37 (1990) 412. W's copy of Ardabîlî's *Poems* appears not to have entered the Rydal Mount library, though C's did (Shaver 313).

13. Ariosto, Ludovico
(i) *Orlando Furioso*
Suggested date of reading: 1788-90; by 1790
References: Schneider 103, 275-6; Shaver 11
Agostino Isola, W's Italian tutor at Cambridge, edited both Ariosto (1789) and Tasso (1786), and under his tutelage W would have read both. W's pocket Ariosto is now in the Wordsworth Library, Grasmere (Shaver 11). It is described on the title-page as 'My Companion in the Alps with Jones. W. Wordsworth'. The title-page is initialled 'W.W.' and 'D.W.', suggesting that Dorothy used it when learning Italian at Racedown. On the last leaf W records that 'I carried this Book with me in my pedestrian Tour in the Alps with Jones. W. Wordsworth'.

Owen reminds me that in the *Thirteen-Book Prelude*, W remembered how, in Blois in 1792, he enjoyed 'earnest dialogues' with Michel Beaupuy, during which he 'slipp'd in thought' into reveries inspired by the writings of Tasso and Ariosto (ix 445-56).

(ii) *Orlando Furioso*
Suggested date of reading: late May 1794 onwards
References: *EY* 121n
W left a number of books with his brother Richard at Staple Inn, London, in 1793. These included copies of Tasso, Ariosto, and an 'Italian Gram.' (*EY* 121n). Richard forwarded them to W in late May 1794, and W would have received them by probably the end of the month. Since DW seems not to have begun reading Ariosto until March 1796 (see next note), W probably wanted the volume for his own reading. This would have been his pocket Ariosto, acquired at Cambridge, now at the Wordsworth Library (see preceding note).

(iii) *Orlando Furioso*
Suggested date of reading: 20 March 1796 onwards
References: *EY* 170; Woof Ph.D. 89
'My Sister would be very glad of your assistance in her Italian studies', W wrote to Mathews on 21 March 1796, 'She has already gone through half of Davila, and yesterday we began Ariosto' (*EY* 170). W's deference suggests that Mathews was the 'better Italian scholar' at Cambridge recalled in 1846 (Grosart iii 456).

Woof suggests that W's meditations on the character of Orlando influenced his portrayal of Rivers in *The Borderers*:

> Both Orlando and Cardenio were examples of men who were in rebellion against their world. But where these were betrayed in love, Rivers has been betrayed in honour. All three men believe that they have a right to love and to honour, as the case may be, and that without it, they have a right to destroy. (Woof Ph.D. 89)

14. Aristophanes, comedies
Suggested date of reading: by 27 Feb. 1799
References: *EY* 255
W refers to Aristophanes in his letter to C of 27 Feb. 1799. Quite possibly he had read Aristophanes as an undergraduate. There was a copy of *Aristophanis comœdiœ duœ, Plutus & Nubes* (1695) at the Rydal Mount library (Shaver 11).

15. *Arthurian Legends*
Suggested date of reading: 1773-9
References: *LY* i 402
In a letter to Allan Cunningham, 23 Nov. 1825, W suggests that, like most children of his time, he read the Arthurian legends as a child:

> Tear me not from the Country of Chaucer, Spencer, Shakespeare and Milton; yet I own that since the days of childhood, when I became familiar with the phrase, 'They are killing geese in Scotland, and sending the feathers to England' which every one had ready when the snow began to fall, and I used to hear in the time of a high wind that
> Arthur's Bower has broken his band
> And he comes roaring up the land
> King of Scotts wi' a' his Power
> Cannot turn Arthur's Bower,
> I have been indebted to the North for more than I shall ever be able to acknowledge.
> (*LY* i 402)

The Rydal Mount library contained a copy of *Great Britain's Glory: Being the History of King Arthur, with the Adventures of the Knights of the Round Table* (?1680), probably the reading of one of the Wordsworth children.

16. Bacon, Francis, essays and other works
Suggested date of reading: by 1785
References: *PW* i 260; *EY* 662; Sheats 3-4
W's earliest extant poem, composed 1785, contains the line, 'Now honour'd Edward's less than Bacon's name' (*Lines Written as a School Exercise* 56), suggesting that he had by that time read (or at least heard of) Bacon. Bacon's *Opera Omnia* (Frankfurt, 1665) survives in the Hawkshead School Library today, and was there in W's time (Wu *CWAAS* 20).

When in 1805 Mrs Thomas Clarkson asked DW whether her brother could recommend suitable reading material, she was told that 'William scarcely knows what Books to recommend to you but you cannot be wrong, he says, if you read the best old writers - Lord Bacon's *Essays*, his *Advancement of Learning* &c., for instance, and if you are fond of History read it in the old Memoirs or old Chronicles' (*EY* 662). W's recommendation of the *Advancement of Learning* suggests that he had by then acquired the copy that appears in the Rydal Mount library catalogue (Shaver 15). Reed notes an interesting echo of Bacon's *Of Studies* (Cornell *13-Book Prelude* 178n).

17. [Baillie, Joanna], *A Series of Plays: in which it is Attempted to Delineate the Stronger Passions of the Mind* **(1798)**
Suggested date of reading: by Oct. 1798
References: see note
W's *There was a boy* has a literary source in Joanna Baillie's play *De Monfort*, published in *A Series of Plays, c.* April 1798. This was first discovered by John Kerrigan and is discussed by Jonathan Wordsworth, *Ancestral Voices* (Spelsbury, 1991), pp. 96-7. Wordsworth concludes that 'a copy of Baillie was available at Alfoxden at the height of the *Lyrical Ballads* period', and that W 'had read Baillie by October 1798'. C and Southey were also

admirers of Baillie's in 1798, even though the plays were published anonymously.[1] I suspect Southey to have been the author of the enthusiastic review of her work published in the *Monthly Magazine* 5 (1798) 507-8, 15 July 1798.

18. Barlow, Joel, *Hume's History of England, with a continuation to the Death of George II. by Dr Smollett, and a Further Continuation to the Present Time by J. Barlow* (5 vols., 1795)
Suggested date of reading: 1795-6
References: see note
W's copy is now at the Wordsworth Library, Grasmere. It contains W's ownership signature, entered *c.* 1795-6; that of Dr Richard Scambler on the title-page of the first volume indicates that the set was presented to him probably some time during the 1810s (Shaver 17).

19. Bartram, William
(i) *Travels through North and South Carolina, Georgia, East and West Florida, the Cherokee Country, the Extensive Territories of the Muscolgulges or Creek Confederacy, and the Country of the Chactaws* (2nd edn, 1794)
Suggested date of reading: *c.* 1797-8
References: Jacobus 189, 198; Shaver 19
Although Bartram's *Travels* was an influence on W's writing during 1797-8, its specific presence in the Alfoxden poetry is not easy to pin down. Jacobus 198 points to its general influence on *Complaint of a Forsaken Indian Woman*. W's copy is now at Cornell University; Healey records that it is 'Listed in the Sale Catalogue of the St. John Collection as from Wordsworth's library' (Healey 2218). C began copying passages from Bartram into his notebooks, June/Sept. 1797 (*Notebooks* i 221); W probably began reading Bartram at about the same time.

(ii) *Travels through North and South Carolina, Georgia, East and West Florida, the Cherokee Country, the Extensive Territories of the Muscolgulges or Creek Confederacy, and the Country of the Chactaws* (2nd edn, 1794)
Suggested date of reading: early 1799
References: see note
Ruth, which W composed at Goslar, probably in early 1799, contains a number of allusions to Bartram. As De Selincourt puts it, 'Mr E. H. Coleridge points out that the whole passage describing the flora of Georgian scenery is a close rendering of Bartram's narrative, and that the frontispiece of the book depicts a chieftain, whose feathers nod in the breeze just as did the military casque of the youth from Georgia's shore' (*PW* ii 510). The frontispiece is reproduced by Bewell, *Wordsworth and the Enlightenment* (New Haven, 1989), p. 33. W's allusions to Bartram are sufficiently detailed to suggest that he took his copy to Germany.

Fagin, *William Bartram: Interpreter of the American Landscape* (Baltimore, 1933), discusses Bartram's influence on *Ruth* at length, pp. 149-76; see also Stein 166-7, 238-9. It is interesting to find C reading Bartram to Sara Hutchinson in late Oct. 1799 (*Notebooks* i 218n; Reed i 274).

---

[1] See *Ancestral Voices*; Griggs i 621; Curry i 168.

20. Bayle, Pierre, *Dictionnaire historique et critique* [Rotterdam, 1697]
Suggested date of reading: spring 1798
References: see note
Bewell suggests that C's interest in Bayle during 1798 may have been shared by W:

> It is surprising that no one has ever noted that *Peter Bell* puns on one of the most
> famous of Enlightenment skeptics, Pierre Bayle (often called Peter Bayle in England)...
> His *Dictionnaire historique et critique* (1695-97), which Coleridge drew from
> extensively as he composed *The Wanderings of Cain*, *Christabel*, and *The Ancient
> Mariner*, was the great source-book of Enlightenment skepticism and impiety, one of
> the most popular works of the eighteenth century.[1]

However, W need not have read Bayle's work to have punned on his name.

21. Beattie, James
(i) 'An Extract from Illustrations on Sublimity'
Suggested date of reading: between 1783 and 1787; by 1787
References: see note
In *The Vale of Esthwaite* (1787), W describes a Lake District storm in particularly apocalyptic
terms:

> [   ]mid the soul appalling scene
> [With] black arm rear'd the clouds between
> [Hig]h from his throne the eternal sire
> [Te]rrific swept the mighty Lyre
> [Of] Nature. With Hell rousing sound
> While shriek'd the trembling strings around
> Or the deep tones struck my ear
> My soul would melt away with fear.
> Or swelld to madness bad me leap
> Down headlong down the hideous steep (*D.C.MS 3* 18v)

W's lines have a source in 'An Extract from Illustrations on Sublimity', *Annual Register* 26
(1783) ii 130-6, where Beattie discusses the various ways in which poetry can aspire to the
sublime:

> Poetry is sublime, when it conveys a lively idea of any grand appearance in art or
> nature. A nobler description of this sort I do not at present remember, than that which
> Virgil gives, in the first book of the Georgick, of a dark night, with wind, rain, and
> lightening: where Jupiter appears, encompassed with clouds and storms, darting his
> thunderbolts, and overturning the mountains ...

He then offers his own translation of the relevant passage from Virgil:

> *High* in the midnight storm enthron'd, *Heaven's Sire*
> Hurls from his blazing *arm* the bolt of fire.
> Earth feels with trembling; every beast is fled;

---

[1] *Wordsworth and the Enlightenment* (New Haven, 1989), p. 120.

And nations prostrate fall, o'erwhelmed with dread.
Athos rolls *headlong*... (*Annual Register* 26 [1783] ii 131)

W also read Crabbe in the *Annual Register*; see note 68.

(ii) *The Minstrel* [1779]
Suggested date of reading: by 1787
References: TWT 344; Fink 72
W was introduced to *The Minstrel* by his teacher, Thomas Bowman (TWT 344), during his schooldays at Hawkshead. De Selincourt emphasizes its influence on the juvenilia - in particular, *The Vale of Esthwaite* (1787). See, for instance, Beattie's Gothicism:

> Young Edwin, lighted by the evening star,
> Lingering and listening wander'd down the vale.
> There would he dream of graves, and corses pale;
> And ghosts that to the charnel-dungeon throng,
> And drag a length of *clanking chain*, and wail,
> Till silenced by the *owl's terrific song* ... (*Minstrel* I st.32 3-8)

At one point in his poem, W borrows Beattie's sound effects:

> And oft as ceased *the owl his song*
> That screamed the roofless walls among
> Spirits yelling from their pains
> And lashes loud and *clanking chains*
> Were heard by minstrel led astray
> Cold wading thro the swampy way ... (*D.C.MS 3* 6v; De Selincourt 51-6)

In 1793 DW identified her brother with Beattie's protagonist (*EY* 100-1).

(iii) *Original Poems and Translations* (1760)
Suggested date of reading: 1779-87; certainly by 1787
References: see note
A number of allusions and echoes in *The Vale of Esthwaite* show that by 1787 W knew Beattie's minor poems. At least one image from the *Vale* - 'perhaps the flickering dove / *Broke from the rustling boughs* above' (*D.C.MS 3* 6v; De Selincourt 67-8) - is borrowed from Beattie's *Retirement*:

> Whence the scared owl on pinions grey
> *Breaks from the rustling boughs* ... (lines 53-4)

Another example can be found in W's description of a cloud:

> And mark the train of *fear* beh[ind]
> Wave her *black banner* to the w[ind] (*D.C.MS 3* 18r; De Selincourt 208-9)

Compare Beattie's *Ode to Hope* 16: 'Where *Fear's black banner* bloats the troubled sky'.
    W can have seen these poems only in the (now rare) first edition of *Original Poems and Translations* (1760), which also contains Beattie's renderings of Lucretius and Horace (see note 160 [i]).

(iv) *The Minstrel*
Suggested date of reading: 1789
References: Cornell *EW* 44
The line of *An Evening Walk* which contains W's allusion to Beattie does not appear in the partial draft of the poem made in 1789 in *D.C.MS 7*. There is no reason, however, to doubt that it was composed in that year.

(v) *The Minstrel*
Suggested date of reading: 1791-2
References: Cornell *DS* 86
The mere fact that W reworks a passage from *The Minstrel* in *Descriptive Sketches* does not prove that he read it at the time (Cornell *DS* 86). He was fond of it, however, and if he took any poetry to France, one would expect him to have taken *The Minstrel*.

22. Beausobre, Isaac de, *Introduction to the Reading of the Holy Scriptures* **[Cambridge, 1779]**
Suggested date of reading: by Dec. 1787
References: Schneider 9
W was examined on this book at St John's College, Cambridge, Dec. 1787.

23. Beccaria Bonesara, Cesare, *An Essay on Crimes and Punishments, Translated from the Italian; with a Commentary, attributed to Mons. de Voltaire, Translated from the French*
Suggested date of reading: by 8 June 1794
References: *EY* 125
On 8 June 1794 W wrote to Mathews suggesting that they collaborate on a monthly journal called *The Philanthropist*. Among the contents, he proposes 'biographical papers' on such figures as Beccaria (*EY* 125). He must therefore have been acquainted with Beccaria's life and work by this time, thanks perhaps to his stay in France, 1791-2. Building on Rousseau's social contract philosophy, Beccaria's *Essay* protested against torture, and demanded penal and legal reform. It had been famous since 1766 when it was translated into French; in 1789 its proposals were implemented by the French National Assembly.

24. Beddoes, Thomas
(i) *A Word in Defence of the Bill of Rights against Gagging Bills* **(2nd edn, Bristol, 1795)**
Suggested date of reading: Nov.-Dec. 1795
References: Pinney Papers; Woof *BWS* 80-1; Chard 219
At the conclusion of his letter to W of 26 Nov. 1795, Azariah Pinney remarks:

> I shall send you by this opportunity Luesdon Hill, and Louvet, but will keep Madame Roland 'till I have the pleasure of seeing you - If there should be any thing I can do for you here, believe me, I shall be very happy to perform it - Beddoes's 2nd. Pamphlet I will also forward to you ... (Pinney Papers, Family Letter Book 13)

Pinney's mention of 'Beddoes's 2nd. Pamphlet' is explained by Woof, who finds that Beddoes' *A Word in Defence of the Bill of Rights against Gagging Bills* was published in two successive editions (Woof *BWS* 80-1). The first was advertised in the *Bristol Gazette*, 19

Nov. 1795; the second contained *A Postscript to the Defence*, the addendum to which is signed 21 Nov. 1795 (see CC *Lectures 1795* 384). It is presumably to the newly-available second edition that Pinney referred when writing to W five days later. C published an extract from Beddoes' *Postscript* in *The Watchman* for 13 May 1796 (CC *Watchman* 344-6); the text of the second edition is reprinted CC *Lectures 1795* 370-84.

Pinney (1775-1803) was tutored by Francis Wrangham, through whom he met W. From the time W moved into Racedown Lodge, Pinney corresponded with him, keeping him informed on events in Bristol. His letter to W of 26 Nov. 1795 describes the uproar in Bristol at the Two Bills; he adds that Beddoes

> published a pamphlet (price 2d.) to explain the nature of the two Bills now pending in Parliament, and recommending the Citizens to meet and frame a Petition, to shew their disapprobation of the measures likely to be adopted by Government ...
>
> (Pinney Papers, Letter Book 13)

Beddoes' pamphlets and the Bristol petition should be seen in the context of a nationwide outcry. Ninety-four petitions, containing over 130,000 signatures, were presented to Parliament before the end of 1795. The Bristol petition is published CC *Lectures 1795* 366-7. Goodwin, *The Friends of Liberty* (1979), pp. 387-93, offers a helpful discussion of the Two Bills within the wider context of increasing protest, while Roe 148-52 elucidates C's and Thelwall's roles at the meeting described by Pinney.

(ii) *Domiciliary Verses*
Suggested date of reading: Aug. 1799; by 2 Sept. 1799
References: see note
Beddoes' *Domiciliary Verses* has the distinction of being probably the first parody of *Lyrical Ballads*. Although it was first printed by Beddoes himself, and inserted into a copy of the Bristol issue of *Lyrical Ballads* (1798)[1] in Sept. or Oct. 1798, W did not read it until it was reprinted in the *Annual Anthology* (1799). Cottle sent W a copy of the *Anthology* in Aug. 1799, and on 2 Sept. he wrote back: 'Pray give yourself no uneasiness about Dr Beddoes's verses - in truth it is a very harmless performance' (Butler *JEGP* 150). For further details see my article, '*Lyrical Ballads* (1798): The Beddoes Copy' (*The Library*, forthcoming 1993).

25. Bell, John, *Classical Arrangement of Fugitive Poetry* Vol. 10 (1789)
Suggested date of reading: by 20 Oct. 1795; shortly after March 1796
References: EY 154, 169
In return for his copy of *Cato's Letters*, W asked Mathews in Oct. 1795 to 'make me a present of that vol: of Bells forgotten poetry which contains The minstrel and Sir martyn' (*EY* 154). He refers to *Bell's Classical Arrangement of Fugitive Poetry* Vol. 10 (1789) which, besides *Sir Martyn* and *The Minstrel*, contains Gloster Ridley, *Psyche*; William Melmoth, *The Transformation of Lycon and Euphormius*; and Moses Mendez, *The Squire of Dames* - all of which were composed in Spenserian stanzas. W must have seen Mathews' copy during his stay in London, Feb.-Aug. 1795, though he knew Beattie's *Minstrel* by 1787, and Mickle's *Sir Martyn* may also have been a favourite with him by then. Mathews had not sent the volume by March 1796 (*EY* 169), but presumably did so shortly after.

---

[1] This is now in the British Library (Ashley 2250).

W included an extract from *Sir Martyn* in the Album he compiled for Lady Mary Lowther in 1819 (*Album* 52-3), and in 1843 remarked that, 'it appears from his poem on Sir Martin, [that Mickle] was not without genuine poetic feelings' (Grosart iii 141).

26. Berkeley, George, philosophy of, inc. *Alciphron*
Suggested date of reading: 1797-8
References: see note

A draft entered in the Alfoxden Notebook in 1798 shows W using Berkeleian ideas to describe the transcendental relationship between the Pedlar and the natural world:

> there would he stand
> Beneath some rock, listening to sounds that are
> The *ghostly language* of the antient earth ... (Cornell *RC* 118-19)

The concept of a natural 'language' which expresses the creative powers of God, was mediated to W through C, who had written, two years earlier, in *The Destiny of Nations*: 'all that meets the bodily sense I deem / Symbolical, one mighty alphabet / For infant minds' (lines 18-20).

Which of Berkeley's works did C read? He borrowed Vol. 2 of the *Works* (1784) frdm the Bristol Library Society, 10-28 March 1796 (Whalley 75; Coffman B97) - indicating, as Whalley suggests, that he was 'already familiar' with the contents of Vol. 1: *Principles of Human Knowledge, Three Dialogues Between Hylas and Philonous, An Essay Towards a New Theory of Vision*, and *Alciphron* (CC *Marginalia* i 409). W may have read the *Works* in 1797-8, but it is hard to prove. However, a remark by Southey attests to the importance of Berkeley to W's writing, and names a work that W may have read. 'I want you, and *pray you*', he wrote to an unknown correspondent in Oct. 1829,

> to read Berkeley's Minute Philosopher; I want you to learn that the religious belief which Wordsworth and I hold, and which - I am sure you know in my case, and will not doubt in his - no earthly considerations would make us profess if we did not hold it, is as reasonable as it is desirable; is in its historical grounds as demonstrable as anything can be which rests upon human evidence; and is, in its life and spirit, the only divine philosophy, the perfection of wisdom; in which, and in which alone, the understanding and the heart can rest.
> (*The Life and Correspondence of the Late Robert Southey* ed. Revd. Charles Cuthbert Southey [6 vols., 1850], vi 76-7; his italics)

Southey was probably aware that the Rydal Mount library contained a copy of Berkeley's *Alciphron; or, the Minute Philosopher, in Seven Dialogues* (Shaver 24). Lyon suggests that *Alciphron* is the source of the Platonic element in *The Excursion* (Lyon 35); Leyburn, 'Berkeleian Elements in Wordsworth's Thought', *JEGP* 47 (1948) 14-28, argues that 'all ideas ultimately important in Wordsworth's poetry, are set forth in *Alciphron*' (p. 14).

Berkeley's *Siris: a Chain of Philosophical Reflexions and Inquiries Concerning the Virtues of Tar Water* is also believed to have influenced W's writings of 1798. A copy was annotated by C, probably in 1808-9 (CC *Marginalia* i 409-10), and the work is mentioned in the letter written by C to himself in *Biographia Literaria* (CC *Biographia* i 303 and n).

14

27. *Bible*

(i)

Suggested date of reading: 1773 onwards
References: Moorman 15

Ann Birkett, W's infant school teacher, apparently expected her charges to memorize passages from the Bible (Moorman 15), and we can be sure that this was one of the first books W read.

The family Bible of the Wordsworth family, purchased by JW Sr in Penrith, is now in the Wordsworth Library, bound up with a Book of Common Prayer. After JW Sr died in 1783, it was retained by Richard Wordsworth of Branthwaite and restored to William and Dorothy in 1805. After W's death it was rebound and on the first page of the 'Epistle Dedicatorie' at the front of the volume, Mary Wordsworth recorded: 'This Book having been taken care of when the House at Cockermouth was broken up, and restored to W. Wordsworth, by his uncle's family. After *his* death in 1850, I got it bound and repaired, by his friend Charles Westly, since dead. Mary Wordsworth 1851' (her italics). It passed subsequently into the library of John Wordsworth, W's son, who gave it, in 1860, to his own daughter, Dora. For further information on this volume, see Wu *Library* JW18 and n.

(ii)

Suggested date of reading: throughout 1779-87
References: Grosart iii 194

In the Fenwick Note to the *Intimations Ode*, W recalled that at school 'I used to brood over the stories of Enoch and Elijah' (Cornell *Poems 1800-1807* 428). Clancey informs me that Hawkshead schoolboys regularly attended Church, and were catechized at least once a week. An early borrowing from the Bible appears at the end of *The Death of the Starling* (composed 1786), based loosely on Catullus, *Carmen* iii:

> For while her days are days of weeping
> Thou in peace in silence sleeping
> In some still world unknown remote,
> The mighty Parent's care hast found
> Without whose tender guardian thought
> No Sparrow falleth to the ground. (lines 11-16; quoted from *D.C.MS 2* 13r)

Where Catullus concludes with a curse upon the shades of Orcus ('malae tenebrae / Orci'), W offers a Christian consolation. The last lines are adapted from Christ's words at *Matthew* 10.29: 'Are not two sparrows sold for a farthing? and one of them shall not fall on the ground without your Father'. For W's knowledge of the Old Testament at this period, see my article, 'Wordsworth's *Orpheus and Eurydice*: The Unpublished Final Line', *N&Q* NS 38 (1991) 301-2.

(iii)

Suggested date of reading: 1791-2
References: Cornell *DS* 80, 100, 110

The allusions in *Descriptive Sketches* show that W either knew his Bible extremely well, or was consulting a copy as he composed.

(iv)
Suggested date of reading: 1796
References: Cornell *B* 152n, 154n

(v)
Suggested date of reading: 1798
References: Mason *LB* 121, 129

28. Blackstone, Sir William, *Commentaries on the Laws of England* **[Oxford, 1765-9]**
Suggested date of reading: c. April 1794 onwards
References: Reed i 149n; *EY* 674; Shaver 28
'Pray ... what is become of the 2 vols of the Commentaries?' Richard Wordsworth wrote W
in 1799, 'It would be a great pitty to break the set. I have the other two volumes here' (*EY*
674). Richard lent his brother Vols. 2 and 4 of Blackstone when W began his residence at
Windy Brow, and that appears to have been the last he saw of the books for some time. The
third edition (4 vols., Oxford, 1768-9) was in the Rydal Mount library (Shaver 28).

29. Blair, Hugh, *Lectures on Rhetoric and Belles Lettres* **(2 vols., 1783)**
Suggested date of reading: 9-26 Feb. 1798
References: see note
As Little points out, W may have known Blair since his schooldays, for the *Lectures* are
extracted in Knox's *Elegant Extracts in Prose*.[1] Even if he did not, the critical consensus
is that he was probably introduced to the *Lectures* in 1797-8 by C. See, among numerous
other discussions, *MH* 263; Parrish 169; and pp. 181-2, below.

30. Boccaccio, Giovanni
(i) *Il Decamerone*
Suggested date of reading: 1789
References: see note
The fact that W thought it worth informing Mathews of the presence of Boccaccio in the
Racedown Lodge library in 1795 (see next note) would suggest that they both read his work
while studying Italian at Cambridge. W retained a copy of *Il Decamerone* at the Rydal
Mount library (Shaver 29).

(ii) *Il Decamerone* **(Venice, 1612)**
Suggested date of reading: Oct. 1795 onwards
References: *EY* 155
'We have a very toler[able] library here', W wrote to Mathews on 24 Oct. 1795, 'Machiavel
Boccacio, D'av[ila] and several other italian books' (*EY* 155). As the Racedown Lodge
Library catalogue shows, W was referring to a copy of *Il Decamerone* (Venice, 1612). He
and Dorothy probably read it together as he tutored her in Italian ('I am studying Italian very
hard', DW wrote in March 1796, *EY* 166). This is consistent with W's remark in Nov. 1805
to Walter Scott: 'It is many years since I saw Boccace, but I remember that Sigismonda is
not married by him to Guiscard' (*EY* 642). The reference is to the Fourth Day of the

---

[1] 'A Note on Wordsworth and Blair', *N&Q* NS 7 (1960) 254-5.

Decameron, where the first tale is told by Guiscardo and Ghismonda. Later in the letter W quotes Boccaccio from memory, showing that he knew the *Decameron* well.

W may have known *Patient Griselda. A Tale. From the Italian of Bocaccio. By Miss Sotheby*, which Cottle published in Bristol in 1798.

31. Boehme, Jacob, works
Suggested date of reading: 1797-8
References: see note
Stallknecht, *Strange Seas of Thought* (Bloomington, Ind., 1958), provides a Behmenist reading of W's work, concluding that 'Wordsworth's attitude toward Nature as expressed in the lyrics of 1798: *Lines Written in Early Spring, To My Sister, Expostulation and Reply* and *The Tables Turned* are steeped in Behmenism. They celebrate in Boehme's language a spontaneous feeling of love and harmony in Nature, which requires no scholarship as its background' (p. 108). W may have learnt about Boehme from C, who had known *Aurora* since childhood. The Rydal Mount library contained Ellistone's translation of *De Signatura Rerum* (1651), and Edward Taylor's commentary on Boehme (see Shaver 29).

32. Boileau-Despréaux, Nicolas, Œuvres
Suggested date of reading: by 21 March 1796
References: *EY* 169; Shaver 30
Writing to Mathews, 21 March 1796, W commented: 'I attempt to write satires! and in all satires whatever the authors may say there will be found a spice of malignity. Neither Juvenal or Horace were without it, and what shall we say of Boileau and Pope or the more redoubted Peter' (*EY* 169). W knew probably all these authors before his Racedown residence. We know that Juvenal and Horace were read at Hawkshead. Boileau and Peter Pindar were probably read by 1795 when he prepared for the Juvenalian imitation he wished to compose with Wrangham. He may have encountered Boileau's work at Cambridge, though there is no proving it.

It is not known whether W read Boileau in translation, but we can be sure that he did read him in the original. On his visit to France in 1802 he acquired a copy of *Œuvres de Boileau Despréaux* (Paris, 1801), now at the Wordsworth Library. In addition, the Rydal Mount Library contained *Les Œuvres de M. Boileau-Despréaux* (3 vols., Paris, 1768), though when and where this was obtained is not known (Shaver 30).

33. *Book of Common Prayer*
Suggested date of reading: 1773-87
References: see note
The Book of Common Prayer was bound up with the Wordsworth family Bible. In later life W mentioned to the Revd. R. P. Graves that 'many of the collects' in the Book of Common Prayer

> seemed to him examples of perfection, consisting, according to his impression, of words whose signification filled up without excess or defect the simple and symmetrical contour of some majestic meaning, and whose sound was a harmony of accordant simplicity and grandeur; a combination, he added, such as we enjoy in some of the best passages of Shakespeare. (Grosart iii 471)

W would certainly have encountered the collects while a schoolboy at Hawkshead. At school he would have possessed his own book of common prayer, like the Morland boys (see p. 164, below).

34. Bowles, William Lisle, *Fourteen Sonnets* (Bath, 1789), and/or *Sonnets Written Chiefly on Picturesque Spots During a Tour* (Bath, 1789)
Suggested date of reading: spring 1789; by Dec. 1789
References: Landon 357; *N&Q* NS 36 (1989) 166-7
At some point after 1828, W told Alexander Dyce that he read Bowles' *Fourteen Sonnets* on publication: 'When Bowles's Sonnets first appeared, - a thin 4to pamphlet, entitled *Fourteen Sonnets*, - I bought them in a walk through London with my dear brother, who was afterwards drowned at sea'.[1] No-one disputes that W read Bowles' sonnets when they were first published. But the questions of which edition W actually read (the first or the second), and precisely when he did so, were raised first by Landon. She concluded that W read both editions: 'if it was in fact the first edition that had originally impressed Wordsworth, he would be likely to get hold of a copy of the second when it came out, with its eight extra sonnets' (Landon 357). In correspondence with me, Owen agrees: 'I favour the suggestion that W had the two editions, even though he drew only on the second' (letter to me). I have followed Landon's dating of W's reading to spring 1789 (Landon 356), although Reed prefers that of Dec. 1789 (Reed i 95). For further discussion of these matters, see my article, 'Wordsworth's Reading of Bowles', *N&Q* NS 36 (1989) 166-7.

35. *British Critic* (Oct. 1799)
Suggested date of reading: after 1 Nov. 1799
References: Reed i 276
This number of the *British Critic* contained a favourable and perceptive review of *Lyrical Ballads* (1798) by Francis Wrangham. W had probably read it by the time he visited Wrangham in early June 1800 (Reed ii 66); if he did not know of it by then, Wrangham probably mentioned it in the letter W had received by 19 Dec. 1800 (Griggs i 657).

36. Brooke, Henry
(i) *The Fool of Quality; or, the History of Henry Earl of Moreland* [1766]
Suggested date of reading: March 1796
References: *EY* 166
On 7 March 1796 DW remarked that 'I am now reading the Fool of Quality which amuses me exceedingly' (*EY* 166). Since *The Fool of Quality* does not appear in the Racedown Lodge Library catalogue of 1793, the copy read by DW may have been sent by friends; indeed, both Azariah Pinney and James Losh were in the habit of sending books to Racedown at this period. It is likely that W also have read the novel, or at least heard parts read by his sister.

(ii) *Gustavus Vasa, the Deliverer of his Country* [1739]
Suggested date of reading: between 21 Sept. 1797 and 6 March 1798
References: *EY* 210

---

[1] *Recollections of the Table-Talk of Samuel Rogers* ed. Revd. Alexander Dyce (1856), p. 261n.

'I have long wished to thank you for your letter and Gustavus Vasa', W wrote to James Tobin on 6 March 1798 (*EY* 210). His phrasing implies that Tobin sent him Brooke's play shortly after visiting Alfoxden, 16-21 Sept. 1797. As Moorman 391 points out, Brooke's verse tragedy made some impression on W, since *The Prelude* recalls 'how Gustavus found / Help at his need in Dalecarlia's Mines' (*Thirteen-Book Prelude* i 212-13). This is a recollection of the play, which begins in the copper mines of Dalecarlia. Williams comments further, *Wordsworth: Romantic Poetry and Revolution Politics* (Manchester, 1989), p. 88.

37. Brown, Dr John

(i) *A Description of the Lake at Keswick (and the Adjacent Country) in Cumberland: Communicated in a Letter to a Friend, by a Late Popular Writer* [Newcastle, 1767]
Suggested date of reading: by 1788
References: see note
W's 1788 description of the Dovedale rocks, 'scattered upon the side of one of the hills of a form perfectly spiral' (*Prose Works* i 11), appears to be influenced by Brown's description of Keswick vale: 'on all sides of this immense amphitheatre the lofty mountains rise round, piercing the clouds in shapes as spiry and fantastic, as the very rocks of Dovedale' (West 192). Only after his death did Dr John Brown (1715-66) become known for his pamphlet describing the Keswick landscape. It was made famous when reprinted, from 1780 onwards, in West's *Guide to the Lakes*, as *Dr. Brown's Letter, Describing the Vale and Lake of Keswick*. W probably knew the pamphlet as well. Bicknell 4.1-4.5.

(ii) *Now Sunk the Sun*
Suggested date of reading: by 1788
References: see note
Brown's *Now Sunk the Sun* was first published by Richard Cumberland in his *Odes* (1776),[1] and reprinted in West's *Guide*, 2nd-11th editions; see Bicknell 11.1-11.2. W first encountered it there, and particularly admired Brown's account of the streams:

> Nor voice nor sound broke on the deep serene,
> But the soft murmur of swift-gushing rills,
> Forth-issuing from the mountain's distant steep,
> (Unheard till now, and now scarce heard) proclaim'd
> All things at rest ...   (lines 15-19)

The phrase 'scarce heard' recurs in W's sonnet of *c.* 1789, 'On the [   ] *village Silence sets her seal*':[2]

> The kine obscurely seen before me lie
> Round the dim horse that crops his later meal
> *Scarce heard* ...   (lines 3-5)

Compare also *Evening Walk* 283: '*Scarce heard*, their chattering lips her shoulder chill'. Averill points out that *Evening Walk* 433-4 echo *Now Sunk the Sun* 17-18 (Cornell *EW* 80). W reprinted Brown's poem in his own *Guide to the Lakes* (*Prose Works* ii 193, 400-1).

---

[1] Eddy, *A Bibliography of John Brown* (New York, 1971), reprints the text published by Cumberland.
[2] A facsimile of the MS draft of this poem can be found in Cornell *Poems 1800-1807* 324-5.

38. Browne, Moses, *Sunday Thoughts*
Suggested date of reading: probably by 1789
References: Cornell *EW* 50
Averill comments on *Evening Walk* 158: 'The phrase "prospect all on fire" is from Moses Browne's *Sunday Thoughts*, which Wordsworth met in John Scott's *Critical Essays* (London, 1785), pp. 348-352' (Cornell *EW* 50). *Evening Walk* 158 is not to be found in the 1789 drafts of the poem that survive in *D.C.MS 7*, but there is no reason to doubt that it was composed at that time.

39. Brydone, Patrick, *A Tour Through Sicily and Malta in a Series of Letters to William Beckford* (2 vols., 1773)
Suggested date of reading: Feb.-March 1796; by 7 March 1796
References: *EY* 166
'Within the last month I have read Tristram Shandy, Brydone's Sicily and Malta, and Moore's Travels in France', DW wrote in March 1796 (*EY* 166). W seems to have read Brydone's *Tour*, or heard parts of it read by his sister, for it was in his mind as he composed the blank verse passage beginning 'There is an active principle alive in all things'[1] in spring 1798: 'The spring and elasticity of the air seems to be lost; and that *active principle that animates all nature*, appears to be dead' (*Tour* i 9-10).

The *Tour* was in great demand at Bristol Library, but the Registers show that the Wordsworths did not obtain their copy from there. Coffman points out that Brydone is cited by C in an unpublished MS (Victoria University Library MS F.14.4).

40. Bürger, Gottfried August
(i) *Des Pfarrers Tochter von Taubenhain* tr. William Taylor
Suggested date of reading: March-April 1797; after 20 March 1797
References: see note
On 20 March 1797, Losh listed in his diary (now at Tullie House, Carlisle) the first consignment of books which he sent W - among them, 'Monthly Magazines from Feby. to December 1796 inclusive'. The issue for April 1796 contained William Taylor's translation of Bürger's *Des Pfarrers Tochter von Taubenhain*, entitled *The Lass of Fair Wone*. Its influence on W's *The Three Graves*, composed in spring 1797, is traced by Jacobus 227-8, who also reprints Taylor's translation (pp. 284-8). It is likely that W read Taylor's rendering of *Lenore* at this time as well (see next note).

W's reading was probably directed by C, who had himself been guided to Taylor by Lamb, July 1796:

> **Have you read** the Balad call'd 'Leonora' in the 2d No. of the **'Monthly Magazine'**? If you have - !!!!!!!!!!!!!! there is another fine song from the same Author (Berger) in the 3d No. of scarce inferior **merit** ... (Marrs i 41)

C must have read the translations between July 1796 and spring 1797, when he recommended them to W.

---

[1] See *William Wordsworth* ed. Stephen Gill (Oxford, 1984), pp. 676-8.

(ii) *Des Pfarrers Tochter von Taubenhain* **and** *Lenore* **tr. William Taylor**
Suggested date of reading: spring 1798
References: Parrish 87, Jacobus 219
The Lass of Fair Wone influenced *The Thorn*; the *Monthly Magazine* for March 1796
contained Taylor's translation of Bürger's *Lenore*, which influenced *The Idiot Boy* (Parrish
87, Jacobus 219). Taylor's translation of *Lenore* is reprinted Jacobus 277-83.

(iii) *Gottfried August Bürgers Gedichte. Herausgegeben von Karl Reinhard* **(2 vols.,
Göttingen, 1796)**
Suggested date of reading: 1 Oct. 1798 onwards; Oct.-Dec. 1798
References: DWJ i 31; *EY* 233-5; Reed i 257n; Shaver 39
'Bought Burgher's poems, the price 6 marks', DW recorded in her journal on Monday 1 Oct.
1798 (*DWJ* i 31). These volumes were given by Mrs Dorothy Dickson to Mr Leo Wiener
in 1956, and are now at the Wordsworth Library; they contain a number of pencil marks,
mainly in the second volume. Their purchase in Oct. suggests that prior to that date W
probably knew Bürger's work mainly, if not exclusively, from Taylor's translations in the
Monthly Magazine (see preceding notes). C purchased a copy of the same edition of Bürger's
Gedichte, probably at the same time (Dendurent 462; CC *Marginalia* i 828; Coffman B259).
   W and DW set about reading '"Leonora" and a few little things of Bürger' more or less
immediately, but were disappointed (*EY* 233). Their letter, which C had received by 20 Nov.
1798, probably mentioned Bürger.

(iv) *Des armen Suschens Traum*
Suggested date of reading: late Nov.-early Dec. 1798
References: EY 234-5
W wrote to C *c.* 15 Nov. 1798 (*EY* 233). C's response has not survived, but in it he
apparently commended *Des armen Suschens Traum*, for in late Nov.-early Dec. 1798, W
wrote back, saying that 'I have read "Susan's Dream," and I agree with you that it is the most
perfect and Shaksperian of his poems, &c., &c.' (*EY* 234-5).
   In late Nov.-early Dec. 1798 W told C that 'Bürger is the poet of the animal spirits. I love
his "*Tra ra la*" dearly; but less of the horn and more of the lute - and far, far more of the
pencil' (*EY* 235; his italics). Shaver notes that W has in mind the opening lines of *Ständchen*:
'Trallyrum larum höre mich!' But *Ständchen* was revised for the 1796 edition of the
Gedichte which the Wordsworths acquired in 1798 (see preceding note), and the lines quoted
by Shaver do not appear there. W might simply have been referring to Bürger's sing-song
rhythms and onomatopoeic style; see, for example, 'Und hurre hurre, hop hop hop!' (*Lenore*
149), 'Und außen, horch! gings trap trap trap' (*Lenore* 97), 'Halloh, Halloh zu Fuß und Roß!'
(*Der wilde Jäger* 2).

41. Burke, Edmund
(i) *A Philosophical Enquiry into the Origin of our Ideas of the Sublime and Beautiful*
Suggested date of reading: by 6-16 Sept. 1790, if not before
References: WC 18 (1987) 114-21
In 'Wordsworth and the Picturesque: A Strong Infection of the Age', *WC* 18 (1987) 114-21,
pp. 117-18, Trott points to a borrowing from Burke's *Enquiry* in W's letter to his sister of
6-16 Sept. 1790. At Hawkshead he would have learnt of the sublime through Gilpin's

Observations on the Lakes, where Burke is frequently cited. And he may have consulted the fourth edition of the *Enquiry* (1764), donated to the Hawkshead School Library in 1789.

(ii) *Reflections on the Revolution in France* [1790]
Suggested date of reading: spring 1791; by spring 1793
References: Roe 33; *Thirteen-Book Prelude* ix 97; *Prose Works* i 53
Roe observes:

> A *Letter to the Bishop of Llandaff* reveals that Wordsworth had read both Burke and Paine, and Book Nine of *The Prelude* recalls that before his second visit to France he 'had read, and eagerly / Sometimes, the master pamphlets of the day' (ix.96-7). The obvious moment for him to have done so was spring 1791, when the *Reflections* was fresh and controversial and the various replies rapidly appearing. (Roe 33)

Burke's *Reflections* was published on 1 Nov. 1790, and W would have read it shortly after. As Roe points out, the *Letter* could not have been written without a knowledge of Burke; see *Prose Works* i 53. Chandler 20-4 argues that, in the *Letter to the Bishop of Llandaff*, W took Watson's *Sermon* to be representative of Burkean thought.

(iii) *A Letter from Mr. Burke, to a Member of the National Assembly* [1791]
Suggested date of reading: by spring 1793
References: *Prose Works* i 49, 65
In the *Letter to the Bishop of Llandaff*, W criticizes 'the unblushing aristocracy of a Maury or a Cazalès' (*Prose Works* i 49) - a satirical reworking of Burke's remarks in his *Letter to a Member of the National Assembly*:

> I assure you, Sir, that, when I consider your unconquerable fidelity to your sovereign, and to your country, the courage, fortitude, magnanimity, and long-suffering of yourself, and the Abbé Maury, and of Mr. Cazales, and of many worthy persons of all orders, in your Assembly, I forget, in the lustre of these great qualities, that on your side has been displayed an eloquence so rational, manly, and convincing, that no time or country, perhaps, has ever excelled. (pp. 52-3)

(iv) *A Letter From the Right Honourable Edmund Burke to A Noble Lord* [1796]
Suggested date of reading: 1796-7; by 1797
References: see note
In *The Borderers*, Rivers proclaims: 'I had within me / A salient spring of energy, a fire / Of inextinguishable thought' (IV ii 118-20). The 'salient spring' echoes Burke's account of his dead son in the *Letter to a Noble Lord*: 'He had in himself *a salient, living spring*, of generous and manly action' (p. 50). The editors of the forthcoming Longman *Wordsworth* judge Rivers' lines to date probably from 1797.

(v) *Two Letters Addressed to a Member of the Present Parliament on the Proposals for Peace with the Regicide Directory of France* [1796]
Suggested date of reading: after 20 March 1797
References: EY 186n
On 20 March 1797, Losh listed in his diary (now at Tullie House, Carlisle) the first consignment of books which he sent W - among them, 'Burke's Two letters to a Member of Parliament'. Shaver's suggestion, that this refers to *A Third Letter on the Proposals for*

Peace with France (1797), cannot be correct since the *Third Letter* was not published until 13 Nov. 1797; Losh's phrasing refers rather to the *Two Letters* (1796) which went through thirteen editions between 1796 and 1800. Erdman finds a review of the *Two Letters* in the *Critical Review* 18 (1796) 201-2 to be 'possibly by C' (CC *Essays* i 396n).

(vi) *A Letter to the Duke of Portland* (1797)
Suggested date of reading: after 20 March 1797
References: EY 186
On 20 March 1797, Losh listed in his diary (now at Tullie House, Carlisle) the first consignment of books which he sent W. This included Burke's 'letter to the Duke of Portland', published 13 Feb. 1797. This was a fresh publication at the time Losh sent it, and it would have been of immediate interest to W.

42. Burns, Robert
(i) *Poems* (either Kilmarnock, 1786, or Edinburgh, 1787)
Suggested date of reading: July-Aug. 1786; 7-23 Oct. 1787
References: TWT 344; *EY* 13
Thomas Bowman Jr states that his father 'lent Wordsworth Cowper's "Task" when it first came out, and Burns' "Poems"' (TWT 344), suggesting that W saw the Kilmarnock *Poems* shortly after publication in July 1786. By Oct. 1787 W had encountered either that or the edition published in Edinburgh in April 1787 - for, as DW wrote to her friend Jane Pollard, he obtained a copy for her through the Penrith Book Club:[1]

> My Br Wm was here at the time I got your Letter, I told him that you had recommended the book to me, he had read it and admired many of the pieces very much; and promised to get it me at the book-club, which he did. I was very much pleased with them indeed, the one which you mentioned to me is I think very comical, I mean the address to a Louse; there is one, to a mountain daisy which is very pretty.
> (*EY* 13)

W was in Penrith, 7-23 Oct. 1787, and must have been acquainted with the works of Burns by then.

I find an echo of Burns in an alternative reading for an unpublished line in the 1787 manuscript of *The Vale of Esthwaite*: 'Ah! I lie me down and sleep' (*D.C.MS 3* 25v). Compare Burns' *Despondency: An Ode* 3: 'I set me down and sigh'.

(ii) *Poems*
Suggested date of reading: 1797-8
References: MH 42; Parrish 173-7; Jacobus 91; Mason *LB* 145, 151
W apparently reread Burns at Alfoxden, for he is alluded to in *The Ruined Cottage* MS D, and the *Lyrical Ballads* were influenced by his poetry.

It was probably at this period that DW acquired her copy of Burns' *Poems, chiefly in the Scottish dialect* (2 vols., 2nd edn, Edinburgh and London, 1793). As Butler *ELN* 303 points out, this is now in The Hugh Walpole Collection, The King's School, Canterbury (Shaver 43).

---

[1] All that remains of the Penrith Book Club today is a catalogue dating from 1808, retained at the Record Office, Carlisle (D/Hud/17/132/2). It makes no mention of Burns.

(iii) *Poems, Chiefly in the Scottish Dialect* **(2 vols., 2nd edn, Edinburgh and London, 1793)**
Suggested date of reading: during Feb. 1799
References: EY 256
W's famous disquisition on German literature in his letter to C of 27 Feb. 1799 led him to discuss Burns (*EY* 255-6). Given his recent study of the German authors there mentioned, it is likely that he also read Burns at this time.

43. Butler, Joseph, *Analogy of Religion, Natural and Revealed, to the Constitution and Course of Nature*
Suggested date of reading: by Dec. 1789
References: Schneider 156
W was examined on this book at St John's College, Cambridge, Dec. 1789.

44. Caesar, *Commentaries*
Suggested date of reading: early 1780s
References: Schneider 68
Schneider writes that W 'probably read' the *Commentaries* at Hawkshead (Schneider 68) - a fairly safe conjecture in view of the widespread use of Caesar, in W's day (and our own), in the classroom.

45. Callistratus
(i) *Harmodiou Melos*
Suggested date of reading: possibly 1786, though more likely 1787-8
References: Woof *SIB* 164-6; Reed i 15-16; *N&Q* NS 38 (1991) 302-3
W's earliest surviving lyric composition, a translation of Callistratus (*PW* i 299-300), celebrates the assassination, in 514 BC, by Aristogiton and Harmodius, of the 'tyrant' Hipparchus. Reed describes it as 'a simple and quite well-known poem ... and this fact along with the character of its emotions make it a poem which a schoolboy would have been likely to meet and wish to translate' (Reed i 303). On this evidence he dates the translation to 1786 (Reed i 15-16), as does Woof *SIB* 165. However, in 'Wordsworth's Translation of Callistratus: A Possible Redating', *N&Q* NS 38 (1991) 302-3, I propose a dating of 1787-8, based on the influence on W's poem of Baynes' *Ode From the Greek of Callistratus*, published in the *European Magazine* for Aug. 1787 (12.142).

Woof *SIB* 165 points out that W's spelling, 'Aristogiton', implies the use of a Latin translation. This is difficult to confirm since W's rendering contains nothing that could derive only from the standard Latin version published in *Selecta ex Poetis Græcis* (2 vols., Eton, 1762), ii 146.

(ii) *Ode From the Greek of Callistratus* **tr. John Baynes**
Suggested date of reading: 1787-8; after 1 Sept. 1787
References: *N&Q* NS 38 (1991) 302-3
See preceding note.

46. Cambridge Intelligencer
Suggested date of reading: c. 31 Dec. 1796
References: see note
Roe tells me that W would have sought out Benjamin Flower's *Cambridge Intelligencer*, because it was controversial and from Cambridge; it was probably in the *Intelligencer* that W first read C's *Ode on the Departing Year* (see note 56 [iv]). The *Ode* was published there on 31 Dec. 1796. The *Intelligencer* was a broadsheet that appeared first on 20 July 1793, at a cost of threepence halfpenny. It carried reports of public events at home and abroad and terminated 18 June 1803.

47. Carter, Elizabeth, *Ode to Spring*
Suggested date of reading: 1773-9
References: Grosart iii 426
In 1836, Justice Coleridge recorded a discussion with W in which 'The first verses from which he remembered to have received great pleasure, were Miss Carter's "Poem on Spring," a poem in the six-line stanza, which he was particularly fond of, and had composed much in, for example, "Ruth"' (Grosart iii 426). Woof tells me that W found Carter's *Ode to Spring* in Anne Fisher's children's anthology, *The Pleasing Instructor or Entertaining Moralist consisting of Select Essays, Relations, Visions, and Allegories collected from the most Eminent English Authors* (1756). This popular collection appeared in new editions in 1760, 1766, 1770, 1775, 1777, and 1780. In addition to Carter's *Ode to Spring*, it contained Gray's *Elegy*, Parnell's *The Hermit*, and Thomson's *Hymn to the Seasons*, as well as poems by Prior, Gay, and Cunningham.

Woof clears up the confusion surrounding W's remark. Legouis incorrectly observed that 'Mrs Carter (1718-1806) only wrote three odes at all corresponding to the description given by Wordsworth. These are the *Ode to Melancholy* (1739), the *Ode to Wisdom* (1749), and the *Ode to Miss Hall* (1749)' (Legouis 125). Moorman 54 suggested that W was confusing Carter with Anna Laetitia Aikin, who published an *Ode to Spring* in 1773.

Our only evidence towards a dating is the recollection of Carter's poem as the 'first verses' from which W 'received great pleasure'. We must presume that the reading took place before W's departure for Hawkshead.

48. Catullus, *Carmina*
Suggested date of reading: 1786-8; by 1786
References: Reed i 16; Woof *SIB* 169-70
Three of W's translations of Catullus survive from between 1786 and c. 1788. These are published by De Selincourt as *Death of a Starling - Catullus* (composed 1786; *PW* i 263); *Lesbia* (composed 1786; *PW* i 306); and *Septimius and Acme* (composed c. 1788; *PW* i 307). Given that he had studied Catullus closely while a schoolboy, it is not surprising that a return visit to Hawkshead in Aug. 1844 revived memories of Catullus, whose *Carmen* lxiii, W remarked, was 'all taken from Greek' (Reed *PBSA* 454). See also note 65.

49. Cervantes Saavedra, Miguel de, *Don Quixote* tr. Tobias Smollett (1782)
Suggested date of reading: 1782-3
References: *Prose Works* iii 372; Shaver 50; Wu *Library* JW33

Of my earliest days at school I have little to say, but that they were very happy ones, chiefly because I was left at liberty, then and in the vacations, to read whatever books I liked. For example, I read all Fielding's works, Don Quixote, Gil Blas, and any part of Swift that I liked ... (*Prose Works* iii 372)

These books were presumably in JW Sr's library at Cockermouth, and W must have read them before his father died in Dec. 1783. Pamela Woof identifies JW Sr's copy of *Don Quixote* as the copy of Smollett's translation (1782) later retained at Dove Cottage and Rydal Mount (*Grasmere Journals* 176; Shaver 50). Although I have accepted it, the evidence for this identification is not conclusive. W owned a copy of Shelton's translation by Jan. 1813 (*MY* ii 75), and by 1829 he had a copy of the Spanish text (Shaver 50).

Woof Ph.D. 89 suggests that Cervantes' Cardenio influenced the portrayal of Rivers in *The Borderers* (see note 13 [iii]).

50. Chapbooks
Suggested date of reading: 1773-9
References: *Thirteen-Book Prelude* v 364-9
Like C, who as a child read *Tom Hickathrift*, *Jack the Giant-Killer*, *Robinson Crusoe*, and *The Seven Champions of Christendom*, W was a reader of chapbooks:

> Oh! give us once again the Wishing-Cap
> Of Fortunatus, and the invisible Coat
> Of Jack the Giant-killer, Robin Hood,
> And Sabra in the Forest with Saint George!
> The Child whose love is here, at least doth reap
> One precious gain, that he forgets himself. (*Thirteen-Book Prelude* v 364-9)

The beggar Fortunatus, owner of the magic purse, had also a hat that would transport him to wherever he wanted to go; Jack the Giant-killer ridded the land of giants by virtue of a coat that made him invisible, shoes that gave him speed, and a magic sword; St George rescued Sabra from a dragon, and married her. For the beneficial effect of fairy-stories and romance, see W's letter on the education of a daughter in which the child's self-importance is to be tempered by 'leaving her at liberty to luxuriate in such feelings and images as will feed her mind in silent pleasure. This nourishment is contained in faery tales, romances ...' (*MY* i 287).

51. Charlevoix, Pierre Francois Xavier de, *The History of Paraguay* (2 vols., 1769)
Suggested date of reading: Aug. 1798; by 14 Sept. 1798
References: BL Add.MS 35,343
When they arrived in London, Aug. 1798, prior to their German trip, W and C met with Joseph Johnson, and, through him, caught up with several books they had not yet encountered. Some of these were sent to Thomas Poole, as his letter to C of 24 Jan. 1799, proves: 'We rec[d] from Johnson, six copies of the poems - the account of Paraguay and the essay on population - but *not* the diversions of Purley - every one admires the poems and I am told they are much admired in London' (BL Add.MS 35,343; his italics). By 'the account of Paraguay', Poole probably means Charlevoix's *History of Paraguay*. Southey borrowed a copy of the book from Bristol Library, 13 April-18 May 1795 (Whalley 47).

52. Chatterton, Thomas
(i) *Poems*
Suggested date of reading: probably by 1787; by Jan. 1788
References: Schneider 77; *PW* i 267-9
It is likely that W read Chatterton as a schoolboy. A copy of Chatterton's *Miscellanies in Prose and Verse* (1778) was owned by his Hawkshead schoolmaster, William Taylor, and survives today at the Armitt Library, Ambleside. It contains a flyleaf inscription by Edmund Irton:

> To the Revd. William Taylor, Master of the Free Grammar School at Hawkshead, to mark my appreciation of his luminous and pertinent reflections on the poets of our time, and especially the unhappy boy whose genius is evident in many of the pieces contained in this slender volume. (Schneider 77)

The statement confirms that Taylor enjoyed the work of 'the poets of our time', and conveyed his enthusiasm to his pupils.
  In the poem published by De Selincourt as *Dirge Sung by a Minstrel* (*PW* i 267-9), composed Jan. 1788, W alludes to Chatterton's *Ælla*:

> Mie love is dedde
> Gone to her deathbedde
> Al under the [wyllowe] tree. (*D.C.MS 2* 36r)

This borrowing is the refrain of the 'Minstrel's Song' from *Ælla*, and is discussed Averill 45. Betz Ph.D. 43 notes another borrowing from Chatterton in an unpublished draft of the *Dirge*.

(ii) *The Battle of Hastings*
Suggested date of reading: 1793
References: *N&Q* NS 23 (1976) 103-4
Celoria, 'Chatterton, Wordsworth and Stonehenge', *N&Q* NS 23 (1976) 103-4, suggests that the opening of *Salisbury Plain* (1793) was influenced by Chatterton's *The Battle of Hastings* II.

53. Chaucer
(i) *The Merchant's Tale* tr. Alexander Pope
Suggested date of reading: by 1785
References: see note

> Nor that vile wretch who bad the *tender age*
> Spurn *Reason's law*, and humour Passion's rage ...
> > (*Lines Written as a School Exercise* 9-10)

This couplet from W's earliest extant poem alludes to Chaucer's *Merchant's Tale* as translated by Pope: Justin is the 'vile wretch' who instructs May, the 'tender age', to surrender to the lust of the old merchant, January ('Passion'). Pope describes May from January's point of view:

> But ev'ry Charm revolv'd within his Mind:
> Her *tender Age*, her Form divinely Fair ... (*January and May* 245-6)

W's phrase, 'Reason's law', also echoes *January and May* 293: 'Let *Reason's Rule* your strong Desires abate'. His reading of Pope's imitation suggests that he may also have read the original before leaving Hawkshead in 1787. He would have been able to consult *The Woorkes of Geoffrey Chaucer, Newly Printed, with Divers Addicions* (1561) in the school library (Wu *CWAAS* 62).

(ii) *Canterbury Tales*
Suggested date of reading: 1787-90
References: *Thirteen-Book Prelude* iii 276-7
In the Fenwick Note to *Yarrow Visited*, W recalls that it was through Anderson's *British Poets*, in Grasmere in 1802, that 'I became first familiar with Chaucer' (Grosart iii 70). He probably means that he first enjoyed a *close* reading in 1802, when he used Anderson for his Chaucer translations. I see no reason seriously to doubt the claim that 'Beside the pleasant Mills of Trompington / I laugh'd with Chaucer' (*Thirteen-Book Prelude* iii 276-7); see also his remark to Henry Crabb Robinson:

> When I began to give myself up to the profession of a poet for life, I was impressed with a conviction, that there were four English poets whom I must have continually before me as examples - Chaucer, Shakspeare, Spenser, and Milton. These I must study, and equal *if I could*; and I need not think of the rest.
>
> (*Memoirs* ii 470; his italics)

While at Hawkshead W may have used the 1561 edition of Chaucer's works, still in the Hawkshead School Library (Wu *CWAAS* 62).

54. Ciceronis, M. Tulii
(i) 'Cicero's Orations 1 Vol.'
Suggested date of reading: before 1787
References: Wu *Library* JW5; Shaver 55
One of the books in JW Sr's library at Cockermouth was a copy of 'Cicero's Orations 1 Vol.' (as it was described in 1805 by Richard Wordsworth of Branthwaite), and it is probable that this volume was used by W and his brothers prior to their time at Hawkshead. It is difficult to identify this volume, but likely candidates must include two titles retained at Rydal Mount: (i) *Orationum Marci Tulli Ciceronis volumen à Joann. Michäele Bruto emendatum* [1636]; (ii) *The Orations of M. Tullius Cicero, translated into English ... By W. Guthrie* (2nd edn, 3 vols., 1745-52).

(ii) *De Officiis Libri Tres. Item, Cato Major, sive de Senectute. Laelius, sive de Amicitia. Paradoxa Somnium Scipionis.* (1754)
Suggested date of reading: 1779-87
References: Schneider 72-6; Shaver 54; Wu *Library* n14
This volume contains *De officiis*, *Cato Major* and *Laelius*, and W's copy is now at the Wordsworth Library, Grasmere. The flyleaf is inscribed, 'John Wordsworths Book 1770', and W has written his own name three times on the verso, twice on the title-page. Numerous markings in pencil and pen indicate that it was well-used by the young Wordsworths as they struggled to translate its contents. The name 'Southey', inscribed on the title-page in pencil, suggests that it was later used by one of the Southey children.

Schneider's analysis of W's earliest surviving poem reveals that by the time of its composition in 1785 he 'had studied and reflected upon Cicero's *De Officiis*' (Schneider 73).

55. Clarke, James
(i) *A Survey of the Lakes of Cumberland, Westmorland, and Lancashire: together with an Account, Historical, Topographical, and Descriptive, of the Adjacent Country* **(2nd edn, 1789)**
Suggested date of reading: by 1789
References: Cornell *EW* 54
W's copy is now in the Wordsworth Library, Grasmere (Shaver 56); it is not known when W acquired it, but my guess would be *c.* 1789. Clarke's *Survey* was an important source for *An Evening Walk*; see Cornell *EW* 54. Bicknell 19.1-19.3.

(ii) *A Survey of the Lakes of Cumberland, Westmorland, and Lancashire: together with an Account, Historical, Topographical, and Descriptive, of the Adjacent Country* **(2nd edn, 1789)**
Suggested date of reading: 1796
References: Cornell *B* 19, 88n, 140n
Clarke's *Survey* was, according to Osborn, 'the single most useful background source' for *The Borderers*. It was probably at his side in 1796.

56. Coleridge, Samuel Taylor
(i) *Moral and Political Lecture* **(Bristol, 1795)**
Suggested date of reading: probably after 27 Feb. 1795
References: Griggs i 152; *EY* 153
In late Feb. 1795, shortly after publication of his *Moral and Political Lecture*, C offered Dyer 'as many Copies as you may choose to give away' (Griggs i 152). Roe suggests to me that 'if Dyer took up this offer, there may have been copies on the table when Wordsworth met Godwin in Dyer's company on 27 Feb. 1795. Evidence enough? Probably not. But Wordsworth certainly knew of C's (and Southey's) reputation *before* he went to Bristol in Aug. 1795; his letter to Mathews (*EY* 153) indicates that both were familiar with Coleridge's name and "talent"' (letter to me). There is reason to think that W at least knew of the *Lecture* at this time (see next note).

(ii) *Poems on Various Subjects* **(1796)**
Suggested date of reading: by April 1796
References: Reed i 345; Shaver 293
W's high opinion of C in Oct. 1795 (*EY* 153) suggests that he had seen C's *Poems* either in MS or proof when they met in Bristol, 1-26 Sept. 1795 (it was published on 16 April 1796). C might have shown him part of *Religious Musings* and (had it been written) *Lines Written at Shurton Bars*, which alludes to *An Evening Walk*.[1] C borrowed frequently from W at this time: the Estlin MS of *Lines Written on an Autumnal Evening* uses an entire couplet from *An*

---

[1] See Reed i 168n and Cornell *EW* 64n.

Evening Walk, as does that of *Songs of the Pixies*.[1] W soon returned the compliment; his *Address to the Ocean* (1796) alludes to C's *Complaint of Ninathoma*, published in *Poems* (1796) as Effusion XXX (Reed i 345).

(iii) *The Watchman* (Bristol, 1796)
Suggested date of reading: c. April 1796
References: Pinney Papers
In his letter to W of 25 March 1796, Azariah Pinney remarks: 'If you should like to have Coleridge's Watchman I will endeavour to have it packed' (Pinney Papers, Family Letter Book 13). W would have wished to acquire *The Watchman* and, I presume, accepted Pinney's offer.

(iv) *Ode for the Last Day of the Year, 1796*
Suggested date of reading: c. 31 Dec. 1796
References: Griggs i 297; *EY* 186
W read C's *Ode* on publication, for as early as 6 Jan. 1797, C told Cottle that he had 'received criticisms' of the *Ode* from 'these Quarters' (meaning W); Griggs takes this to indicate that W and C 'were in correspondence' (Griggs i 297).

The *Ode* was published on 31 Dec. 1796, as a quarto pamphlet entitled *Ode on the Departing Year*, and in the *Cambridge Intelligencer*, as *Ode for the Last Day of the Year, 1796* (EHC i 160). It is likely that W read it first in the *Intelligencer*, for he did not acquire the pamphlet until Losh sent him one on 20 March 1797; its dispatch is recorded in Losh's diary (now at Tullie House, Carlisle): 'Coleridge's ode to the new year'.

Losh's own copy of the pamphlet is at the Wordsworth Library, and contains his ownership signature dated 1797.

(v) *Ode on the Departing Year* (1796)
Suggested date of reading: after 20 March 1797
References: see preceding note.

(vi) *Conciones ad Populum* (Bristol, 1795)
Suggested date of reading: after 20 March 1797
References: *EY* 186
On 20 March 1797, Losh listed in his diary (now at Tullie House, Carlisle) the first consignment of books which he sent W - among them, C's 'Conciones ad Populum', published 3 Dec. 1795. If W sought out the *Conciones* at this late date, it is likely that he also knew the *Moral and Political Lecture*.

(vii) *The Plot Discovered* (Bristol, 1795)
Suggested date of reading: April 1797
References: see note
On 20 March 1797, Losh listed in his diary (now at Tullie House, Carlisle) the first consignment of books which he sent W - among them, 'Protest against certain Bills - by Coleridge'. Patton and Mann point out that 'Several surviving copies of [*The Plot*

---

[1] See Woof *BWS* 83-8, Cornell *EW* 32n, and Averill, 'Another Early Coleridge Reference to *An Evening Walk*', *ELN* 13 (1976) 270-3.

Discovered] ... have a wrapper on which is printed: "A Protest against Certain Bills"' (*CC Lectures 1795* 278); the copy sent to W evidently possessed such a wrapper.[1]

It is curious that W took so long to acquire a copy of this response to the uproar over the Two Bills in Bristol. He may have seen the pamphlet before 1797, but did not possess his own copy. Kitson, 'Coleridge's *The Plot Discovered*: A New Date', *N&Q* NS 31 (1984) 57-8, notes that it was published 4-6 Dec. 1795, despite its being dated 28 Nov.

(viii) *Osorio* in MS
Suggested date of reading: probably between 4 and 7 June 1797
References: Reed i 198
In June 1797, DW wrote to Mary Hutchinson, telling her that, as soon as C arrived at Racedown Lodge, 'he repeated to us two acts and a half of his tragedy *Osorio*' (*EY* 189). This suggests a dating of between 4 and 7 June 1797, though Reed prefers that of 'between June 6 and July 2'. Newlyn 13-14 discusses W's influence on *Osorio*.

(ix) *This Lime-Tree Bower my Prison* in MS
Suggested date of reading: probably between 7 and 14 July 1797; spring 1798
References: Griggs i 332-7; Reed i 201
Despite the dating of June 1797 which C later gave for Lamb's visit to Nether Stowey, it is clear from his letters that the correct dating is probably 7-14 July. *This Lime-Tree Bower* was composed and read to W probably during that week. Newlyn 39 finds echoes of the poem in W's lines about the Pedlar, composed spring 1798.

(x) *The Wanderings of Cain* in MS
Suggested date of reading: probably by 13 Nov. 1797
References: see note
This prose fragment of Nov. 1797 has its source in Gessner, whose *Der Tod Abels* has affinities with *The Ruined Cottage*. Reed points out that work on *The Wanderings of Cain* would have begun 'within a few days' of the walking tour to the Valley of Rocks (Reed i 208). Since *The Wanderings of Cain* was part of a projected collaboration with W, it would have been shown to him shortly after, in early Nov. - probably by 13 Nov., when W, DW, and C set out on another walking tour.

(xi) *Kubla Khan* in MS
Suggested date of reading: Nov. 1797; by 1 Oct. 1798
References: *DWJ* i 34; Reed i 208-9
On 1 Oct. 1798, Dorothy described her arrival with W in Goslar:

> He brought me his pockets full of apples, for which he paid two bon gros, and some excellent bread. Upon these I breakfasted and carried *Kubla* to a fountain in the neighbouring market-place, where I drank some excellent water. (*DWJ* i 34; her italics)

De Selincourt suggests that Dorothy's '*Kubla*' is 'a MS. copy of Coleridge's *Kubla Khan*'; Moorman, however, believes that it is 'a *can* for drinking, humourously named after Coleridge's builder of the pleasure-dome' (Moorman 413; her italics). In any case, the

---

[1] Shaver omits this item from his account of the books sent to W by Losh (*EY* 186n).

Wordsworths were familiar with C's poem by 1 Oct. 1798; they probably read it soon after composition in early Nov. 1797.

Kubla's 'pleasure dome' is recalled at *Thirteen-Book Prelude* viii 130-1: 'Domes / Of Pleasure spangled over'.

(xii) *The Dungeon* **in MS**
Suggested date of reading: after 13 Nov. 1797
References: Jacobus 80
The plan for *Lyrical Ballads* was evolved on 13 Nov. 1797; C extracted passages from *Osorio* soon after.

(xiii) *The Foster Mother's Tale* **in MS**
Suggested date of reading: after 12 Nov. 1797; by spring 1798
References: Jacobus 80
See preceding note. Newlyn 39 detects 'a radical rereading' of this poem in W's lines about the Pedlar, composed spring 1798.

(xiv) *Frost at Midnight* **in MS**
Suggested date of reading: Feb. 1798; by July 1798
References: see note
When C published this poem in late 1798 he dated it 'February 1798', and it was probably seen in MS by W at that time. W must have read it by July since, as Parrish observes, 'Coleridge's autobiographical reflection served as a model for *Tintern Abbey*'. *Frost at Midnight* is quoted at the beginning and end of the *Two-Part Prelude* (Cornell *Prelude 1798-9* 43n, 66n).

(xv) *The Ancient Mariner* **in MS**
Suggested date of reading: 23 March 1798
References: Reed i 228; *DWJ* i 13
'He brought his ballad finished', wrote Dorothy of *The Ancient Mariner* on 23 March 1798 (*DWJ* i 13). Since W had been instrumental in its conception,[1] the Wordsworths probably heard earlier versions as well. Newlyn 52n36 finds that W alludes to *The Ancient Mariner* in a cancelled passage in *Ruined Cottage* MS B, composed spring 1798; she finds also that lines from *Peter Bell* are inspired by C's poem (Newlyn 50).

(xvi) *Fears in Solitude* **in MS**
Suggested date of reading: April-May 1798
References: Griggs i 409
Although C reported the completion of *Fears in Solitude* to his brother George on 14 May 1798 (Griggs i 409), its published title suggests that it was written in April: 'Fears in Solitude. Written, April 1798, during the alarms of an invasion'.

(xvii) *The Nightingale* **in MS**
Suggested date of reading: 10 May 1798, or shortly after
References: Griggs i 406
C sent W a copy of the poem, 10 May 1798.

---

[1] See the Fenwick Note to *We are Seven* (*PW* i 360-2).

(xviii) *Fears in Solitude, Written in 1798 ... To which are added, France, an Ode; and Frost at Midnight* (1798)
Suggested date of reading: perhaps shortly after 27 July 1799; probably by Dec. 1799
References: Butler *JEGP* 27
In his letter of 27 July 1799, W suggests to Cottle, 'If you put any trifle in the poem or pamphlet way into the parcel with your Vol: of original poetry, it would be very welcome: I mean without expence to yourself: for example: Coleridges "Fears in Solitude" which we have not seen' (Butler *JEGP* 27). Joseph Johnson published C's *Fears in Solitude* in late 1798. I presume that W acquired a copy before the end of the year.

57. Coleridge, Samuel Taylor, Charles Lamb and Charles Lloyd, *Poems by S. T. Coleridge, Second Edition. To which are now Added Poems by Charles Lamb and Charles Lloyd* (1797)
Suggested date of reading: after 28 Oct. 1797; probably by 9 May 1798
References: EY 217-18
This volume was published on 28 Oct. 1797, though W may have been acquainted with some or all of its contents in proof or MS prior to that date. On 9 May 1798 he told Cottle that 'We regularly received Charles Lloyds works' (*EY* 217-18) - meaning, presumably, that he had received a copy of this volume.

58. Collins, William
(i) *Odes* [1746]
Suggested date of reading: 1779-87; by 1785
References: Sheats 5
The influence of Collins' *Odes* is widely evident in the juvenile works; the young W greatly admired the *Ode to Evening*, *Ode to Fear*, and the *Ode Occasion'd by the Death of Mr Thomson*. For example, a couplet from *The Vale of Esthwaite* (1787) is modelled on lines by Collins:

> And since that hour the world unknown
> The world of shades is all my own (*D.C.MS 3* 10r)

Compare Collins' *Ode to Fear* 1-2: 'Thou, to whom the World unknown / With all its shadowy Shapes is shown'. Betz Ph.D. 44 discusses the influence of Collins on W's *Dirge Sung by a Minstrel* (1787).

(ii) *Odes*
Suggested date of reading: 1787-90
References: Cornell *EW* 66; *PW* i 322
Collins was an influence on W's Cambridge verse, and echoes from him can be found in an early sonnet later revised to form *Remembrance of Collins* and *Lines Written near Richmond, upon the Thames,*[1] *at Evening* (both published in *Lyrical Ballads*). This sonnet, which Reed calls *Lines Written while Sailing in a Boat at Evening* (Reed i 22), survives in *D.C.MS 11* in a draft made some time after its original composition.[2] It concludes:

---

[1] W's Fenwick Note points out that the poem was actually inspired by a walk along the Cam (*PW* i 324).
[2] It is published in my article, 'Wordsworth's Reading of Bowles', *N&Q* NS 36 (1989) 166-7, p. 167.

> Witness that son of grief who in these glades
> Mourned his dead friend - suspend the dashing oar (lines 11-12)

The phrase 'suspend the dashing oar' alludes to Collins' *Ode Occasion'd by the Death of Mr Thomson* 13-16:

> Remembrance oft shall haunt the Shore
> When Thames in Summer-wreaths is drest,
> And oft *suspend the dashing Oar*
> To bid his gentle Spirit rest!

Collins' *Ode Occasion'd by the Death of Mr Thomson* played an even larger part in the final version of W's poem.[1]

The Rydal Mount library contained a copy of the 1747 edition of Collins' *Odes on Several Descriptive and Allegoric Subjects* (Shaver 63) - a rare book, for almost all 1000 copies of the edition were destroyed when they failed to sell. In Sept. 1808 W expressed his sympathy: 'What safe had Collins' Poems during his lifetime, or during the fourteen years after his death, and how great has been the sale since! the product of it if secured to his family, would have been an independence to them' (*MY* i 266). See also *LY* iii 626.

(iii) *An Ode on the Popular Superstitions of the Highlands of Scotland* [1788]
Suggested date of reading: c. April 1788
References: *LY* i 648
W's well-informed letter to Alexander Dyce of 29 Oct. 1828 describes the bibliographical history of Collins' *Ode on the Popular Superstitions of the Highlands* - still useful to modern editors of the poem (see Lonsdale 498, 515n). W recalls that

> in 1788 the Ode was first printed from Dr Carlyle's copy, with Mr Mackenzie's supplemental lines - and was extensively circulated through the English newspapers, in which I remember to have read it with great pleasure upon its first appearance.
>
> (*LY* i 648; his underlining)

Lonsdale confirms that the *Ode* was first published from a MS belonging to Dr Alexander Carlyle in the first volume of the *Transactions of the Royal Society of Edinburgh* 2 (1788) 63-75. W states that 'I never saw the Edinburgh Transactions, in which Dr C.'s copy was printed' (*LY* i 649). The *Ode*, he correctly recalls, was reprinted in a selection of newspapers and magazines, including the *European Magazine* 13 (1788) 241-6, the *Gazeteer*, 4 April 1788, and the *London Chronicle*, 1-3, 3-5 April 1788.

(iv) *Odes*
Suggested date of reading: 1791-2
References: Cornell *DS* 70, 80

59. Colman, George, *The Iron Chest* (1796)
Suggested date of reading: after 23 July 1796
References: *WC* 4 (1973) 31-5

---

[1] See *PW* i 41 and 324; see also Healey 2797 and plate following Healey p. 400; Stein 19-29.

The Iron Chest was first performed on 12 March 1796, and its popularity depended partly on that of Godwin's *Caleb Williams*, on which it was based. W visited London in June and met with Godwin several times (Reed i 182-4), when Colman's play may have arisen in conversation. Whether or not W saw the play, he probably read it after it had been published on 23 July 1796. Pollin, 'Permutations of Names in *The Borderers*, or hints of Godwin, Charles Lloyd, and a real renegade', *WC* 4 (1973) 31-5, discusses the play's influence on *The Borderers*.

60. Condorcet, Antoine-Nicolas, *Outline for an Historical Picture of the Progress of the Human Mind* (1795)

Suggested date of reading: possibly 1795-6
References: Chard 98-9; Roe 78
Chard argues that Condorcet's ideas were known to W through Girondin friends:

> by starting with a belief in the innate goodness of man, Condorcet and his predecessors evolved an optimistic philosophy heavily emphasizing reason and education; it culminated with the theory 'that the perfectibility of man is truly indefinite'... It must be kept in mind, furthermore, that though *The Progress of the Human Mind* was published posthumously in 1795 (in both England and France), Condorcet made his opinions known both as a member of the Legislative Assembly from 1791 to 1792 and in his subsequent attempts to devise a permanent Constitution for the nation... *The Progress of the Human Mind* was essentially a final statement of the author's ideals, which ideals Wordsworth may easily have noted either in the reports of political affairs while he was in Blois or Orléans, or in the Assembly itself while he was in Paris.
>
> (Chard 98-9)

This is supported by Roe, who suggests that W's claim in the *Letter to the Bishop of Llandaff* that Louis XVI occupied 'that monstrous situation which rendered him unaccountable before a human tribunal' (*Prose Works* i 32) echoes Condorcet's call in Nov. 1792 for a 'tribunal ... chosen by all the departments' to ensure Louis an 'impartial trial' in the eyes of the nation (Roe 78).

The *Outline* was published by Joseph Johnson in May 1795; he advertised imported copies of the French text in the *Morning Chronicle*, 19 Aug. 1795.

61. Congreve, William, works, inc. *The Old Bachelor*

Suggested date of reading: by 8 June 1788
References: Grosart iii 94; Reed i 86n
'I remember how', W recalled in the Fenwick Note to his *Sonnet at Florence*,

> during one of my rambles in the course of a college vacation, I was pleased on being shown at [   ] a seat near a kind of rocky cell at the source of the river [   ], on which it was said that Congreve wrote his 'Old Bachelor'. One can scarcely hit on any performance less in harmony with the scene; but it was a local tribute paid to intellect by those who had not troubled themselves to estimate the moral worth of that author's comedies; and why should they? He was a man distinguished in his day; and the sequestered neighbourhood in which he often resided was perhaps as proud of him as Florence of her Dante ... (*PW* iii 499)

Reed points out that, 'Of the several places which vie for the honor of having been the location for the composition of *The Old Bachelor*, the one which W visited must have been that at Ilam, four miles northwest of Ashbourne' (Reed i 86n).[1] W visited Ashbourne on 8 June 1788 (see *Prose Works* i 10-11), and must have visited Ilam that evening or the following day. The visit implies a reading of Congreve, including *The Old Bachelor*. If W had read Congreve by June 1788, he had probably read other Restoration dramatists. He knew Farquhar by 1796; see note 102.

62. Constant, Benjamin, *Observations on the Strength of the Present Government of France, and upon the Necessity of Rallying Round It* tr. James Losh (Bath, 1797)
Suggested date of reading: Jan./Feb. 1797
References: *EY* 186
W was in correspondence with Losh while this pamphlet was in preparation (see Reed i 194-6). Losh wrote to W on 7 Jan. 1797, and on 3 March (having published Constant's *Observations* on 26 Jan.), and sent at least two parcels of books to W during spring 1797. It is likely that his own publications were among them.

Even if W did not know the *Observations* at first hand, he would have heard about them from C. In early Feb. 1797, C told Thelwall:

> That good man, James Losh, has just published an admirable pamphlet translated from the French of Benjamin Constant entitled 'Considerations on the Strength of the present Government of France'. (Griggs i 308)

W's letter to Losh of 11 March 1798 confirms 'how deeply interested [C] is in e[very]thing relating to you' (*EY* 213).

63. Cooper, Anthony Ashley, 3rd Earl of Shaftesbury, *Characteristicks* [1711]
Suggested date of reading: by 1785
References: see note
It is indicative of the sophistication of W's juvenile poetry that in *Lines Written as a School Exercise* (1785) he praises the power of Education

> To teach on rapid wings the curious Soul
> To roam from Heav'n to Heav'n, from Pole to Pole,
> From thence to search the mystic cause of things
> And follow Nature to her secret springs ... (lines 73-6)

W's diction can be traced to the 'argument from design' drawn in rational eighteenth-century proofs of God's existence - for he echoes Shaftesbury's deduction of a 'Universal Mind' from the 'Universal System' of Nature:

---

[1] Reed cites Boswell's *Life of Johnson* as evidence that *The Old Bachelor* was composed at Ilam: 'I recollect a very fine amphitheatre, surrounded with hills covered with wood, and walks neatly formed along the side of a rocky steep, on the quarter next the house, with recesses under projections of rock, overshadowed with trees; in one of which recesses, we were told, Congreve wrote his "Old Bachelor"' (*Boswell's Life of Johnson* ed. George Birkbeck Hill, rev. L. F. Powell [6 vols., Oxford, 1934-50], iii 187).

For can it be suppos'd of any one in the World, that being in some Desart far from Men, and hearing there a perfect Symphony of Musick, or seeing an exact Pile of regular Architecture arising gradually from the Earth in all its Orders and Proportions, he shou'd be persuaded that at the bottom there was no Design accompanying this, no *secret Spring of Thought*, no active Mind? (*Characteristicks* ii 290)

This suggests that W encountered *Characteristicks* whilst a schoolboy, by 1785. There was a copy in the Rydal Mount library in 1829 (Shaver 65); W's 1800 Preface borrows from Shaftesbury (see *Prose Works* i 175; Owen, *Wordsworth's Preface to Lyrical Ballads* [Copenhagen, 1957], pp. 50-1).

64. Cottle, Joseph

(i) *Malvern Hills: a poem* (1798)
Suggested date of reading: Feb.-March 1798
References: Reed i 226; *EY* 214; *WC* 13 (1982) 98
Malvern Hills was lent by Cottle to the Wordsworths in Feb. 1798, and returned to him *c.* 13 March. This suggests that the Wordsworths had acquired their own copy of the poem by then. In 'Two Addenda', *WC* 13 (1982) 98, Owen reprints *Malvern Hills* 38-64, with suggestions as to how it may have influenced *The Thorn*.

Writing to Cottle in Jan. 1829, W claimed that *Malvern Hills* 'was always a favourite of mine - some passages - and especially one, closing "to him who slept at noon and wakes at Eve" [*Malvern Hills* 921-56], I thought superexcellent' (*LY* ii 10). This is borne out by the fact that *Malvern Hills* 952-6 are incorporated into the *Fourteen-Book Prelude* viii 48-52. Owen identifies other borrowings in both the Thirteen and Fourteen-Book versions of the poem (Cornell *14-Book Prelude* 160n). The Rydal Mount auction catalogue records that W's copy of the first edition (now lost) contained 'MS. Notes by Mr. Wordsworth' (Park 57).

(ii) *Alfred* in MS
Suggested date of reading: 1798
References: Butler *JEGP* 149; *CLB* NS 73 (Jan. 1991) 19-21
On 27 July 1799, W told Cottle that 'Looking over some old monthly Magazines I saw a paragraph stating that your "Arthur" was ready for the press! I laughed heartily at this idle story' (Butler *JEGP* 149). Explaining this unkind remark, Butler points out that W is referring to Cottle's *Alfred*, 'which was not published until 1800, although Cottle had been working on it for some time'. W's remark would suggest that he had known of its progress for a while, and that he had perhaps heard or read sections in MS during spring or summer 1798. Since the idea for the poem had been suggested to C by Poole's brother, Richard, and passed on to Cottle by C, it is likely that W heard regular reports of its progress during 1798; for further details of its origins, see my article, 'Cottle's *Alfred*: Another Coleridge-Inspired Epic', *CLB* NS 73 (Jan. 1991) 19-21.

Reed notes that W's consideration of Mithradates as a subject at *Thirteen-Book Prelude* i 186-202 was inspired not only by Mallet and Gibbon (see notes 167 and A10), but by Joseph Cottle's long note on Mithradates and Odin at the opening of *Alfred*. He would presumably have read this in the published volume. As Reed observes, although W had not seen the printed volume as of 19 Dec. 1800 (see Butler *JEGP* 153), 'He probably did see the book, sooner or later, but when is unknown' (Cornell *13-Book Prelude* i 17n).

(iii) *The Killcrop*
Suggested date of reading: Aug. 1799; by 2 Sept. 1799
References: Butler *JEGP* 149-50
See note 9.

65. Cowley, Abraham, *The Works of Mr Abraham Cowley* **(7th edn, 1681)**
Suggested date of reading: 1789-90
References: *Prose Works* iii 71
Septimius and Acme, W's 1788 translation of Catullus, *Carmen* xlv, apparently follows
Cowley's rendering, particularly in the way W chooses to expand some of Catullus' lines.
For instance, Catullus *Carmen* xlv 16, 'ignis mollibus ardent in medullis', is translated by
Cowley: 'It reigns not only in my heart, / But runs, like life, through ev'ry part' (*Ode* 35-6).
W characteristically eschews the *double entendre*, but offers his own expansion, where love

> Burns at my heart - with more resistless sway
> Thrills through my bones and melts away my frame (lines 19-20)

In 1815 W recalled that on his first visit to London 'the booksellers' stalls ... swarmed with
the folios of Cowley' (*Prose Works* iii 71). We cannot say for sure whether he purchased one
of these, but he would have been more likely to remember this detail if he had. He owned
a copy of Cowley's *Works* by Oct. 1801, when C entered numerous marginalia in it. This
is now at the Lilly Library, University of Indiana. Its whereabouts is not mentioned by the
Shavers (Shaver 68), and the copy is not listed by Noyes, *The Indiana Wordsworth
Collection: A Catalogue* (Boston, 1978). But a full account is given by Whalley, *CC
Marginalia* ii 102-3; see also Coffman C170.

66. Cowper, William
(i) *Poems* **(1782)**
Suggested date of reading: 1782-5
References: TWT 344
Thomas Bowman Jr recalls that his father provided W with a copy of Cowper's *Task* when
it first came out (TWT 344); such avid interest in Cowper's latest publication implies some
knowledge on W's part of his earlier work. He may at least have read *Poems* (1782).

(ii) *The Task* **(1785)**
Suggested date of reading: *c.* July 1785
References: TWT 344; Lienemann 87
Bowman lent W a copy of this work 'soon after' its first publication (TWT 344). *The Task*
was published at the beginning of July 1785, and W can be presumed to have read it during
the summer. Lienemann 87 detected echoes of *The Task* in the revised extract from *The Vale
of Esthwaite* published in 1815 as *Extract from the Conclusion of a Poem, Composed in
Anticipation of Leaving School*:

> Der Lektüre von Cowpers 1785 ershienenen Dichtung *The Task* muß sich Wordsworth
> bald nach ihrem Erscheinen hingegeben haben, denn Anklänge finden sich schon in dem
> Anfängergedicht 'Dear native regions, I foretell' (1786).

Lienemann does not specify what these echoes may be, and I have not found them.

(iii) *The Task*
Suggested date of reading: 1789
References: *PW* i 323
De Selincourt points out that the owl's 'boding note' at *Evening Walk* 392 recalls *Task* i 205-6: 'and ev'n the *boding* owl / That hails the rising moon [has] charms for me'.

(iv) poems inc. *The Task*
Suggested date of reading: 1791-2
References: Cornell *DS* 98

(v) *John Gilpin*
Suggested date of reading: spring 1797
References: see note
In *The Baker's Cart* Fragment (Cornell *RC* 463), composed spring 1797, W wrote:

> I have seen the Baker's horse
> As he had been accustomed at your door
> Stop with the loaded wain, when o'er his head
> *Smack went the whip* ... (lines 1-4)

Roe points out to me that W is recalling *John Gilpin* 41: '*Smack went the whip*, round went the wheels ...'

(vi) *John Gilpin*
Suggested date of reading: spring 1798
References: Mason *LB* 160

(vii) *Table Talk*
Suggested date of reading: spring 1798
References: see note
In blank verse lines composed spring 1798, W described the Pedlar's transcendent state:

> Accordingly he by degrees perceives
> His feelings of aversion softened down
> *A holy tenderness pervade his frame* (Cornell *RC* 261)

The last line is borrowed from Cowper, *Table Talk* 485: 'A tender sympathy pervades the frame'.

(viii) *The Task*
Suggested date of reading: *c.* Dec. 1798
References: see note
Owen, 'Understanding *The Prelude*', *WC* 22 (1991) 100-9, points out that *Two-Part Prelude* i 226-7 echoes *Task* iv 308-10: 'We remember, too, as Wordsworth must have remembered, that this passage from *The Task* is the basis of Coleridge's "Frost at Midnight," from which Wordsworth had already quoted in this book' (p. 107). In addition, Owen tells me that the phrase 'craggy ridge' at *Two-Part Prelude* i 100 is borrowed from *Task* iv 57, and that the screaming fiddle at *Two-Part Prelude* i 39 is borrowed from *Task* iv 478 (letter to me). This suggests that W read *The Task* (at least Book IV) either shortly before or during composition of *The Two-Part Prelude*, which was begun in Dec. 1798.

67. Coxe, William, *Travels in Switzerland. In a Series of Letters to William Melmoth, Esq.* (3 vols., 1789)
Suggested date of reading: 1790-1
References: *N&Q* 195 (1950) 144-5; Gill 45n
Coe suggests that Coxe helped determine the route taken by W and Jones on their tour:

> While outlining the itinerary of his journey, Wordsworth explains to Dorothy: 'You have undoubtedly heard of these celebrated scenes, but if you have not read of them, any description which I have here room to give you must be altogether inadequate.' [*EY* 33] Doesn't this suggest that Wordsworth had read some description of these 'celebrated scenes' and was in a position to compare his own account of them in the letter with the more detailed accounts to be found in a book like Coxe's?[1]

Gill agrees that W was guided by Coxe, but points out that his *Travels* went through a number of different versions, and suggests that W is most likely to have used the first:

> It is not clear which edition of Coxe W knew in 1790. The book appeared as William Coxe, *Sketches of the Natural, Civil, and Political State of Swisserland: In a series of letters to William Melmoth, Esq.* (London, 1779; 2nd edn. 1780). It was translated as *Lettres de M. William Coxe à M. W. Melmoth, sur l'état politique, Civil et naturel de la Suisse: Traduites de l'anglois, et augmentées des observations faites dans le même pays par le traducteur* [Ramond de Carbonnières] (2 vols., Paris, 1781; 2nd edn. 1782). A further English version appeared as *Travels in Switzerland: In a Series of Letters to William Melmoth, Esq.* (3 vols., London, 1789). A copy of this last book was given to Hawkshead School by William and Christopher Raincock in 1792. W certainly knew the French edition by 1792, as he acknowledges his indebtedness to it in *Descriptive Sketches*, and by then he would have been fluent enough in French to read it with ease. It seems likely, however, that on his 1790 tour he was guided by the first and simplest English version. (Gill 45n)

There is broad agreement that W's itinerary on his walking tour implies a reading of Coxe. This is supported by a note to *Descriptive Sketches*: 'For most of the images in the next sixteen verses I am indebted to M. Raymond's interesting observations annexed to his translation of Coxe's Tour in Switzerland' (Cornell *DS* 74). W turned to Coxe as he composed *Descriptive Sketches* in Blois because he had read the *Travels* in preceding years.

'Tour in Switzerland' is the title usually cited when W refers to Coxe (see, for instance, *EY* 235), and it is closest to the edition published as *Travels in Switzerland: In a Series of Letters to William Melmoth, Esq.* (3 vols., 1789). I doubt whether W knew Coxe's earlier *Sketches of Swisserland* (1779; 2nd edn, 1780).

68. Crabbe, George, 'An Extract from THE VILLAGE, a Poem by the Rev. G. CRABBE, Chaplain to his Grace the Duke of Rutland, &c.'
Suggested date of reading: 1783-7
References: TWT 344

---

[1] 'Did Wordsworth Read Coxe's *Travels in Switzerland* Before Making the Tour of 1790?', *N&Q* 195 (1950) 144-5.

On 21 Oct. 1809 Sir Walter Scott wrote to Crabbe, recalling his boyhood encounter with his poetry:

> Among the very few books which fell under my hands was a volume or two of Dodsley's Annual Register, one of which contained copious extracts from 'The Village' and 'The Library,' particularly the conclusion of book first of the former, and an extract from the latter ...
> (*The Poetical Works of the Revd. George Crabbe* ed. George Crabbe Jr [8 vols., 1834], i 191; his italics)

In Feb. 1834 W wrote to George Crabbe Jr, revealing that

> I first became acquainted with Mr Crabbe's Works in the same way, and about the same time, as did Sir Walter Scott ... and the extracts made such an impression upon me, that *I* can also repeat them. The two lines
> 'Far the happiest they
> The moping idiot and the madman gay'
> struck my youthful feelings particularly - tho' facts, as far as they had then come under my knowledge, did not support the description; inasmuch as idiots and lunatics - among the humbler Classes of society - were not to be found in Workhouses - in the parts of the North where I was brought up, - but were mostly at large, and too often the butt of thoughtless Children. (*LY* ii 691-2; his italic)

Scott and W correctly recall two extracts from *The Village* in the *Annual Register* 26 (1783) ii 183-9, which appeared as 'An Extract from THE VILLAGE, a Poem by the Rev. G. CRABBE, Chaplain to his Grace the Duke of Rutland, &c.' (hereafter *Extract*). The lines that stuck in W's mind were from Crabbe's description of the poorhouse:

> Their's is yon house that holds the parish poor,
> Whose walls of mud scarce bear the broken door;
> There, where the putrid vapours, flagging, play,
> And the dull wheel hums doleful through the day;
> There children dwell who know no parents' care,
> Parents, who know no children's love, dwell there;
> Heart-broken matrons on their joyless bed,
> Forsaken wives and mothers never wed;
> Dejected widows with unheeded tears,
> And crippled age with more than childhood-fears;
> The lame, the blind, and, far the happiest they!
> The moping idiot and the madman gay. (*Extract* 57-68)

69. Crakanthorpe, Richard, *Vigilius Dormitans ... a Treatise on the Fifth General Council, Held at Constantinople, anno 553 ... published and set forth by his brother, Geo: Crakanthorpe* [1631]
Suggested date of reading: 1794
References: Reed i 149n; *EY* 674; Shaver 28
We know the titles of at least two books W possessed at Windy Brow because he left them behind, and they were identified by the caretaker, Mr Ianson, as '1st Guide Du Voyageur En

41

Suisse - 2nd Treatise of the fifth Genl council held at Constantinople Anno 553 by G. Crackanthorp' (*EY* 674). A copy of Crakanthorpe was present in the old library of Hawkshead Grammar School (Wu *CWAAS* 77).

70. *Critical Review*
(i) July 1793; Aug. 1793
Suggested date of reading: Aug., Sept. 1793
References: Reed i 146, 148
An Evening Walk was reviewed in the *Critical* for July, and *Descriptive Sketches* for Aug.

(ii) March 1798; April 1798
Suggested date of reading: April, May 1798
References: Erdman *BNYPL* 575-87
Erdman *BNYPL* 575-87 attributes two reviews in the *Critical Review* 1798 to C: (1) Sir William Jones, *Institutes of Hindu Law*, published March 1798; (2) M. G. Lewis, *The Castle Spectre*, published April 1798. If these reviews were by C, W may have read them. It is likely, in any case, that W was reading the *Critical Review* at this period.

(iii) Oct. 1798
Suggested date of reading: by *c.* 27 May 1799
References: Butler *JEGP* 145
'Southeys review I have seen', W wrote to Cottle, *c.* 27 May 1799 (Butler *JEGP* 145). Southey's unfavourable account of *Lyrical Ballads* was published in the *Critical Review* for Oct. 1798, and published *c.* 1 Nov 1798.

71. Crowe, William, *Lewesdon Hill* (Oxford, 1788)
Suggested date of reading: Nov.-Dec. 1795
References: Pinney Papers; *EY* 166n; Shaver 71
At the conclusion of his letter to W of 26 Nov. 1795, Azariah Pinney promises: 'I shall send you by this opportunity Luesdon Hill' (Pinney Papers, Family Letter Book 13). W probably had the poem by the end of the month, or during the first week of Dec. at the latest.

Crowe's *Lewesdon Hill* would have been of interest to Pinney and the Wordsworths because it describes the countryside around Racedown. Its account of the 'prospect' from the top of Lewesdon Hill is a forerunner of the Wordsworthian view along the Wye (compare, for instance, Crowe's 'tufted orchards' with W's 'orchard-tufts', *Tintern Abbey* 11). Williams, *Wordsworth: Romantic Poetry and Revolution Politics* (Manchester, 1989), pp. 10-18, discusses Crowe's political background and his influence on W.

72. Daniel, Samuel, *History of the Civil Wars between the houses of York and Lancaster* [1595]
Suggested date of reading: by 13 July 1798
References: Mason *LB* 213
Mason *LB* 213 finds that 'Nature never did betray / The heart that loved her' (*Tintern Abbey* 123-4) echoes Daniel, *Civil Wars* ii 225-6:

> Here have you craggy Rocks to take your Part,
> That never will betray their Faith to you ...

This is the earliest reminiscence of Daniel in W's poetry thus far discovered, and supports my suspicion that W had by 13 July 1798 acquired his copy of *The Poetical Works of Mr. Samuel Daniel* (2 vols., 1718), now at the Wordsworth Library (Shaver 73). It was at Dove Cottage by 31 Dec. 1803, when C consulted it (CC *Marginalia* i 116-17), and it was probably from this set that Mary Hutchinson read *Musophilus* on 24 Nov. 1801 (*Grasmere Journals* 41). Both volumes contain the undated ownership inscription, 'W. Wordsworth', in a hand dating apparently from the 1790s. The title-page contains the deleted inscription of a former owner of the set, while the third flyleaf of Vol. 1 contains that of W's grandson:

> W^m. Wordsworth Jr.
> Rydal Mount. March 1858.
> This copy of the works of Daniel is from the library at Rydal Mount. the volumes were among my Grandfathers especial favorites and were frequently in his hands. W.W.

Turning to the *History of the Civil Wars* in Vol. 2 it is interesting to find the stanza containing the lines recalled in *Tintern Abbey* marked heavily in pencil. Numerous pencil markings and some annotations by W may be found in both volumes.

If W did not own his copy of Daniel by 1798, he might still have read the *Civil Wars* in C's copy of Anderson's *British Poets* Vol. 4 (see note 7). This may be the implication of his later comment that had it not been for Anderson 'I should have known little of Drayton, Daniel, and other distinguished poets of the Elizabethan age, and their immediate successors, till a much later period of my life' (*PW* iii 451).

73. Dante Alighieri
(i) *La Divina Commedia*
Suggested date of reading: by 1793, possibly before
References: *N&Q* NS 27 (1980) 204-5; *WC* 3 (1972) 3-16

> The thoughts which bow the kindly spirits down
> And break the springs of joy, their deadly weight
> Derive from memory of pleasures flown
> Which haunts us in some sad reverse of fate ... (*Salisbury Plain* 19-22)

Sturrock, 'Wordsworth: An Early Borrowing from Dante', *N&Q* NS 27 (1980) 204-5, argues that these lines from *Salisbury Plain* (1793) were influenced by Dante:

> Nessun maggior dolore
> che ricordarsi del tempo felice
> ne la miseria ... (*Inferno* v 121-3)

Owen points out to me that 'Dante might be relevant, but the sentiment is commonplace' (letter to me). In his article, 'Literary Echoes in *The Prelude*' he traces it back to Chaucer and, ultimately, Boethius (*WC* 3 [1972] 3-16). Sturrock is aware of the Chaucerian and Boethian examples (independently of Owen, apparently) but states that 'Wordsworth is not known to have been acquainted with the *De Consolatione Philosophiae* of Boethius, on which Dante based this passage' (p. 205). She argues against W having borrowed the sentiment from Chaucer on the grounds that he 'first became familiar with Chaucer from Robert Anderson's *Works of the English Poets*, which was not published until 1795' (p. 205). In fact, W encountered Chaucer first at Cambridge or Hawkshead (see note 53 [i]), when he might have read any number of editions of the *Works*; and the mere fact that he is 'not known' to have read Boethius does not necessarily mean that he did not. Whatever W's source in *Salisbury Plain*, the most likely time for a reading of Dante is during the course of his Italian studies at Cambridge. His 'strong predilection' for Dante, mentioned by Hazlitt in 1800 (Howe iv 276), suggests that he had known *La Divina Commedia* for some time. His remarks to Landor in 1824 also imply a long acquaintance with Dante's work: 'his style I used to think admirable for conciseness and vigour, without abruptness; but I own that his fictions often struck me as offensively grotesque and fantastic, and I felt the Poem tedious from various causes' (*LY* i 245-6).

(ii) *Purgatorio*
Suggested date of reading: spring 1798
References: see note
The editors of the Longman *Wordsworth* suggest that the 'little boat' in the Prologue to W's *Peter Bell* recalls 'la navicella del mio ingegno' from the opening lines of the *Purgatorio*.

74. Darwin, Erasmus
(i) *The Botanic Garden* Part II, *The Loves of the Plants* (1789)
Suggested date of reading: 1789
References: Cornell *EW* 56
W's allusion to Darwin appears at *Evening Walk* 199, which does not appear in the drafts of the poem dating from 1789, *D.C.MS 7*. However, there is no cause to doubt that they were composed at that time, or that W saw Darwin's poem soon after publication.

(ii) *The Botanic Garden* Part II, *The Loves of the Plants* (1789)
Suggested date of reading: 1791-2
References: see note

> The cross with hideous laughter Demons mock,
> By angels planted on the aëreal rock ... (*Descriptive Sketches* 70-1)

W imitates *The Loves of the Plants* iii 107-8:

> While from dark caves infernal Echoes mock,
> And fiends triumphant shout from every rock!

(iii) *The Botanic Garden* Part I, *The Economy of Vegetation* (1792)
Suggested date of reading: between June and Dec. 1792; by Dec. 1792
References: see note
In *Descriptive Sketches* W refers to 'Th' *indignant waters* of the infant Rhine' (line 185), borrowing from Darwin's description of the Alps: 'Where round dark crags *indignant waters* bend' (*Economy of Vegetation* iii 113). There are other similarities between W's poem and *The Economy of Vegetation* (dated 1791, though in fact published June 1792), but it is hard to believe that he had time to absorb the influence of Darwin's 2,500 line poem between his return from France, Nov./Dec. 1792, and the publisher's deadline, Dec. 1792/Jan. 1793 (*An Evening Walk* and *Descriptive Sketches* were published on 29 Jan. 1793). The most likely explanation is he acquired a copy during his stay in France. English books were sold there, and the popular ones were easy to find in Paris.

(iv) *Zoönomia; or, the Laws of Organic Life* (**2 vols., 1794-6**)
Suggested date of reading: 1796-7; after April 1796
References: EY 214
On either 28 Feb. or 7 March 1798, W asked Joseph Cottle to 'contrive to send me Dr Darwin's Zoönomia *by the first carrier*. If it is not in your power to borrow it I wish you would send to Cote House with my compliments to John Wedgwood and say that I should be much obliged to him if he would let me have it for ten days, at the end of which time it shall certainly be returned' (*EY* 199; his italics). (One of the case-histories described by Darwin provided the source for *Goody Blake and Harry Gill*.) Apart from the copy at Cote House, Westbury, several miles north of Bristol, there were at least two others in the vicinity: there was one at the Bristol Library Society, and another in the Pinney house in Great George Street. It was probably the latter W had in mind when he asked Cottle to 'borrow it'. The speed with which it 'answered the purpose' (by 13 March - see *EY* 214-15) indicates that W knew precisely what he wanted, having read it previously, possibly on a visit to Bristol in 1796-7. The passage which informs *Goody Blake and Harry Gill* appears in Part II, published in April 1796 during W's Racedown residence.

W may have been told of the case-history by C, who would also have known of the copy at Cote House, which he had visited as recently as 30 Jan. 1798 (Griggs i 380).

(v) *Zoönomia; or, the Laws of Organic Life* (**2 vols., 1794-6**)
Suggested date of reading: 10-13 March 1798
References: EY 214
See preceding note. See also Averill, 'Wordsworth and "Natural Science": The Poetry of 1798', *JEGP* 77 (1978) 232-46; Matlak, 'Wordsworth's Reading of *Zoonomia* in Early Spring', *WC* 21 (1990) 76-81; and Mason *LB* 174.

(vi) *The Botanic Garden* **Part I,** *The Economy of Vegetation* (**1792**)
Suggested date of reading: c. Dec. 1798
References: see note
Owen informs me that *Two-Part Prelude* i 156-7, 'All shod with steel / We hissed along the polished ice', recollects Darwin, *Economy of Vegetation* iii 596-70:

> On step alternate borne, with balance nice
> Hang o'er the gliding steel, and hiss along the ice.

I would go so far as to suggest that *Two-Part Prelude* i 150-69 was inspired by Darwin's passage, lines 561-70. Perhaps W reread Darwin shortly before, or during, composition of the *Two-Part Prelude*.

75. Davila, Enrico Caterina, *Historia delle Guerre Civili di Francia ... nella quale si contengono le operationi di quattro rè, Francesco II., Carlo IX., Henrico III. e Henrico IV. cognominato il Grande* (**Venice, 1642**)
Suggested date of reading: Oct. 1795-spring 1796
References: EY 155, 170
In Oct. 1795, W told Mathews: 'We have a very toler[able] library here. Machiavel Boccacio, D'av[ila] and several other italian Books' (*EY* 155). Since W and Mathews probably knew these authors from their Italian studies at Cambridge, it was natural that W should use them in teaching DW. On 21 March 1796, he told Mathews that DW 'has already

gone through half of Davila' (*EY* 170). At Rydal Mount W possessed his own copy of Davila, in the original Italian, published at Venice, 1646 (Shaver 74).

76. Delille, Jacques, *Les Jardins*
Suggested date of reading: by Dec. 1792
References: Cornell *DS* 112
A note to *Descriptive Sketches*, probably added in Dec. 1792 shortly before the poem's printing, describes the banks of the River Loiret:

> The hand of false taste has committed on its banks those outrages which the Abbé de Lille so pathetically deprecates in those charming verses descriptive of the Seine, visiting in secret the retreat of his friend Watelet. (Cornell *DS* 112)

Legouis incorrectly identifies this as an allusion to Delille's *Inscription en vers pour Moulin Joli*; in fact, W had before him a copy of *Les Jardins*, for his phrasing closely echoes Delille's 'En visite en secret la retraite d'un sage' (iii 348). The 'charming verses' read as follows:

> Tu traitas sa beauté comme une vierge pure
> Qui rougit d'être nue, & craint les ornemens.
> Je crois voir le faux-goût gâter ces lieux charmans.
> Ce moulin, dont le bruit nourrit la rêverie,
> N'est qu'un son importun, qu'une meule qui crie;
> On l'écarte. Ces bords doucement contournés,
> Par le fleuve lui-même en roulant façonnés,
> S'alignent tristement. Au lieu de la verdure
> Qui renferme le fleuve en sa molle ceinture,
> L'eau dans des quais de pierre accuse sa prison;
> Le marbre fastueux outrage le gazon,
> Et des arbres tondus la famille captive
> Sur ces saules vieillis ose usurper la rive.
> Barbares, arrêtez, & respectez ces lieux.
> Et vous, fleuve charmant, vous, bois délicieux,
> Si j'ai peint vois beautés, si dès mon premier âge
> Je me plûs à chanter les prés, l'onde & l'ombrage,
> Beaux lieux, offrez long temps à votre possesseur
> L'image de la paix qui règne dans son cœur. (*Les Jardins* iii 352-70)

Perhaps W read *Les Jardins* in 1791 in the copy of Delille's *Œuvres* later retained at Rydal Mount (Shaver 75). He returned to Delille in later years: Legouis points out that he consulted *Les Jardins* while composing *The Reverie of Poor Susan* (Legouis 143n), and Owen suggests that he referred to the 'Discours Preliminaire' to Delille's *Georgiques*, while composing the Preface to *Lyrical Ballads* (*Prose Works* i 179, 185). See also Hearn, *The Road to Rydal Mount* (Salzburg, 1973), pp. 173-82.

77. Demosthenes
(i) *Orations*

Suggested date of reading: Aug. 1786 onwards
References: Shepherd MSS; TWT 91; Reed i 68
The accounts of Christopher Crackanthorpe Cookson (1745-1799), now among the Shepherd
MSS at the Wordsworth Library, record the purchase of W's Demosthenes for four shillings:

1786 Aug 8th P^d. Anthony Soulby a Demosthenes for William 0.4.0

It is interesting to find Soulby's name here. JW Sr purchased four volumes of *Gil Blas* from
him in 1781 (see note 150); Soulby also ran the Penrith Book Club used by W in summer
1787.
    W's study of Demosthenes was certainly under way by spring 1787, for *D.C.MS 3* (in use
at that time) contains a Latin and Greek exercise on Demosthenes' *De Corona* in his hand.
Clancey assures me that W read *De Corona* at this time, and draws my attention to the copy
of *Aischinou ho kata Ktesiphontos kai Demosthenous ho peri stephanou logos* (2nd edn,
Oxford, 1715), retained at the Rydal Mount library (Shaver 4). This volume, Clancey writes,

> is clearly a school text and typical of the classics texts used by Wordsworth as a boy
> at Hawkshead. It has a Latin 'interpretation', probably a fairly close translation of the
> Greek into Latin. It also has the more difficult words 'explained'. This is the 1715
> edition. Might it be the Demosthenes Wordsworth was given at Hawkshead, or is it
> more likely a volume he picked up when tutoring his son John? (letter to me)

Leland's translation of the *Orations* (3rd edn, 1777) was also in the Rydal Mount library
(Shaver 75); it is not possible to say when it was acquired.

(ii) *Demosthenis selectæ orationis. Ad codices MSS. recensuit, textum, scholiasten, &*
versionem plurimis in locis castigavit. notis insuper illustravit Ricardus Mounteney
[Cambridge, 1731]
Suggested date of reading: by Dec. 1789
References: Schneider 156
W was examined on this book at St John's College, Cambridge, Dec. 1789. It contains
Olynthiacs I-III and *Philippics* I, and reached its 9th edition in 1791; see p. 168, below.

78. Denham, Sir John, *Cooper's Hill* [1642]
Suggested date of reading: probably summer or autumn 1789; by May 1798
References: Owen *LB* 180
Owen *LB* 180 finds that W's *Lines written near Richmond, upon the Thames, at evening* 23-4
echoes *Cooper's Hill* 189-92. The echo does not occur in earlier versions of W's poem; the
version which appeared in *Lyrical Ballads* (1798) was composed, Reed writes, 'between 29
Mar 1797 and 30 May 1798' (Reed i 23). It is likely, however, that W had known Denham's
widely anthologized poem since his Hawkshead schooldays; it is discussed in Scott's *Essays*,
which he probably read in the summer or autumn of 1789 (see note 220 [i]).

79. Doddridge, Philip, *Three Sermons on the Evidences of the Gospel; Preached at Northampton*
Suggested date of reading: c. Dec. 1787
References: Schneider 9
W was examined on this book at St John's College, Cambridge, Dec. 1787; see p. 167, below.

80. Donne, John, *Death be not proud*
Suggested date of reading: 1798
References: Reed i 327n
W copied a brief quotation from Donne's *Death be not proud* into *D.C.MS 16* (in use at Alfoxden, and in which he drafted *The Ruined Cottage* MS B); it reads in full:

Sonnet from Dr Donne
Death! be not proud, though some have called thee
Mighty and dreadful (*D.C.MS 16* 117r)

Only these lines appear in the notebook, but W apparently meant to copy out the entire poem (the tenth of Donne's *Holy Sonnets*). Although the quotation is too brief to allow us to speculate with certainty on which edition he was consulting, it is significant that the punctuation and orthography coincide precisely with that in Anderson's *British Poets* iv 22.

Donne's *Sermons* in the Hawkshead Grammar School Library in W's time (Wu *CWAAS* 87-8). Writing to Dyce in 1833, W commended *Death be not proud* as 'eminently characteristic' of Donne, 'weighty in thought, and vigorous in the expression' (*LY* ii 604).

81. Donovan, Edward, *The Natural History of British Insects; explaining them in their several states, with the period of their transformations, their food, œconomy, etc. together with the history of such minute insects as require investigation through the microscope* **(1792)**
Suggested date of reading: by 1798
References: Shaver 79
W's copy of this book is now in the possession of Jonathan Wordsworth and contains an early signature on the flyleaf, 'W Wordsworth', probably dating from the late 1790s. The signature of a previous owner appears above W's, indicating that he bought his copy secondhand.

82. Drayton, Michael
(i) *The Owle*
Suggested date of reading: by 1789
References: Cornell *EW* 74
Although, according to Averill, W's allusion to Drayton's *Owle* at *Evening Walk* 377-8 may owe something to his reading of an article in the *European Magazine*, it is possible that W read more of Drayton's poem than the mere three lines there quoted. See note 97 (ii).

(ii) *England's Heroical Epistles*
Suggested date of reading: 1796
References: Cornell *B* 17
Osborn suggests that the names of Mortimer and Matilda in *The Borderers* were suggested by a reading of *England's Heroical Epistles* (Cornell *B* 17). C acquired his set of Anderson's *British Poets* in 1796, to which W might have had access; *England's Heroical Epistles* appears in Vol. 3. See Cornell *Poems 1807-1820* 527 and *Prose Works* i 65n and 89.

83. Drummond, William, *The Most Elegant, and Elabourate Poems of That Great Court-Wit, Mr. William Drummond* **(1659)**

Suggested date of reading: 1787 onwards
References: Shaver 81; Park 59
W acquired this volume at Cambridge, and retained it at Rydal Mount. Its present whereabouts is unknown, but the Rydal Mount Sale Catalogue records that it contained a 'curious MS. note by Mr. Wordsworth while at St. John's Coll. Cambridge' (Park 59).

84. Dryden, John
(i) *Alexander's Feast*
Suggested date of reading: by Aug. 1786
References: Landon 226
In a draft conclusion to his 1786 imitation of Anacreon, W wrote: "'Tis Pity melted into love' (*D.C.MS* 2 9r). Landon 226 notes that this echoes Dryden, *Alexander's Feast* 96: 'For Pity melts the Mind to Love'.

(ii) *A Song for St Cecilia's Day, 1687*
Suggested date of reading: by Sept. 1798
References: *Prose Works* i 97
A comic moment occurs in W's *Conversations with Klopstock*: 'I spoke of Dryden's Cecilia, but he did not seem familiar with our writers' (*Prose Works* i 93). W's reference does not necesarily prove that he was reading the poem at Hamburg; in fact, I suspect that he had known the *Song* since his Hawkshead days. This is consistent with his comment to Walter Scott on 7 Nov. 1805: 'I have read Dryden's Works (all but his plays) with great attention, but my observations refer entirely to matters of taste' (*EY* 642).

85. Dumouriez, Charles, *On the Republic, a Continuation of the Political Survey of the Future Condition of France* [tr. James Losh] (Bath, 1796)
Suggested date of reading: Sept/Oct 1796
References: *EY* 186n
W was in contact with Losh while this pamphlet was in preparation (see Reed i 194-6). Losh's diary records letters sent to W at Racedown on 5 July, 20 Aug., 7 Oct., and 18 Nov. 1796, some of which must have mentioned his translation of Dumouriez, which was published in Sept. Losh wrote again on 7 Jan. 1797, and on 3 March (having published his translation of Constant's *Observations* on 26 Jan.), and sent at least two parcels of books to W during spring 1797. It is likely that his own publications were among them.

86. Dyche, Thomas, *The Youth's Guide to the Latin Tongue: or, an explication of Propria quæ maribus, Quæ genus, and As in præsenti. Wherein the rules are made plain and easy to the Capacity of young Learners, by A new Verbal Translation, the Examples declin'd, and the Sense illustrated with useful Notes and Observations from the best Grammarians.* (4th edn, 1766)
Suggested date of reading: 1779
References: see note
W's copy of Dyche was retained in the Rydal Mount library (Shaver 294), and is now in the possession of Mark L. Reed, who describes it as follows:

> The Dyche's Latin Grammar, 4th edn, is scribbled with numerous signatures, but has almost no other sorts of inscriptions. The signatures are on the title page, the front and

rear pastedowns, and blank space on many pages, miscellaneously, in between. All are in schoolboyish or -girlish hands. The earliest dated signature is at the foot of p. 132: 'William Wordsworth / 1779'. The dominant title-page signature is 'Richard Wordsworth / Hawkshead / 1784'. On the front pastedown is written twice 'William Wordsworth'. On the rear pastedown are written 'William Wordsworth' and 'Richard Wordsworth / 1780' and 'James Longmire'. On p. 120 is written 'James Longmire Book / 1791'; on p. 130 is written 'John Wordsworth Book / 1782'. On p. 63 is written 'Ann Wordsworth' (probably W's cousin Ann of Whitehaven, 1771-1841). Other signatures of William and Richard and John are found elsewhere, without dates or other supplement. One or two insignificant Latin scribbles appear, in an unidentified hand that does not appear to resemble the samples of W's that are present. (letter to me)

W probably covered the material in this elementary Latin primer fairly quickly before passing it on to his brother, Richard. Clancey suggests that Taylor encouraged the use of Dyche, and that upon his appointment as Headmaster in 1786 Bowman phased it out in favour of the Eton Grammar.

87. Dyer, George
(i) *Dissertation on the Theory and Practice of Benevolence* (1795)
Suggested date of reading: March 1795 onwards
References: Roe 193; Shaver 84
Roe points out that 'When Wordsworth met Dyer on 27 February [1795], he was actually preparing the *Dissertation* for publication' (Roe 193). I suspect that the copy of the first edition retained in the Rydal Mount library was acquired at the time of publication; it is at least likely that W saw the volume when it was published in March.

Like Wrangham, Dyer was a mutual friend of both W and C before they first met. He probably introduced W to C's published work in Feb. 1795. It is no surprise that C ordered 10 copies of the *Dissertation* from Cottle in late Feb. 1795 (Griggs i 152). Roe, 'Radical George: Dyer in the 1790s', *CLB* NS 49 (Jan. 1985) 17-26, argues for Dyer's influence on *Tintern Abbey*, and Chard 196ff provides a compelling discussion of W's friendship with Dyer in 1795, pointing to Dyer's influence on the Preface to *Lyrical Ballads*.

The Wordsworth Library possesses a copy of Dyer's *Poems* (1792) bearing the inscription, 'With G.D.ˢ respects'. It was probably given to W in Oct. 1804 when Dyer visited Grasmere (*EY* 511).

(ii) *Memoirs of the Life and Writings of Robert Robinson* (1796)
Suggested date of reading: 1796
References: Chard 155; Morley i 4
'He wrote one good book', Crabb Robinson recalled of Dyer, 'the *Life of Robert Robinson* (I have heard Wordsworth speak of it as one of the best books of biography in the language)' (Morley i 4). Dyer presented W with a copy of the *Life of Robinson*, probably in 1796, which subsequently passed into the Rydal Mount library (Shaver 84); its present whereabouts is unknown.

Although Dyer's contemporaries regarded him as a ludicrous figure endowed with immense and redundant learning, W had a special respect for him arising out of the fact that he had been a contemporary of his schoolteacher, William Taylor, at Emmanuel College, Cambridge (see pp. 162-3, below). Like Taylor, Dyer attended William Bennett's lectures at Cambridge, which advocated the Horatian style that informs the Preface to *Lyrical Ballads*. This style is commended in the Preface to the *Life of Robinson*: 'The language of equality is adopted in this volume: it is the language of truth and soberness' (p. vii). Dyer continues: 'My language, therefore, will appear naked and unadorned, and my periods will want the harmony, that accompanies a great name. Among writers I appear, as a native of Botany Bay, or Otaheite, among civilised nations' (p. ix). For more on Dyer and Robinson see Roe 90-1, and Morley i 4.

88. Dyer, John
(i) *Grongar Hill*
Suggested date of reading: 1791-2
References: Cornell *DS* 48
It is likely that W knew this poem at Hawkshead. It was widely anthologised, and is discussed by Scott in his *Critical Essays* (see note 220 [i]).

(ii) *The Ruins of Rome*
Suggested date of reading: 1796
References: *PW* i 370
In the Fragment of the *Gothic Tale*, W wrote:

> The unimaginable touch of time,
> Or shouldering winds, had split with ruin deep
> The towers that stately stood as in their prime,
> Though shattered, stood of undiminished height ... (lines 68-71)

In his annotations to this poem, De Selincourt observed that 'The image of Time splitting the towers of a ruin was probably suggested by the lines in Dyer's *Ruins of Rome*' (*PW* i 370):

> The pilgrim oft
> At dead of night, 'mid his oraison hears
> Aghast the voice of time, disparting tow'rs,
> Tumbling all precipitate down-dash'd,
> Rattling around, loud thund'ring to the Moon ... (lines 38-42)

89. Ebert, Johann Arnold, *Johann Arnold Eberts Episteln und vermischte Gedichte* **(Hamburg, 1795)**
Suggested date of reading: 21 or 26 Sept. 1798 onwards
References: Reed i 250; Shaver 84-5
This book was given to W by Klopstock on either 21 or 26 Sept. 1798. It is now at the Wordsworth Library and contains the title-page inscription: 'Wm Wordsworth given him Anno 1798 by Klopstock -'. It was an appropriate gift, since Klopstock 'mentioned Ebert's translation of Leonidas and Young's Night Thoughts as the best translation from English which they had. By the bye, Ebert was his particular friend' (*Prose Works* i 92). The volume contains, at pp. 73-104, Ebert's correspondence to and from Edward Young, Richard Glover and Robert Ferguson, all of whose works Ebert rendered into German.

90. Edda, *Icelandic Poetry; or, the Edda of Saemund translated into English Verse, by Amos Simon Cottle* **(Bristol, 1797)**

Suggested date of reading: Nov. 1797 onwards
References: Reed i 211; Shaver 85; Butler *JEGP* 141
Shortly before the publication of this book on 15 Nov. 1797, Joseph Cottle sent two advance copies to C, entrusting him with the task of giving one to W. Although W must have received it before the walking tour of early Nov., he did not thank Cottle until 13 Dec., because 'I begged Coleridge to return you my best thanks for it' (Butler *JEGP* 141). W's copy is now at the British Library (C.61.b.14), and his inscription appears on the title-page; at some point it passed into Southey's possession, for his handwriting is on the label affixed to the back of the volume. For more details see p. 179, below. The editors of the Longman *Wordsworth* detect a number of echoes of Southey's *To A. S. Cottle from Robert Southey*, which appears at the front of the volume, in W's poetry of spring 1798.

91. Eden, Sir Frederick, *The State of the Poor; or, An History of the Labouring Classes in England, from the Conquest to the Present Period* (3 vols., 1797)
Suggested date of reading: 1797-8; by 5 March 1798
References: Griggs i 634
C's letter to Poole of 11 Oct. 1800, remarking that 'You have Sir Frederic Eden's book' (Griggs i 634), implies that Poole's copy of *The State of the Poor* was acquired while he and C were neighbours at Nether Stowey, 1797-8. If this is the case, it would have been within W's reach, for as DW's Alfoxden journal indicates, the Wordsworths frequently visited Poole.

The case for W's reading of *The State of the Poor* is supported by Trott's lecture, '*The Old Cumberland Beggar*: The Poor Law and the Law of Nature', delivered at the Wordsworth Winter School 1989, in which she discussed Eden's influence on *The Old Cumberland Beggar*. She found evidence that W read Eden by 5 March 1798, when *The Old Cumberland Beggar* was completed (Reed i 27).

There was a copy of Eden at the Bristol Library Society (*BLS* 31).

92. Edwards, Bryan, *The History, Civil and Commercial, of the British Colonies in the West Indies* (2 vols., 1793-4)
Suggested date of reading: summer 1797-spring 1798
References: Jacobus 229-30
C borrowed this book from Bristol Library, 14 July-7 Aug. 1795 (Whalley 64), and seems to have returned to it when composing *The Three Graves* in spring 1798; as he recalled in *The Friend*,

> I had been reading Bryan Edwards's account of the effects of the *Oby* Witchcraft on the Negroes in the West Indies, and Hearne's deeply interesting Anecdotes of similar workings on the imagination of the Copper Indians ... and I conceived the design of shewing, that instances of this kind are not peculiar to savage or barbarous tribes, and of illustrating the mode in which the mind is affected in these cases, and the progress and symptoms of the morbid action on the fancy from the beginning.
>
> (CC *Friend* ii 89; his italics)

Two factors lead me to believe that W also saw this volume. Firstly, the other volume mentioned here, Samuel Hearne's *A Journey from Prince of Wales's Fort in Hudson's Bay to the Northern Ocean, Undertaken ... for the Discovery of Copper Mines, a North West Passage, etc. in the Years 1769-1772* (1795), was seen by W in 1798 (see note 127). The second factor is that *The Three Graves* was a poem on which W and C collaborated, so that W can be presumed to have been aware of such an important influence upon it.

See Jacobus 229-30; CC *Friend* i 431-2, and C's reference to Edwards in a notebook entry of 7 Dec. 1804 (*Notebooks* ii 2297 and n).

93. Engel, Johann Jacob, works
Suggested date of reading: Sept. 1798
References: *Prose Works* i 95, 98
Klopstock told W that 'Nicolai & Engel had, in different ways, contributed to disenchant the Nation' of Kant (*Prose Works* i 95). W probably knew who Engel was; if he did not, he would have found out after seeing Klopstock.

94. Erskine, Thomas, *A View of the Causes and Consequences of the Present War with France* (1797)
Suggested date of reading: after 20 March 1797
References: *EY* 186
On 20 March 1797, Losh listed in his diary (now at Tullie House, Carlisle) the first consignment of books which he sent W; this included 'Erskine's view of the causes and consequences of the present War', published 9 Feb. 1797. Perhaps W requested a copy from Losh after seeing the excerpt in *The Weekly Entertainer* 29 (27 Feb. 1797) 161-5. Erskine defended Thomas Paine on 18 Dec. 1792, when Paine was found guilty of High Treason and sentenced to death *in absentia*. He also acted for the defence in the treason trials of 1794.

95. Estlin, John Prior
(i) *Evidences of Revealed Religion, and Particularly Christianity, Stated, with Reference to a Pamphlet Called the Age of Reason, in a Discourse Delivered December 25, 1795* **(Bristol, 1796)**
Suggested date of reading: after 20 March 1797; by 10 June 1797
References: Griggs i 327; *EY* 186
On 20 March 1797, Losh listed in his diary (now at Tullie House, Carlisle) the first consignment of books which he sent W - among them, 'Estlin's Evidences of Christianity'. W had read the *Evidences* by 10 June 1797, when C told Estlin that W preferred it to *The Nature and Causes of Atheism* (see next note).

The *Evidences* expresses views that C shared. Patton and Mann suggest that 'C may have had a hand in the writing of Estlin's pamphlet' (CC *Lectures* 152n), and its intellectual range reflects C's reading as much as its author's. The presentation inscription in C's copy, now at Victoria University Library, reads: 'From the Author to his highly valued friend Mr. S. T. Coleridge to whose judicious suggestion this Discourse is indebted for the quotation from Sir Isaac Newton' (*Notebooks* i 88n; Coffman E42; Dendurent 478).

(ii) *The Nature and the Causes of Atheism, Pointed out in a Discourse, Delivered at the Chapel in Lewin's-Mead, Bristol* **(Bristol, 1797)**
Suggested date of reading: probably between 4 and 10 June 1797
References: Griggs i 327; Chard 219
'This is a lovely country', C told Estlin on 10 June 1797, '& Wordsworth is a great man. - He admires your sermon against Payne much more than your last - I suppose because he is

more inclined to Christianity than to Theism, simply considered' (Griggs i 327). This shows that W had read both Estlin's *Evidences of Revealed Religion* and *The Nature and Causes of Atheism* by 10 June 1797, and that he preferred the former.

It is likely that W read C's copy of *The Nature and Causes of Atheism*, which C probably took to Racedown between 4 and 7 June. This would imply a date of reading of between 4 and 10 June 1797. It had been recently published: Cottle advertised it in *Felix Farley's Bristol Journal*, 25 March 1797, and it was advertised in the *Morning Chronicle*, 30 March.

Incidentally, John Carter's 1829 catalogue of the Rydal Mount library lists 'Estlin's Sermons', which the Shavers believe to be Estlin's *Sermons, Designed Chiefly as a Preservative from Infidelity and Religious Indifference* (Bristol, 1802). However, it seems to me that Carter's entry could refer to Estlin's two sermons of 1797 - the *Evidences of Revealed Religion* and *The Nature and Causes of Atheism*.

96. Euclid
(i) *Elements* I-IV, VI
Suggested date of reading: 1785 onwards
References: Ann Tyson's Account Book; TWT 90; Shaver 90; Wu *Library* JW20
W recollected that at Hawkshead he was given a thorough grounding in Euclidean mathematics in preparation for the Cambridge curriculum: 'When at school, I, with the other boys of the same standing, was put upon reading the first six books of Euclid, with the exception of the fifth; and also in algebra I learnt simple and quadratic equations' (*Prose Works* iii 373). This is consistent with Ann Tyson's account book for 1785, now at the Hawkshead Grammar School, which records the purchase of 'A Euclid' for W, costing four shillings and sixpence (see p. 169, below). The volume appears to have been retained in the Rydal Mount library (Shaver 90).

(ii) *Elements*
Suggested date of reading: June and Dec. 1788
References: Schneider 15
When he got to Cambridge W was already familiar with one of the most important University texts, the *Elements*. He probably did not need to work hard for the College examinations in June and Dec. 1788, when Euclid appeared on the syllabus (see p. 167, below).

97. *European Magazine*
(i) 1786-7
Suggested date of reading: 1786-7
References: Averill 33
Averill suggests that W's first published poem, the *Sonnet, on Seeing Miss Helen Maria Williams Weep at a Tale of Distress*, was prompted by the review in the *European Magazine* 10 (1786) 89-93, 177-80, of her *Poems, in Two Volumes* (1786):

> The short poem of recognition to a fellow poet was a minor genre popular in the late eighteenth century. In the works of most of Wordsworth's contemporaries, one finds poems like Coleridge's 'To Schiller' and, in a perverse vein, Blake's challenge to Klopstock. Certainly the genre flourished in the poetry section of the *European Magazine*. In 1786, six such poems appear, five of them addressed to poetesses. There are 'Stanzas to Mrs. Barbauld,' a 'Sonnet, Addressed to Miss Seward,' three sonnets to

Mrs. Smith, and an 'Ode to the Author of the Triumph of Benevolence.' Probably the *European*'s evident interest in Helen Maria Williams and its publication of several other similar poems encouraged Wordsworth to send his sonnet to the magazine in late 1786 or early 1787. (Averill 33)

(ii) Sept. 1786

Suggested date of reading: 1788-9; by 1788
References: see note

> Till pours the wakeful bird her solemn strains
> Heard by the night-calm of the watry plains. (*Evening Walk* 377-8)

In the first edition of *An Evening Walk*, W provided an annotation to line 378: '"Charming the night-calm with her powerful song". A line of one of our older poets.' Averill identifies the source as Drayton's *The Owle*: 'Wordsworth evidently remembered the line from an article on Drayton in *The European Magazine* 10 (1786) 153' (Cornell *EW* 74). The quotation as printed in the *European Magazine* reads:

> -------The warbling Throstle-cock,
> The Ousel and the Nightingale among,
> *That charms the night-calm with her powerful song.*
> DRAYTON's Owl.

The article 'On Michael Drayton' appears first in the *European Magazine* for Sept. 1786, pp. 153-5, and is continued in Nov., pp. 361-2. The quotation is to be found at p. 153, with a number of other poetical descriptions of birds: Drayton, *Noah's Flood* 370-3; Donne, *The Progress of the Soul* 231-5; *Paradise Lost* vii 438-42; and Thomson, *Spring* 778-82. In a notebook used during W's Cambridge years, there are two fragments that echo the line from Drayton's *The Owle* cited in the *Evening Walk* annotation:

> The nightingale
> Was hush'd, and immelodious were the passing gales
> All nature slept & not a sound was heard
> To break the solemn *night calm*. The raven
> Moved thro' the silent waters (*D.C.MS 2* 92v)

> gently steal
> Soft sounds along the deep green woods, and spread
> *Charming* the quiet vales of listening night (*D.C.MS 2* 93r)

I have italicized those words which echo the lines from Drayton quoted in the *European Magazine*. Both fragments date from *c.* 1788, prior to composition of *An Evening Walk*.

(iii) Jan. 1788

Suggested date of reading: after 1 Feb. 1788
References: Fink 139

This number of the *European Magazine* contains a review of Gilpin's *Observations*, cited by Christopher Wordsworth in his notebook (Fink 139), *c.* 1788. It would have been of interest to W, who probably kept up with the *European* at Cambridge.

(iv) Sept. 1793
Suggested date of reading: Oct. 1793
References: Reed i 149
A review of *An Evening Walk* appeared in the *European Magazine* for Sept. 1793.

98. Evans, Evan, *Llys Ifor Hael* in MS
Suggested date of reading: either June 1791 or Aug. 1793
References: WC 13 (1982) 35-6
Bement, 'Simon Lee and Ivor Hall: A Possible Source', *WC* 13 (1982) 35-6, puts forward the case for the influence on *Simon Lee* of a Welsh poem by Evan Evans, *Llys Ifor Hael*:

> Wordsworth was in North Wales in 1791 and again in 1793, sightseeing and visiting his friend Robert Jones... During one of these visits, it is not certain which, he called on Thomas Pennant at Downing... Apart from this meeting with one of Evan Evans's patrons, it is possible that Wordsworth had other opportunities to hear of Evans's poem on Ivor's Hall, perhaps even to see it in translation. At its first printing in 1793, the Welsh version only appeared, and the English translation was not printed until 1824, but the poem was circulating fairly widely in manuscript. (p. 35)

Bement puts forward an interesting case, but the evidence remains circumstantial.

99. Evelyn, John, *Sylva, or a Discourse of Forest Trees, and the Propagation of Timber in His Majesties Dominions; to which is annexed Pomona* (2nd edn, 1670)
Suggested date of reading: 1780s; by July 1787
References: TWT 344
This was one of the books in the Hawkshead Grammar School Library which W is believed to have read during his time there (TWT 344). This is consistent with the fact that a copy of the 2nd edn was in the Library in 1788 (Wu *CWAAS* 101). In later years he read Evelyn's *Diary* and described its author as 'accomplished' (*Prose Works* iii 341).

100. Farish, Charles
(i) poems in MS
Suggested date of reading: 1784-5
References: see note
W probably saw the poetry of Charles Farish at Hawkshead, where both boys were taught by William Taylor. There, *c.* 1784, Farish composed a poem *On the Vacation*. At about the same time W composed his first verses, on the same subject: 'It may be perhaps as well to mention, that the first verses which I wrote were a task imposed by my master; the subject, "The Summer Vacation;" and of my own accord I added others upon "Return to School." There was nothing remarkable in either poem' (*Prose Works* iii 372). W and Farish were almost certainly acquainted at Hawkshead, and probably knew each other's work. Farish went up to Cambridge in 1785.

(ii) poems in MS
Suggested date of reading: 1787-91
References: see note

During his Cambridge years, W heard Charles Farish read the poetry of his dead brother, John Bernard Farish (see next note). This suggests that he heard Charles read his own work too.

101. Farish, John Bernard
(i) poems in MS
Suggested date of reading: 1787-91
References: TWT 319-21
W's note to *Guilt and Sorrow* 81 acknowledges a borrowing 'From a short MS. poem read to me when an under-graduate, by my schoolfellow and friend Charles Farish, long since deceased. The verses were by a brother of his, a man of promising genius, who died young' (Cornell *SP* 126n). Charles Farish's brother, John Bernard Farish, was indeed a prolific and inventive poet during his schooldays. The reading of Farish's *The Heath*, which W recalled in 1842, must have taken place during W's time at Cambridge, 1787-91. For further details on the Farishes, see TWT 311-21, and my article, 'William Wordsworth and the Farish Brothers', *Bodleian Library Record* 14 (1991) 99-101.

(ii) *The Heath* in MS
Suggested date of reading: Sept.-Nov. 1795
References: Cornell *SP* 126; TWT 319-21
See preceding note. The image of a body swinging in irons, borrowed from John Bernard Farish's *The Heath*, appears first in W's poetry in *Adventures on Salisbury Plain*, composed between 26 Sept. and 20 Nov. 1795 (Reed i 25). This implies a rereading of Farish's poem, though W might simply have recalled the image itself - for, as Owen tells me, W probably saw, while a schoolboy at Hawkshead, the gibbet at Priest-pot described in the *Unpublished Tour* (*Prose Works* ii 333). For a discussion of this gibbet, see *Prose Works* ii 445-6.

102. Farquhar, George, *The Beaux' Strategem*
Suggested date of reading: by April 1796
References: EY 174n
W's imitation of Juvenal VIII alludes to *The Beaux' Stratagem* (*EY* 174n). The imitation was composed between 7 March and April 1796 (Reed i 26), by which time he must have known Farquhar's play. W read Congreve at Cambridge and, I suspect, encountered other Restoration dramatists at that time. Perhaps he saw productions of Restoration plays in London; *The Beaux' Stratagem* was performed at the Kings' Theatre, Haymarket, 19 Nov. and 20 Dec. 1792, during one of W's visits to the capital.

103. Fawcett, Joseph, *The Art of War* (1795)
Suggested date of reading: spring or summer 1795
References: Cornell *SP* 154; Cornell *B* 22
In the Fenwick Note to *The Excursion*, W identified 'Mr Fawcett, a preacher at a dissenting meeting-house at the Old Jewry', as his model for the character of the Solitary. He adds that 'He published a Poem on War, which had a good deal of merit, and made me think more about him than I should otherwise have done' (*PW* v 374-5). This suggests that W read Fawcett's *The Art of War* soon after publication in spring or summer 1795.[1] It was probably

---

[1] It was advertised in the *Morning Chronicle*, 23 March 1795.

at his side during composition of *Adventures on Salisbury Plain* and the Fragment of a *Gothic Tale* in 1795-6 (see Cornell *SP* 154 and Cornell *B* 22), and like them deals with the guilt and self-loathing that follows violent acts. At one point Fawcett depicts a murderer before his crime when, 'to the scene / Of his dark act, with a light-falling foot, / Ghost-like he glides' (lines 1026-8). After the crime,

> He is 'afraid to think on what he has done;'
> That 'twere undone, is his devoutest wish.
> Of heaven and earth he feels himself accurst. (lines 1032-4)

Compare Mortimer's final speech, *Borderers* V iii 264-75.

Beatty, 'Joseph Fawcett: The Art of War', *University of Wisconsin Studies in Language and Literature* 2 (1918) 224-69, reprints the text of Fawcett's poem with useful annotations; Jacobus 155-6 discusses its influence on *Adventures on Salisbury Plain*.

104. Fawkes, Francis, *An Elogy on Sir Isaac Newton* **[1761]**
Suggested date of reading: by 1785
References: see note
In *Lines Written as a School Exercise* (1785), W says that Education will 'lead the mind to those Elysian plains / Where, Thron'd in Gold, immortal Science reigns' (lines 69-70). Thomas and Ober suggest that 'What the Elysian plains have to do with Science and the discoveries of Science' is explained by Francis Fawkes' *An Elogy on Sir Isaac Newton* - a translation of Halley's Latin poem prefixed to editions of Newton's *Principia*:

> Lend, lend your aid, ye bright superior powers,
> That live embosom'd in *Elysian bowers*,
> Lend your sweet voice to warble Newton's praise,
> Who search'd out truth thro' all her mystic maze ... (lines 57-60)

Thomas and Ober explain: 'The original Latin makes no mention of Elysian bowers: these were Fawkes's geographic gaffe as he translated lines which called upon those "who now upon heavenly nectar fare"'.[1] The case for W's reading of Fawkes is strengthened by the fact that *School Exercise* 75 uses the same diction as *Elogy* 60.

105. Fielding, Henry, *The Works*
Suggested date of reading: 1779-83
References: *Prose Works* iii 372; *EY* 8; Wu *Library* JW31
Towards the end of his life, W recalled:

> Of my earliest days at school I have little to say, but that they were very happy ones, chiefly because I was left at liberty, then and in the vacations, to read whatever books I liked. For example, I read all Fielding's works ... (*Prose Works* iii 372)

This reveals that an edition of Fielding must have been in his father's library at Cockermouth, and that W must have read it before his father's death in 1783. At that point it passed first into the hands of DW (*EY* 8), and subsequently to Richard Wordsworth of Branthwaite, who

---

[1] *A Mind For Ever Voyaging* (Edmonton, 1989), p. 52.

returned it to Grasmere in 1805. Richard Wordsworth's inventory of 1805 describes it as 'Fieldings Works 8 or 9 Vols'; this was probably the copy of 'Fielding's Works: 9 odd Vol:', recorded in the Rydal Mount library in 1829 by John Carter (Shaver 93). The second edition of Fielding's *Works* (1762) was issued in 8 volumes; the third, of 1766, was in 12. Thus the set owned by JW Sr at Cockermouth must have dated from at least 1766, if not later.

DW and W always held Fielding in high regard. In 1831 W expressed regret that neither Fielding nor Smollett had 'been surrounded with any due marks of respect in the close of life'.[1]

106. Finch, Anne, Countess of Winchelsea, *Miscellany Poems* (1713)

Suggested date of reading: by 1789
References: see note
The earliest detectable borrowing from Finch in W's poetry occurs in a sonnet dating from c. 1789, '*On the [   ] village Silence sets her seal*':[2]

> The kine obscurely seen before me lie
> Round the dim horse that crops his later meal
> Scarce heard ... (lines 3-5)

As early as 1840, David Lester Richardson[3] compared W's image with Finch's *A Nocturnal Reverie* 31-2, who mentions a horse

> Whose stealing Pace, and lengthen'd Shade we fear,
> Till torn up Forage in his Teeth we hear ...

There is a more explicit allusion to Finch's *A Nocturnal Reverie* in *An Evening Walk* (Cornell *EW* 76), confirming that W knew her poem by 1789; see also *Prose Works* iii 73.

A copy of the *Miscellany Poems* (1713) was present in the Rydal Mount library by 1829 (Shaver 94).

107. Foxe, John, *Acts and Monuments of Matters Most Special and Memorable* (3 vols., 1641)

Suggested date of reading: 1780s; by July 1787
References: TWT 344
W read the copy preserved today in the Hawkshead Grammar School Library, published in three volumes by the Company of Stationers, 1641 (TWT 344; Wu *CWAAS* 112). His boyhood enjoyment of it is shared by the Pedlar:

> Yet greedily he read & read again
> Whate'er the rustic vicar's shelf supplied
> The life & death of Martyrs who sustained
> Intolerable pangs ... (Cornell *RC* 162-3)

---

[1] Lockhart, *Memoirs of the Life of Sir Walter Scott* (2nd edn, Edinburgh, 1842), p. 731.
[2] A facsimile of the MS draft of this poem can be found in Cornell *Poems 1800-1807* 324-5.
[3] *Literary Leaves or Prose and Verse* (1840), pp. 133-4.

Miss Wordsworth, the schoolteacher in Britten's *Albert Herring*, gives Albert a copy of Foxe's *Book of Martyrs*.

108. Frend, William, *Peace and Union* (1793)
Suggested date of reading: 1793-5; by 27 Feb. 1795
References: see note
'Wordsworth would have sought out Frend's *Peace and Union* at some time in these years', Roe writes,

> It was controversial; it was a Cambridge publication; he was acquainted with Frend after Feb. 1795, if not before [see Reed i 164]. I think for the same reason he would have been acquainted with Benjamin Flower's *Cambridge Intelligencer* after its first appearance in 1793. (letter to me)

The controversy surrounding Frend and his pamphlet attracted nationwide attention, and was the concern of so many of W's friends and acquaintances that he cannot have been ignorant of it. He would have known, for instance, that his former tutor at Cambridge, James Wood, led the outcry against Frend. Among Frend's defenders were C and Wrangham. And in addition to *Peace and Union*, Wrangham possessed several pamphlets published during the controversy, including Frend's own *An Account of the Proceedings in the University of Cambridge, Against William Frend ... for publishing a pamphlet intitled Peace and Union, &c., containing the proceedings in Jesus College, the trial in the Vice-Chancellor's Court, and in the Court of Delegates. Published by the defendant* (Cambridge, 1793). If, as I suspect, Wrangham acquired these at the time of publication, he might well have shown them to W when he visited Wrangham in Cobham in late July 1795 (see Reed i 166).

As Roe points out, the strongest evidence for a reading of *Peace and Union* is W's visit to Frend's lodgings in London on 27 Feb. 1795, where he met Godwin, Holcroft and Dyer, among others. This provides the most likely terminal date for W's reading of Frend.

Peace and Union was published in Cambridge on 12 or 13 Feb. 1793 and led, within ten days, to Frend's condemnation by the University authorities. Roe writes that 'Frend's downfall lay in his unequivocal support for parliamentary reform, and his readiness of draw comparisons between Britain in 1793 and the recent course of the French Revolution' (Roe 103). Knight, *University Rebel* (1971) quotes Frend's own account of the pamphlet:

> The reforms recommended were classed under three heads, representation, law and religion. Under the first, the shortening of the duration of parliaments, increase of votes in boroughs, extension of the rights of suffrage to copy holders as well as freeholders, and the antient system of government introduced by ... the king, were recommended. Under the second head, some evils in the modern system of law were enumerated... Under the third head, some changes in the religious establishment were desired. (p. 120)

109. Fuller, Thomas, *The History of the Holy Warre* (2nd edn, 1640)
Suggested date of reading: 1796
References: Cornell *B* 86n; Shaver 98
Osborn notes that W's reference to the siege of Antioch at *Borderers* I i 146-55 'may have come from' Fuller (Cornell *B* 86n). The fact that a copy of the *History* was retained in the Racedown Lodge Library makes this likely. It is interesting that the Lodge possessed the

second edition of 1640, and that W should have owned a copy of the same edition at Rydal Mount (Shaver 98).

110. Gastrell, Francis, Bishop of Chester, *The Christian Institutes; or, the Sincere Word of God. Being a Plain and Impartial Account of the Whole Faith and Duty of a Christian. Collected out of the Writings of the Old and New Testament.* **(7th edn, 1748)**
Suggested date of reading: 1780
References: Shaver 100; Wu *Library* JW16
W's copy of this volume is now at the Wordsworth Library. Its inscriptions show that it was originally the property of JW Sr, and was given to Richard and William Wordsworth in 1780. That on the title-page reads, 'Wordsworth Penrith 1756', and beneath it, in an adult hand: 'R & Wm. Wordsworth'. Someone else has written William's name, and the date 1780, on the inside front cover. This volume passed into the Rydal Mount library (Shaver 100).

111. *Gazette Nationale, ou le Moniteur Universel*
Suggested date of reading: 1791-2
References: EY 128
Describing the height of the Revolution in *The Prelude*, W recalled 'the hour, / The most important of each day, in which / The public News was read' (*Thirteen-Book Prelude* ix 156-8). He probably read the *Gazette Nationale, ou le Moniteur Universel*, for in June 1794 he recommended that Mathews 'procure a perusal of *the french monitor*' (*EY* 128). Copies were available in London; one bookseller advertising in the Morning Chronicle of 17 Feb. 1797 even offered complete runs of 'Collection Complette du Moniteur Francais'.

The *Moniteur* was founded on 24 Nov. 1789 by Charles-Joseph Panckoucke; Jeremy Popkin points out that this,

> the one important, folio-sized newspaper of the Revolution, was distinctly un-English. It carried no advertising, quickly abandoned its original promise to print English-style political controversy, and eventually became the Revolution's semiofficial newspaper of record, devoting most of its columns to transcripts of Assembly debates, which were published several days after smaller papers had reported the essence of the proceedings. At twice the price of ordinary newspapers, the *Moniteur* had little impact on French public opinion.[1]

It is likely that W read at least two other French newspapers (although there is insufficient evidence for them to be entered them on the list):
1. *Annales Patriotiques*. Gilchrist and Murray describe this as 'one of the most popular papers in the early days of the Revolution' (p. 26). It began publication on 3 Oct. 1789 under the editorship of L. S. Mercier and Jean-Louis Carra. Carra was a prominent member of the Girondins from 1792, and is mentioned with Gorsas at *Thirteen-Book Prelude* ix 179.
2. *Courrier des Départements*. Edited by Antoine-Joseph Gorsas, and 'best known for the speed with which Gorsas transcribed the speeches from the Assembly and converted them into the pages of his paper' (Gilchrist and Murray 26). Peter Swaab has observed that, in

---

[1] 'Journals: The New Face of News', *Revolution in Print: The Press in France 1775-1800* ed. Robert Darnton and Daniel Roche (Berkeley, Calif., 1989), pp. 141-64, p. 151.

W's copy of Burke's *Works* (now in the Wordsworth Library), W scribbled the words, 'I knew this man', next to Gorsas' name.

The Jacobins of Blois subscribed to both these journals.[1]

112. *Gentleman's Magazine*
(i) April-Dec. 1789
Suggested date of reading: May 1789-Jan. 1790; by 1792
References: Cornell *DS* 80
W's note to *Descriptive Sketches* 428 reads: 'These summer hamlets are most probably (as I have seen observed by a critic in the Gentleman's Magazine) what Virgil alludes to in the expression "Castella in tumulis"' (Cornell *DS* 80). W refers to a dispute over the word 'castella', as used by Virgil (*Georgics* iii 475), conducted in the *Gentleman's Magazine* from April to Dec. 1789 between two correspondents, 'THW' and 'BLA'. It is BLA who remarks, in May, that Virgil used 'castella' to refer to 'towns and castles so frequently both in Noricum and Italy constructed on high hills' (*Gentleman's Magazine* 59 [1789] 410). It is possible that W saw this exchange when it took place, but we can be certain only that he knew of it by the time he prepared *Descriptive Sketches* for the press in Dec. 1792.

(ii) March 1794
Suggested date of reading: April 1794
References: Reed i 151; Cornell *EW* 9-10
The *Gentleman's Magazine* for March 1794 contained a review of *An Evening Walk* that W would probably have read in April or May. The review is in the form of a letter from one of W's Cambridge contemporaries, and compares the landscape of the Lake District with that of *An Evening Walk*. It is signed 'Peregrinator'.

113. Gessner, Salomon, *Der Tod Abels*
Suggested date of reading: by Nov. 1797
References: *PW* i 360; EHC i 286-7; *MH* 263; Parrish 170; Reed i 208
While on their short walking tour to Lynton in early Nov. 1797, C and W planned to write a prose tale in the manner of Gessner's *Der Tod Abels*, to be called *The Wanderings of Cain*. W later recalled that, 'as our united funds were very small, we agreed to defray the expense of the tour by writing a Poem, to be sent to the New Monthly Magazine set up by Phillips the bookseller, and edited by Dr. Aikin'[2] (*PW* i 360). C recounted that

> The title and subject were suggested by myself, who likewise drew out the scheme and the contents for each of the three books or cantos, of which the work was to consist, and which, the reader is to be informed, was to have been finished in one night! My partner undertook the first canto: I the second: and which ever had *done first*, was to set about the third. (EHC i 286)

Both of them must therefore have read Gessner by early Nov. 1797. This is consistent with Jonathan Wordsworth's suggestion that one of Gessner's 'New Idylles, *Amyntas*, has close

---

[1] See Kennedy, *The Jacobin Clubs in the French Revolution: The First Years* (Princeton, 1982), p. 365.
[2] W refers to *The Monthly Magazine*, published by Richard Phillips (1767-1840) in 1796, and sold by Joseph Johnson.

affinities with the opening of *The Ruined Cottage*' (*MH* 263n), and by Parrish's comment that 'Wordsworth and Coleridge must have talked about [Gessner] at the start of their collaboration, for *The Ancient Mariner* echoes *Der erste Schiffer*' (Parrish 170). W refers to Gessner at *Thirteen-Book Prelude* vii 559-60.

Gessner was perhaps a greater influence on C than on W. The fact that C translated Gessner's *Der erste Schiffer* in 1802 (Griggs ii 808-11) would appear to support Sultana's claim that, 'although there is no evidence that he did so, [Coleridge] used one of the idylls of Gessner for *The Picture*'.[1] Hibberd argues that *The Picture* is an imitation of Gessner's *Der feste Vorsatz*.[2] Both W and C would have been aware of Blair's approval of Gessner.[3]

114. Gilbert, William
(i) *The Hurricane: A Theosophical and Western Eclogue* (Bristol, 1796)
Suggested date of reading: 1796
References: see note
On 19 Sept. 1839, W told John Peace that Gilbert 'lived some time at Bristol, between the year -95 and -98, at which time I often conversed with him, and admired his genius though he was in fact insane' (*LY* iii 726). This suggests that W read *The Hurricane* at the time of its publication, when I suspect he acquired the copy later retained in the Rydal Mount library (Shaver 102). He was probably aware of the extracts published by C in *The Watchman*, 13 May 1796 (CC *Watchman* 350). A note to *The Brothers* (1800) reveals that 'This description of the Calenture is sketched from an imperfect recollection of an admirable one in prose, by Mr. Gilbert, author of the *Hurricane*' (*PW* ii 2). W's phrasing confirms that he read Gilbert's poem before 1800, probably at the time of publication.

For more on Gilbert, see Kaufman, '*The Hurricane* and the Romantic Poets', *English Miscellany* 21 (1970) 99-115. It is interesting that Thelwall's advance copy of *The Hurricane* fell into C's hands (Coffman G27d).

(ii) *The Hurricane: A Theosophical and Western Eclogue* (Bristol, 1796)
Suggested date of reading: July 1798
References: Mason *LB* 209

115. Gillies, John, *The History of Ancient Greece, its Colonies, and Conquests from the Earliest Accounts till the Division of the Macedonian Empire in the East, Including the History of Literature, Philosophy, and the Fine Arts* (2nd edn, 4 vols., 1787)
Suggested date of reading: c. 1787
References: TWT 144-5, 353; Reed i 72
Woof reports that this volume was a joint gift to the Hawkshead School Library from W, Robert Hodgson Greenwood, Thomas Gawthrop and John Millar, all of whom went up to Cambridge in 1787 (TWT 353). It is likely that W knew the volume, which may have been recommended at Cambridge. It was also in the Stowey Book Society (see p. 174, below). In later years W became a friend of R. P. Gillies, Gillies' nephew (*PW* iii 425; *MY* ii 169ff).

---

[1] *Samuel Taylor Coleridge in Malta and Italy* (New York, 1969), p. 61.
[2] *Salomon Gessner: His Creative Achievement and Influence* (Cambridge, 1976), p. 138.
[3] *Lectures on Rhetoric and Belles Lettres* (2 vols., 1783), ii 348-9.

116. Gilpin, William
(i) *Observations, Relative Chiefly to Picturesque Beauty, Made in the Year 1772, on Several Parts of England; Particularly the Mountains, and Lakes of Cumberland, and Westmoreland* **(2 vols., 1786)**
Suggested date of reading: 1787-9
References: BWS 371; WC 18 (1987) 114-21
Gilpin's painterly way of viewing the landscape is evident in *The Vale of Esthwaite* (1787):

> While winds faint rippling paint it white
> The long lake lengthening stretches on the sight[1]
> While many a dark calm sleeping bay
> Blends with the shore and fades away (*D.C.MS 3* 7v; De Selincourt 131-4)

W's images, and his use of the metaphor, 'paint' (line 131), recall the detailed light effects described by Gilpin. Compare, for instance, Gilpin's account of the 'tremulous shudder' that runs 'in lengthened parallels' across the surface of a lake, giving 'the painter an opportunity of throwing in those lengthened lights and shades which give the greatest variety and clearness to water' (i 100), or the description of Bassenthwaite by night, presented as an example of sublimity:

> a lake ... appeared through the uncertainty of the gloom, like something of ambiguous texture, spreading a lengthened gleam of wan, dead light under the dark shade of the incumbent mountains: but whether this light was owing to vapours arising from the valley; or whether it was water ... to the uninformed traveller would appear matter of great uncertainty. (ii 21-2)

W had read Gilpin by the time he wrote *An Evening Walk* 341-50 in 1789; see Trott, 'Wordsworth and the Picturesque: A Strong Infection of the Age', WC 18 (1987) 114-21. Woof observes that Gilpin was related by marriage to Charles Farish, W's friend at Hawkshead and Cambridge (TWT 312). W's copy of this book was probably acquired by the time he went up to Cambridge; see Shaver 103. Bicknell 18.1-18F.

(ii) *Observations, Relative Chiefly to Picturesque Beauty, Made in the Year 1776, on Several Parts of Great Britain; Particularly the High-lands of Scotland* **(2 vols., 1789)**
Suggested date of reading: 1789
References: Cornell EW 68
Evening Walk 317, 'The sugh of swallow flocks that twittering sweep', is noted by W:

> Sugh, a Scotch word, expressive, as Mr. Gilpin explains it, of the sound of the motion of a stick through the air, or of the wind passing through the trees. See Burn's Cotter's Saturday Night. (Cornell EW 68)

W had been introduced to Burns' poetry by Bowman, *c.* 1787 (TWT 344), and purchased a copy of Burns' poems for DW in Oct. (*EY* 13). He was reminded of *The Cotter's Saturday Night* by its complete reprinting in Gilpin's *Observations, Relative Chiefly to Picturesque Beauty, Made in the Year 1776, on Several Parts of Great Britain; Particularly the High-*

---

[1] This couplet was revised for *Thirteen-Book Prelude* iv 170-1.

lands of Scotland (2 vols., 1789), i 215-21. Line 10 of the poem - 'November chill blaws loud wi' angry sugh' - is annotated by Gilpin:

> *Sugh* is a very expressive word, which we want in English, signifying the sound, which the wind makes, when it is resisted: as when you strike a stick through it; or when it blows against trees. (i 215; his italics)

Evening Walk 317 appears in the manuscript of the poem dating from 1789, *D.C.MS 7*, suggesting that W read Gilpin's book as soon as it was published, and borrowed from it immediately. Bicknell 23.1-23.3.

(iii) *Observations, Relative Chiefly to Picturesque Beauty, Made in the Year 1776, on Several Parts of Great Britain; Particularly the High-lands of Scotland* **(2 vols., 1789)**
Suggested date of reading: 1791-2
References: Cornell *DS* 72

(iv) *Observations, Relative Chiefly to Picturesque Beauty, Made in the Year 1772, on Several Parts of England; Particularly the Mountains, and Lakes of Cumberland, and Westmoreland* **(2 vols., 1786)**
Suggested date of reading: 1791-2
References: Cornell *DS* 44
W alludes to Mason's *Caractacus* at *Descriptive Sketches* 56. The same allusion is made by Gilpin in his *Observations*, i 122. Nabholtz, 'Wordsworth and William Mason', *RES* 15 (1964) 297-302, insists that the evidence points towards a reading of *Caractacus* itself:

> it seems certain that Wordsworth was remembering the phrase 'sober Reason' not from Gilpin, but from a reading of Mason; for the dramatic situation at the opening of the play and the sentiments expressed by the speaker exactly parallel the effect Wordsworth was trying to reach in describing the desecration of the famous religious site. (p. 299)

Since it is likely that W possessed his own copy of Gilpin by 1792, this reading is listed both here and under Mason; see note 173 (ii).

(v) *Observations, Relative Chiefly to Picturesque Beauty, Made in the Year 1772, on Several Parts of England; Particularly the Mountains, and Lakes of Cumberland, and Westmoreland* **(2 vols., 1786)**
Suggested date of reading: spring-autumn 1796
References: *EY* 170; Cornell *B* 18
When he left London for Racedown in Aug. 1795, W left a number of books with Basil Montagu. In March 1796 he wrote to Mathews asking him to retrieve them: 'Gilpin's tour into Scotland, and his northern tour, each 2 vol., ought to be amongst the number', he wrote (*EY* 170). Woof has observed that W returned to London in June 1796, so that even if the volumes were not sent to him in March, he could have retrieved them himself a few months later (see Woof Ph.D. 66).

(vi) *Observations, Relative Chiefly to Picturesque Beauty, Made in the Year 1776, on Several Parts of Great Britain; Particularly the High-lands of Scotland* **(2 vols., 1789)**
Suggested date of reading: spring-autumn 1796
References: *EY* 170; Cornell *B* 82n; Woof Ph.D. 64-5

See preceding note. Woof Ph.D. 64-5 regards this as a 'pregnant source' for *The Borderers*. He cites, in particular, Gilpin's remarks on the borderers' expertise in 'the arts of rapine, and plundering' (i 41-2), and his description of the Highlander (i 211-12).

(vii) *Observations on the River Wye ... Relative Chiefly to Picturesque Beauty: Made in the Summer of the Year 1770* **(2nd edn, 1789)**
Suggested date of reading: July 1798
References: Jacobus 110-11; Moorman 402n
Jacobus and Moorman both observe the influence of Gilpin on *Tintern Abbey*. W seems to have owned a copy of the second edition of Gilpin's *Observations on the River Wye* (Shaver 103). It eventually took its place on the shelves of the Rydal Mount library, alongside Thomas Dudley Fosbroke's *The Wye Tour; or, Gilpin on the Wye, with Picturesque Additions, from [Francis] Wheatley, [R.A.], [John] Price, &c.* (3rd edn, Ross, 1826). See also Jacobus, '"Tintern Abbey" and Topographical Prose', *N&Q* NS 18 (1971) 366-9.

117. Glover, Richard, *Leonidas* **[1737]**
Suggested date of reading: by 21 Sept. 1798
References: *Prose Works* i 96
W recorded that Klopstock 'preferred the blank verse of Glover ... to that of Milton' (*Prose Works* i 91); W had presumably read Glover's epic poem, *Leonidas*, by 21 Sept. 1798, when Klopstock made this remark.

118. Godwin, William
(i) *An Enquiry Concerning Political Justice* **(2 vols., 1793)**
Suggested date of reading: by June 1794
References: Reed i 141; *EY* 124
Roe writes that in summer 1794 'Wordsworth had told William Mathews that "every enlightened friend of mankind" had a duty to "diffuse by every method a knowledge of those rules of political justice", and elaborated plans for their journal the *Philanthropist* in terms that demonstrate his familiarity with Godwin's book (*EY* 124)' (Roe 11). This would appear to confirm the implication of *Thirteen-Book Prelude* x 805ff., where W recalls his attraction to 'the Philosophy / That promised to abstract the hopes of man / Out of his feelings, to be fix'd thenceforth / For ever in a purer element' (lines 806-9). The implication is that W became a Godwinian after Robespierre's execution in July 1794, though he must have read *Political Justice* by June. The final stanza of *Salisbury Plain*, composed at about that time, refers to Reason as the chief weapon of radical thought.

(ii) *Caleb Williams* **(3 vols., 1794)**
Suggested date of reading: by Feb. 1795
References: Reed i 163; Cornell *B* 31-2
The period Feb.-Aug. 1795 is, as Reed observes, 'that of W's firmest adherence to the doctrines of William Godwin' (Reed i 163); W must by then have read *Caleb Williams*.

(iii) *Caleb Williams* **(3 vols., 1794)**
Suggested date of reading: 1796
References: Woof Ph.D. 89; *BWS* 403-5

Woof suggests that W's characterization of Rivers in *The Borderers* 'undoubtedly drew upon figures of Gothic Romance, as cruel as the Marquis in Mrs. Radcliffe's *Romance of the Forest*, and as subtle as Falkland in Godwin's *Caleb Williams*' (Woof Ph.D. 89). Osborn agrees: 'In the context of Rivers' developing role as initiator, Godwin's novel is of the first importance' (*BWS* 403). The editors of the Longman *Wordsworth* detect echoes of the novel in W's play, as when Rivers exclaims, 'A blow! I would have killed him ...' (IV iii 33); compare Falkland in *Caleb Williams*: 'All are but links of one chain. A blow! A murder!' (p. 135).

(iv) *An Enquiry Concerning Political Justice* (2nd edn, 2 vols., 1795)
Suggested date of reading: March 1796
References: EY 170
'I have received from Montagu, Godwyn's second edition', reports W on 21 March 1796:

> I expect to find the work much improved. I cannot say that I have been encouraged in this hope by the perusal of the second preface, which is all I have yet looked into. Such a piece of barbarous writing I have not often seen. It contains scarce one sentence decently written. I am surprized to find such gross faults in a writer who has had so much practise in composition. (*EY* 170-1)

W's condemnation of the 'barbarous' writing of the preface is the first sign of a reaction against Godwin.[1] The second edition was published 26 Nov. 1795, and its revisions were wholesale. As Locke points out: 'no single chapter emerges unscathed, new ones are added, old ones deleted, and others so thoroughly altered that, of the eight Books, "the four first and the last may, without impropriety, be said to be rewritten"'. Locke cites De Quincey's comment that 'The second edition, as regards principles, is not a re-cast, but absolutely a travesty of the first; nay, it is all but a palinode' (*A Fantasy of Reason* [1980], pp. 92-3).

(v) *Memoirs of the Author of a Vindication of the Rights of Woman* (1798)
Suggested date of reading: 14 April 1798 onwards
References: DWJ i 15; EY 212; Reed i 232
Godwin's *Memoirs* was published 7 Feb. 1798. On 6 March 1798 W told Tobin that he had 'not yet seen the life of Mrs. Godwyn' (*EY* 212), soon after which Tobin must have mailed him a copy, for on 14 April DW noted: 'Mary Wollstonecraft's life, etc., came' (*DWJ* i 15).

119. Goethe, Johann Wolfgang von
(i) *Sorrows of Young Werther*
Suggested date of reading: 1779-87; by 1784
References: TWT 344; *Prose Works* i 93
The Sorrows of Young Werther had been popular since its first English translation in 1779. It was read by Southey at Westminster (Simmons 25), and W probably read it at Hawkshead. We know that W read Charlotte Smith's *Elegiac Sonnets* (1784) when first published, which included translations of five sonnets 'Supposed to be written by Werter'. W knew the *Sorrows of Young Werther* by Sept. 1798, when Klopstock mentioned to him that Goethe's 'sorrows of Werter was his best work, better than any of his dramas' (*Prose Works* i 93).

[1] They remained on cordial terms, however, and met in London on 7, 18, 19, and 25 June 1796.

(ii) *The Wanderer* tr. William Taylor
Suggested date of reading: June 1798
References: see note
Taylor's translation of Goethe's *Der Wandrer* (1774) was not published until Aug. 1798, when it appeared in the *Monthly Magazine*. Jonathan Wordsworth reprints it (*MH* 264-8), arguing that it circulated in MS prior to publication, and influenced parts of *The Ruined Cottage* composed *c.* March 1798:

> The clearest influence of *The Wanderer* is ... on the central section of *The Ruined Cottage*, which was probably written after the arrival of Coleridge at Racedown in June 1797, and it is very much easier to believe that a connection existed between Coleridge and Taylor, or between literary society in Bristol and Norwich, than between Taylor and Wordsworth himself. (*MH* 263)

However, it is unlikely that any contact existed between C and Taylor as early as 1798, for their correspondence began *c.* 1800 (Griggs i 564-6). If W and C saw Taylor's translation of *Der Wandrer* during the spring and summer of 1798, prior to publication in the *Monthly Magazine*, it was probably through Southey. Southey's mention of Goethe in his letter to Henry Herbert Southey of 7 March 1798 suggests that he was reading Taylor's translation of Goethe's *Iphigenia in Tauris* (1793). And on 27 May 1798 he told Grosvenor Charles Bedford that 'I had two days conversation with William Taylor, a man whose whole character and conduct has very much interested me. I go to visit him on Wednesday and remain till the Tuesday following - so directez vous to me at Mr Taylors, Surrey Street, Norwich' (Curry i 165). In his first letter subsequent to this week-long visit, dated 24 July 1798, Southey reveals that Taylor has read him his translation of *Der Wandrer*:

> What you told me of the German eclogues, revived some almost forgotten plans, and enabled me to correct them. I purpose writing some, which may be called English, as sketching features peculiar to England; not like the one which you read to me of Goethe, which would suit any country with Roman ruins. (Robberds i 213)

This is generally taken to be a reference to Goethe's *Der Wandrer*, a copy of which Southey could have shown C and W in June 1798 at the earliest. Jonathan Wordsworth quotes a parallel remark in *Southey's Common-place Book* ed. John Wood Warter (4 vols., 1851), iv 95, in which Southey meditates on 'the Idylls of Gessner and Voss, and the translation he [Taylor] has shown me of one by Goethe' (*MH* 262). Southey remained in close touch with Taylor for many years, and their correspondence (published by Robberds) reveals a vigorous exchange of unpublished work.

DW had known various members of the Taylor circle, such as the Martineau family (*EY* 42) and the Revd. William Enfield (*EY* 22). But that was some years before, and the more likely connection is through Southey. W may have known Taylor's translation of Goethe's *Iphigenia*, which Joseph Johnson published in April 1793.

(iii) 'different fragments'
Suggested date of reading: 1797-8
References: EY 255
On 27 Feb. 1799, W told C that 'My internal prejudg[ments con]cerning Wieland and Goethe ... were, as your letter has convinced me, the result of no *negligent* perusal of the different

fragments which I had seen in England' (*EY* 255; his italics). This indicates that W read Goethe prior to his residence in Germany, probably during 1797-8 at Alfoxden. Beddoes' library in Bristol, to which he and C may have had access, was well-stocked with German texts. W was conversant with Goethe's works by the time he discussed them with Klopstock in Sept. 1798 (*Prose Works* i 97).

120. Goldsmith, Oliver
(i) *Poems*
Suggested date of reading: by 1785
References: see note
Of W's Hawkshead years, De Quincey writes:

> At another period of the year, when the golden summer allowed the students a long season of early play before the studies of the day began, he describes himself as roaming, hand-in-hand, with one companion, along the banks of Esthwaite Water, chanting, with one voice, the verses of Goldsmith and of Gray ... which, at that time of life, when the profounder feelings were as yet only germinating, filled them with an enthusiasm
> 'More bright than madness and the dreams of wine.' (Masson ii 264-5)

There is a borrowing from Goldsmith's *The Traveller* in W's earliest surviving poem, *Lines Written as a School Exercise* (1785):

> No longer steel their *indurated hearts*
> To the mild influence of the finer arts. (lines 59-60)

The phrase 'indurated hearts' recalls Goldsmith's account of the 'low' morals of the Swiss peasants, *Traveller* 231-2:

> And love and friendship's finely pointed dart
> Fall blunted from each *indurated heart.*

(ii) *Poems*
Suggested date of reading: 1789
References: Cornell *EW* 66

(iii) *Poems*
Suggested date of reading: 1791-2
References: Legouis 150

> Were there, below, a spot of holy ground,
> By Pain and her sad family unfound ... (*Descriptive Sketches* 1-2)

The opening couplet of *Descriptive Sketches* refers us back to Goldsmith:

> But where to find that happiest spot below,
> Who can direct, when all pretend to know? (*The Traveller* 63-4)

Later in *Descriptive Sketches* W writes: 'While fill each pause the ringing woods of morn' (line 147), echoing the 'village murmur' of Goldsmith's *Deserted Village* 124 which 'filled each pause the nightingale had made'.

(iv) *The Deserted Village*
Suggested date of reading: June 1797
References: *MH* 89-91, 126-7
Jonathan Wordsworth argues for Goldsmith's influence on *The Ruined Cottage*.

121. Gray, Thomas
(i) *The Poems of Mr Gray* **ed. William Mason [2 vols., York, 1775]**
Suggested date of reading: 1779-87
References: Sheats 11; Masson ii 265
For De Quincey on W's childhood love of Gray's poetry, see note 120 (i). During composition of *The Vale of Esthwaite* (1787), W had access to Mason's edition of Gray's *Poems* (2 vols., York, 1775). At one point W addresses the Vale:

> My soul shall cast the wistful view
> The lingering look alone on you (*D.C.MS 3* 26r; De Selincourt 506-7)

The couplet recalls the last line of a rejected stanza from Gray's *Elegy*, printed by Mason in the notes to his edition: 'With wistful eyes pursue the setting sun' (*Poems* ii 108). W's 'lingering look' alludes to *Elegy* 88: 'Nor cast one longing *ling'ring look* behind'.

(ii) *Journal of the Lakes*
Suggested date of reading: by 1787
References: see note
W probably read Gray's *Journal* while at Hawkshead. He certainly read West's *Guide to the Lakes* which, from the second edition of 1780 onwards, reprinted *Mr. Gray's Journal* from Mason's edition of Gray in Appendix (or Article) III. Bicknell 10.1-10a.

(iii) *Journal of the Lakes*
Suggested date of reading: 1789
References: Cornell *EW* 80
Gray's letters describing his Lake District tour were available in the *Poems* ed. Mason, and in West's *Guide to the Lakes*, where they were reprinted.

(iv) *The Poems of Mr Gray* **ed. William Mason [2 vols., York, 1775]**
Suggested date of reading: 1790
References: Moorman 134-5
Moorman suggests that Gray influenced the itinerary of W's continental tour:

> At Lyons they set forward once more on foot, and turning this time eastwards, they reached on August 4th a place that left an ineffaceable impression on Wordsworth's mind - the monastery of the Grande Chartreuse. As already pointed out, in planning their route Wordsworth must have deliberately included this place, for he would have known it by description from the letters of the poet Gray - a favourite volume with him as it contained also Gray's *Journal of a Tour in the Lakes*. Gray and Horace Walpole had visited the Chartreuse in 1739, and Gray's record of it was of exactly the kind to attract and excite Wordsworth. (Moorman 134-5)

Trott points to echoes of Gray's journal in W's description of the Schaffhausen Fall in his letter to Dorothy, Aug. 1790: 'Magnificent as this fall certainly is I must confess I was disappointed in it. I had raised my ideas too high' (*EY* 35). 'Wordsworth probably got his high ideas from Coxe', Trott tells me, 'in whose opinion the Fall "far surpassed [the] most sanguine expectations." But W's diction is borrowed from Gray, who in 1740 wrote to his mother from Rome, "As high as my expectation was raised, *I confess*, the *magnificence* of this city infinitely surpasses it"'. W can have known Gray's remarks only from Mason's edition of the *Poems* (1775), pp. 81, 84.

(v) *Poems*
Suggested date of reading: 1791-2
References: Cornell *DS* 40, 52

(vi) *The Poems of Mr Gray* ed. William Mason [2 vols., York, 1775]
Suggested date of reading: Feb.-March 1798
References: see note

> Him had I seen the day before - alone
> And in the middle of the public way
> Standing to rest himself. His eyes were turn'd
> Towards the setting sun ... (Cornell *RC* 326-7)

These lines on the Pedlar, composed *c.* Feb. 1798, recall the discarded stanza to Gray's *Elegy*, which W could have known only from the notes to Mason's edition of the *Poems*:

> Him have we seen the greenwood side along,
> While o'er the heath we hied, our labour done,
> Oft as the woodlark pip'd her farewell song,
> With wistful eyes pursue the setting sun. (*Poems* [1775] ii 108)

W's borrowing implies that he had a copy of Mason's edition at Alfoxden, though it should be remembered that W had echoed these lines as early as 1787 in *The Vale of Esthwaite* (see [i], above).

122. Greenwood, William, *A Poem Written During a Shooting Excursion on the Moors* (Bath, 1787)
Suggested date of reading: by 1789
References: Cornell *EW* 44
W probably knew Greenwood, who was a Fellow of St John's, W's Cambridge College.

123. 'Guide Du Voyageur En Suisse'
Suggested date of reading: 1790, certainly by 1794
References: *EY* 674
When W left Windy Brow he left two books behind him. One of them was described by the caretaker, Mr Ianson, as 'Guide Du Voyageur En Suisse' (*EY* 674). Woof suggests that this refers to one of the following volumes:
　(i) Reynier, Jean Louis Antoine, *Les guides de voyageurs en Suisse. Précédé d'un discours sur l'état politique du pays [par J. L. A. Reynier].* (Paris, 1790; 2nd edn, 1791)
　(ii) The more likely of the two titles is *Guide du voyageur en Suisse*, which is a translation of Thomas Martin's *Sketch of a Tour through Switzerland* (1787). There was a new edition of 1788 'to which is added A short account of an expedition to the summit of Mont Blanc

by Monsieur de Saussure'. Woof has seen a French edition of 1794, which 'describes itself as a troisième édition'; it lacks Saussure's account of his expedition. This guide may have been used during W's 1790 tour of the continent.

124. Harrington, James, *The Common-wealth of Oceana* [1656]
Suggested date of reading: 1791-2
References: Chard 86, 91; Shaver 115
Chard 84-91, points out that Milton, Sidney and Harrington were essential reading among the Girondins with whom W associated in France 1791-2, and it is likely that W read their works. This is supported by the presence of the first English edition of *Oceana* (1656) in the Rydal Mount library (Shaver 115). This may have been acquired during the early 1790s. Fink, 'Wordsworth and the English Republican Tradition', *JEGP* 47 (1948) 107-26, p. 108, notes French translations of Milton's *Theorie de la royaute* (Paris 1789, 1791); Sidney, *Discourses* (1702), and Harrington, *Oceana* (1737).

125. Hartley, David, *Observations on Man, His Frame, His Duty, and His Expectations* [1749]
Suggested date of reading: c. 1787-90
References: Schneider 109n
Schneider remarks that 'most of the [Cambridge] undergraduates knew of [Hartley's] existence and probably of his famous theory of association' (Schneider 109n). Whether or not W knew of Hartley's application of the theory, associationism can be found in W's poetry as early as *The Vale of Esthwaite* (1787); see my article, 'Wordsworth's Poetry of Grief', *WC* 21 (1990) 115-17, p. 117.

126. Hayley, William, *The Poetical Works of William Hayley, Esq.* (3 vols., Dublin, 1785)
Suggested date of reading: by Aug. 1786
References: Landon 224; *EY* 8; Shaver 117
In *Anacreon Imitated* (composed Aug. 1786), W compares Sir Joshua Reynolds with the classical painter, Apelles (lines 1-8). Landon 224 observes that 'The names of Reynolds and Apelles had been linked in Hayley's *Poetical Epistle to an Eminent Painter*':

> And Grace, the first attendant of her train,
> She, whom Apelles wooed, nor wooed in vain,
> To Reynolds gives her undulating line,
> And Judgment doats upon his chaste design. (ii 123-6)

DW possessed a copy of Hayley's poems in 1787 (3 vols., Dublin, 1785), presumably the legacy of her father (*EY* 8), which later entered the Rydal Mount library (Shaver 117).

127. Hearne, Samuel, *A Journey from Prince of Wales's Fort in Hudson's Bay to the Northern Ocean, Undertaken ... for the Discovery of Copper Mines, a North West Passage, etc. in the Years 1769-1772* (1795)
Suggested date of reading: April/May 1798; by mid-May 1798
References: *PW* ii 513-14; Jacobus 242
Hearne's account of the Chipewyan Indians provided the inspiration for W's *Complaint of a Forsaken Indian Woman*. We cannot be sure whether it was C who first read Hearne's

Journey, and then recommended it to W, but the evidence points that way. In *The Friend* C remembered reading 'Bryan Edwards's account of the effects of the *Oby* Witchcraft on the Negroes in the West Indies, and Hearne's deeply interesting Anecdotes of similar workings on the imagination of the Copper Indians' (CC *Friend* ii 89; his italics) during work on *The Three Graves*, probably in April 1798.[1] He had known Edwards' volume from a Bristol Library borrowing made in 1795 (Whalley 64), and was therefore in a position to recommend it to W, who composed the *Complaint* shortly before mid-May 1798.

In later years a copy of the *Journey* was on the shelves at Rydal Mount (Shaver 118); another containing C's marginalia dating from *c.* 1824 is at the Harvard University Library (CC *Marginalia* ii 985-7; Coffman H49).

128. Hederich, Benjamin, *Graecum lexicon manuale ... cura J. A. Ernesti, nunc iterum recensitum et ... auctum a T. Morell* (1778)
Suggested date of reading: March 1786 onwards
References: Shepherd MSS; TWT 91; Reed i 66; Shaver 118
The accounts of Christopher Crackanthorpe Cookson, now among the Shepherd MSS at the Wordsworth Library, record the purchase of this book, for £1, from the Penrith Bookseller, Anthony Soulby:

1786 March 13th P^d. Anthony Soulby for a Hedrick's Lexicon for William   1.0.0

This may have been the quarto edition of 1778 which entered the Rydal Mount library (Shaver 118). W's Greek education was well under way by March 1786, when he would have used the *Lexicon* for his reading of Xenophon. He almost certainly took the *Lexicon* to Cambridge, where it would have come in handy for his studies of Xenophon (examined Dec. 1787), Sophocles (Dec. 1788) and Demosthenes (Dec. 1789).

129. Hentzner, Paul, *A Journey into England* tr. Horace Walpole (Strawberry Hill, 1757)
Suggested date of reading: by autumn 1796
References: Cornell B 348-65
Several extracts from Hentzner are copied into MS 1 of *The Borderers*, D.C.MS 12, in the hand firstly of W and then of DW. Since the extracts predate the drafts towards *The Borderers*, they must have been entered by autumn 1796. There were two editions of the *Travels* that W might have read:
   (i) *A Journey into England* (Strawberry Hill, 1757)[2]
   (ii) *Paul Hentzner's Travels in England* (1797; published by Edward Jeffrey)
In determining which of these the Wordsworths were working from, Osborn observes that they

probably obtained a text of the rare Strawberry Hill edition, since the entry of the extracts appears to predate Jeffrey's reissue, though variations from the text of the Jeffrey volume are consistent with copyist error. (Cornell B 349n)

[1] The dating of *The Three Graves* is slightly vexed. I follow Jacobus, who suggests that C 'began work in the summer of 1797, but Parts III and IV reflect the activities of the Alfoxden spring so clearly that the bulk of composition must belong to this period' (Jacobus 228n).
[2] Osborn erroneously records of the Strawberry Hill edition, 'date unknown' (Cornell B 349n).

The conclusion is sound - the Wordsworths do seem to have worked from the first edition of 1757 - but not all the variations between the various texts can be put down to copyist error. I have collated the MS with both editions, and find that the Wordsworths' capitals and punctuation are closer to 1757 than to 1797. One substantive variant confirms 1757 as the most likely source. At *D.C.MS 12* 40r, reproduced at Cornell *B* 360-1, DW transcribes from Hentzner the phrase, 'Jack w^h. Lanthorns'. Where 1797 modernizes to 'Jack-w'-a-lanterns' (p. 74), 1757 has 'Jack-w'-a-lanthorns' (p. 101). It is unlikely that DW would have entered the archaic 'lanthorn' unless prompted to do so by her source.

The fact that the Wordsworths were copying from a rare edition may explain why they made the copy in the first place - the book was probably not theirs, and they wished to have a copy of a passage they admired. It is not easy to guess where they saw the *Journey*, since it appears neither in the Racedown Lodge Library catalogue, nor in that of the Bristol Library Society.

130. Herd, David, ed. *Ancient and Modern Scottish Poems* **(2 vols., Edinburgh, 1776)**
Suggested date of reading: spring 1798; by early 1801
References: PW ii 513-14; N&Q NS 4 (1957) 400-5; Woof Ph.D. 236; Jacobus 242
Moorman, 'Wordsworth's Commonplace Book', *N&Q* NS 4 (1957) 400-5, reports that the commonplace book used by W after 1800 contains 'four verses from a ballad in Herd's *Ancient and Modern Scottish Songs* (1776) which he had certainly known in earlier years and probably used as part of his material for *The Thorn* (1798)' (p. 402). The ballad is called *The Cruel Mother* and is quoted by Jacobus, who touches on its influence (Jacobus 242); Woof Ph.D. 236 suggests that it was entered in the Commonplace Book in early 1801.

131. Heron, Robert, *Observations Made in a Journey through the Western Counties of Scotland* **(2 vols., Perth, 1793)**
Suggested date of reading: spring 1798
References: Parrish 171; Cornell *RC* 479-80; N&Q NS 4 (1957) 400-5
The precise date of W's reading of Heron is in question, and no-one has so far proved that it was read, or even necessary to W, when he composed lines on the Pedlar in spring 1798. I nevertheless enter it here as a possible reading.

In fact, the available evidence suggests that W read Heron in spring 1800, when it provided one of the first entries in his Commonplace Book - an entry that included, apparently, the extract that appears in the Note to *The Excursion* (Cornell *RC* 479-80); see Moorman, 'Wordsworth's Commonplace Book', *N&Q* NS 4 (1957) 400-5, p. 401. An 1800 reading is further supported by Mendilow's finding (discussed Parrish 170-1) that a number of ideas and expressions in W's 1800 Preface may be traced to Heron; see Mendilow, 'Robert Heron and Wordsworth's Critical Essays', *MLR* 52 (1957) 329-38. For Heron's later influence, see Coe, 'A Source for Wordsworth's *Effusion in the Pleasure-Ground*', *N&Q* 196 (1951) 80-1.

132. Holbach, Paul Heinrich Dietrich, Baron d', *Système de la Nature ou des lois du monde physique et du monde moral* **[2 vols., 1781]**
Suggested date of reading: 1791-2
References: Chard 97-8; Reed ii 301n; Shaver 125; Wu *Library* JW15
JW Sr owned a copy of this book, which passed into W's possession in Oct. 1805, and then into the Rydal Mount library (Shaver 125). Even if W had not read his father's copy by

1791, it is likely that he was acquainted with its contents by then. Chard 97-8 writes convincingly about its importance to the Girondin group with which W was associated.

Starting with a philosophy of atheistic materialism, Holbach showed how the state was obliged to nurture, in every way, the virtues of mutual co-operation on which the good of society depended. The government was a means to that end, and if it failed the people were entitled to overthrow and replace their rulers.

133. Holcroft, Thomas, *The Man of Ten Thousand* **(1796)**
Suggested date of reading: by 21 March 1796
References: EY 171
W read Holcroft's play shortly after publication: it was listed in the *Monthly Magazine* as a new publication in Feb. 1796; on 21 March 1796 W told Mathews that 'I have attempted to read Holcroft's *Man of Ten Thousand*, but such stuff! Demme hey, humph' (*EY* 171). W alludes to it at *Thirteen-Book Prelude* xii 91 (Cornell *13-Book Prelude* i 306n).

134. Home, John, *Douglas*
Suggested date of reading: 1791-2
References: Cornell *DS* 58
W may have encountered Home's play first at Hawkshead, since it was extracted in Knox's *Elegant Extracts*.

135. Homer
(i) '2 Vol Homer' (probably *The Iliad* **and** *The Odyssey*)
Suggested date of reading: between Feb. 1784 and Aug. 1787
References: Shepherd MSS; TWT 91; Schneider 68
In old age, W recalled his schoolboy reading: 'As to Homer, I was never weary of travelling over the scenes through which he led me' (Cornell *Poems 1807-1820* 544). In his accounts, now among the Shepherd MSS at the Wordsworth Library, Richard Wordsworth of Whitehaven (1733-1794) records the purchase of two volumes of Homer and one of Lucian 'for my Nephews', totalling eight shillings and ninepence (see pp. 169-70, below). The 'Nephews' must be W and his brother, Richard, both of whom may by this time have been learning Greek: W was 14, Richard 16. In Christmas 1785, Richard left Hawkshead to become articled as a clerk to his cousin Richard Wordsworth, attorney, of Branthwaite (1752-1816). W would then, presumably, have taken possession of these books.

W apparently gave them to DW in summer 1787 when he had finished at Hawkshead, and was visiting her prior to going to Cambridge. In Aug. 1787 she referred to them as 'the Iliad, the Odyssey' (*EY* 8). At that time she reported that 'I am at present [reading] the Iliad', which would imply that the volumes contained facing translations of the original (she knew no Greek).

(ii) *The Iliad* **and** *The Odyssey* **tr. Alexander Pope**
Suggested date of reading: by June 1785
References: see note
W's earliest extant poem, *Lines Written as a School Exercise*, displays a thorough knowledge of Pope's *Homer*; line 28, 'Through all my frame the pleasing accents ran', echoes Pope's *Odyssey* xxiv 367: 'Quick *thro'* the father's heart *these accents ran*'. In *School Exercise* 30,

Superstition 'fled indignant to the shades of night', echoing Pope, *Iliad* v 360: 'The Soul indignant seeks the Realms of Night'. Compare also *School Exercise* 39-40: 'The god of day in all the pomp of light / Moves through *the vault of Heav'n* and dissipates the night', with Pope, *Iliad* xvi 938-9:

> Now flaming from the Zenith, Sol had driv'n
> His fervid Orb thro' half *the Vault of Heav'n* ...

W probably read Pope's *Homer* in a copy owned by one of his teachers, for it was not in the School Library. In 1827 he declared: 'As far as Pope goes, he succeeds; but his Homer is not Homer, but Pope' (Grosart iii 460).

136. Horatius Flaccus, Quintus

(i) *Q. Horatii Flacci Opera*

Suggested date of reading: 1779-87; by 1786
References: see note

One of the epigraphs for W's juvenile poem, *The Dog: An Idyllium* (1786), 'Fies nobilium tu quoque' (*D.C.MS 2* 23r), is from Horace's famous ode to the Bandusian fountain (*Ode* III xiii 13), which W may have translated as a schoolboy. It translates as: 'You shall be ranked among the most celebrated'. By omitting the final word of the original Latin, 'fontium' (fountains), W applies the phrase to his dog.

Among the rough drafts for the poem there appears a conclusion in which he curses the waters in which the dog was drowned: 'And may the panting dog-star with his tongue of fire / Lash thy frighted waves' (*D.C.MS 2* 109r). This reverses the blessing bestowed by Horace on the Bandusian fountain ('Te flagrantis atrox hora Caniculae Nescit tangere', lines 9-10), translated by Watson as: 'The burning Heat of the Dog-star shall not affect you'.[1]

(ii) *Ars Poetica* or *Epistles* I or II

Suggested date of reading: c. Dec. 1787
References: Schneider 9; *PW* i 371

In W's first College examination at Cambridge (the only one in which he was placed in the first class) he answered questions on either Horace's *Ars Poetica* or *Epistles* I or II.

(iii) *The Works of Horace. Translated into English prose, for the use of those who are desirous of acquiring or recovering a competent knowledge of the Latin language. By Christopher Smart* (2 vols., Dublin, 1772)

Suggested date of reading: 1787-90
References: *N&Q* NS 38 (1991) 303-5; Shaver 129; Wu *Library* JW7

W's copy of volume 2 of this set survives today in the library of Pembroke College, Cambridge. It contains an early ownership signature that probably dates from his Cambridge years. Full details can be found in my article, 'Wordsworth's Copy of Smart's Horace', *N&Q* NS 38 (1991) 303-5.

In spring 1789 W translated Horace's *Ode to Apollo* (*Ode* I xxxi), with the help of Smart's translation. Smart's translation of this *Ode* includes the line, 'not those countries, which the

---

[1] *The Odes, Epodes, and Carmen Seculare of Horace* tr. Philip Watson (2 vols., 1741), i 295.

still river Liris eats away with its silent streams'. W develops the reference to the erosion of the riverbank in his own translation:

Nor fields where kiss'd by Liris' tide
As still his evening waters glide
Drops in the quiet stream the crumbling mold ... (*D.C.MS 7* 7v)

(iv) *Odes*
Suggested date of reading: 1794
References: Cornell *EW* 135
W's translation of Horace's Ode to the Bandusian Fountain (*Ode* III xiii) appears in a manuscript dating from his time at Windy Brow in 1794 (Cornell *EW* 135). Averill observes that it follows the text in the 'standard eighteenth-century schoolboy Horace, the one that Alexander Boswell used at Eton in 1792 ... the *Opera* published in London by Rivington, Dilly, Johnson, *et al.*, [which] in 1788 ... was in its tenth edition' (Cornell *EW* 135). W probably acquired his copy in Cambridge. For Darbishire's account of W's use of the form, 'Blandusian', which suggests a reading of Thomas Warton's translation, see *PW* iii 492.

137. Hutchinson, William, *An Excursion to the Lakes, in Westmoreland and Cumberland, August 1773* (1774)
Suggested date of reading: 1796
References: Cornell *B* 18
According to Osborn, this is a book on which W drew during composition of *The Borderers*; see Cornell *B* 18, and Marijane Osborn, 'Wordsworth's "Borderers" and the Landscape of Penrith', *Transactions of the Cumberland and Westmorland Antiquarian and Archaeological Society* 76 (1976) 144-58, p. 155. Bicknell 6-7.

138. Isola, Agostino, *Pieces Selected from the Italian Poets by Agostino Isola and Translated into English verse by some Gentlemen of the University* (2nd edn, Cambridge, 1784)
Suggested date of reading: 1787-90; by 1788
References: Moorman 99; Shaver 201
Sturrock, 'Wordsworth's Italian Teacher', *Bulletin of the John Rylands University Library of Manchester* 67 (1985) 797-812, points out that W's copy of *Pieces Selected from the Italian Poets* is now at the Fitzwilliam Museum, Cambridge (a fact not noted by the Shavers - see Shaver 201). It was in use during W's Cambridge years, and in 1802-3, when W copied into it the versions of Metastasio composed for Stuart (see Woof *SIB* 185-9).

Isola's translations from Petrarch, Ariosto, Tasso, Tassoni, Guarini, Metastasio, and Marino, give a good idea of W's Cambridge reading. In later years he recalled: 'My Italian master was named Isola, and had been well acquainted with Gray the poet. As I took to these studies with much interest, he was proud of the progress I made' (*Prose Works* iii 373).

139. 'Italian Gram.'
Suggested date of reading: late May 1794 onwards
References: *EY* 120-1n
W left a number of books with his brother Richard at Staple Inn, London, in 1793. These included copies of Tasso, Ariosto, and an 'Italian Gram.' (*EY* 121n). Richard forwarded these

to W in late May 1794, and W would probably have received them by the end of the month. They were needed for the Italian tutorials which W gave his sister during the summer of 1794. All three volumes were probably acquired during W's Cambridge years.

140. James I, *Demonology* (1603)
Suggested date of reading: July 1795
References: EY 175
A couplet from the earliest surviving draft of W's imitation of Juvenal's eighth satire, made in *D.C.MS 11* during March 1796,[1] reads:

> Or whet his kingly faculties to chase
> Legions of devils through a keyhole's space ... (*D.C.MS 11* 5v)

This survives in the fair copy sent to Francis Wrangham, Feb. 1797, and, as Shaver points out, alludes to *Demonology* (*EY* 175). W never owned a copy himself, but Wrangham did. John Cole, *A Bibliographical and Descriptive Tour from Scarborough to the Library of a Philobiblist* (Scarborough, 1824), catalogues some of the titles in Wrangham's library and mentions 'James I. on Demonologie (1603)' (p. 59). Wrangham's own catalogue, *The English Portion of the Library of the Ven. Francis Wrangham, M.A., F.R.S., Archdeacon of Cleveland* (Malton, 1826), also includes 'James the First, on Dæmonologie 1603' (p. 68). Wrangham had probably acquired the volume by the time W visited him in Cobham in July 1795, and showed it to him then. At Sotheby's auction of Wrangham's collection, 12 July 1843, the volume went to 'A. Hatfield' for the princely sum of five shillings. Its present whereabouts is unknown.

141. Johnson, Samuel
(i) prose
Suggested date of reading: between July 1782 and June 1786
References: LY iii 492; Morley i 103
On 15 Dec. 1837, W told Elizabeth Fisher that

> One of my Schoolmasters, whom I most respected and loved, was, unfortunately, for me, a passionate admirer of Dʳ Johnson's prose; and having not been much exercised in prose myself, I have not till this day got over the ill effects of that injudicious [ ] upon my own way of expressing myself. (*LY* iii 492)

The reference to a teacher 'whom I most respected and loved' suggests that W has in mind William Taylor. If this identification is correct, W's early readings of Johnson must have occurred between July 1782 (when Taylor's predecessor, Edward Christian, resigned) and July 1786 (when Taylor died). *Rasselas* appears to have been on W's mind in spring 1798; see Mason *LB* 99.

(ii) *The Vanity of Human Wishes* (?and other poems)
Suggested date of reading: by 1794
References: Sheats 96; Cornell *EW* 153
In his 1794 revisions to *An Evening Walk*, W writes:

---

[1] For dating see Reed i 340-1.

So Virtue, fallen on times to gloom consigned,
Makes round her path the light *she cannot find.* (lines 680-1)

This echoes *The Vanity of Human Wishes* 368: 'And *makes* the happiness *she does not find*'. I suspect that W read *The Vanity of Human Wishes* long before 1794, probably at Hawkshead, and that he had also read *London*, if not other poems by Johnson. He might have returned to Johnson's imitations of Juvenal prior to his final College examinations at Cambridge in June 1790, when *Satires* III-XV were on the syllabus (see p. 168, below), and must have been acquainted with Johnson's imitations of Juvenal by 1795 (see next note). Details of the early publishing history of *The Vanity of Human Wishes* are given in *Samuel Johnson: Poems* ed. E. L. McAdam Jr, with George Milne (New Haven and London, 1964), p. 91.

(iii) poetry, especially *The Vanity of Human Wishes* and *London*
Suggested date of reading: by 1795
References: LY iii 516
On 26 Jan. 1838, W wrote to Robert Shelton Mackenzie:

> when I was a very young Man the present Archdeacon Wrangham and I amused ourselves in imitating jointly Juvenile's Satire upon Nobility - or rather parts of it. How far the choice of a Subject might be influenced by the run at that time against Aristocracy, I am unable to say, and am inclined to think that if the 3ᵈ and 10ᵗʰ Satire had not been so well imitated by Dʳ Johnson, we might as easily have chosen one of them to amuse ourselves and try our skill upon. Not a word of this essay was ever, to my knowledge, printed, and fierce poems upon political subjects from *my* pen, could never have been suppressed or forgotten for they were never written.
>
> (*LY* iii 516; his italics)

This letter indicates that W had read Johnson's *London* (imitation of Juvenal, *Satire* III) and *The Vanity of Human Wishes* (imitation of Juvenal, *Satire* X) by 1795 - most probably at Hawkshead, some time before 1787.

142. Juvenalis, Decimus Junius
(i) *Mores Hominum, the Manners of Men, Described in Sixteen Satyrs* tr. Sir Robert Stapylton (1660)
Suggested date of reading: early 1780s
References: Wu CWAAS 158
This title was retained at the Hawkshead Grammar School Library during W's day, when it was in frequent use by schoolboys. During the latter part of the eighteenth century it was customary for them to inscribe their names in books they read, and this volume, which survives in the Library today, contains the signatures of 'Isaac Leathes Dec.ʳ 6ᵗʰ 1782' (p. 326); 'Chris: Wilson 1782' (p. 330); and W's friend, 'Flet.ʳ Raincock Dec.ʳ 6ᵗʰ 1782' (p. 327).[1] Besides these and other names, it contains an inscription I believe to be W's, probably entered at around the same time as the others in the volume, *c*. 1782-6. The inscription, which is dated, appears on the right hand margin of p. 227, though it is no longer

---

[1] W hunted ravens' eggs with Fletcher Raincock; see TWT 211.

distinct since it was erased and, later, cropped when the book was rebound. The following, however, may still be discerned:

William W[   ]
    May 3[ ]
    178[ ]

No other pupil of the early 1780s, so far as I can to discover, shared W's initials.

(ii) *Satires* III-XV
Suggested date of reading: by June 1790
References: Schneider 167
W was examined on Juvenal, *Satires* III-XV at St John's College, Cambridge, June 1790; see p. 168, below.

(iii) *D. Iun. Iuvenalis et Auli Persii Flacci Satyrae, ex doct: virorum emendatione* (1683)
Suggested date of reading: late Feb.-26 Sept. 1795
References: Reed i 340-1; Shaver 143
As Reed points out, 'W and Wrangham very likely worked out an imitation of a large part of Juvenal VIII.1-86 while W was in London in 1795'; Juvenal VIII.87-124 was composed, 'probably in Bristol', by 26 Sept. 1795 (Reed i 340).

During the summer of 1795 W saw much of his old friend William Mathews, and it was probably then that Mathews gave W the 1683 edition of Juvenal's *Satires* (now in the Wordsworth Collection, Cornell University) which, on its flyleaf, bears the inscription, 'W. Mathews to W. Wordsworth'. Beneath it, W recalls that

> This friend of mine was the elder son of Mr Mathews, Bookseller near Northumberland House, Strand. He went to practise as a Barrister in the West Indies, and died almost immediately on his arrival there. W. Wordsworth. (Healey 2247; Shaver 143)

W and Mathews did not, apparently, meet or correspond between March 1796 (*EY* 170) and Mathews' premature death from yellow fever in 1801. For more on Mathews, see Gill 432.

(iv) *Satires*
Suggested date of reading: 7 March-April 1796
References: Reed i 341
'A date of 7 Mar-Apr 1796 would probably include virtually all W's work on *Juvenal* 29-162' (Reed i 341). 'I have either lost or mislaid my Juvenal', W told Wrangham on 25 Feb. 1797 (*EY* 176). This is presumably a reference to the copy given to him by Mathews (see preceding note). The loss, as Shaver observes, must have occurred between summer 1796 and Feb. 1797 (*EY* 172n); it was probably repaired in March 1797 when Wrangham responded to W's plea to 'Send Copy of Lat. Juvenal' (*EY* 172). W soon recovered the volume he had been given by Mathews because it passed into the Rydal Mount library (Shaver 143).

143. Kant, Immanuel, works inc. *The Critique of Judgement*
Suggested date of reading: by 26 Sept. 1798
References: Prose Works i 95
'I asked him what he thought of Kant', W recorded of his last meeting with Klopstock, which took place on 26 Sept. 1798. Trott suggests that W may have read F. A. Nitsch's defence

of Kant, *Monthly Magazine* 2 (1796) 702-5; Nitsch's *A General and Introductory View of Professor Kant's Principles* (1796), or A. F. M. Willich's *Elements of the Critical Philosophy* (1798), a copy of which Willich presented to Cottle in 1798.[1] Kant's *Project for a Perpetual Peace* was published 20 Feb. 1797. W apparently had the *Critique of Judgement* in mind while composing his *Guide to the Lakes*, 1811-12 (*Prose Works* ii 456-7). Significantly, C's earliest marginalia on Kant may date from as early as 1800 (CC *Marginalia* iii 236).

144. Klopstock, Friedrich Gottlieb
(i) *Messias* [Halle, 1749]
Suggested date of reading: by 21 Sept. 1798
References: *Prose Works* i 96; Reed i 251; Shaver 338
'Went to Remnant, the English bookseller, where I procured the analytical review in which is contained the review of Cumberland's Calvary. I remembered to have read there some specimens of a blank verse translation of the Messiah. I had mentioned this to Mr Klopstock, and he had a great desire to have a sight of them' (*Prose Works* i 92). W's first visit to Klopstock took place on 21 Sept. 1798. He went to Remnant's bookshop between then and 26 Sept., when he showed Klopstock the translation of his *Messias* (Reed i 250-1). W may have been referred to the translation in the *Analytical* by Joseph Johnson, and it is likely that he read at least parts of the *Messias* in German prior to meeting its author. Perhaps he read C's copy, probably acquired 1798-9, which entered the Rydal Mount library (Shaver 338).

On 13 July 1802, C told Sotheby that he had written a 'malicious Motto ... on the first page of Klopstock's·Messias' (Griggs ii 811). The motto comes from Virgil, *Eclogues* v 45-6, and translates: 'Your song, oh divine poet, is no less delightful to me than sleeping'.

(ii) *Oden*
Suggested date of reading: 21 Sept. 1798
References: *Prose Works* i 91
On 21 Sept. 1798, Klopstock read to W and C 'some passages from his odes in which he has adopted the latin measures' (*Prose Works* i 91). Perhaps W went on to read some of these in print; this is supported by the fact that C purchased the *Oden*, and was acquainted with the first two volumes of Klopstock's *Werke* (*Notebooks* i 339n, 340).

145. Knight, Richard Payne, *The Progress of Civil Society, A Didactic Poem* (1796)
Suggested date of reading: late Jan. 1798
References: see note
Reed reported that the Alfoxden Notebook (*D.C.MS 14*) contained 'a pair of quotations, one from Boswell. In default of evidence to the contrary, these materials on the pages of the Nb may be supposed to date from late Jan 1798' (Reed i 322). The 'pair of quotations' have since been identified by Dr Robert Woof as a single transcription from Richard Payne Knight's *The Progress of Civil Society*, and this has been reported by Michael C. Jaye.[2] The transcription is in W's hand and reads as follows:

---

[1] Cottle's copy is now at Victoria University Library (Dendurent 565). Willich's *Elements* was in the shops by Christmas 1797, and it provides 'a view of all the works published by ... Professor Immanuel Kant'.
[2] 'William Wordsworth's Alfoxden Notebook: 1798', *The Evidence of the Imagination* ed. Donald H. Reiman, Michael C. Jaye, and Betty T. Bennett (New York, 1978), pp. 42-85, p. 77.

Dr Johnson observed, that in blank
verse, the language suffered
more distortion to keep it out
of prose than any inconveni=
=ence or limitation to be   [5]
apprehended from the shackles
& circumspection of rhyme.
Boswells life. Vol 1st. p.584.
This kind of distortion is
the worst fault that poetry   [10]
can have; for if once the
natural order & connection
of the words is broken, & the
idiom of the language violated,
the lines appear manufactured, [15]
& lose all that character
(*D.C.MS 14* 20v)

of enthusiasm & inspiration,
without which they become
cold & vapid, how sublime
soever the ideas & images   [20]
may be which they express

These lines occur a few
pages before the preceding
note
See, of Reviews & Baviads in   [25]
    despite,
Each month new swarms of
    Bavius's write
(*D.C.MS 14* 20r)

Lines 1-21 are a copy of the footnote on p. 71 of Knight's poem; lines 22-4 are W's; lines 25-8 are *Progress of Civil Society* iii 395-6. W may have read the copy in the Bristol Library Society (*BLS* 55).

146. Knox, Vicesimus, *Extracts, Elegant, Instructive, and Entertaining, in Poetry, from the Most Approved Authors* [*c*. 1770]
Suggested date of reading: ?1780s
References: *Prose Works* ii 84; Fink 127
In 1810 W observed that Knox's *Elegant Extracts* was 'known to most of my Readers, as it is circulated every where and in fact constitutes at this day the poetical library of our Schools' (*Prose Works* ii 84). This suggests that it was used by W himself at Hawkshead; if so, he probably had his own copy. Even if he did not, he would have had access to the 1789 Dublin

edition owned by his brother Christopher (see Fink 34), which may have been that recorded in the Rydal Mount library catalogue by John Carter in 1829 (Shaver 147).

Knox's *Elegant Extracts in Verse and Prose* was the standard textbook anthology of the day, and contained, apart from extracts from Spenser, Shakespeare, and Milton, poems by Pope, Gray, Collins, Goldsmith, Elizabeth Carter, John and Anna Laetitia Aikin, and virtually every other significant writer of the eighteenth century. It was first published *c.* 1770, and updated with each edition. Zall identifies Knox as the source for the text of *The Babes in the Woods*, as quoted in the Preface to *Lyrical Ballads* (*WC* 10 [1979] 345-7).

147. Kotzebue, August Friedrich Ferdinand von, works
Suggested date of reading: 1796-7; by 1800
References: see note
Kotzebue was one of the most prolific and successful dramatists of the 1790s, and it is likely that as he worked on *The Borderers*, W encountered Kotzebue's work. He knew of it by 1800 when, in the Preface to *Lyrical Ballads*, he criticized 'sickly and stupid German tragedies' (*Prose Works* i 129). This is consistent with his attack on 'superficial' writing on 9 March 1840: 'Kotzebue was acted and read at once from Cadiz to Moscow; what is become of him now?' (*LY* iv 43). C reviewed a translation of Kotzebue's *The Negro Slaves* in Jan. 1797 (Erdman *BNYPL* 520-7).

148. Langhorne, John
(i) *Poetical Works* (2 vols., 1766)
Suggested date of reading: ?1780s; by March 1787
References: TWT 344
Bowman introduced W to Langhorne's poems (TWT 344), and their influence is evident in the opening lines of W's first published poem, *Sonnet, on Seeing Miss Helen Maria Williams Weep at a Tale of Distress* (composed by March 1787):

She wept. - *Life's purple tide* began to flow
In languid streams through every thrilling vein ...

The heightened diction derives from Langhorne's translation of Bion's *The Death of Adonis*, where Venus weeps over her dying lover: 'she saw *Life's purple tide*, / Stretch'd her fair arms, with trembling voice she cry'd' (lines 49-50). See also Cornell *DS* 72 and n.

(ii) *The Country Justice* [1771-4]
Suggested date of reading: by 1789
References: PW i 322
An Evening Walk describes a war widow who

Shakes her numb arm that slumbers with its weight,
And eyes through tears the mountain's shadeless height;
And bids her soldier come her woes to share,
Asleep on Minden's charnel plain afar ... (lines 251-4)

The errata to the first edition corrects 'Minden's charnel plain' to 'Bunker's charnel hill'. Bunker Hill (1775) was a comparatively recent battle, and moves the widow's story from the

Seven Years' War (1756-63) to the American War of Independence. W's alteration suppresses a borrowing from *The Country Justice*:

Cold on Canadian Hills, or *Minden's Plain*,
Perhaps that Parent mourn'd her Soldier slain;
Bent o'er her Babe, her Eye dissolv'd in Dew,
The big Drops mingling with the Milk He drew ... (i 161-4)

I suspect that W first encountered *The Country Justice* at Hawkshead - a likely possibility, since he also knew Langhorne's *Poetical Works* at that time.

(iii) *Owen of Carron* **(1778)**
Suggested date of reading: early 1788
References: see note
D.C.MS 2 105v contains rough drafts connected with fair copy extracts made from *The Vale of Esthwaite* during early 1788. Among them W has jotted 'The morn is on the mountains spread' - a line from Langhorne's *Owen of Carron*:

The Morn is on the Mountains spread,
The Wood-lark trills his liquid Strain -
Can Morn's sweet Music rouse the dead?
Give the set Eye it's Soul again? (lines 309-12)

De Selincourt notes echoes of *Owen of Carron* in *She Dwelt Among the Untrodden Ways* (*PW* ii 30).

(iv) *The Country Justice* **and** *Owen of Carron*
Suggested date of reading: 1791-2
References: Cornell *DS* 72, 118

(v) *The Country Justice*
Suggested date of reading: summer or autumn 1793
References: see note
In *Salisbury Plain* (composed 1793), the traveller finds 'No brook to wet his lips or *soothe his ear*' (line 47); Williams points out that W's phrasing appears to echo Langhorne's 'The Stream, to *soothe thine Ear*, to cool thy Breast' (*Country Justice* ii 147).[1] This echo indicates a rereading of Langhorne's poem in summer or autumn 1793.

(vi) *The Country Justice*
Suggested date of reading: autumn 1795
References: *N&Q* NS 1 (1954) 302-4
The influence of *The Country Justice* on *Adventures on Salisbury Plain* (1795) is discussed by Sharrock, 'Wordsworth and John Langhorne's *The Country Justice*', *N&Q* NS 1 (1954) 302-4.

(vii) *The Country Justice*
Suggested date of reading: March-May 1798
References: Mason *LB* 118

---

[1] *Wordsworth: Romantic Poetry and Revolution Politics* (Manchester, 1989), pp. 79-80.

149. Latin primers
Suggested date of reading: 1776 onwards
References: *Prose Works* iii 372
In old age W recalled: 'I was very much indebted to one of the ushers of Hawkshead School, by name Shaw, who taught me more of Latin in a fortnight *than I had learnt during two preceding years at the school of Cockermouth*' (*Prose Works* iii 372). This remark suggests not only that W studied Latin as soon as he arrived at Hawkshead in 1779, but that since 1777 he had been learning the language at Revd. Gilbanks' Grammar School in Cockermouth. In fact he attended Gilbanks' School from 1776; JW Sr's account book (now at the Wordsworth Library) records, among his payments to Gilbanks:

1776 22ᵈ. Octʳ. William half a Year ... - 15.0 (50v)

On this basis Reed notes that 'there is no evidence that W attended Gilbanks' school except Apr-Oct 1776', and speculates that after this period 'the boys were surely receiving schooling somewhere', perhaps at Penrith or elsewhere in Cockermouth (Reed i 44-5n). However, Reed appears to have overlooked the History of All Saints and Christ Church, Cockermouth, which, according to Wilkinson, states that W was taught at Cockermouth Grammar School, 1776-8.[1] The likely explanation is that after 1776 JW Sr recorded expenditure on his childrens' education separately from his other accounts, in a volume since lost.

150. Le Sage, Alain Rene, *Histoire de Gil Blas de Santillane*
Suggested date of reading: between 27 Dec. 1781 and Dec. 1783; by Dec. 1783
References: JW Sr's Account Book; *Prose Works* iii 372; *EY* 8; Reed i 54; Wu *Library* JW26
Towards the end of his life, W recalled:

> Of my earliest days at school I have little to say, but that they were very happy ones, chiefly because I was left at liberty, then and in the vacations, to read whatever books I liked. For example, I read all Fielding's works, Don Quixote, Gil Blas, and any part of Swift that I liked ... (*Prose Works* iii 372)

JW Sr recorded the purchase of *Gil Blas* in his account book:

1781 Decʳ. 27ᵗʰ. A. Soulby for 4 Volˢ. of Gil Blas 0.8.0 (82v)

In other words, on 27 Dec. 1781, he paid Anthony Soulby, the bookseller in Penrith, eight shillings for a four-volume set of *Gil Blas*. The set may not necessarily have been purchased new; indeed, JW Sr was in the habit of purchasing books second-hand. In all likelihood this is the copy of 'Gil Blas (in French)', mentioned by DW in her letter to Jane Pollard of 6 and 7 Aug. 1787 (*EY* 8). Copies of the French text of this immensely popular novel were widely available by the 1780s; the NUC and BN list editions published in Edinburgh, Paris, Amsterdam and London. The set apparently passed into Dorothy's possession at JW Sr's death in 1783; shortly after it came into the hands of Richard Wordsworth of Branthwaite,

---

[1] *The Wake of the Bounty* (1953), p. 129. The History records that 'Joseph Gilbanks was from 1778 to 1795 Master of Cockermouth Grammar School, which occupied the site of the present Church Room. He had under him Christopher Wordsworth, afterwards Master of Trinity; William the poet; Fearon Fallows, missionary and astronomer at the Cape; the brothers Quickett (one being Dickens' model curate): and also Fletcher Christian, Lieutenant of the *Bounty* and founder of the Pitcairn Colony' (p. 129).

who sent it to Dove Cottage in 1805. It was not the same as that retained in the Rydal Mount library, also in four volumes, and published 'a Paris, 1794' (Park 68).

151. Lessing, Gotthold Ephraim
(i) *Nathan der Weise*
Suggested date of reading: by 26 Sept. 1798
References: *EY* 255; *Prose Works* i 93, 97
While conversing with Klopstock on 26 Sept. 1798, W 'complained of Nathan [   ] as tedious' (*Prose Works* i 93) - indicating that he had read Lessing's play. *Nathan der Weise* was privately printed in William Taylor's translation (1791), though W might also have seen R. E. Raspe's rendering (1781).

(ii) works
Suggested date of reading: Jan.-Feb. 1799
References: *EY* 255
On 27 Feb. 1799 W told C, 'Of the excell[ence] of Lessing I can form no distinct idea' (*EY* 255). This suggests some acquaintance with his works, perhaps through C's copy of the *Fabeln* (Berlin, 1759), purchased in 1798 (Griggs i 340; Coffman L59).

Both C and W returned to Lessing in subsequent years. C referred to the *Fabeln* in his *Morning Post* essay of 25 Jan. 1800 (CC *Essays* i 130). Five days later Southey told Poole that C was 'clogged by the life of Lessing' (Curry i 220), and on 7 Aug. 1800 Josiah Wedgwood told Poole:

> I have heard from Coleridge with a short account of his situation. He says his preface or introduction to the life of Lessing will soon appear. I entertain great expectations of that work & consider it of the utmost importance for his reputation.
>
> (BL Add.MS 35,345 171v)

On 4 Sept. 1800, Losh recorded in his diary that C 'tells me that he is engaged in a life of Lessing which he means to be in fact an history of German literature'. However, as Southey told Taylor in March 1805, 'Coleridge never began his "Life of Lessing".... He has certainly given up the intention altogether' (Robberds ii 75-6).

The Wordsworths had assumed possession of C's copy of the *Fabeln* by 1802 (see *Notebooks* i 340 and n; also Shaver 340), and may have seen his copy of the *Leben* (CC *Marginalia* iii 640). In her Journal entry of 6 Feb. 1802, DW records that she 'translated 2 or 3 of Lessing's Fables', and on 25 Feb., 'I read a good deal of Lessing's Essay' (*Grasmere Journals* 63, 72). The prose *Fables* were a natural starting-point for a student of the German language. They were published, with Lessing's treatises on the Fable, in 1759.

152. Lewis, Matthew Gregory
(i) *The Monk: a romance* (3 vols., 1796)
Suggested date of reading: 1797-8; by 8 Nov. 1800
References: see note
Since C reviewed *The Monk* for the *Critical Review* in Feb. 1797 (Erdman *BNYPL* 436-9), W might have read his copy (Coffman L65), 1797-8. W's visit to the Theatre Royal, Bristol, to attend a performance of *The Castle Spectre* on 21 May 1798 (see next note) suggests that he had a particular interest in its author, possibly inspired by a reading of Lewis' popular

novel. The Wordsworths appear to have read *The Monk* by 8 Nov. 1800, when DW recorded in her journal: 'Wm & I walked out at 4 o clock - went as far as Rothay Bridge met the Butcher's man with a l[ette]r from Monk Lewis' (*Grasmere Journals* 31). C and W's esteem for Lewis was such that he was sent a presentation copy of *Lyrical Ballads* (1800) (Reed ii 108).

(ii) *The Castle Spectre* (1797)
Suggested date of reading: Feb.-March 1798
References: EY 210-11; Griggs i 378-9
The records of the Theatre Royal, Bristol, now at the Theatre Collection, University of Bristol, show that *The Castle Spectre* was one of its most popular productions in 1798. W attended the performance of Monday 21 May 1798 at the Theatre Royal, when it preceded *The Rival Soldiers*[1] on a double bill. He had arrived in Bristol, 18 May, and returned to Alfoxden on 22 May, to meet Hazlitt for the first time. Years later, Hazlitt recalled that W 'had been to see the *Castle Spectre* by Monk Lewis, while at Bristol, and described it very well. He said "it fitted the taste of the audience like a glove"' (Howe xvii 118). Some idea of this production may be gleaned from a Theatre Royal playbill of 28 Sept. 1798, which announces that *The Castle Spectre* contains music 'composed by Mr. KELLY', and 'Scenery, Dresses, Machinery, and Decorations' (Bristol Record Office 8982[3]). Mr Kelly was the Irish composer Michael Kelly (?1764-1826), who in 1813 provided the music for Coleridge's *Remorse* (*Notebooks* ii p. xviii). C read *The Castle Spectre* in Jan. 1798 (Griggs i 379) and reviewed it (Erdman *BNYPL* 583-5). His copy of *The Castle Spectre* contains an ownership signature dated 20 Jan. 1798 - a week after its publication date (Coffman L63).

153. Livy, *History of Rome* XXI
Suggested date of reading: by June 1789
References: Schneider 105-6
W was examined on Livy at St John's College, Cambridge, June 1789; see pp. 167-8, below.

154. Lloyd, Charles, the Younger
(i) *Edmund Oliver* (2 vols., Bristol, 1798)
Suggested date of reading: May-June 1798
References: EY 218; Shaver 160
The *Morning Chronicle* announced the publication of Lloyd's controversial novel on 4 May 1798; W had received his copy by 9 May: 'Of the novel I can say nothing as I have not yet read it' (*EY* 218). I presume that he read it during the ensuing weeks; it was the gift of his publisher, Joseph Cottle.

(ii) *Poems on Various Subjects* (Carlisle, 1795)
Suggested date of reading: April-May 1798
References: WC 4 (1973) 31-5; EY 217; Jacobus 17; Shaver 161
'We regularly received Charles Lloyds works', W told Cottle on 9 May 1798 (*EY* 217). His previous surviving letter to Cottle dates from 12 April, suggesting that the period during

---

[1] I am unable to discover its author; it was not apparently published. It was billed as a 'musical farce' in Bath in 1812, and the *Morning Chronicle* for 10 Oct. 1797 described it as 'a Musical Piece, in one act'.

which Lloyd's works had arrived at Alfoxden was between 12 April and 9 May 1798. W probably read Lloyd's poetry during that time.

Pollin, 'Permutations of Names in *The Borderers*, or Hints of Godwin, Charles Lloyd, and a Real Renegade', *WC* 4 (1973) 31-5, suggests that the change of name from 'Rivers' to 'Oswald' in *The Borderers* may have been inspired by Lloyd's *Oswald, a Poem*, published in the 1795 *Poems*. Pollin also suggests a resemblance between *Oswald* and W's *Peter Bell*, which would be consistent with a reading of April-May 1798.

(iii) *Poems on the Death of Priscilla Farmer* (Bristol, 1796)
Suggested date of reading: 12 April-9 May 1798
References: *EY* 217; Shaver 161
See preceding note. This volume and the *Poems on Various Subjects* are presumably the 'works' W received from Cottle between 12 April and 9 May 1798.

155. Locke, John
(i) *An Essay Concerning Humane Understanding* [1690]
Suggested date of reading: by spring 1787
References: Fink 97, 144; Sheats 4
W's Hawkshead notebook, in use during spring-summer 1787, contains a rough draft which aims to explain the formation of artistic taste in the individual mind:

> The muses gave when first they placd
> Their pencil in the hand of taste
> Fair on the *mental tablet* throws
> Each Beauty art and Nature knows
> In tints whose strength tho time efface
> [?He] blends them into softer grace (*D.C.MS 3* 30v)

W's 'mental tablet' recalls Locke's *tabula rasa*: 'Let us then suppose the Mind to be, as we say, white Paper, void of all Characters, without any Ideas'.[1] Christopher Wordsworth's mention of 'The conduct of the human understanding' in his Hawkshead notebook supports the notion that Bowman taught his pupils about Lockean philosophy.

(ii) *An Essay Concerning Humane Understanding* [1690]
Suggested date of reading: June 1789
References: Legouis 72n; Schneider 106-11
W was examined on Locke at St John's College, Cambridge, in June 1789; see pp. 167-8, below. In 1827 he described the *Essay* as the 'best of Locke's works ... in which he attempts the least' (Grosart iii 462).

156. *London Gazette Extraordinary*
Suggested date of reading: 12-15 Sept. 1793
References: Reed i 148

---

[1] *An Essay Concerning Human Understanding* ed. Peter H. Nidditch (Oxford, 1975), p. 104. The sentence begins the second paragraph of Book II Chapter 1.

In the *Thirteen-Book Prelude* x 258-63, W writes of how he 'Exulted in the triumph of my soul' when he heard of the defeat of the British at the Battle of Hondeschoote. Reed points out that 'News concerning the battle itself would not have reached Plas-yn-Llan before 14 Sept; the first general report in England was in a *London Gazette Extraordinary* of 12 Sept' (Reed i 148). W probably read the *London Gazette Extraordinary* at about this time.

157. Louvet de Couvray, Jean-Baptiste, *Narrative of the Dangers to Which I have been Exposed, since the 31st of May, 1793. With historical memorandums. By John-Baptist Louvet, one of the representatives proscribed in 1793. Now President of the National Convention.* (1795)
Suggested date of reading: Nov.-Dec. 1795
References: Pinney Papers, Family Letter Book 13; *EY* 166
At the conclusion of his letter to W of 26 Nov. 1795, Azariah Pinney promises: 'I shall send you by this opportunity Luesdon Hill, and Louvet' (Pinney Papers, Family Letter Book 13). He was as good as his word, for DW reported on 7 March 1796 that 'I have also read lately ... Louvet and some other french things - very entertaining' (*EY* 166). W almost certainly read these books too; Gill points out that the fact that 'Madame Roland and Louvet figure so strikingly in *The Prelude*'s account of the Revolution, far more than their historical importance warrants, may be due in part to W's familiarity with these books' (Gill 444). In *The Thirteen-Book Prelude* W recalled seeing copies of Louvet's famous speech denouncing Robespierre sold on the streets of Paris, 30 Oct. 1792 (x 83-106).

Louvet begins his *Narrative* by warning the youth of Paris to be 'on your guard against rushing headlong too soon upon obstacles, and in going in quest of them where they do not exist' (pp. vi-vii). His attack on 'atheism reduced to principle' (p. 70) would have reassured W as he entered his post-Godwinian period; Louvet may also have influenced *The Borderers*. The *Narrative* was published by Joseph Johnson, 29 June 1795, who advertised imported copies of the French text in the *Morning Chronicle*, 15 June 1795.

158. Lowth, Robert, *Lectures on the Sacred Poetry of the Hebrews* tr. George Gregory (1787)
Suggested date of reading: March 1798; by 30 Sept. 1800
References: Mason *LB* 39
Mason *LB* 39 finds Lowth's mistranslation of *Judges* 5.28-30, and approval of 'the utmost elegance in the repetitions' (i 293), to be followed by W in his Note to *The Thorn*. This suggests that W read Lowth before composing the Note, which was finished by 30 Sept. 1800 (Reed ii 21), but I am not convinced that W needed to have read Lowth to compose *The Thorn* itself. In the absence of further evidence, I record Lowth here as a possible reading in March 1798, when *The Thorn* was written. It is significant that C borrowed the Latin version of Lowth from Bristol Library, 16-22 Sept. 1796 (Whalley 84), so that W may have had access to his notes. The *Lectures* were published by W's old friend Joseph Johnson.

159. Lucian of Samosata, '1 Vol.'
Suggested date of reading: between Feb. 1784 and 1787
References: Shepherd MSS
In his accounts, now among the Shepherd MSS at the Wordsworth Library, Richard Wordsworth of Whitehaven (1733-94) records the purchase of two volumes of Homer and one

of Lucian 'for my Nephews', totalling eight shillings and ninepence. The 'Nephews' must be W and his brother, Richard, both of whom may by this time have been learning Greek: W was 14, Richard 16. In Christmas 1785 Richard left Hawkshead to become articled as a clerk to his cousin Richard Wordsworth, attorney, of Branthwaite (1752-1816), son of Richard Wordsworth of Whitehaven. W would then, presumably, have taken possession of these books.

W's Lucian may have been the volume of the *Dialogorum Selectorum* (1685) with texts in Greek and Latin, retained in the Rydal Mount library (Shaver 164). Clancey tells me that 'W invariably used a Latin translation when he was learning the Greek' (letter to me).

160. Lucretius
(i) *The Beginning of the First Book of Lucretius* **tr. James Beattie (1760)**
Suggested date of reading: by 1787
References: see note
The diction of a couplet of *The Vale of Esthwaite* echoes Beattie's translation of Lucretius:

> Peace to that noisy brawling *din*
> That *jars* upon the dirge within (*D.C.MS 3* 20v; De Selincourt 398-9)

Compare Beattie, *The Beginning of the First Book of Lucretius* 45-6: 'O hush the dismal *din* of arms once more, / And calm the *jarring* world from shore to shore!' While at Hawkshead, W may also have read the poem in the original. W could have known the translation only in Beattie's *Original Poems and Translations* (1760); see note 21 (ii).

(ii) *De Rerum Natura*
Suggested dates of reading: 1791-2, 1793-4
References: N&Q NS 30 (1983) 219-22
Kelley, 'Wordsworth and Lucretius' *De Rerum Natura*', N&Q NS 30 (1983) 219-22, puts forward a convincing case for the influence of Lucretius on W's poetry. He points out that not only did *De Rerum Natura* v 1386-7 provide the epigraph for *Descriptive Sketches*, but that it influenced the first two stanzas of *Salisbury Plain*:

> Lucretius' images of primitive man living in forests, at the mercy of wind and rain, sleeping naked on open ground, and terrified when woken at night by fierce animals, all seem to have contributed to Wordsworth's description. (p. 220)

Even parts of the revisions to *An Evening Walk* in 1794, Kelley suggests, 'may be an earlier translation of Lucretius modified'. Clancey suggests that *De Rerum Natura* was a model for *The Recluse* - a plausible notion, given W's regard for the poem. Emerson visited W on 28 Aug. 1833, and later recorded: 'Lucretius he esteems a far higher poet than Virgil: not in his system, which is nothing, but in his power of illustration' (*English Traits* [1856], p. 26).

161. Lyly, John, *Alexander and Campaspe*
Suggested date of reading: by 1786
References: Landon 224
In *Anacreon Imitated*, W uses the word 'Shadow'd' to mean 'depict':

> Shadow'd here her picture see
> Shadow'd by the muse and me (lines 3-4)

Landon 224 suggests that he follows Lyly's *Alexander and Campaspe*:

Apelles: Were you ever *shadow'd* before of any?
Campaspe: No: and would you could so now *shadow* me, that I might not be perceived of any. (*Select Collection of Old Plays* ed. Dodsley, 2nd edn, 1780; ii 115)

162. Lyttelton, George, Baron Lyttelton, *To the Memory of a Lady Lately Deceased: a Monody*

Suggested date of reading: by 1786
References: Landon 247
Landon observes that the last line of W's *The Dog: An Idyllium* (1786), 'We were the happiest pair on earth', is a 'reminiscence' of Lyttelton's *Monody* 252: 'We were the happiest pair of human kind'. She remarks that 'Wordsworth adapted the line ... to describe the joyful sense of community that he felt existed between himself and the dog' (Landon 235). The poem remained a favourite: in the *Essays upon Epitaphs*, he remarks that 'We know from other evidence that Lord Lyttelton dearly loved his wife: he has indeed composed a monody to her memory which proves this' (*Prose Works* ii 75), and goes on to discuss the *Monody*. It was frequently anthologized, and appeared in Knox's *Elegant Extracts*.

163. Machiavelli, Niccolò

(i) *Tutte le Opere*

Suggested date of reading: 1789-90; by June 1794
References: RES 31 (1980) 285-304
The evidence for a reading of Machiavelli at Cambridge is circumstantial, but the case made by Hill, 'Wordsworth and the Two Faces of Machiavelli', *RES* 31 (1980) 285-304, is convincing:

Wordsworth, as an undergraduate at Cambridge, must surely have come across Machiavelli long before his political ideals were awakened by the 'pedestrian tour' to France in 1790. No student of the Italian language could have afforded to ignore him, least of all the pupil of Agostino Isola, a liberal who shared Machiavelli's ideal of a united Italy. (pp. 287-8)

The fact that W informed Mathews of the presence of 'Machiavel' in the Racedown Lodge library in Oct. 1795 (*EY* 155) suggests that both had encountered Machiavelli while at Cambridge. This is supported by a letter to Mathews of June 1794 in which W refers to Machiavelli as one of 'those distinguished for their exertions in the cause of liberty' (*EY* 125). There was a copy of Machiavelli's works in Italian (Florence, 1680) in the Rydal Mount library (Shaver 165).

(ii) *Machiavel's Discourses upon the First Decade of T. Livius, Translated out of the Italian. To which is Added his Prince: with some Marginal Animadversions Noting and Taxing his Errors. By E[dward]. D[acres].* (2nd edn, 1674)

Suggested date of reading: Aug. 1795 onwards
References: EY 155
This edition of Machiavelli's *Discourses* and *The Prince* was in the Racedown Lodge library, and W's reference to it in his letter to Mathews of Oct. 1795 suggests that both had studied

Machiavelli at Cambridge (*EY* 155). W probably returned to Machiavelli at Racedown, since the *Discourses* concern themselves with a side of human nature explored in *Adventures on Salisbury Plain* (1795) and *The Borderers*. For instance, chapter 42 of Dacres' translation discusses 'How easily Men may be corrupted ... though at first good, and well brought up'; while chapter 46 proposes that 'Men arise by degrees from one ambition to another, and first they aim no further than that they themselves suffer no harm of others, afterwards they strive to be able to harm others'.

164. Mackintosh, James, *Vindiciæ Gallicæ. Defence of the French Revolution and its English Admirers* (1791)
Suggested date of reading: 1792; by spring 1793
References: *Prose Works* i 54
Owen and Smyser write that, in the *Letter to the Bishop of Llandaff*, 'Wordsworth's recognition of the need for violence in effecting a major revolution parallels James Mackintosh, *Vindiciæ Gallicæ* ... and innumerable speeches in the National Convention' (*Prose Works* i 54). A comparison of the passages in Mackintosh and the *Letter* reveals a close similarity of argument and rhetorical style. Owen and Smyser point out another parallel with Mackintosh at *Prose Works* i 66. As Roe observes, Mackintosh was among the Godwin circle during 1794-5, and may well have met W during his time in London (Roe 191, 245). In addition, Roe tells me that *Vindiciæ Gallicæ* was one of the 'master Pamphlets of the day' that W remembered having read in the *Thirteen-Book Prelude* ix 97. This is supported by the fact that a copy of *Vindiciæ Gallicæ* (1792) turned up at the auction of the Rydal Mount library (Shaver 167; Park 8).

165. Macpherson, James 'Ossian', *Fingal* [1762]; *Temora* [1763]
Suggested date of reading: by 1787
References: Landon (1970) 363-4
'All hail, Macpherson! hail to thee, Sire of Ossian!'
   The narrator of *The Vale of Esthwaite* (1787) describes his meeting with a spectre-guide who leads him into a Virgilian underworld beneath Helvellyn:

   [B]lack were his bones seen through his skin
   As the pale moonbeam wan and thin
   Which through *a chink of rock* we view
   On a lone sable blasted yew (*D.C.MS 3* 19v; De Selincourt 330-3)[1]

As Landon (1970) 363-4 points out, the 'chink of rock' recalls the sleeping highlanders in *Temora*, who 'thought they heard the voice of the dead. This voice of the dead, however, was, perhaps, no more than a shriller whistle of the winds in an old tree, or in the *chinks of a neighbouring rock*' (p. 79). In *Fingal*, Cuchullin remarks: 'I sighed as the wind in the *chink of a rock*' (p. 32). This is discussed by Landon, *BWS* 363, and in my article, 'Wordsworth's Poetry of Grief', *WC* 21 (1990) 114-17, pp. 114-15. Although a number of borrowings from Macpherson may be found in the juvenilia, none occurs earlier than 1787.

---

[1] De Selincourt's text differs from mine because he uses a revised fair copy dating from 1788, where I prefer the 1787 drafts.

166. Mallet, David, *Poems*
Suggested date of reading: by 23 March 1787
References: Jacobus 214
Jacobus 214 notes the influence of Mallet on W's early poem, *A Ballad* (*PW* i 265-7), composed 23-4 March 1787. Borrowings from Mallet can be found in both *A Ballad* and *Dirge Sung by a Minstrel*, composed Jan. 1788 (*PW* i 267-9). In *A Ballad* Mary's 'clay-cold hand' (line 51) echoes the phrase with which Mallet describes Margaret's ghost: 'And *clay-cold was her lily-hand*, / That held her sable shroud' (*William and Margaret* 7-8). The distinctive first line in W's *Dirge Sung by a Minstrel*, 'List! the bell-Sprite stuns my ears', imitates Mallet's *Edwin and Emma*:

> Alone, appall'd, thus had she pass'd
> The visionary vale -
> When *lo! the death-bell smote her ear*,
> Sad sounding in the gale! (lines 85-8)

W must have read Mallet's verse before 23 March 1787, when *A Ballad* was composed (Reed i 20).

167. Mallet, Paul-Henri, *Northern Antiquities* **tr. Thomas Percy (2 vols., 1770)**
Suggested date of reading: 1797-8
References: Butler *WC* 59; Shaver 299
The copy of Mallet which W gave Cottle is now at the Rosenbach Foundation, Philadelphia. It contains a flyleaf inscription, 'Joseph Cottle from Wm Wordsworth', and annotations in W's hand at i 133 and ii 170. It was probably given to W during 1797-8 (Shaver 299).
The volume contains Percy's translation of the Edda, which Cottle's brother Amos translated and published in 1797. Had W used Mallet as a crib to help him assess Amos' rendering, it would have been appropriate to present the volume to Joseph shortly before his departure for Germany.
W apparently referred to Mallet while composing the *Thirteen-Book Prelude*:

> Sometimes, more sternly mov'd, I would relate
> How vanquish'd Mithridates northward pass'd,
> And, hidden in the cloud of years, became
> That Odin, Father of a Race by whom
> Perish'd the Roman Empire ... (i 186-90)

The merging of Mithradates and Odin is probably taken from Mallet, who tells us that,

> Mithridates by flying, had drawn Pompey after him into those desarts. The king of Pontus sought there for refuge, and new means of vengeance. He hoped to arm against the ambition of Rome, all the barbarous nations his neighbours, whose liberty she threatened. He succeeded in this at first; but all those people, ill-united as allies, ill-armed as soldiers, and still worse disciplined, were forced to yield to the genius of Pompey. Odin is said to have been of this number. He was obliged to withdraw himself by flight from the vengeance of the Romans; and to go seek in countries unknown to his enemies, that safety which he could no longer find in his own. (i 59-60)

See also notes 64 (ii) and A10.

168. Malthus, Thomas Robert, *Essay on the Principles of Population as it Affects the Future Improvement of Society, with Remarks on the Speculations of Mr. Godwin, M. Condorcet, and Other Writers* **(1798)**
Suggested date of reading: Aug. 1798; by 14 Sept. 1798
References: BL Add.MS 35,343; Griggs i 517-19
When they arrived in London, Aug. 1798, prior to their German trip, W and C met with Joseph Johnson, and, through him, caught up with several books they had not yet encountered. Some of these were sent to Thomas Poole, as his letter to C of 24 Jan. 1799, proves:

> We rec^d from Johnson, six copies of the poems - the account of Paraguay and the essay on population - but *not* the diversions of Purley - every one admires the poems and I am told they are much admired in London. (BL Add.MS 35,343; his italics)

The 'essay on population' was Malthus' *Essay*, published by Johnson as recently as 23 June 1798. It was read by C prior to his departure for Germany (Griggs i 517-19), and was probably seen by W. A copy of the 1803 edition containing C's marginalia is in the British Library (CC *Marginalia* iii 805). W argued against Malthus in 1835 (*Prose Works* iii 234).

169. Marino, Giovanni Battista, poems
Suggested date of reading: 1788-9
References: EY 56
On 3 Aug. 1791, W wrote to Mathews from Wales saying that if he had an Italian dictionary and grammar he might gather 'sea weed from Marino' (*EY* 56). Both had probably read Marino's *L'Adone* (1623) while at Cambridge, 1788-9. This is supported by Marino's appearance in Isola's anthology of Italian verse (note 138); see Schneider 103.

170. Marlowe, Christopher
(i) *The passionate shepherd to his love*
Suggested date of reading: by March 1798
References: see note
The editors of the Longman *Wordsworth* find that *The Thorn* 67, 'But thou wilt live with me in love', echoes Marlowe, *The passionate shepherd to his love* 1: 'Come live with me, and be my love'. I have not been able to discover where W encountered this poem.

(ii) *Edward II*
Suggested date of reading: 1798
References: Reed i 325; Coffman M43
At the front of *D.C.MS 16*, in use during 1798, DW copied Marlowe's *Edward II*, V v 55-108, with some omissions. As in all transcriptions I have supplied line numbers. Act and Scene references are also included here (within square brackets) to give the reader an idea of how many lines DW omits from her source, Dodsley's *Select Collection of Old Plays*:

> From C. Marlows Edward 2nd
> Edward in Prison
> *Edward.* (to his murderer)
> The dungeon, where they keep me, is the sink
> Wherein the filth of all the Castle falls;   [5]
> [V v 55-6]

And there, in mire and puddle have I stood
This ten day's space; and, lest that I should sleep,
One plays continually upon a drum.
They give me bread and water, being a King,
So that for want of sleep and sustenance   [10]
My mind's distempered, and my body's numbed
And whether I have limbs or no, I know not.
Would my blood drop out from every vein
As does this water from my tattered robes.
Tell Isabel the queen I looked not thus   [15]
When, for her sake, I ran at tilt in France
And there unhorsed the Duke of Clairmont.
[V v 58-69]

Murderer. You're overwatched, my Lord, lie down & rest.
Edward. But that grief keeps me waking I should sleep
For not these ten days have these eye-lids closed   [20]
Now while I speak they fall and yet with fear
Open again. Oh! wherefore sitt'st thou here?
Murderer. If you mistrust me I'll be gone, my Lord.
Edward. No, no, for if thou mean'st to murder me
Thou wilt return again, and therefore stay.   [25]
Murderer. He sleeps.
Edward. Let me not die yet, stay. Oh! stay a while
Murderer. How now, my Lord?
Edward. Something still buzzeth in mine ears
(*D.C.MS 16* 1r)

And tells me if I sleep I never wake   [30]
This fear is that which makes me tremble thus,
And therefore tell me wherefore art thou come?
Murderer. To rid thee of thy life. Molrevis come
Edward. I am too weak and feeble to resist
Assist me sweet God! and receive my soul!   [35]
[V v 91-106]
(*D.C.MS 16* 1v)

The extract was copied from Dodsley's *Select Collection of Old Plays*, which W may have known since his schooldays. There were two editions available: the first (1744), and the second (1780). I have collated both against the draft, and the most striking difference comes at line 14, where 1744 gives 'tattered', and 1780 restores the earlier reading, 'tottered'. This would suggest that DW was following the first edition of 1744.

171. Martial, *Epigrams*
Suggested date of reading: 1787
References: Landon 28-9

On the inside front cover of W's fair copy notebook *D.C.MS 2*, in use during 1786-8, he copied the motto: 'Hæc novimus esse nihil'. The ink and hand suggest that it dates from 1787, and Landon 28-9 traces it to Martial's *Epigrams* xiii 2: 'nos haec novimus esse nihil' ('I know these efforts of mine are nothing worth'). Landon 28 observes that this was Mickle's epigraph for *Hengist and Mey*; it was also that of Southey's *Metrical Tales* (1805). A copy of Martial's *Epigrams* was retained in the Hawkshead Grammar School Library in 1788 (Wu *CWAAS* 176).

172. Marvell, Andrew, *Instructions to a Painter, about the Dutch Wars, 1667*, probably in *The Works of Andrew Marvell, Esq.* ed. Thomas Cooke (2 vols., 1772)
Suggested date of reading: late July 1795
References: see note
The terminal date for this reading is 25 Feb. 1797, when W told Wrangham that his contribution to their imitation of Juvenal contained 'some lines about Andrew Marvel' (*EY* 176). Reed, however, dates the composition of these lines to 'between 7 Mar and Apr 1796' (Reed i 26). W's reference to 'a freak or brawl of the Duke of Monmouth ... [which] is mentioned in Andrew Marvels Poems' in his letter to Walter Scott, 7 Nov. 1805 (EY 641-2), shows that he knew the poem published by Thomas Cooke as *Instructions to a Painter*:

> We in our glorious bacchanals dispose
> The humbled fate of a plebeian nose. (iii 31-2)[1]

Cooke's edition footnotes this couplet: 'See letter the third to a friend, concerning Sir John Coventry' (ii 162). Marvell's letter to William Popple of 24 Jan. 1671,[2] to which this refers, also appears in Cooke. The relevant passage begins by describing an eventful exchange in the House of Commons:

> Sir John Coventry having moved for an imposition on the playhouses, Sir John Berkenhead, to excuse them, sayed they had been of great service to the king. Upon which Sir John Coventry desired that gentleman to explain, whether he meant the men or women players. Hereupon it is imagined, that, the house adjourning from Tuesday before till Thursday after Christmas day, on the very Tuesday night of the adjournment twenty five of the Duke of Monmouth's troop, and some few foot, layed in wait from ten at night till two in the morning, by Suffolk street, and as he returned from the Cock, where he supped, to his own house, they threw him down, and with a knife cut off almost all the end of his nose; but company coming, made them fearful to finish it, so they marched off. (ii 221-2)

W was correct in observing that this 'freak or brawl of the Duke of Monmouth' was mentioned in the poem he knew as Marvell's *Instructions to a Painter, about the Dutch Wars, 1667*. But he was evidently remembering an earlier reading of Marvell's poem and the letter to Popple: 'This I remember is mentioned in Andrew Marvels Poems, which I have not seen these many years' (*EY* 641-2).

---

[1] Quotations from Marvell are from Cooke's edition (2 vols., 1772). These lines appear in Margoliouth's edition as *Further Advice to a Painter* 37-8.

[2] The dating is Margoliouth's.

Since W did not have a copy of Marvell at Dove Cottage or Rydal Mount, the copy he had read by April 1796 probably belonged to someone else, the most likely candidate being Wrangham, whose 1826 library catalogue includes Marvell's *Works* ed. Thomas Cooke (2 vols., 1772).[1] W had ample opportunity to examine Wrangham's library when he visited Cobham shortly before 24 July 1795. Wrangham had cause to show him Marvell's *Instructions to a Painter*, for it uses the same couplet form, and is cast in the same satirical style, as the imitation of Juvenal. W seems also to have seen Wrangham's copy of James I, *Demonology* (1603); see note 140. For further discussion, see my article, 'Wordsworth's Reading of Marvell', *N&Q* (forthcoming, March 1993). *Prelude* MS W contains a copy of Marvell's *Horatian Ode* (D.C.MS 38, rectos of leaves 2-7).

173. Mason, William
(i) *Poems*
Suggested date of reading: 1785-7; by spring 1785
References: RES 15 (1964) 297-302
Nabholtz, 'Wordsworth and William Mason', *RES* 15 (1964) 297-302, points out that Mason is one of the earliest detectable influences on W's poetry. In his *Elegy to a Young Nobleman Leaving the University*, Mason writes:

Go to the wayward world; complete the rest;
Be, what the purest Muse would wish to sing.
Be still thyself; that open path of Truth,
Which led thee here, let Manhood firm pursue;
Retain the sweet simplicity of Youth,
And, all thy virtue dictates, dare to do. (lines 59-64)

W borrows several of Mason's phrases in his earliest extant poem, *Lines Written as a School Exercise* (1785). Mason's 'Go to the wayward world' becomes 'Go to the world' (*School Exercise* 85), while Mason's image of a path, the rhyme of 'pursue' and 'do', the moral, and Mason's line 64, all recur in W's couplet:

Oft have I said, the paths of Fame pursue,
And all that Virtue dictates, dare to do ... (*School Exercise* 83-4)

Echoes of other Mason poems are detectable in *The Vale of Esthwaite* (1787).

(ii) *Caractacus*
Suggested date of reading: 1791-2
References: Cornell *DS* 44; Shaver 171
W's allusion to *Caractacus* in *Descriptive Sketches* is well-documented; see Cornell *DS* 44 and Nabholtz, 'Wordsworth and William Mason', *RES* 15 (1964) 297-302.

(iii) *Caractacus*
Suggested date of reading: c. autumn 1796
References: Cornell *B* 420-21

---

[1] Wrangham 346; see Appendix IV.

W copied a series of references to various books under the heading, 'Druids', into *D.C.MS 12*, in use during autumn 1796 and spring 1797 as MS 1 of *The Borderers*; this is reproduced in facsimile, Cornell *B* 420-1. This 'bibliography on Druids', as Osborn describes it, contains a series of references copied from Mason's 'Illustrations' to *Caractacus*. These are scholarly annotations that, as Mason says, 'explain some of the passages in the Drama of CARACTACUS, that respect the manners of the Druids; and which, the general account of their customs, to be found in our histories of Britain, does not include.'[1] The 'illustrations' appeared in *Caractacus* for the first time in the fourth edition of Mason's *Poems* (York, 1774).

174. Massinger, Philip, *Dramatick Works* ed. J. M. Mason (4 vols., 1779)
Suggested date of reading: April/May 1798
References: *EY* 218; Whalley 95, 108
Cottle sent Massinger's *Works* to W, *c.* April/May 1798. As Shaver points out, the only editions available to W at the time were those edited by Thomas Coxeter (4 vols., 1759) and John Monck Mason (4 vols., 1779). The edition Cottle sent can be deduced from a short extract from Massinger's *The Picture* (III v 211-19), copied by DW into *D.C.MS 16*:

> I find myself
> Strangely distracted with the various stories,
> Now well, now ill, then doubtfully, by my guests
> Delivered of my Lord. And like poor Beggars
> That in their dreams find treasure, by reflection   [5]
> Of a wounded fancy make it questionable
> Whether they sleep or not; yea tickled with
> Such a fantastic hope of happiness
> Wish they may never wake (Massinger. The Picture)
> (*D.C.MS 16* 117r)

I have collated this draft with the texts in Coxeter (ii 150) and Mason (i 58). Mason evidently drew his text from Coxeter's, since he follows the punctuation and even the layout of the older text very closely; he did, however, modernize its orthography. Where, in line 8, Coxeter preserves 'phantastick', Mason gives 'fantastick'; and, more importantly, where Coxeter renders 'Whither' in line 7, Mason gives 'Whether'. DW was probably following the text as it appears in Mason - the edition Cottle probably sent W. In her transcription DW made an emendation of her own: where Mason and Coxeter read 'yet' in line 7, she transcribes 'yea'. See also pp. 177, 184, below.

175. Mickle, William Julius, *Sir Martyn*
Suggested date of reading: by Oct. 1795
References: *EY* 154, 169
In return for his copy of *Cato's Letters*, W asked Mathews in Oct. 1795 to 'make me a present of that vol: of Bells forgotten poetry which contains The minstrel and Sir martyn' (*EY* 154). W knew Beattie's *Minstrel* by 1795, and Mickle's *Sir Martyn* was probably also a favourite with him by then (I suspect that W first encountered *Sir Martyn* during his

---

[1] *Poems* (4th edn, York, 1774), p. 287.

98

Hawkshead years). Mathews had not sent the volume by March 1796 (*EY* 169), but presumably did so shortly after.

W included an extract from *Sir Martyn* in the Album he compiled for Lady Mary Lowther in 1819 (*Album* 52-3), and in 1843 remarked that, 'it appears from his poem on Sir Martin, [that Mickle] was not without genuine poetic feelings' (*PW* iii 527). See also note on Martial, note 171.

176. Milton, John
(i) selections
Suggested date of reading: 1774-9
References: *Memoirs* i 34
As Christopher Wordsworth Jr points out, three of the most important influences on W's writing were encountered during the pre-Hawkshead years: 'the Poet's father set him very early to learn portions of the works of the best English poets by heart, so that at an early age he could repeat large portions of Shakspeare, Milton, and Spenser' (*Memoirs* i 34). These 'portions' might have been learned from such anthologies as Knox, *Elegant Extracts*.

(ii) *Works*
Suggested date of reading: 1779-87
References: see note
The juvenile poetry contains numerous echoes and allusions to Milton. In *The Vale of Esthwaite* (1787), W writes, 'I soon shall be with them that rest' (*D.C.MS 3* 25r; De Selincourt 445), recalling Samson: 'I shall shortly be with them that rest' (*Samson Agonistes* 598). Earlier in the poem, W writes:

> When Twilight wrappd in dusky s[hroud]
> Slow journey'd from her cave of cloud (*D.C.MS 3* 7r; De Selincourt 77-8)

The images echo those in Milton's account of the creation of light in *Paradise Lost*, though the time of day is altered:

> and from her Native East
> To *journie* through the airie gloom began,
> *Spheard in a radiant Cloud* ... (vii 245-7)

(iii) *Paradise Lost* ed. Thomas Newton (1763)
Suggested date of reading: 1787-90
References: *TLS* (4 Oct. 1947) 507; Shaver 299
The *Works* which W owned at Cambridge is now at the Wordsworth Library, Grasmere. It is autographed 'Wordsworth Cambridge', and on the same page, 'M. Wordsworth Aug 27. 1822'. Beneath this there is a fragment of poetry in W's hand, in ink, which De Selincourt published as *Fragment of an Intended Poem on Milton* (*PW* v 362, 485). The book's discovery was announced by Darbishire, 'Milton and Wordsworth', *TLS* (4 Oct. 1947) 507. Shaver has shown how Newton's annotations influenced the 1815 Preface, 'Wordsworth's Debt to Thomas Newton', *MLN* 62 (1947) 344.

The title-page of this volume reveals that the poem is 'CORRECTLY PRINTED FROM THE TEXT / OF / THOMAS NEWTON, D.D.' On the title-page of Sara Hutchinson's copy (now owned by Jonathan Wordsworth), W has underlined 'correctly', and written underneath: 'shamefully incorrect. W.W.'

(iv) *Poetical Works*
Suggested date of reading: 1791-2
References: Cornell *DS* 40, 46, 66, 78, 80
Milton is an important influence on *Descriptive Sketches*.

(v) *Areopagitica*
Suggested date of reading: 1791-2
References: Cornell *EW* 32; Cornell *DS* 114
Although it is likely that W knew *Areopagitica* at Hawkshead or Cambridge, the earliest time when he certainly read it was during his stay in France in 1791-2. Chard suggests that those parts of *An Evening Walk* 'with their increased debt to Milton (above all, *Areopagitica*), were likely added in France when he first began to study politics' (Chard 84).

In 1791-2 Milton's political prose was popular among the Girondins with whom W associated; Fink, 'Wordsworth and the English Republican Tradition', *JEGP* 47 (1948) 107-26, p. 108, notes a French translation (Paris, 1792).

(vi) *Sonnet on the Lord General Fairfax*
Suggested date of reading: by summer 1793
References: *PW* i 341; Cornell *SP* 37n

(vii) *Works*
Suggested date of reading: Sept. 1795-6
References: Cornell *SP* 149; Cornell *B* 293
Milton was a continuing influence on W's Racedown poetry.

(viii) *Paradise Lost* (2nd edn, 1674)
Suggested date of reading: 1797-8
References: see note
W probably acquired his copy of the second edition of *Paradise Lost* (1674) in 1798. This is the date assigned the flyleaf signature by Bishop Hunt, who adds that the Welsh names of its previous owners, also on the flyleaf, indicate that it came either from the West Country or from Wales:

> Even in 1800, the second edition would have been a comparatively rare book. One possible source - though it should be emphasized that this is the purest conjecture - is Joseph Cottle, the bookseller and publisher of *Lyrical Ballads*, with whom Wordsworth was in constant touch while living at Alfoxden. The surviving letters show that Wordsworth often asked Cottle to get books for him ...
>
> ('Wordsworth's Marginalia on *Paradise Lost*', *BNYPL* 73 [1969] 167-83, p. 168)

The volume is at the Wordsworth Library, Grasmere (Shaver 176), and its marginalia are published and analysed by Hunt.

(ix) *The Judgment of Martin Bucer*
Suggested date of reading: by 13 July 1798
References: *PW* ii 517-18

177. Montesquieu, Baron de, *De l'Esprit des Lois*
Suggested date of reading: Dec. 1791-2, probably by summer 1793
References: *Prose Works* i 33, 53; Chard 95-6; Legouis 207
W's comments on 'the statues of the laws' in *A Letter to the Bishop of Llandaff* appear to recall Montesquieu (*Prose Works* i 33, 53). Chard 95-6 argues that Montesquieu helped W 'to form a political ideal centered on the natural and the moral' (p. 96).

178. *Monthly Magazine*
(i) Feb.-Dec. 1796
Suggested date of reading: March 1797 onwards
References: EY 186
On 20 March 1797 Losh listed in his diary (now at Tullie House, Carlisle) the first consignment of books which he sent W - among them, 'Monthly Magazines from Feby to December 1796 inclusive'. These contain C's *On a Late Connubial Rapture* (2 [1796] 647, pub. Sept. 1796), and *Reflections on Entering into Active Life* (2 [1796] 732, Oct. 1796), later retitled *Reflections on Having Left a Place of Retirement*, and reprinted in C's *Poems* (Bristol, 1797). The issues for March and April 1796 contain translations by William Taylor of Norwich of two poems by Bürger: *Lenore* (1 [1796] 135-7) and *The Lass of Fair Wone* (1 [1796] 223-4). Both translations influenced poems composed by W from March 1797 onwards (see notes 40 [i]-[ii]), and they are reprinted Jacobus 277-88.

Trott 208-9 argues that Arthur Aikin's 'Pedestrian Tour in North Wales' (1 [1796] 191-4) is an important source for the Climbing of Snowdon in *Thirteen-Book Prelude* Book XIII.

(ii) Jan.-April 1797
Suggested date of reading: April 1797; by March 1798
References: see note
In her discussion of *Goody Blake and Harry Gill*, Jacobus suggests that W saw Hannah More's prospectus for the *Cheap Repository* ballad-tracts, published in the *Monthly Magazine*, Jan. 1797 (Jacobus 238). Chandler thinks that W read the reports in the *Monthly Magazine* for April 1797 on the proceedings of the French National Institute (Chandler 226). It is perfectly likely that these issues of the *Monthly* may have been in the second parcel sent to W by Losh on 14 April 1797.

(iii) Feb. 1796-April 1797
Suggested date of reading: 1797-8
References: Griggs i 381-2; Jacobus 219
W took his copies of the *Monthly* to Alfoxden, and read them during spring 1798, while composing the Lyrical Ballads (see Jacobus 238, 243, 250-3). C's Nehemiah Higginbottom sonnets appeared in the issue for Nov. 1797. Chandler discusses W's interest in the reports on the proceedings of France's National Institute in the issues for March, Sept., and Nov. 1796 (Chandler 224-7).

(iv) Jan.-Aug. 1798
Suggested date of reading: Feb.-Sept. 1798
References: see note
There is some reason to think that W was reading the *Monthly* prior to his departure for Germany in Sept. 1798. For one thing, he was in touch with Joseph Johnson, its publisher

(*EY* 228). In addition, C had been reviewing for the *Monthly* since 1796, and in late 1797 W considered writing for it too. In the Fenwick Note to *We are Seven*, W recalled the circumstances of the walking tour he made with DW and C in Nov. 1797:

> In the spring of the year 1798, he, my Sister, and myself, started from Alfoxden, pretty late in the afternoon, with a view to visit Linton and the valley of Stones near it; and as our united funds were very small, we agreed to defray the expense of the tour by writing a Poem, to be sent to the New Monthly Magazine[1] set up by Phillips the bookseller, and edited by Dr. Aikin. (*PW* i 360)

If W was reading the *Monthly* during the first half of 1798, he would have found some help with his study of German. In a letter to C of 27 Feb. 1799 he remarks that 'My internal prejudg[ments con]cerning Wieland and Goethe ... were, as your letter has convinced me, the result of no *negligent* perusal of the different fragments which I had seen in England' (*EY* 255; his italics). The most likely place for W to have seen 'different fragments' of either poet is a periodical. The *Monthly* for June 1798 contains a letter from A. F. M. Willich claiming that 'French and English translations from the German, *generally* are deficient, both in point of sense and diction' (his italics); to illustrate his point, Willich provides an extract from Wieland's *Oberon* together with two translations of it - one by Sotheby, the other by himself.[2]

I suspect that W also found inspiration in the *Monthly* for the record of his conversations with Klopstock. While visiting Germany in autumn 1798, he visited Klopstock in Hamburg three times between 21 and 26 Sept. 1798. What motivated him to seek out this poet in particular? And why did he decide to record the contents of his conversations with the German poet?

The Monthly Magazine for April 1798 contains an article entitled 'Original Anecdotes and Remains of Eminent Persons', subtitled 'Some Account of the Lives and Writings of Eminent Foreign Literati, now living', by T.D.[3] The first of the eminent foreign literati to be profiled is Klopstock, and the article is evidently based on a personal encounter with him. If W read the article, it may have given him the idea of recording his own conversations with the German poet. W's account records that 'I was somewhat disappointed in his countenance, in which I was not able to discover the marks either of sublimity or enthusiasm' (*Prose Works* i 91). Why should he have supposed Klopstock's countenance to be sublime? Perhaps he had read T.D.'s account in which it is claimed that

> His countenance is highly pleasing, and reflects *that calm tranquillity, that divine peace of mind*, so forcibly depicted in his verses, and which nothing but the consciousness of a well spent life can bestow. (p. 281)

It is likely that W also saw Thelwall's essay, 'The Phenomena of the Wye, during the Winter of 1797-8', published in the *Monthly Magazine* during May and July 1798; an important part of the essay is reprinted and discussed by Roe, *Politics of Nature* (1992), pp. 134-6.

---

[1] W means the *Monthly*, although he and C consistently refer to it as the New Monthly Magazine.
[2] *Monthly Magazine* 5 (1798) 399-400. In 1798 Willich was acquainted with Joseph Cottle (Dendurent 565).
[3] *Monthly Magazine* 5 (1798) 280-3.

(v) Feb. 1796-April 1797
Suggested date of reading: between 24 June and 27 July 1799
References: Butler *JEGP* 149
When they went to Germany in 1798, the Wordsworths left most of their books in England. Some, presumably, were left in London with W's brother Richard. Among these, I suspect, were the *Monthly Magazines* W had accumulated. When the Wordsworths returned from Germany they would no doubt have retrieved their books, including the *Monthly Magazines*. These they took with them to Sockburn, where they stayed with the Hutchinson family. Thus, on 27 July 1799, W wrote to Cottle: 'Looking over some old monthly Magazines I saw a paragraph stating that your "Arthur" was ready for the press! I laughed heartily at this idle story' (Butler *JEGP* 149). His previous letter to Cottle is dated 24 June 1799, so he must have been reading the magazines between that date and 27 July.

(vi) 1798 supplement
Suggested date of reading: some time after 12 Jan. 1799
References: Reed i 262
A review of *Lyrical Ballads*, probably by Dr Aikin, appeared in the 1798 supplement to the *Monthly Magazine*.

179. *Monthly Review*
(i) Oct. 1793
Suggested date of reading: Nov. 1793
References: Reed i 149; Cornell *EW* 131
The *Monthly* for Oct. contains a review of both *An Evening Walk* and *Descriptive Sketches*, both of them by Thomas Holcroft.

(ii) June 1799
Suggested date of reading: some time after 31 July 1799
References: Reed i 270
Charles Burney's review of *Lyrical Ballads* appeared in the *Monthly Review* for June 1799. In a letter postmarked 31 July 1799, W told Cottle that he had heard of its contents: 'I am told they have been reviewed in the Monthly review, but I have not heard in what style, I suspect not so as to be likely to push the sale or you would have told me' (Butler *JEGP* 149). The implication of this remark is that Cottle kept W and C abreast of the more favourable reviews of their book. W is likely to have sought out the review some time after writing to Cottle.

180. Moore, John, either *A Journal During a Residence in France, from the Beginning of August, to the Middle of December, 1792* (1793) or *A View of Society and Manners in France, Switzerland, and Germany* (1779)
Suggested date of reading: between 7 Feb. and 7 March 1796
References: *EY* 166
On 7 March 1796, DW wrote that 'Within the last month I have read ... Moore's Travels in France' (*EY* 166). Shaver is not sure whether this refers to *A Journal During a Residence in France* (1793) or *A View of Society and Manners in France, Switzerland, and Germany* (1779), so I have entered both titles (though the reference is, arguably, to the more recent). W is likely either to have read, or to have heard DW read out, passages from the volume.

181. *Morning Chronicle*
(i)
Suggested date of reading: Dec. 1792 onwards
References: *EY* 137-8
James Perry and James Gray purchased the *Morning Chronicle* about 1789, and turned it into the leading organ of the Whig Party. W appears to have known them in 1792-3 (Reed i 138), but no-one has yet discovered who might have introduced him to them at that early date.

He had at least two friends who knew Gray and Perry: (i) Francis Wrangham, whose acquaintance with the editors would prove useful in 1795 (see next note); (ii) Joshua Lucock Wilkinson (see note 263). The latter connection is indicated by a copy of one of Wilkinson's books, *Political Facts, Collected in a Tour, in the Month of August, September, and October, 1793, Along the Frontiers of France* (1793), now in the Bodleian Library, which bears the inscription, 'M^r. Perry With the Author's Com[pliments]'.[1] It was probably a gift to Perry, who would have had an interest in the volume since he too was a recent visitor to revolutionary France. Since W did not apparently meet Wrangham until 1795 (Reed i 163), his acquaintance with Gray and Perry from Dec. 1792 onwards probably came through Wilkinson. The contact would have been advantageous; at this period W was composing his *Letter to the Bishop of Llandaff*, and no doubt shared Wilkinson's journalistic (and pamphleteering) ambitions. After the publication of *An Evening Walk* and *Descriptive Sketches* in Jan. 1793, members of the literary world would have been interested in meeting him.

W was probably familiar with the *Chronicle* and its editors in London, 1792-3; he might have read it at Windy Brow, 1794; read it in London, 1795; and possibly received complimentary copies at Racedown, 1795-7. The *Chronicle* was the chief Whig paper of the time, founded 1769. In early July 1796, Perry invited C to write regularly for it, and possibly replace Gray as co-editor. Although C accepted the plan fell through (see Griggs i 226).

(ii)
Suggested date of reading: 1795-7
References: *EY* 137-8
In late Nov. 1795, W wrote to Wrangham:

> You flattered me with a hope that by your assistance, I might be supplied with the morning Chronicle; have you spoken to the editors about it? If it could be managed I should be much pleased, as we only see here a provincial weekly paper, and I cannot afford to have the Chronicle at my own expence. (*EY* 159)

This suggests that while at Racedown W sought out, and may have found, copies of the *Morning Chronicle*. It was his preferred daily paper, and as late as 1804 Dorothy wrote to John Wordsworth, then in London, pointing out that 'William has desired me to remind you about sending the Morning Chronicles - we wish for them very much' (*EY* 523).

182. *Morning Post*
Suggested date of reading: Dec. 1797-May 1798
References: see note

---

[1] Although the inscription was damaged when the volume was rebound, it is still readable.

Since W and C were publishing poetry and articles in the *Morning Post* throughout much of 1798, they probably read it on a regular basis. Visitors to Dove Cottage today can find an entire room papered with copies of it. For W and C's poetry in the *Morning Post* at this time, see CC *Essays* iii 285-8.

183. Moschus
(i) *Lament for Bion*
Suggested date of reading: by spring 1789
References: Reed i 85
During the spring or summer of 1789, W translated Moschus' *Lament for Bion* (usually published as *Idyllium* III). Only lines 99-104 of the *Lament* were entered *c.* spring 1789 into the MS containing *An Evening Walk*. Presumably he was working on a fuller version in another notebook, now lost. For text and bibliographical details, see *PW* i 286-7 and Wu D.Phil. 560-4.

W read (in Langhorne's translation) Bion's *Death of Adonis* by 1786 - the poem on which the original *Lament* was based (see note 148 [i]), suggesting that he may have known the *Lament* itself during his Hawkshead days.

(ii) *The Idyllia, Epigrams, and Fragments, of Theocritus, Bion, and Moschus, with the Elegies of Tyrtæus* **tr. Revd. Richard Polwhele (Exeter, 1786)**
Suggested date of reading: by spring 1789
References: see note
W's translation of Moschus' *Lament for Bion* (see preceding note) concludes:

> *But we the great the mighty and the wise*
> Soon as we perish in the hollow earth
> Unwakeable unheard of undisturbd
> *Slumber* a vast interminable sleep (*D.C.MS 7* 8r)

His phrasing derives from Polwhele's recent version of the poem:

> *But We, the Great, the Valiant, and the Wise,*
> When once the Seal of Death hath clos'd our Eyes,
> Lost in the hollow Tomb obscure and deep,
> *Slumber*, to 'wake no more, one long unbroken Sleep! (Moschus, *Idyllium* iii 129-32)

184. Nepos, Cornelius, works
Suggested date of reading: 1779-87
References: *MY* ii 8; Shaver 184; Wu *Library* JW8
In spring 1812 W described his disappointment at the unremarkable intellects of his children:

> As to their intellectual Powers they are none of them remarkable except the eldest, who is lamentably slow: This is to me a mortification as I promised myself much pleasure in rubbing up my Greek with him, and renewing my acquaintance with Nepos and Ovid etc. (*MY* ii 8)

JW Sr owned a copy of Nepos, which W almost certainly read as a child. This may have been the copy of *Vitae Excellentium Imperatorum* containing John Clarke's facing English translation that entered the Rydal Mount library (Shaver 184).

185. *New Annual Register* ... *For the Year 1786* (Part II)
Suggested date of reading: July-Aug. 1795
References: Cornell *SP* 307-10; Woof Ph.D. 40-1
Gill explains that the story of Jarvis Matcham, reported in the *New Annual Register*, provided the source for W's sailor in *Adventures on Salisbury Plain* (Cornell *SP* 307-10). Woof suggests that Godwin pointed W to the *New Annual Register*:

> what has not been observed is that Godwin's *History of England* appeared as a serial in that magazine and was the principal contribution to it (it was meant to rival Burke's in the *Annual Register*). Nothing is more possible than that Godwin should point out the suitability of the story of Jarvis Matcham for inclusion in a poem whose setting was Salisbury Plain and whose purpose was to expose the vices of war and the criminal code. (Woof Ph.D. 40-1)

186. 'a newspaper'
Suggested date of reading: Oct. 1796/spring 1798
References: Cornell *PB* 3
W recalled that *Peter Bell* was 'Founded upon an anecdote, which I read in a newspaper, of an ass being found hanging his head over a canal in a wretched posture. Upon examination a dead body was found in the water and proved to be the body of its master' (Cornell *PB* 3). In his lecture, 'Peter Bell', delivered at the Wordsworth Winter School 1991, Woof identified the newspaper as *The Sportsman's Magazine*, and quoted the article mentioned by W. I am unable to confirm the existence of such a magazine at this period.

187. Newton, Sir Isaac
(i) *Opticks*
Suggested date of reading: 1784-7
References: TWT 344
Bowman once left the young W in his study for a moment and returned to find him reading the *Opticks* (TWT 344). Since this book was not kept in the Old School Library it probably belonged to Bowman. The recollection dates from W's schooldays, supporting the argument that his studies anticipated the Cambridge syllabus.

The Pedlar, who shares W's boyhood passion for Foxe's *Book of Martyrs* (see note 107), had also, 'before his twentieth year was passed', attempted to reconcile the Newtonian science of optics with his own perceptions:

> I have heard him say
> That at this time he scann'd the laws of light
> With a strange pleasure of disquietude
> Amid the din of torrents where they send
> From hollow clefts, up to the clearer air
> A cloud of mist which in the shining sun
> Varies its rainbow hues. (Cornell *RC* 172-3)

(ii) *Opticks*
Suggested date of reading: by Dec. 1789
References: Schneider 160-1

W was examined on the *Opticks* at St John's in Dec. 1789; see p. 168, below. He thought well of its author; Muirhead recalled that W thought Newton 'perhaps the most extraordinary man that this country ever produced... he was an excellent linguist, but never sought display, and was content to work in that quietness and humility both of spirit and of outward circumstances in which alone all that is truly good was ever done' (Muirhead 741).

(iii) *Principia*
Suggested date of reading: spring 1790
References: Schneider 168-71
Schneider provides a sound argument for W's knowledge of this book, but the evidence remains far from conclusive.

188. Newton, John
(i) *An Authentic Narrative of Some Remarkable and Interesting Particulars in the Life of [the Revd. J. Newton] Communicated in a Series of Letters to the Revd. T. Haweis* [1764]
Suggested date of reading: 1796
References: Jacobus 26 and n
Jacobus puts forward the case for the influence of this work on *The Borderers*, suggesting a reading of 1796.

(ii) *An Authentic Narrative of Some Remarkable and Interesting Particulars in the Life of [the Revd. J. Newton] Communicated in a Series of Letters to the Revd. T. Haweis* [1764]
Suggested date of reading: 1798
References: see note
There is an apparent reminscence of the *Narrative* in MS B of *The Ruined Cottage*, dating from Feb. 1798 (*PW* v 384), suggesting that W took his copy to Alfoxden from Racedown, where it had influenced *The Borderers* (see preceding note). In 1798-9, DW copied an extract from the *Narrative* into *D.C.MS 16*. It reads as follows:

> From a narrative of various events of the life of
> the Revd. Mr Nelson.
> One thing though strange is most true. Though des=
> =titute of food and clothing, depressed to a degree beyond
> common wretchedness, I could sometimes collect my   [5]
> mind to mathematical studies. I had bought Bar=
> =row's Euclid at Plymouth; it was the only volume
> I brought on shore; it was always with me and I used
> to take it to remote corners of the Island by the sea-side
> and draw my diagrams with a long stick upon   [10]
> the sand. Thus I often beguiled my sorrows and
> almost forgot my feeling, and thus, without any
> other assistance I made myself, in a good measure,
> Master of the first six books of Euclid. - (*D.C.MS 16* 1v)

This passage, which forms the conclusion to Letter V of the *Narrative*, is the source of *Thirteen-Book Prelude* vi 160-74. I have collated the draft against the 3rd (1765), 6th (1786) and 7th (1790) editions. The punctuation and orthography of each differs, but that of the 6th (1786) is closest to DW's draft. Why she should have regarded the *Narrative* as the work of 'the Revd. Mr Nelson' remains a mystery - though Newton's name does not appear on the title-page, and she may simply have been misinformed.

189. Nicolai, Christoph Friedrich, works
Suggested date of reading: Sept. 1798
References: *Prose Works* i 95, 98
Klopstock told W that 'Nicolai & Engel had, in different ways, contributed to disenchant the Nation' of Kant (*Prose Works* i 95). W probably knew who Nicolai was; if he did not, he would have found out after seeing Klopstock; see also CC *Marginalia* iii 954.

190. Nicolson, Joseph, and Richard Burn, *The History and Antiquities of the Counties of Westmorland and Cumberland* (1777)
Suggested date of reading: 1796
References: *PW* i 344; Cornell *B* 18
De Selincourt suggests that this volume suggested to W the names Mortimer, Marmaduke, Matilda, Idonea, and Clifford, in *The Borderers* (*PW* i 344). W probably acquired his copy of the book at about this period (Shaver 186). Bicknell 12.

191. *The Oeconomist, or Englishman's Magazine*
Suggested date of reading: shortly after 9 May 1798
References: *EY* 214, 218
On 11 March 1798 W complained to Losh that 'I have not yet seen any numbers of the *Economist*, though I requested Cottle to transmit them to me' (*EY* 214), and on 9 May he asks Cottle to 'Be so good as to remember to send all the numbers of the Economist by the next opportunity' (*EY* 218). Since no further mention is made of them, Cottle probably obliged, and sent W his copies.

The title-page reads, 'Printed by M. Angus, Newcastle upon Tyne, and sold by Johnson, London; Cottle, Bristol; Jollie, Carlisle; and by the booksellers at York, Durham, Stockton, Cambridge, Edinburgh, Manchester, &c.' *The Oeconomist* had principally radical leanings, and contained articles about the education of the poor and extracts from *The Task*. It is entertaining enough, but next to the *Monthly Magazine* or the *Analytical*, seems tame and unoriginal. It completed a second volume and folded in Dec. 1799.

192. Ogilvie, John, *Poems on Several Subjects* (2 vols., 1769)
Suggested date of reading: 1787-91; by 1791
References: Shaver 189
A series of inscriptions show that these volumes were acquired in Cambridge and retained throughout W's life. The preliminary leaves of both volumes contain the inscription, in ink: 'Wordsworth St Johns'. The flyleaf of volume 1 reads: 'Wm Wordsworth Grasmere', and that of volume 2: 'Wm Wordsworth Rydal'. They are now in the possession of a scion of the Wordsworth family in New Zealand.

193. Ovidius Naso, Publius
(i) *Metamorphoses*
Suggested date of reading: 1779-87
References: *PW* iv 422

Late in life, W remembered that he discovered Ovid before Virgil: 'Before I read Virgil I was so strongly attached to Ovid, whose Metamorphoses I read at school, that I was quite in a passion whenever I found him, in books of criticism, placed below Virgil' (Cornell *Poems 1807-1820* 544). Ovid appears to have been a standard school textbook at Hawkshead (see p. 164, below). Lienemann 222-3 identifies a number of allusions and echoes from Ovid in the later poetry.

The Rydal Mount Library contained numerous copies of Ovid, some of which may have been in use during W's schooldays (Shaver 191-3). His copy of Nathan Bailey's *Ovid's Metamorphoses ... with the arguments and notes of John Minellius* (7th edn, 1787), now at the Wordsworth Library, contains on its flyleaf an ownership signature that dates probably from the 1810s. The Hawkshead Grammar School Library possessed a copy of Minellius' edition (Wu *CWAAS* 190).

(ii) *Ovid's Metamorphosis Englished, Mythologiz'd, and Represented in Figures, and an Essay to the Translation of Virgil's Aeneis* by George Sandys (Oxford, 1632)
Suggested date of reading: 1780s
References: TWT 344
When Thomas Bowman Jr remarked that W read the copy of 'Ovid's "Metamorphosis"' in the School Library (TWT 344), he was referring to Sandys' translation, which the Library possessed in a first edition of 1632 (Wu *CWAAS* 191).

(iii) *Metamorphoseon series compendiosa. Ex Gulielmi Canteri novis lectionibus* (1772)
Suggested date of reading: by Aug. 1795
References: see note
W was given this book by John Tweddell, the distinguished classical scholar, probably during his stay in London, Feb.-Aug. 1795. The Rydal Mount sale catalogue notes: 'with Autographs of John Tweddell and W. Wordsworth, given to him by John Tweddell who died at Athens' (Park 65). Its present whereabouts is unknown (Shaver 192). Tweddell left England on 24 Sept. 1795, never to return, and died of a fever in Athens on 25 July 1799; see Roe 245-7; *EY* 213.

194. Paine, Thomas
(i) *Common Sense* [1776]
Suggested date of reading: spring 1791; by spring 1793
References: *Prose Works* i 53
In their annotations to the *Letter to the Bishop of Llandaff*, Owen and Smyser show that W was probably aware of Paine's *Common Sense*. It was probably one of the 'master Pamphlets of the day' that W remembered having read in the *Thirteen-Book Prelude* ix 97. The most likely date of reading is spring 1791.

(ii) *Rights of Man* Part I (1791)
Suggested date of reading: spring 1791; by spring 1793
References: Roe 32-3
Paine's *Rights of Man* came out on 22 Feb. 1791. By selling 200,000 copies through working-men's clubs, it became the most effective answer to Burke's *Reflections*. As Roe points out to me, it was probably one of the 'master Pamphlets of the day' that W remembered having read in the *Thirteen-Book Prelude* ix 97: 'Wordsworth was not only in

London when *The Rights of Man* first appeared on the bookstalls, he was moving in circles likely to be receptive to Paine's ideas' (Roe 32). The probable date of reading is spring 1791; it was published by Joseph Johnson, who W probably knew by then. W had read this book by the time he composed the *Letter to the Bishop of Llandaff*; see *Prose Works* i 62.

(iii) *Rights of Man* Part II (1792)
Suggested date of reading: spring 1792-3; by spring 1793
References: *Prose Works* i 53; Roe 68-9
The second part of *The Rights of Man* was published 17 Feb. 1792, and W probably read it in a French edition some time during the spring or summer. On 21 May both parts of the book were banned in England, and Paine charged with sedition. He was tried and sentenced to death *in absentia*, 18 Dec., at about the time W returned to England. Roe 68-9 points to the influence of *Rights of Man* Part II on *Descriptive Sketches*. A *Letter to the Bishop of Llandaff* (composed Feb.-June 1793) reveals a knowledge of both parts of the banned work; see *Prose Works* i 62.

195. Paley, William, *The Principles of Moral and Political Philosophy* [1785]
Suggested date of reading: by Jan. 1791
References: Schneider 182-5
W was examined on Paley at St John's College, Cambridge, Jan. 1791.

W's opinion of Paley in subsequent years fluctuated. In the 1798 *Essay on Morals*, he classed *Moral Philosophy* with Godwin's *Political Justice* as 'impotent [?in *or* ?to] all their intended good purposes; to which I wish I could add that they were equally impotent to all bad one[s]' (*Prose Works* i 103). However, Hazlitt reported W's approval of Paley's works in 1800 (Howe iv 277).

In 1829, John Carter recorded that the Rydal Mount library contained 'Paley's Nat: Philoso:' (Shaver 346). I question whether this refers to Paley's *Natural Theology* (1802), as the Shavers think; it is more likely to have been *The Principles of Moral and Political Philosophy* (1785).

196. Percy, Thomas
(i) *Reliques of Ancient English Poetry* [3 vols., 1765]
Suggested date of reading: 1780s
References: TWT 344; Moorman 67
As a schoolboy, W read Bowman's copy of Percy (TWT 344) - presumably the first edition of 1765, though we cannot be sure. (In 1792 the Hawkshead Grammar School Library acquired the third edition [3 vols., 1775]). The fact that W purchased his own copy in Hamburg in 1798 would suggest that he had not possessed one before then (see next note).

(ii) *Reliques of Ancient English Poetry*
Suggested date of reading: 1797-8
References: Parrish 121-5; Griggs i 379; Woof Ph.D. 303
C referred to his copy of the *Reliques* in his letter to W of 23 Jan. 1798 (Griggs i 379n). As Woof observes, 'It can be inferred ... that Wordsworth did not have a copy of Percy when the 1798 edition of *Lyrical Ballads* was being prepared, but that Coleridge did' (Woof Ph.D. 303). For 'some verbal resemblances' between some of Percy's *Reliques* and the Lyrical Ballads, see Owen *LB* 142-3 and Mason *LB* 132.

(iii) *Reliques of Ancient English Poetry* **(3 vols., 4th edn, 1794)**
Suggested date of reading: 1 Oct. 1798 onwards
References: Reed i 253; *DWJ* i 31; Shaver 198
'Bought Percy's ancient poetry, 14 marks', DW recorded in her journal for Monday 1 Oct. 1798 (*DWJ* i 31). The copy is now at Harvard University Library, and contains a note recording its purchase in Hamburg, 1798, 'by William Wordsworth' (Shaver 198; Coffman P39). This is consistent with Woof's suggestion that 'Wordsworth seems to have been only generally acquainted with Percy in 1798, but after that his knowledge seems to have increased' (Woof Ph.D. 303). Stein 176 discusses the influence of Percy on W's poetry of 1799.

197. Petrarch
(i) *Sonnets*
Suggested date of reading: 1789-91
References: Schneider 103; *EY* 56
W composed a loose translation of Petrarch, *Se la mia vita da l'aspro tormento* in 1789-90 while learning Italian with Agostino Isola. See Woof *SIB* 166-7, Reed i 23. By 3 Aug. 1791, when he wrote to Mathews admitting that he was not equipped with an Italian grammar or dictionary, W seems to have lost touch with the language.

(ii) *Sonnets*
Suggested date of reading: Dec. 1792
References: Cornell *DS* 54
W's declaration in Feb. 1794 to 'resume' his Italian studies (*EY* 112) suggests that they were dropped during his stay in France, 1791-2, and that he had not returned to them since he left Cambridge. The footnoted allusion to Petrarch in *Descriptive Sketches* was probably added immediately prior to publication, *c*. Dec. 1792. It is not clear whether, when he began teaching DW Italian at Windy Brow in 1794, he returned to Petrarch; the next confirmable reading took place in Dec. 1803 (*EY* 425-6).

198. Phaedrus, *Fabularum Æsopiarum Libri Quinque* **(1765)**
Suggested date of reading: 1787
References: Butler *WC* 59; Shaver 200
W's copy is in the Wells Wordsworth Collection, Swarthmore College. Butler reports that an inscription on the front cover reads: 'This was one of Wordsworth's school Books. It was bought at his Sale' (Butler *WC* 59). Clancey, who examined it in autumn 1989, describes it in detail:

> This is a very much used and dirty text. There are no comments (as nearly as I could find from examining each page) made by Wordsworth. His signature first appears on the inside of the cover. 'Wordsworth' is scrawled a bit awkwardly. Facing this inside cover is page v and here are found two signatures: at the top of the page, 'George George Benn' (I cannot be sure of the spelling). At the first free space in the text is to be found: 'W. Wordsworth', in a much firmer hand than the 'Wordsworth' scrawled on the inside of the cover. The 'Benn' signature is that of a young person, I would think. In the text on page three is another signature which looks like 'John Mitchell'. This text is typical of the Wordsworth texts I've seen. It has a literal parsing of each word in the

text in alphabetical order in the rear. My thesis is that Wordsworth's teachers followed a consistent pattern of getting him into the classical texts as quickly as possible with good English translations close at hand. He was taught in this way because it is such an efficient way to teach one to read the classical texts and because it so quickly and naturally teaches good English idiom and style. The disadvantage is that one does not learn to explicate grammatically in the detail which other systems require and one does not necessarily learn how to write in Latin and Greek. (letter to me)

199. The Philanthropist
Suggested date of reading: 1795-6
References: see note
In June 1794, W made tentative plans to launch up his own periodical, to be called *The Philanthropist: a Monthly Miscellany* (*EY* 125). From 16 March 1795 to 25 Jan. 1796, Daniel Isaac Eaton, the well-known radical publisher, issued a journal of that name, and a number of critics and scholars have posited a Wordsworthian connection. He may at least have read it. In 1950, Stockwell remarked:

> Though there is nothing in *The Philanthropist* to show that Mathews, and much less Wordsworth, had any connection with it, the opinions expressed on a wide range of subjects are remarkably similar to Wordsworth's during 1793 and 1794.
> ('Wordsworth's Politics' [B.Litt. thesis, 1950], p. 337)

See also Roe 276-9; Johnston, 'Philanthropy or Treason? Wordsworth as "Active Partisan"', *SIR* 25 (1986) 371-409; and Thompson, 'Wordsworth's Crisis', *London Review of Books* 10 (8 Dec. 1988) 3-6.

200. Plinius Caecilius Secundus, Caius, *Epistolarum*
Suggested date of reading: 1787-91
References: Cornell *DS* 50; *EY* 348
W's comment to C in 1802 suggests a first reading of Pliny's letters years before, possibly at Cambridge: 'I remember having the same opinion of Plinys letters which you have express'd when I read them many years ago' (*EY* 347-8). Although translations were readily available (Melmoth's had been in print since 1747), W probably read the original Latin text. He mentions Pliny in his description of Lake Como in *Descriptive Sketches*:

> Heedless how Pliny, musing here, survey'd
> Old Roman boats and figures thro' the shade ... (lines 116-17)

This is a reference to Pliniana, a villa on Lake Como, which is mentioned in Coxe's *Travels* iii 5; see note 67.

201. Pope, Alexander
(i) *Poetical Works*
Suggested date of reading: by 1785
References: *PW* i 366; Potts 30-8
W's *Lines Written as a School Exercise* (1785) was, he recalled, 'but a tame imitation of Pope's versification, and a little in his style' (*PW* i 366). Pope continued to be a strong

influence on W's juvenilia. A favourite passage was Pope's portrait of Melancholy in *Eloisa to Abelard*:

> Black Melancholy sits, and round her throws
> A death-like silence, and a dread repose:
> Her gloomy presence saddens all the scene,
> Shades ev'ry flow'r, and darkens ev'ry green,
> Deepens the murmur of the falling floods,
> And breathes a browner horror on the woods. (lines 165-70)

These lines inspired W's portrait of Superstition in *The Vale of Esthwaite*:

> At noon I hied to gloomy glades
> Religious woods and midnight shades
> Where brooding Superstition frown'd
> A cold and awful horror round
> While with black arm and nodding head
> She wove a stole of sable thread (*D.C.MS 3* 6r; De Selincourt 25-30)

(ii) *Poetical Works*
Suggested date of reading: 1791-2
References: Cornell *DS* 44, *EY* 55.

(iii) *Poetical Works*
Suggested date of reading: 1795-8
References: *EY* 169, 174; Cornell *B* 72
W probably reread Pope in preparation for the *Imitation of Juvenal* (see Reed i 340-1). Apart from the epigraph to *The Borderers* (Cornell *B* 72), he draws also on Pope's *Epistle to Cobham* 39-40, at *Borderers* III ii 25-6 (Cornell *B* 184; see also Kelley, 'Wordsworth and Pope's *Epistle to Cobham*', *N&Q* NS 28 [1981] 314-15), and Mason *LB* 100.

202. 'provincial weekly paper'
Suggested date of reading: Aug. 1795 onwards
References: *EY* 159
In late Nov. 1795, W told Wrangham that at Racedown 'we only see here a provincial weekly paper' (*EY* 159).

203. Quintilian, *Institutio Oratoria*
Suggested date of reading: by Feb. 1798
References: see note
Lindenberger traces Quintilian's influence on W to MS JJ, the first MS of *The Prelude*, composed in late 1798.[1] The editors of the forthcoming Longman *Wordsworth* go back earlier:

> And further, by contemplating these forms
> In the relations which they bear to man

---

[1] *On Wordsworth's Prelude* (Princeton, 1963), p. 25.

We shall discover what a power is theirs
To stimulate our minds, & multiply
The spiritual presences of absent things ... (Cornell *RC* 262-3)

These lines, originally drafted as part of a conclusion to *Ruined Cottage* MS B, *c.* Feb. 1798, recollect Quintilian, *Institutio Oratoria* VI ii 29: 'visiones ... per quas imagines rerum absentium ita repraesentantur animo, ut eas cernere oculis ac praesentes habere videamur'. W recalled the same passage in the Preface to *Lyrical Ballads* 1802, when he mentioned the poet's 'disposition to be affected more than other men by absent things as if they were present' (*Prose Works* i 138). His familiarity with Quintilian may even go back to Hawkshead days.

A motto from Quintilian appears on the title-page of *Lyrical Ballads* (1800), and W quotes from Quintilian in his letter to Charles James Fox, 14 Jan. 1801 (*EY* 315). During the late 1790s or early 1800s W perhaps acquired one or both of the editions of Quintilian retained in the Rydal Mount library (Shaver 209).

In 1799, Montagu recommended that Azariah Pinney read Quintilian (Pinney Papers); might his interest in the author have been aroused by C? It is possible that W was also referred to Quintilian by C.

204. Racine, Jean, *Athalie*

Suggested date of reading: 1791-2; by summer 1793
References: *Prose Works* i 33; Shaver 210

'I flatter myself I am not alone', W writes in the *Letter to the Bishop of Llandaff*, 'when I wish that it may please the almighty neither by the hands of his priests nor his nobles (I allude to a striking passage of Racine) to raise his posterity to the rank of his ancestors and reillume the torch of extinguished David' (*Prose Works* i 33). In other words, he hopes that the monarchy of France will not be restored. On the facing verso of the MS, he directs the reader to 'See *Athalie*, Scene second', and copies out *Athalie* I ii 278-82, 292-4, where Joad is speaking. W almost certainly read *Athalie* in 1792 before returning to England, and was always to admire the play. This is clear from an anecdote recorded by Thomas Moore, who encountered W in Paris on 24 Oct. 1820:

> A young Frenchman called in, and it was amusing to hear him and Wordsworth at cross purposes upon the subject of 'Athalie;' Wordsworth saying that he did not wish to see it acted, as it would never come up to the high imagination he had formed in reading it, of the prophetic inspiration of the priests, &c. &c.; and the Frenchman insisting that in acting alone could it be properly enjoyed, - that is to say, in the manner it was acted *now*; for he acknowledged that till the Corps de Ballet came to its aid, it was very dull, even on the stage, - *une action morte*.
>
> (*Memoirs, Journal, and Correspondence of Thomas Moore* ed. Rt. Hon. Lord John Russell, MP [8 vols., 1853-6], iii 159; his italics)

See also *LY* ii 197. Woof points out to me that W acquired a four volume set of Racine's works, probably on his 1802 visit to France, of which the volume containing *Athalie* is now missing. The remaining volumes are now at the Wordsworth Library (Shaver 210). This suggests, firstly, that W did not possess his own copy of *Athalie* before 1802, and secondly, that the volume containing *Athalie* was in such frequent use that it went missing.

205. Radcliffe, Ann
(i) *The Romance of the Forest* [3 vols., 1791]
Suggested date of reading: by summer 1793
References: see note

> The man half raised that stone by pain and sweat,
> Half raised; for well his arm might lose its force
> Disclosing the grim head of a new murdered corse. (*Salisbury Plain* 151-3)

In these lines, the editors of the Longman *Wordsworth* find a parallel with Radcliffe's *Romance of the Forest*, in which La Motte finds a large chest 'which he went forward to examine, and, lifting the lid, he saw the remains of a human skeleton. Horror struck upon his heart, and he involuntarily stepped back' (i 135). Later in *Salisbury Plain* the Female Vagrant 'seemed transported to another world' (line 371), not unlike Adeline, the heroine of Radcliffe's novel, who 'seemed as if launched into a new world' as she stands on the deck of a ship (ii 169). A copy of *The Romance of the Forest* was in the Stowey Book Society (see p. 174, below), and a two-volume set, published in 1810, turned up in the sale of the Rydal Mount library (Shaver 268).

(ii) *The Romance of the Forest* [3 vols., 1791]
Suggested date of reading: c. late 1796
References: Legouis 272; Moorman 307-8; Cornell *B* 28, 162n; Woof Ph.D. 68
In his synopsis of *The Borderers*, W writes: 'Smugglers seen on the top of the walls - Another part of the castle Smugglers have overheard resolve to prevent scheme' (Cornell *B* 308-9). Woof believes that 'The smugglers no doubt were fed into Wordsworth's imagination by certain situations in Mrs. Radcliffe's *Romance of the Forest*' (Woof Ph.D. 68). This would suggest a reading of *The Romance of the Forest* c. late 1796 (Reed i 26).

Legouis observes that Radcliffe offers 'our best source of information on what the reader of the moment considered a faithful representation of a criminal' (Legouis 271), and quotes at length from her portrayal of the villainous Marquis Philip de Montalt. In his introduction to the Cornell *Borderers*, Osborn develops the connection suggested by Legouis between Montalt and Rivers (Cornell *B* 29).

(iii) *The Italian* (3 vols., 1797)
Suggested date of reading: spring 1797-summer 1798
References: Masson iii 206; Griggs i 318
Attacking W's 'one-sidedness' in 1840, De Quincey records:

> One of Mrs Radcliffe's romances, viz. 'The Italian,' he had, by some strange accident, read, - read, but only to laugh at it; whilst, on the other hand, the novels of Smollett, Fielding, and Le Sage - so disgusting by their moral scenery and the whole state of vicious society in which they keep the reader moving: these, and merely for the ability of the execution, he read and remembered with extreme delight. (Masson iii 206)

W's affection for Smollett, Fielding, and Le Sage owes much to his boyhood reading of them.

De Quincey's expression, 'by some strange accident', suggests that W read someone else's copy. The most likely candidate is C, who told Bowles in March 1797 that 'I have been lately reviewing the Monk, the Italian, Hubert de Sevrac & &c & &c' (Griggs i 318; Coffman

R3). C's review of *The Italian* was published in the *Critical Review* for June 1798,[1] and W could have read his copy at any point between spring 1797 and summer 1798. In later years W professed scorn for 'that want of taste, which is universal among modern novels of the Radcliffe school' (*MY* ii 232); see also C's formula for 'a Romance in Mrs Radcliff's style' (Griggs iii 294-5).

206. Ramond de Carbonnières, Louis François Elizabeth
(i) *Lettres de M. William Coxe à M. W. Melmoth sur l'état politique, civil, et naturel de la Suisse; traduits de l'Anglais, et augmentées des observations faites dans le même pays par le traducteur* (2 vols., 2nd edn, Paris, 1782)
Suggested date of reading: 1790-2
References: Shaver 69; Cornell *DS* 74
W owned and read the French translation of Coxe during his residence in France, 1791-2. It was at his side as he composed *Descriptive Sketches* (see Cornell *DS* 74-5; Legouis 475-7; Sheats 59-74), and subsequently passed onto the shelves of the Rydal Mount Library (Shaver 69). There is no proof that W possessed a copy of Coxe, but it is likely that he did. He recommended Ramond de Carbonnières to Robinson, 28 Nov. 1828 (*LY* i 674).

(ii) *Lettres de M. William Coxe à M. W. Melmoth sur l'état politique, civil, et naturel de la Suisse; traduits de l'Anglais, et augmentées des observations faites dans le même pays par le traducteur* (2 vols., 2nd edn, Paris, 1782)
Suggested date of reading: mid Dec. 1798
References: *EY* 235
W had his copy with him in Germany, where he was consulting it (*EY* 235).

207. Reynolds, Sir Joshua, *Discourses*
Suggested date of reading: by July 1798
References: *Prose Works* i 116
Reynolds' first discourse was published in 1769, and 14 more followed before his death in 1792. It is impossible to say exactly when W first read the discourses, but the earliest hint that he had done so is his apostrophe to Reynolds in *Anacreon Imitated* (1786).
The first clear indication that he knew the *Discourses* occurs in the 1798 Advertisement to *Lyrical Ballads*:

> An accurate taste in poetry, and in all the other arts, Sir Joshua Reynolds has observed, is an acquired talent, which can only be produced by severe thought, and a long continued intercourse with the best models of composition. (*Prose Works* i 116)

This could refer, Owen points out, to any of at least three of Reynolds' *Discourses* (see *Prose Works* i 186). Owen tells me that W 'may have used Malone's 1797 edition of the *Works* for his essay on the *Sublime and Beautiful* in 1812 (*Prose Works* ii 358, 457), but more probably the third edition (1801), which Beaumont gave him in 1804 (*EY* 490-1; Shaver 214). Whether he had access to the 1797 edition in 1798 is uncertain; his remarks on his desultory reading of the *Discourses* (*EY* 490-1) suggest that he probably did not' (letter to me). A copy of the 1797 edition was on the shelves of the Bristol Library Society in 1798 (*BLS* 85).

---

[1] Reprinted Raysor, *Coleridge's Miscellaneous Criticism* (1936), pp. 378-82.

208. Richardson, Samuel, *Clarissa*
Suggested date of reading: 10-16 Jan. 1791
References: Memoirs i 48; Reed i 116
Christopher Wordsworth Jr wrote of W: 'The week before he took his degree he passed his time in reading Clarissa Harlowe' (*Memoirs* i 48). On this evidence Reed dates the reading to *c.* 10-16 Jan. 1791. DW read the novel at the age of 14 (*MY* i 161), *c.* 1785.

209. Ridpath, George, *The Border History of England and Scotland* **(1776)**
Suggested date of reading: 1796
References: Cornell *B* 814; Woof Ph.D. 66
In 1843, W recalled his research for *The Borderers*:

> Nevertheless I do remember that having a wish to colour the manners in some degree
> from local history more than my knowledge enabled me to do I read Redpath's history
> of the Borders but found there nothing to my purpose. I once made an observation to
> Sir Walter Scott in which he concurred that it was difficult to conceive how so dull a
> book could be written on such a subject. (Cornell *B* 814)

Woof suggests that 'the number of pilgrims in the play (and in the earlier drafts these have greater importance), owes something to Ridpath, but this is little enough' (Woof Ph.D. 66). This book was not in the Racedown Lodge library, the Bristol Library Society or, in later years, the Rydal Mount library.

210. Rogers, Samuel
(i) *The Pleasures of Memory* **(1792)**
Suggested date of reading: between May 1792 and Jan 1793
References: Cornell *DS* 44; Legouis 144-5
Legouis observes that W's early couplet poems owe 'most to Samuel Rogers' *Pleasures of Memory*, of which he makes no mention' (Legouis 144). *The Pleasures of Memory* was first published in May 1792, and became an instant success; a second edition was published on 26 July 1792. W must have read the poem between May 1792 and early Jan 1793, when he would have drafted final versions of *An Evening Walk* and *Descriptive Sketches*. This supports the argument that, although *An Evening Walk* was composed largely at Cambridge in 1789, W continued work on it prior to publication in 1793. Since *Descriptive Sketches* was largely written 1792-3, there is no reason why it should not reflect Rogers' influence. W was in France when *The Pleasures of Memory* was first published, but he might easily have obtained a copy in Paris; alternatively, one might have been sent to him from England.

The inside back cover of W's fair copy notebook, *D.C.MS 2*, contains a jotting which dates from *c.* 1792: 'And the dead friend is present in his shade'. This is apparently a recollection of *Pleasures of Memory* i 252, 'And the lost friend still lingers in his shade!'

There are good reasons why W should have found Rogers' poem interesting. Like W, Rogers followed the picturesque principles of Gilpin, whose influence is evident throughout *The Pleasures of Memory*. Also, Rogers was a known radical, having been signatory to a resolution for constitutional reform proposed by the Whig Friends of the People on 11 April 1792 (Erdman 159). Like W, Rogers visited Paris in 1791 (during Jan. and Feb.) - at which time he met, among others, Condorcet, whom he described as 'a very sensible but very plain man' (Clayden, *The Early Life of Samuel Rogers* [1887], p. 136).

117

(ii) *The Pleasures of Memory ... with some other poems* **(6th edn, 1794)**
Suggested date of reading: 18 Aug. 1795 onwards
References: *EY* 151; Shaver 219
In her letter of 2 and 3 Sept. 1795, DW tells Mrs John Marshall how William Rawson, the
Halifax merchant and husband of her distant 'Aunt' Threlkeld, bought this book for her (*EY*
151). It survives today at the Wordsworth Library, but is not bound up with Akenside's
Pleasures of Imagination, as stated by Pamela Woof (*Grasmere Journals* 176). The flyleaf
inscription reads: 'D Wordsworth / The Gift of Mʳ. Wᵐ. Rawson / August 18.ᵗʰ 1795'.

211. Roland de la Platière, Marie Jeanne, *An Appeal to Impartial Posterity, by Citizenness*
Roland **(2 vols., 1795)**
Suggested date of reading: Jan. 1796
References: Pinney Papers, Family Letter Book 13, *EY* 166
At the conclusion of his letter to W of 26 Nov. 1795, Pinney remarks: 'I shall send you by
this opportunity Luesdon Hill, and Louvet, but will keep Madame Roland 'till I have the
pleasure of seeing you' (Pinney Papers, Family Letter Book 13). Pinney brought Roland's
Appeal to Racedown in Jan. 1796, for in March 1796 DW reported that 'I have also read
lately Madame Roland's *Memoirs*, Louvet and some other french things - very entertaining'
(*EY* 166). W almost certainly read these books as well; Gill points out that the fact that
'Madame Roland and Louvet figure so strikingly in *The Prelude*'s account of the Revolution,
far more than their historical importance warrants, may be due in part to W's familiarity with
these books' (Gill 444; see *Thirteen-Book Prelude* x 352-4). This book was in great demand
at the Bristol Library Society during 1795-6, as Azariah knew (his brother, John, was a
subscriber). The copy he gave the Wordsworths was probably his own, since the Bristol
Library registers show that it did not come from there. Poole read the *Appeal* in March 1796;
writing to Henrietta Warwick on 2 April, he revealed that 'I have lately perused with much
delight *La Citoyenne Roland*' (Sandford i 167). His comments suggest that he read the work
in French; this was possible since the publisher of the translation, Joseph Johnson, advertised
imported copies of the French text in the *Morning Chronicle*, 21 July 1795.

212. Rosset, Pierre Fulcrand de, *L'Agriculture. Poëme.* **(Paris, 1774-82)**
Suggested date of reading: by spring 1789
References: Cornell *EW* 46; Legouis 143n

> In this description of the cock, I remembered a spirited one of the same animal in the
> l'Agriculture ou Les Georgiques Françoises, of M. Rossuet. (note to *EW* 129)

As Averill points out, Rosset's poem has no such subtitle (Cornell *EW* 46), and W is probably
confusing it with Jacques Montanier Delille, *Œuvres de M. l'Abbé de Lille, contenant les*
géorgiques de Virgile, en vers françois, et Les jardins, poème (1788); see note 76. The
passage Wordsworth recalls in his note occurs in *L'Agriculture* I Chant Sixième:

> Que le Coq, de ses sœurs & l'époux & le Roi,
> Toujours marche à leur tête & leur donne la loi.
> Il peut dix ans entiers les aimer, les conduire;
> Il est né pout l'amour, il est né pour l'empire.
> En amour, en fierté le Coq n'a point d'égal.

Une crête de poupre orne son front royal;
Son œil noir lance au loin des vives étincelles;
Un plumage éclatant peint son corps & ses ailes,
Dore son cou superbe, & flotte en longs cheveux:
De sanglans éperons arment ses pieds nerveux:
Sa queue en se jouant du dos jusqu'à la crête,
S'avance, & se recourbe en ombrageant sa tête. (lines 91-102)

Compare *Evening Walk* 129-36. The description of the cock is present in Wordsworth's Cambridge notebook (*D.C.MS 7*), in use during the spring and summer of 1789 (see Cornell *EW* 122-3); he must therefore have read Rosset by that time.

213. Rousseau, Jean Baptiste, *Ode à la Fortune*
Suggested date of reading: by Feb. 1799
References: *Prose Works* i 93, 97
In 1799, W noted that Klopstock 'called Rousseau's ode to Fortune a moral dissertation in stanzas' (*Prose Works* i 93). Owen points out to me that, 'as Klopstock made the reference, it doesn't follow that W knew the poem, but his phrasing doesn't suggest that it was quite unknown to him' (letter to me). W's conversations with Klopstock took place in Feb. 1799.

214. Rousseau, Jean Jacques
(i) *The Social Contract*
Suggested date of reading: Nov. 1791-2; by spring 1793
References: *Prose Works* i 36, 56
W quotes from *The Social Contract* in *A Letter to the Bishop of Llandaff* (*Prose Works* i 36, 56). The argument that he probably read Rousseau in France in 1791-2, and imbibed his ideas from Beaupuy and other Girondin thinkers, is supported by Chard's observation that, in *A Letter to the Bishop of Llandaff*, W takes the Girondin line in opposition to Rousseau. Like the Girondins, W seldom emphasizes the notion of a social contract, nor that of the rule of law, and, unlike Rousseau, refuses to limit liberty to certain types of nations. On the other hand he shares with Rousseau a belief in thegeneral will, and uses Rousseau's concept of man in a state of nature (see for instance the opening stanzas of *Salisbury Plain* or *Two-Part Prelude* i 17-26). It is likely that W read Rousseau before 1791.

(ii) *Discourse on Inequality*
Suggested date of reading: by spring 1793
References: *N&Q* NS 24 (1977) 323
Kelley, 'Rousseau's *Discourse on the Origins of Inequality* and Wordsworth's *Salisbury Plain*', *N&Q* NS 24 (1977) 323, points to the influence of the *Discourse* on the *Letter to the Bishop of Llandaff* (see *Prose Works* i 23, 56-7, 59-60), and on the opening of *Salisbury Plain*. W had apparently read the *Discourse* by spring 1793.

(iii) *Emile*
Suggested date of reading: 1796
References: Cornell *B* 63
In the Preface to *The Borderers*, W remarked: 'A child, Rousseau has observed, will tear in pieces fifty toys before he will think of making one' (Cornell *B* 63). Osborn notes that W

is alluding to Rousseau's *Emile*. Perhaps he and Dorothy were reading books on education as an aid to bringing up Basil Caroline Montagu. Betz suggests to me that W's teacher at Hawkshead, William Taylor, was probably influenced by *Emile*.

215. 'Rudiments of the Italian Tongue'
Suggested date of reading: by 1788-90
References: Shaver 221; Park 49
When it was auctioned after W's death, this volume was described only as 'Rudiments of the Italian Tongue'. Since its present whereabouts are unknown, we do not know what exactly it was. Mary Wordsworth's flyleaf inscription is recorded in the Rydal Mount auction catalogue: 'This book was much valued as belonging to my dear husband when he studied the language at Cambridge, M.W.' (Park 49). It may have been the 'Italian Gram.' that RW forwarded to W (then at Windy Brow) in May 1794 (see *EY* 120-1n). The Shavers suggest that it was a translation of Domenico Soresi, *I rudimenti della lingua Italiana* (Milano, 1756).

216. Russell, Thomas, *Sonnets and Miscellaneous Poems* ed. W. Howley (Oxford, 1789)
Suggested date of reading: 1789-90; by 1793
References: *Prose Works* i 163; Hunt 9
Hunt points to W's use of Russell's sonnets in the Appendix on Poetic Diction (*Prose Works* i 163), suggesting that 'Since Russell's sonnets first appeared in 1789 and were not reprinted until 1808, Wordsworth may well have seen them at roughly the same time as those of Bowles and Charlotte Smith' (Hunt 9). It is likely that W first encountered Russell's sonnets when composing his own in 1789-90 at Cambridge. I have therefore included Russell here as a speculative entry. In support of this I find an allusion to Russell at the end of *Salisbury Plain*: 'Must Law with *iron scourge* / Still torture crimes that grew a monstrous band' (lines 519-20). Ultimately, the iron scourge of Law must derive from Spenser's Talus, 'Who in his hand an yron flale did hould, / With which he thresht out falshood, and did truth vnfould' (*Faerie Queene* V i xii 8-9), but W alludes to Russell's *Sonnet X*, quoted in the Appendix on Poetic Diction: 'Beneath th' Oppressor's *iron scourge* to mourn' (line 7). *Salisbury Plain* (1793) thus provides a date by which W read Russell's *Sonnets*.
A copy of this volume was in Wrangham's library (2047 in Sotheby's auction catalogue).

217. St Pierre, Jacques Henri Bernardin de, *Paul and Virginia* tr. Helen Maria Williams (1796)
Suggested date of reading: shortly after July 1796
References: see note
Williams' translation of St Pierre's novel was in print by July 1796 and W probably read it soon after. Jonathan Wordsworth tells me that W's copy survives in a private collection in England, and contains an ownership inscription dating from 1796-7. This makes Racedown the most likely place for W's first reading of *Paul and Virginia*, which is consistent with the argument that it influenced *The Ruined Cottage*.[1] It was serialised in the *Weekly Entertainer*, 27 Feb.-29 May 1797, at a time when W was reading the *Entertainer* regularly.

---

[1] See Wordsworth, *Ancestral Voices* (Spelsbury, 1991), pp. 66-8.

In summer 1803 W denied borrowing the idea of *Poems on the Naming of Places* from *Paul et Virginie* (Reed ii 215; Howe xvii 115-16). At least two copies were at Rydal Mount: one in Spanish, another in Italian (Florence, 1795) - the latter being a gift from W to his daughter, Dora (Patton 261). Gittings and Manton, *Dorothy Wordsworth* (Oxford, 1985), discuss *Paul and Virginia* and its resemblances to Dorothy's Journal, concluding that she had read it by 1800.

218. Sandys, George, *A Relation of a Journey Begun 1610. Foure Bookes. Containing a Description of the Turkish Empire, of Ægypt, of the Holy Land, of the Remote Parts of Italy and Ilands Adjoyning* (1679)
Suggested date of reading: 1784-7
References: TWT 344
Bowman recalled that W read this book in the Hawkshead Grammar School Library. There was a copy in the Library in 1788, but it does not survive today (Wu *CWAAS* 230).

219. Schiller, Johann Christoph Friedrich von
(i) *The Robbers* tr. Alexander Fraser Tytler (1792)
Suggested date of reading: by March 1797
References: Cornell *B* 28, 128n
'My God! Southey!', wrote C to Southey in Nov. 1794, 'Who is this Schiller? This Convulser of the Heart? Did he write his Tragedy amid the yelling of Fiends?' (Griggs i 122). C stayed up until one o'clock in the morning to read Tytler's translation of *The Robbers*; he introduced W to it in 1797 for, as Osborn points out in his discussion of *The Borderers*, 'Schiller's *Robbers* appears to have become a direct source for *The Borderers* only in the later stages of composition, possibly as a result of Wordsworth's visit to Coleridge in March [1797]' (Cornell *B* 11n). Osborn suggests also that Mortimer's band of border outlaws was 'borrowed from Schiller's *Robbers*' (Cornell *B* 11), and that Schiller's Francis and Spiegelberg influenced Rivers (Cornell *B* 28).

(ii) *Don Carlos* [1787]
Suggested date of reading: spring/summer 1798; by Sept. 1798
References: Prose Works i 97-8
In the *Conversations with Klopstock* W reports Klopstock's opinion of Schiller:

> Schiller's robbers he found so extravagant that he could not read it. I spoke of the scene of the setting sun. He did not know it. He said Schiller could not live. He thought Don Carlos might be the best of his dramas, but said that the plot was inextricable - It was evident he knew little of Schiller's work[?s], indeed he said he could not read them.
>
> *(Prose Works i 93)*

Klopstock was apparently being quizzed about a German author he did not much admire. W, on the other hand, did admire him, and knew a great deal about his work; in fact, he had probably read *The Robbers* and *Don Carlos*, since he appears to have asked Klopstock quite specifically about both plays.
Don Carlos appeared in two English translations in 1798; one by H. D. Symonds, the other by Georg Heinrich Noehden and John Stoddart. The latter, which was published 10 July, is the one probably read by C and W. C's brother, Edward, was Stoddart's schoolteacher, and

C met Stoddart at Oxford in 1794, when they probably discussed Schiller. During the 1790s Stoddart moved in similar circles to W and C - in June 1796 Lamb described him as 'a cold hearted well bred conceited disciple of Godwin' (Marrs i 22). Given that W was reading *The Robbers* in 1797, he would probably have read *Don Carlos* soon after publication in spring 1798. He must in any case have known it by the time he met Klopstock in the early autumn. Stoddart and Noehden's translation of Schiller's *Fiesco* had been published by Joseph Johnson in 1796; C had probably read it by the time he gave Stoddart *Christabel* in MS, Oct. 1800 (*Notebooks* ii 2121n).

220. Scott, John
(i) *Critical Essays on Some of the Poems of Several English Poets* (1785)
Suggested date of reading: by summer or autumn 1789
References: Cornell *EW* 50; Legouis 131n
W had access to the *Critical Essays* as he composed *An Evening Walk*. Stewart quotes a letter of 1783 in which Scott told Beattie that his forthcoming *Critical Essays*

> will consist of a series of essays on several celebrated poems, by an investigation of whose beauties and defects I have exemplified the difference between good and bad composition. My criterion of merit is classical simplicity; that is to say, the manner of Homer, the Greek tragic poets, Virgil, Milton, Pope, in contradistinction to every species of false ornament. There never was a time when it was more necessary to counteract the public taste, which is now running wild after this fashionable *clinquant*, as I think it is termed by Addison. The poems I have criticised are, Denham's Cooper's-Hill, of which I have nothing to praise, and all to censure; Milton's Lycidas, and Dyer's Ruins of Rome, which I have vindicated from the censure of Dr. Johnson, and given the praise they merit; Pope's Windsor Forest, Collin's Oriental Eclogues, Gray's Elegy, Goldsmith's Deserted Village, and Thomson's Seasons; in all which I have much to applaud, and something to blame.
>
> (*John Scott of Amwell* [California, 1956], p. 165; his italics)

The published volume also contains an essay on Dyer's *Grongar Hill*. Scott's emphasis on 'classical simplicity', and opposition to 'false ornament', allies him with the Horatian tradition in which W was brought up. W's agreement with Scott is indicated by the footnote to *An Evening Walk* instructing the reader to 'see Scott's Critical Essays' (Cornell *EW* 50). A copy of the *Critical Essays* was given to the Hawkshead School Library in 1789; perhaps W saw it there while visiting Hawkshead during summer or autumn 1789, during work on *An Evening Walk*; see TWT 143.

(ii) *Moral Eclogues*
Suggested date of reading: by summer 1788
References: Landon 338

> Oft by still midnight waters have we heard
> Shrieks from high rocks warbling to the moon
> Then warbling nature's music solemn airs
> Pour down the mountain sid[e]
> Till every rock is haunted with a voice
> Surpassing human sweet[ness] (*D.C.MS* 2 93r)

This untitled fragment appears in W's fair copy notebook of Hawkshead and Cambridge years, and was probably composed in summer 1788. As Landon 338 points out, its first line echoes Scott's second *Moral Eclogue*:

> Sweet is the nightingale's love-soothing strain,
> *Heard by still waters on the moonlight plain*! (lines 67-8)

221. Ségur, Alexandre Joseph P., Vicomte de, *L'Education de l'Amour*
Suggested date of reading: by 21 Aug. 1795
References: Reed i 24n
The evidence for dating W's translation of Ségur's poem is contradictory. Although Southey wrote that it was composed while W was 'at the University', 1787-91,[1] Wrangham, who introduced it when it was published with the French text in the *Morning Chronicle*, 21 Aug. 1795,[2] made a different claim: 'To make amends in some measure for a very long silence, I send you what I consider as a most exquisite Imitation of some beautiful French Verses, done lately by a Friend of mine. I am not aware that the original has ever appeared in print. - The English certainly has not.' Perhaps W told Wrangham that the French text had not previously been published, or perhaps Wrangham provided W with a MS copy of it. Either way, the translation could have been 'done lately', in spring or summer 1795. Although Reed suggests, on the grounds of its appearance in the Windy Brow Notebook, that it was composed by 23 May 1794 (Reed i 24), the Notebook was in use well after this date (Cornell *EW* 158), and I see no reason why a dating of summer 1795 might not be plausibly advanced.

222. Shakespeare, William
(i)
Suggested date of reading: 1774-9
References: Memoirs i 34
As Christopher Wordsworth Jr points out, three of the most important influences on W's writing were encountered during the pre-Hawkshead years: 'the Poet's father set him very early to learn portions of the works of the best English poets by heart, so that at an early age he could repeat large portions of Shakspeare, Milton, and Spenser' (*Memoirs* i 34). These 'portions' might have been learned from such anthologies as Knox's *Elegant Extracts*.

(ii) *Love's Labours Lost*
Suggested date of reading: by 1786
References: see note
In *Anacreon Imitated* (1786), W describes his mistress' waving hair, as he wishes it painted by Sir Joshua Reynolds:

> *Waving in the wanton air,*
> Black and shining, paint her hair ... (lines 9-10)

---

[1] Review of Wrangham, *Poems* (1795), *Annual Review* 1 (1803) 655-7, p. 657. Accordingly, Christensen, 'The Date of Wordsworth's "The Birth of Love"', *MLN* 53 (1938) 280-2, places composition 'before 1791' (p. 281).

[2] The introduction is unsigned, but Reed must be correct in observing that it is 'plainly by Wrangham' (Reed i 24n). Wrangham was acquainted with the editors of the *Chronicle*; see p. 104, above.

The allusion is to *Love's Labours Lost*:

Love, whose month is ever May,
Spied a blossom passing fair
Playing in the wanton air ... (IV iii 100-2)

Like Shakespeare, Wordsworth uses 'wanton' to mean 'playful, frolicsome'; the word has no equivalent in Anacreon's *Ode* XXVIII, his source. *The Prelude* suggests that W first saw Shakespeare performed during his Hawkshead years:

When, at a Country Play-house, having caught,
In summer, through the fractured wall, a glimpse
Of day-light, at the thought of where I was
I gladden'd more than if I had beheld
Before me some bright Cavern of Romance,
Or than we do when on our beds we lie
At night, in warmth, when rains are beating hard. (*Thirteen-Book Prelude* vii 482-8)

(iii) *Pericles*
Suggested date of reading: by 1787
References: see note
Describing his grief at his father's death in *The Vale of Esthwaite* (1787), W wrote:

Flow on - in vain thou hast not flow'd
But eas'd me of an *heavy load* (*D.C.MS 3* 25r; De Selincourt 428-9)

The italicized phrase appears to echo Shakespeare's reference to grief in *Pericles*:

Nor come we to add sorrow to your tears,
But to relieve them of their *heavy load* ... (I iv 90-1)

(iv) works
Suggested date of reading: 1787-90
References: PW i 323; Cornell EW 38
An Evening Walk alludes to passages in Shakespeare that W probably knew by heart (*Tempest* IV i 155-6 and *As You Like It* II i 31-2). In *The Prelude*, W recalled seeing Shakespeare acted on stage during his Cambridge years - 'some beauteous Dame'

or mumbling Sire,
A scare-crow pattern of old Age, patch'd up
Of all the tatters of infirmity,
All loosely put together, hobbled in,
Stumping upon a Cane, with which he smites,
From time to time, the solid boards, and makes them
Prate somewhat loudly of the whereabout
Of one so overloaded with his years... (*Thirteen-Book Prelude* vii 455-62)

The 'scare-crow pattern of old Age' suggests Lear or Adam (in *As You Like It*), and the allusion in the penultimate line indicates that one of the plays he saw during these years was *Macbeth*: 'The very stones *prate of my whereabout*' (II i 58).

(v) works
Suggested date of reading: Dec. 1791-2
References: Cornell *DS* 84, 116

(vi) works
Suggested date of reading: July 1793-spring 1794
References: Cornell *EW* 140; Cornell *SP* 33; Mason *LB* 142

(vii) *The Winter's Tale*
Suggested date of reading: spring-summer 1796; winter 1798-9
References: see note
Woof points out to me that W's *Address to the Ocean* (composed, Reed suggests, between mid-April and mid-Nov. 1796) contains an echo of *The Winter's Tale*. The poem begins:

> How long will ye round me be roaring
> Once terrible waves of the sea (*D.C.MS 2* 9v)

The phrase, 'waves of the sea' is borrowed from *The Winter's Tale*: 'When you do dance, I wish you / A wave o' th' sea' (IV iv 140-1). The same phrase was in W's mind as he composed *The Two April Mornings* between 6 Oct. 1798 and 23 Feb. 1799 (Mason *LB* 142).

(viii) *Sonnets, Hamlet, Macbeth*
Suggested date of reading: 1796-7
References: *EY* 168, 173n; Cornell *B* 22, 148n

(ix) works
Suggested date of reading: spring and summer 1798
References: Cornell *RC* 62
Shakespeare's influence can be found not only in *The Ruined Cottage* but in a number of the Lyrical Ballads written in 1798 including *The Idiot Boy*, *Goody Blake and Harry Gill*, *Tintern Abbey*, *The Last of the Flock*, and *Simon Lee*. See Bate, *Shakespeare and the English Romantic Imagination* (Oxford, 1986), pp. 97-102; Mason *LB* 101, 125, 213, 292.

223. Shaw, Cuthbert, *Monody to the Memory of a Young Lady*
Suggested date of reading: by 1787
References: Landon 376
W's earliest echo of Shaw occurs in *The Vale of Esthwaite*: 'For I must never prove / A tender parent's guardian Love' (*D.C.MS 3* 26r; De Selincourt 514-15). This poignant acknowledgement that W has been orphaned borrows the phrasing of Shaw's address to his child, whose mother,

> Alas, is gone; yet shalt thou prove
> A father's dearest, tenderest love ... (*Monody to the Memory of a Young Lady* 248-9)

W follows Shaw in using 'prove' to mean 'experience'.
　　Another early borrowing can be found in a sonnet of c. 1789, '*On the [   ] village Silence sets her seal*':

> oh my friends restrain
> Those busy cares that must renew my pain

Go rear the [   ] plant - quick shall it feel
The *fond officious* touch, and droop again. (Cornell *Poems 1800-1807* 324-5)

As Landon 376 points out, the italicized phrase is borrowed from Shaw's *Monody to the Memory of a Young Lady*:

Forbear, my *fond officious* friends, forbear
To wound my ears with the sad tales you tell ... (lines 37-8)

224. Shelvocke, George, *A Voyage Round the World by the Way of the Great South Sea, Performed in the Years 1719-1722* (1726)
Suggested date of reading: c. 11-12 Nov. 1797
References: *PW* i 361; Reed i 210; Lowes 224-6
As W recalled in the Fenwick Note to *We are Seven* (*PW* i 361), his reading of Shelvocke's *Voyages* inspired the killing of the albatross in C's *Ancient Mariner*. W dates this reading 'a day or two before' the walking tour to Lynton - which would make it c. 11-12 Nov. 1797. A copy of Shelvocke was retained in the Rydal Mount library (Shaver 234).

225. Shenstone, William, *The Schoolmistress* [1742]
Suggested date of reading: by Feb. 1799
References: *EY* 255
Although W refers first to this poem in Feb. 1799, he surely read it before then. I suspect that he read it at Hawkshead, since it was a favourite children's anthology piece, and appeared in Knox's *Elegant Extracts* (see note 146). In the absence of further evidence, however, I find no alternative but to enter it under the terminal date of Feb. 1799. See also *Prose Works* iii 28, 76. Numerous editions of Shenstone's poetical works were published from 1764 onwards.

226. Sidney, Algernon, *Discourses Concerning Government, by Algernon Sidney, Son to Robert Earl of Leicester, and Ambassador from the Commonwealth of England to Charles Gustavus King of Sweden. Published from an Original Manuscript of the Author* [1698]
Suggested date of reading: 1789; by spring 1793
References: Hunt 46; *JEGP* 47 (1948) 107-26; *Prose Works* i 60; *EY* 125
Hunt 46 observes that W wrote Sidney's name in his copy of Smith's *Elegiac Sonnets* (5th edn, 1789), suggesting a Cambridge reading of the *Discourses*. W had read Sidney by spring 1793, since he is an influence on the *Letter to the Bishop of Llandaff*:

The office of king is a trial to which human virtue is not equal. Pure and universal representation, by which alone liberty can be secured, cannot, I think, exist together with monarchy. (*Prose Works* i 41)

Fink, 'Wordsworth and the English Republican Tradition', *JEGP* 47 (1948) 107-26, suggests that Sidney is W's source:

Man is of an aspiring nature, and apt to put too high a value upon himself; they who are raised above their Brethren, tho but a little, desire to go farther; and if they gain the name of King, they think themselves wronged and degraded, when they are not suffer'd to do what they please. (*Discourses Concerning Government* [1698], p. 148)

Chard suggests another quotation that may have been in W's mind: 'absolute power ... is a burden which no man can bear; and ... no wise or good man ever desired it' (Chard 90). W probably encountered the *Discourses* when discussing revolutionary politics with Beaupuy; Sidney was immensely important to the Girondins, and was on W's mind when planning *The Philanthropist* in June 1794 (*EY* 125).

A copy of the *Discourses* was in the Racedown Lodge library when W moved in, Aug. 1795; it was removed by John Pinney Sr on 15 June 1796 (Pinney Papers). Joseph Johnson reprinted the *Discourses* in 1795 - might he have been prompted to do so by W?

227. Sidney, Sir Philip, *Astrophil and Stella*
Suggested date of reading: by 1787
References: see note
The Vale of Esthwaite (1787) contains a highly poeticised description of the moon:

> The moon with wan and watery face
> Wades through the skies with heavy pace (*D.C.MS 3* 18r, De Selincourt 238-9)

This is a lightly reworked version of Sidney's famous lines from *Astrophil and Stella*, Sonnet 31, 1-2:

> With how sad steps, ô Moone, thou climb'st the skies,
> How silently, and with how wanne a face ...

In 1806 W began a sonnet of his own with Sidney's lines.

228. Smith, Charlotte
(i) *Elegiac Sonnets* (1784)
Suggested date of reading: 1784-7; by 1787
References: TWT 344
The *Elegiac Sonnets* were first published in 1784, and W is said to have read them at that time (TWT 344). He certainly knew them by the time he composed *The Vale of Esthwaite* (1787):

> Twas done. The scene of woe was oer
> *My breaking soul could bear no more* (*D.C.MS 3* 20r; De Selincourt 358-9)

The italicized line derived ultimately from Charlotte Smith's best-known sonnet, *To the South Downs* (1784):

> But can they peace to this sad breast restore,
> For one poor moment sooth the sense of pain,
> *And teach a breaking heart to throb no more*? (lines 6-8)

Helen Maria Williams had adapted it first for *An American Tale* (1786) - 'My panting soul can bear no more' (line 107), and then for *Peru*, when Aciloe exclaims, at the sight of her tortured father: '*My heart, my breaking heart can bear no more*' (v 148).

W remained fond of Smith's poems for the rest of his life, and as late as 1830 advised Alexander Dyce to include her in his *Specimens of British Poetesses* (*LY* ii 260).

(ii) *Elegiac Sonnets, and Other Essays* **(5th edn, 1789)**
Suggested date of reading: 1789 onwards
References: Hunt; *EY* 68n; Shaver 237
W's copy of Smith's *Elegiac Sonnets* (5th edn, 1789) is now at the Wordsworth Library. It is autographed, 'Wm Wordsworth St. John's', and farther down the page, 'To Dora Wordsworth from her affectionate Father Wm Wordsworth'. Overleaf there is a portion of an early autograph, 'W Wordsw[   ]': the pages of the book were cropped by about a third of an inch when the volume was rebound. To the list of subscribers whose names were 'received too late for insertion', W added:

W. Wordsworth   St John's
John Myers   Cambridge '89

John Myers was W's first cousin, the son of his father's sister Anne, and entered St John's with W in the autumn of 1787. 'We went to College together', W recalled, 'and were inseparables for many years' (*LY* i 3).

(iii) poems in MS
Suggested date of reading: late Nov. 1791
References: Hunt 51-2; Reed i 123n
On the rear flyleaf of his copy of *Elegiac Sonnets* (see preceding note), W copied two more of Smith's compositions, both of which were first published in her novel, *Celestina* (1791), and reprinted as XLIX and LI in *Elegiac Sonnets* (6th edn, 1792). These are in W's hand, in ink, and are preserved on a leaf not cropped during rebinding. W's copies vary from both texts as published. Hunt points out that

> These variations are enough to suggest the possibility that Wordsworth may have seen the two sonnets in manuscript (and in a version not yet corrected for publication in the collected edition of 1792) when he visited Charlotte Smith at Brighton in late November, 1791... In all probability, then, Charlotte Smith showed some of her uncollected or unpublished verse to her young admirer. This is what Wordsworth meant by saying that she had shown him 'every possible civility' [*EY* 68] during his visit. (Hunt 51-2)

See also Reed i 123 and n.

(iv) *The Emigrants* **(1792)**
Suggested date of reading: between May 1793 and April/May 1794
References: *WC* 1 (1970) 85-103
Hunt, 'Wordsworth and Charlotte Smith', *WC* 1 (1970) 85-103, proposes *The Emigrants* as a general influence on *Tintern Abbey*, and as a specific influence on *Inscription for a Seat by a Roadside* at Windy Brow, composed April/May 1794. The publication of *The Emigrants* was announced in the *Morning Chronicle* at the end of May 1793; given W's enthusiasm for Smith's earlier works, he may have sought it out shortly after.

229. Smollett, Tobias
(i) *Ode to Leven-water*
Suggested date of reading: Dec. 1791-2
References: Cornell *DS* 90
The *Ode* was published in Knox's *Elegant Extracts*, which W may have read at Hawkshead.

(ii) *Humphry Clinker*
Suggested date of reading: by Feb. 1798
References: see note
The editors of the Longman *Wordsworth* suggest that W's Discharged Soldier (described in verse dating from Feb. 1798) is modelled on Lieutenant Lismahago in Smollett's *Humphry Clinker*, mentioned in Melford's letter of 10 July 1771 (p. 188).

230. Sophocles, *Oedipus at Colonus*
Suggested date of reading: by Dec. 1788
References: Schneider 95-6
W was examined on Sophocles at St John's in Dec. 1788 and, according to the report, 'had considerable merit'. Schneider interprets this to indicate that he 'must have read Sophocles' *Oedipus Coloneus*' (Schneider 95). I would add only that it raises the possibility of his having also read *Oedipus Rex*.

Yarnall reports that in 1849 W 'spoke with great animation of the importance of the study of the classics - Greek especially. "Where," said he, "would one look for a greater orator than Demosthenes, or finer dramatic poetry, next to Shakespeare, than that of Æschylus and Sophocles, not to speak of Euripides?"' (*Wordsworth and the Coleridges* [New York, 1899], p. 38). There was a copy of Sophocles at the Rydal Mount library (Shaver 240).

231. Southey, Robert, see also Coleridge, Samuel Taylor
(i) *Joan of Arc* in MS or proof
Suggested date of reading: 18 Aug.-26 Sept. 1795; by 26 Sept. 1795
References: EY 153
Southey, W told Mathews in Oct. 1795, 'is about publishing an epic poem on the subject of the Maid of orleans. From the specimens I have seen I am inclined to think it will have many beauties' (*EY* 153-4). W would have seen *Joan of Arc* in proof or in MS during his stay in Bristol, 18 Aug.-26 Sept. 1795 (Reed i 167).

(ii) *Joan of Arc* (Bristol, 1796)
Suggested date of reading: Jan.-March 1796
References: EY 153; Shaver 242; Reed i 177
Joan of Arc was printed 21 Nov. 1795 and published in Bristol *c.* 1 Dec.; it was available in London by 23 Dec. Writing from Racedown in Jan. 1796, W thanked Cottle for 'the highly acceptable present of Southey's Joan of Arc, with which you honoured me by the hands of Mr Pinney' (*EY* 163). Azariah Pinney brought a number of other books for the Wordsworths when he visited Racedown in Jan. 1796. W's reading of *Joan of Arc* changed his opinion of Southey both as a man and a poet; in March 1796 he told Mathews: 'You were right about Southey, he is certainly a coxcomb,[1] and has proved it completely by the preface to *his Joan of Arc*, an *epic* poem which he has just published. This preface is indeed a very conceited performance and the poem though in some passages of first-rate excellence is on the whole of very inferior execution' (*EY* 169; his italics).

W's copy is now lost; that in the Wordsworth Library belonged to James Dykes Campbell, and contains copies of C's annotations made by Campbell from C's copy, also now lost.

---

[1] W refers to Mathews' earlier remark to this effect, mentioned in W's letter of Oct. 1795, *EY* 154.

(iii) *Poems* (Bristol, 1797)
Suggested date of reading: by April 1797
References: Reed i 192n; Griggs vi 1009
W's criticism, reported by C to Cottle in April 1797, provides a date by which he can be assumed to have read Southey's *Poems*: 'Wordsworth complains with justice, that Southey writes *too much at his ease*' (Griggs vi 1009; his italics). This represents a development of his earlier judgment that Southey 'is certainly a coxcomb' (see preceding note).

(iv) *Joan of Arc* (Bristol, 1796)
Suggested date of reading: c. April 1797
References: see note
Thompson notes that the central story of *The Ruined Cottage* was drawn from Southey's *Joan of Arc*.[1] Butler adds that the lines in question (*Joan of Arc* vii 320-31) were excerpted in the first issue of *The Watchman*, which W probably read c. April 1796 (Cornell *RC* 5-6); see note 56 (iii), CC *Watchman* 45. W also owned a copy of *Joan of Arc* itself; see note (ii), above.

(v) *Hannah* in MS
Suggested date of reading: Sept. 1797
References: MH 63; Griggs i 345
Jonathan Wordsworth notes the similarities between *The Ruined Cottage* and *Hannah*, observing that 'Direct connection between the two poems is possible, but would be difficult to prove' (*MH* 63). *Hannah* was sent in MS to C before 15 Sept. 1797 (Griggs i 345), and may thus have been available to W. It was published in the *Monthly Magazine* 4 (1797) 287, Oct. 1797, and in the *Morning Chronicle*, 14 Nov. 1797; it is reprinted *MH* 63-4.

(vi) *To A. S. Cottle from Robert Southey*
Suggested date of reading: Nov./Dec. 1797
References: see note
Southey's verse epistle to Amos Cottle appeared at the front of Cottle's translation of the *Edda*, of which W owned a copy (see note 90), and was described by C as 'very [plea]sing' c. 20 Nov. 1797. The editors of the Longman *Wordsworth* find it echoed in W's poetry of Feb.-March 1798.

(vii) *Poems: The Second Volume* (Bristol, 1799)
Suggested date of reading: July 1799; by 27 July 1799
References: Butler *JEGP* 149
On 27 July 1799 W thanked Cottle for the book parcel sent earlier that month: 'We were much obliged to you for the Lyrical Ballads and Southey's second volume which we received safe' (Butler *JEGP* 149). 'Southey's second volume' refers to Southey, *Poems: The Second Volume* (1799), published by Cottle.

232. 'my Spanish Grammar'
Suggested date of reading: 1788-91
References: EY 52, 56

[1] 'Disenchantment or Default? A Lay Sermon', *Power and Consciousness* ed. Conor Cruise O'Brien and William Dean Vanech (1969), pp. 149-81, p. 151.

In June 1791, DW noted that W 'reads Italian, Spanish, French, Greek and Latin, and English' (*EY* 52). In Aug. that year W wrote to his Mathews from Plas-yn-llan, that 'I regret much not having brought my Spanish Grammar along with me' (*EY* 56). In fact, he seems to have stopped reading Spanish by Aug. 1791, and had not resumed by the time he wrote to Mathews on 17 Feb. 1794: 'Of Spanish I have read none these three years' (*EY* 112).

233. *The Spectator*
(i)
Suggested date of reading: 1773-6
References: Moorman 15
In her Memoranda of the Hutchinson and Monkhouse Families (1851), Mary Wordsworth recalled the books given her by her Aunt Gamage:

> Long before she died, she from dimness of sight, became unable to read even her Prayer book, the one so often referred to - it was therefore with other books she possessed, sent by herself to me among which were the Guardians, Tatlers & Spectators, 'Addison's Works,' as she used to call them, '& which would never be out of fashion'.
> The Spectators she used to lend us to take to School as being approved by our Dame, as a 'reading' book! What would our modern Teachers say, to the Spectator being used by Children under 8 years of age? - But this old Lady tho' no bad Teacher, was indifferent to method. (*D.C.MS 167* 36v; her underlining)

W too attended Ann Birkett's dame school at this time, and would also have read *The Spectator* at this period. The best account of the school is given by Moorman 15.

(ii)
Suggested date of reading: 1788-9
References: *Prose Works* iii 373
In later years, W recalled that under Agostino Isola 'I translated the Vision of Mirza, and two or three other papers of the Spectator, into Italian' (*Prose Works* iii 373).

(iii)
Suggested date of reading: spring 1793
References: *Prose Works* i 31, 50
W begins his *Letter to the Bishop of Llandaff* (1793):

> Alluding to our natural existence, Addison, in a sublime allegory well known to your Lordship, has represented us as crossing an immense bridge, from whose surface from a variety of causes we disappear one after another, and are seen no more.
> *(Prose Works* i 31)

As Owen and Smyser point out, W was recalling 'The first Vision of Mirzah', *Spectator* 159 (*Prose Works* i 50).

234. Spenser, Edmund
(i)
Suggested date of reading: 1774-9
References: *Memoirs* i 34

As Christopher Wordsworth Jr points out, three of the most important influences on W's writing were encountered during the pre-Hawkshead years: 'the Poet's father set him very early to learn portions of the works of the best English poets by heart, so that at an early age he could repeat large portions of Shakspeare, Milton, and Spenser' (*Memoirs* i 34). Spenser is a far more important influence on W's poetry than has hitherto been recognized, and it is possible here only to suggest the full extent of his significance.

(ii) *The Faerie Queene*
Suggested date of reading: 1787-90
References: Cornell *EW* 68; *Thirteen-Book Prelude* iii 279-82
W thought highly of Una's story in *Faerie Queene* Book I (see *Thirteen-Book Prelude* ix 459-64 and the Dedication to *The White Doe of Rylstone*). He also admired Book II Canto xii, and Book VI.

(iii) *The Faerie Queene*
Suggested date of reading: July-Sept. 1793
References: Cornell *SP* 23

(iv) *The Faerie Queene*
Suggested date of reading: Sept.-Nov. 1795
References: Cornell *SP* 149

235. Statius, *Silvae*
Suggested date of reading: 1787
References: Landon 28-9
Landon observes that on the inside front cover of W's fair copy notebook *D.C.MS 2*, in use during his last year at Hawkshead and first year at Cambridge, 1787-8, he has copied the motto: 'Amantes carmina somnos'. The ink and hand suggest a dating of 1787. Landon traces the motto to *Silvae* I iii 23, where Statius describes the River Anio passing the villa of Manilius Vopiscus:

> ipse Anien - miranda fides - infraque superque
> saxeus his tumidam rabiem spumosaque ponit
> murmura, ceu placidi veritus turbare Vopisci
> Pieriosque dies et *habentes carmina somnos* (lines 20-3)

236. Sterne, Lawrence
(i) *Tristram Shandy*
Suggested date of reading: 1787-91; by 3 Aug. 1791
References: *EY* 56
In his letter to Mathews of 3 Aug. 1791, W somewhat effacingly claims only to have read 'in our language three volumes of *Tristram Shandy*, and two or three papers of the *Spectator*' (*EY* 56). He probably encountered Sterne's novel at Hawkshead, but this is his earliest mention of it.

(ii) *Tristram Shandy*
Suggested date of reading: Feb. 1796
References: *EY* 166

In March 1796, DW wrote that 'Within the last month I have read Tristram Shandy' (*EY* 166). I presume that W shared his sister's delight at this classic novel, and took the opportunity of her reading to reacquaint himself with it.

237. Stobaeus, Johannes, *Sententiae*
Suggested date of reading: Feb. 1796
References: BRH 87 (1986-87) 482-8
Curtis, 'Wordsworth, Coleridge, and *Lines, left upon a Seat in a Yew-tree*', *BRH* 87 (1986-87) 482-8, observes that 'On folio 8r of MS.11 the name "Johannes Stobæus," in Coleridge's hand, appears in the midst of draft for *The Ruined Cottage...* Its situation on the page suggests that Coleridge jotted the name down first; the draft for *The Ruined Cottage* was later entered around it by Dorothy Wordsworth' (p. 483). He suggests that 'the most likely time' for the jotting is the period of Coleridge's visit to Racedown in June 1797, and adds:

> Coleridge used a passage from the *Sententiae* by this fifth-century Christian writer (John of Stobi) as the Greek epigraph for an essay 'On the Communication of Truth' [CC *Friend* i 44]. But he knew of Stobaeus in 1796 and had read the *Sententiae* by December or January 1800-1801. The presence of the name in Coleridge's hand in the very notebook Wordsworth was using for drafts of *Lines* strongly suggests that they discussed Stobaeus while Wordsworth was working on his portrait of the 'lost man' ...
> (p. 485)

Curtis relates Stobaeus to the *Lines Left upon a Seat in a Yew-tree* and *The Borderers*, and provides facsimiles of the MS.

238. Swift, Jonathan
(i) *The Works*, inc. *Gulliver's Travels* and *Tale of a Tub*
Suggested date of reading: 1779-Dec. 1783; by Dec. 1783
References: *Prose Works* iii 372; Wu *Library* JW34
Towards the end of his life, W recalled that during his 'earliest days at school' he read 'any part of Swift that I liked; Gulliver's Travels, and the Tale of the Tub, being both much to my taste' (*Prose Works* iii 372). A set of Swift's works was presumably in his father's library at Cockermouth, and W would have read them before his father's death in Dec. 1783.

This may have been the edition of thirteen volumes (Edinburgh, 1768), retained at Rydal Mount (Shaver 250). By 1829 Vol. 1 of the set was missing; still minus its first volume, the set was sold in 1859 to William Wordsworth Jr. The present whereabouts of Vol. 5 only is known: it is in the George A. Aitken Collection at the University of Texas, Austin (Park 52).

(ii) *Letters, Written by the Late Jonathan Swift, D.D. Dean of St. Patrick's, Dublin, and Several of his Friends. From the Year 1703 to 1740. Published from the Originals; with Notes Explanatory and Historical, by John Hawkesworth, L.L.D.* (3 vols., 1766)
Suggested date of reading: Oct.-Dec. 1792
References: Cornell *DS* 112
'The river Loiret', W tells us in his annotation to *Descriptive Sketches* 760, 'rises out of the earth at a place, called La Source':

> The walks of La Source, where it takes its rise, may, in the eyes of some people, derive an additional interest from the recollection that they were the retreat of Bolingbroke

during his exile, and that here it was that his philosophical works were chiefly composed. The inscriptions, of which he speaks in one of his letters to Swift descriptive of this spot, are not, I believe, now extant. (Cornell *DS* 112)

The letter W has in mind appears in *Letters, Written by the Late Jonathan Swift, D.D. Dean of St. Patrick's, Dublin, and Several of his Friends. From the Year 1703 to 1740. Published from the Originals; with Notes Explanatory and Historical, by John Hawkesworth, L.L.D.* (3 vols., 1766), ii 229. Further details may be found in my article, 'Wordsworth's Reading of Swift's Letters', *N&Q* NS 39 (1992) 161-2. Moorman and Reed suggest that W visited La Source in Oct. 1792 (Moorman 201; Reed i 136); the lines describing his visit, and the annotation to them, must therefore have been composed between then and Dec., when W prepared his fair copy of *Descriptive Sketches* for publication in Jan. 1793.

239. Tasso

(i) *Gerusalemme Liberata*
Suggested date of reading: 1788-9; by July 1788
References: Schneider 103; Cornell *EW* 46
Agostino Isola, W's Italian tutor at Cambridge, edited Ariosto (1789) and Tasso (1786), and under his tutelage W would have read both. In my article, 'Tasso, Wordsworth, and the Fragmentary Drafts of 1788', *N&Q* NS 37 (1990) 409-11, I demonstrate Tasso's influence on a series of MS drafts described by Reed as the 'heroic fragments'. These were probably composed during the summer of 1788 which W spent in Hawkshead, and reflect the influence of *Jerusalem Delivered*, which he is likely to have read both in the original and in Hoole's translation. They also provide a terminal date for a first reading of Tasso, which W probably studied alongside Hoole's translation. The copy of Hoole which he donated to the Hawkshead School Library a year before would have been available to him in 1788 (TWT 353-4).

W's allusion to Tasso in *An Evening Walk* (Cornell *EW* 46) confirms a 1789 reading. The copy of Isola's edition of Tasso (2 vols., Cambridge, 1786) with 'MS. Notes by Mr. Wordsworth' (Park 69) retained at Rydal Mount may have been in use during W's Cambridge years.

(ii) *Jerusalem Delivered* tr. John Hoole
Suggested date of reading: 1788-9
References: TWT 144-5, 353-4; Reed i 72
Agostino Isola apparently encouraged his students to study *Gerusalemme Liberata* alongside Hoole's translation, for W gave a copy to Hawkshead Grammar School Library in 1789. For further discussion of Hoole's influence on W's poetry during the Cambridge years, see my article, 'Tasso, Wordsworth, and the Fragmentary Drafts of 1788', *N&Q* NS 37 (1990) 409-11.

(iii) *Gerusalemme Liberata*
Suggested date of reading: summer 1794 (from the end of May onwards)
References: EY 121n
W left a number of books with his brother Richard at Staple Inn, London, in 1793. These included copies of Tasso, Ariosto, and an 'Italian Gram.' (*EY* 121n). Richard forwarded these to W in late May 1794, and W would presumably have received them by the end of the

month. W apparently taught DW Italian during the summer of 1794, and they were probably required for this purpose. It is likely that their reading of Tasso was conducted with a copy of Hoole's translation, and that it extended into their residence at Racedown Lodge.

240. Thelwall, John
(i) *The Rights of Nature against the Usurpation of Establishments: a Series of Letters on the Recent Effusions of the Right Hon. Edmund Burke* (1796)
Suggested date of reading: April 1797; by July 1797
References: Roe 240
Losh sent two parcels of books to W at Racedown. He listed the contents of the first in his diary, 20 March 1797, but not those of the second, sent 14 April 1797. Roe conjectures that Thelwall's *Rights of Nature* was in the second parcel:

> These pamphlets [in the first parcel] most likely belonged to Losh himself, for he noted that he had read them all in his diary during the previous year. The following month he dispatched 'another large parcel of pamphlets' to Racedown, but did not list the contents in his diary. To judge by his previous reading of pamphlets not included in his first parcel, it might have comprised a pamphlet by Thomas Beddoes, Helen Williams' *Letters from France*, copies of the *Watchman*, and John Thelwall's *Rights of Nature*, all of which Losh had recently read at Bath. (Roe 240)

In correspondence with me, Roe insists: 'I am sure Wordsworth read Thelwall's *Rights* about this time - and Coleridge did too'. In fact, C's reading can be confirmed: on 22 June 1796, C told Thelwall that 'Your answer to Burke is, I will not say, the best - for that would be no praise - it is certainly the only good one; & it is a very good one. In style, and *in reflectiveness* it is, I think, your chef d'œuvre' (Griggs i 221; his italics). By the time Thelwall visited Alfoxden and Nether Stowey in July 1797, W must also have known the *Rights*.

(ii) *The Peripatetic* (1793)
Suggested date of reading: 1797-8
References: see note
In his diary for 12 Feb. 1815, Henry Crabb Robinson records a visit to Thelwall, who 'talked of "The Excursion" as containing finer verses than there are in Milton, and as being in versification most admirable; but then Wordsworth borrows without acknowledgement from Thelwall himself!!' (Sadler i 473). Crabb Robinson refers, among other things, to the subtitle of Thelwall's book, *Sketches of the Heart, of Nature and Society; in a Series of Politico-sentimental Journals, in Verse and Prose, of the Eccentric Excursions of Sylvanus Theophrastus* which, as Lyon says, 'suggests both the title of *The Excursion* and Wordsworth's description of the subject matter of *The Recluse*, "Man, Nature and Society"'[1] (Lyon 36). Finch has discussed the importance of *The Peripatetic* to the conception of *The Recluse* in 1798: 'Behind *The Recluse* stand Thelwall's *The Peripatetic* ... and Coleridge's 1797 idea for "The Brook"'.[2] Lyon points to some of the similarities between Thelwall's work and *The Excursion*; both contain characters called The Wanderer,

---
[1] W's proposed title on 11 March 1798 was *The Recluse or Views of Nature, Man, and Society* (*EY* 214).
[2] 'Wordsworth, Coleridge, and The Recluse, 1798-1814' (Ph.D. thesis, 1964), p. 65.

Both works present philosophical and social views through dialogue; both show great interest in local topography... *The Peripatetic* has a passage on the observation of regular living habits as a key to health, much as *The Excursion* does. There is a long passage on the advantages and disadvantages of commerce in *The Peripatetic*, just as in *The Excursion*. There is also a strikingly similar graveyard scene in *The Peripatetic*, in which the characters moralize over selected graves somewhat as they do in *The Excursion*, Books VI and VII. (Lyon 36)

Thelwall's copy of *The Excursion* is now in a private collection, and contains annotations by him.

W was probably introduced to *The Peripatetic* by C, who told its author in June 1796 that it 'let me into *your heart*' (Griggs i 221; his italics). He probably read C's copy, which had entered the Rydal Mount library by 1829 (Shaver 356).

241. Theocritus
(i) *Idyllia*
Suggested date of reading: by 1785
References: see note
W's earliest extant poem, *Lines Written as a School Exercise* (1785), borrows a line from Theocritus: 'Hush'd are the winds, and silent are the tides' (line 38). Broughton points out that it derives from *Idyllium* ii 38: 'Lo, silent is the deep, and silent the winds'.[1] See *Thirteen-Book Prelude* x 1015-27.

(ii) *Epigram* XIX
Suggested date of reading: between 6 Oct. 1798 and 23 Feb. 1799
References: *TLS* (11 Sept. 1937) 656; *PW* iv 414; Mason *LB* 318
Casson, 'Wordsworth and Theocritus', *TLS* (11 Sept. 1937) 656, was the first to notice the 'remarkable parallel' between Theocritus *Epigram* xix and *A Poet's Epitaph*, composed between 6 Oct. 1798 and 23 Feb. 1799. It is likely that W had a copy of Theocritus with him in Germany, for he mentions him in his letter to C of 27 Feb. 1799 (*EY* 255).

242. Thomson, James
(i) *The Seasons*
Suggested date of reading: 1779-87; by Aug. 1786
References: Schneider 82; Shaver 257
The rhetorical tradition in which W was educated, running through Richard Bentley, William Bennett, and William Taylor, held Thomson in high esteem. The unsigned 'Memoir of William Wordsworth, Esq.', *New Monthly Magazine* 11 (1819) 48-50,[2] recalls that,

Before the morning hour of repairing to school, he has been often seen and heard in the sequestered lane, either alone, or with a favourite companion, repeating aloud beautiful passages from Thomson's Seasons, and sometimes comparing, as they chanced to occur, the actual phenomena of nature with the descriptions given of them by the poet. (p. 48)

[1] *The Theocritean Element in the Works of William Wordsworth* (Halle, 1920), p. 158.
[2] The principal informant for the memoir was Mr Richard Scambler, the apothecary from Ambleside who attended the Wordsworth children.

Thomson is an important influence on W's *Lines Written as a School Exercise* (1785), which draws on *The Seasons* and *Liberty*. For instance, within W's poem, enlightenment is dependent on the Dissolution of the Monasteries: 'No jarring Monks to gloomy cell confin'd' (line 49). This is almost certainly a recollection of Thomson's praise of Bacon:

> The great Deliverer he! who from the Gloom
> Of cloister'd Monks, and Jargon-teaching Schools,
> Led forth the true Philosophy ... (*Summer* 1543-5)

In *Liberty*, Thomson is more specific in his criticism of monkishness; there, they are responsible for weakening the Saxon warrior:

> But Superstition first, and Monkish Dreams,
> And Monk-directed Cloyster-seeking Kings,
> Had eat away his Vigour ... (iv 726-8)

W's stylistic model may be Pope, but the Thomson of *Summer* is closest to him in thought. The celebration of enlightenment thought at *Summer* 1531-63 - beginning with Bacon, continuing with Shaftesbury, Boyle and Locke, and culminating with Newton - provides a model for W. For more on this, see Wu D.Phil. 2-4. Numerous borrowings from Thomson can be found in subsequent works of the 1780s and 1790s.

(ii) poems
Suggested date of reading: 1787-9
References: Cornell *EW* 52; Sheats 51-4
Thomson was a crucial influence on W's poetry leading up to *An Evening Walk*. In a sonnet of 1789, *'When slow from pensive twilight's latest gleams'*,[1] W describes how 'vanish'd woods a lulling murmur make' (line 5), borrowing the phrasing of Thomson's *Castle of Indolence*:

> Mean time unnumber'd glittering Streamlets play'd,
> And hurled every-where their Waters sheen;
> That, as they bicker'd through the sunny Glade,
> Though restless still themselves, *a lulling Murmur made*. (i 24-7)

(iii) *Castle of Indolence*
Suggested date of reading: between 6 Oct. 1798 and 23 Feb. 1799
References: Mason *LB* 319

243. Tickell, Thomas, *Colin and Lucy*
Suggested date of reading: by 1787
References: Jacobus 214
Jacobus 214 points out that W's *'Ballad* of 1787 is simply an adaptation of the tales of broken vows told by Mallet and Tickell', and quotes the third stanza of Tickell's *Colin and Lucy* to show how he reworked 'the gothic portents of Tickell's ballad'. Other traces of Tickell's influence can be found in *A Ballad*. The virgins who visit Mary after her death ('Her knell was rung - the Virgins came / And kissed her in her shroud', lines 57-8) derive

---

[1] The sonnet is published in my article, 'Wordsworth's Reading of Bowles', *N&Q* NS 36 (1989) 166-7.

from Tickell's *Colin and Lucy*, where the dying Lucy 'bespoke / The virgins weeping round' with warnings (lines 23-4). W's *Dirge Sung by a Minstrel* (1788) also shows Tickell's influence:

> For nine times the death-bell's Sprite
> Sullen for the Virgin cried ... (lines 5-6)

Compare Tickell, *Colin and Lucy* 17-18:

> Three times all in the dead of night
> A bell was heard to ring ...

In July 1831 W described Tickell as 'one of the best of our minor Poets' (*LY* ii 414).

244. Tooke, John Horne, *Diversions of Purley* [1786]
Suggested date of reading: Aug. 1798; by 14 Sept. 1798
References: BL Add.MS 35,343
When they arrived in London, Aug. 1798, prior to their German trip, W and C met with Joseph Johnson, and through him caught up with several books they had not yet encountered. Some of these were sent to Thomas Poole, as his letter to C of 24 Jan. 1799, proves:

> We rec[d] from Johnson, six copies of the poems - the account of Paraguay and the essay on population - but *not* the diversions of Purley - every one admires the poems and I am told they are much admired in London. (BL Add.MS 35,343; his italics)

Horne Tooke's *Diversions of Purley* had been published as long ago as 1786, and C first read it in Jan. 1792, when he borrowed it from the library of Jesus College, Cambridge.[1] Perhaps the copy acquired in London was intended for W. For W's disapproval of Tooke's conduct during the treason trials of 1794, see *EY* 137. Like W, Tooke was an alumnus of St John's, Cambridge.

245. *The Town and Country Magazine; or Universal Repository of Knowledge, Instruction, and Entertainment*
Suggested date of reading: 12 Feb. 1796 onwards
References: Pinney Papers, Account Book 1687
W borrowed *Town and Country* from Joseph Gill, the caretaker at Racedown Lodge. Gill's diary mentions a 'hoard of Newspapers' perhaps left by earlier occupants, and on 12 Feb. 1796, he reports that '[John] F[rederick Pinney] had a great part of my hoard of Newspapers to pack up his picture of Leda Naked[2] for Bristol & my Town & Country Magazines for Mr Wordsworth &c Amusement' (Pinney Papers, Account Book 1687). W and DW borrowed Gill's copies of *Town and Country* on 12 Feb. 1796; the phrase, '&c', suggests that the Wordsworths and Pinneys were reading to each other.

---

[1] Mays, 'Coleridge's Borrowings From Jesus College Library, 1791-94', *Transactions of the Cambridge Bibliographical Society* 8 (1981-5) 557-81, p. 567.
[2] This painting, a family heirloom, may have shown Leda bathing in the River Eurotas, watched by Jupiter. Evans and Pinney, 'Racedown and the Wordsworths', *RES* 8 (1932) 1-18, suggest: 'Perhaps Dorothy did not approve of it' (p. 17).

Town and Country was founded in Jan. 1769 and folded in Aug. 1795; it was a periodical miscellany containing extracts from travel books, original articles, poems, and letters. Among its contributors it could boast Chatterton and Holcroft. In 1793 it carried an extract from Wollstonecraft's *Vindication of the Rights of Woman*.

246. Trenchard, John and Thomas Gordon, *Cato's Letters*

Suggested date of reading: by summer 1795
References: EY 154

W's letter to Mathews of Oct. 1795 (*EY* 154) shows that he owned a copy of *Cato's Letters* during his stay in London that summer, and left it with him on his departure for Racedown. In Oct. 1795 he swapped it for Mathews' copy of Bell's *Classical Arrangement of Fugitive Poetry*. His reference to 'my edition of Cato's Letters' (*EY* 154) suggests that it was either the 1724 reprint of the 2nd edn, which was the first to go under the title *Cato's Letters*, or one published subsequently. His willingness to part with it may owe something to the fact that there was another on the shelves of the Racedown Lodge library - a fact he did not reveal to Mathews.

I suspect that Trenchard and Gordon informed the thinking behind *The Borderers*; in 'Considerations on the Weakness and Inconsistencies of human Nature', Cato writes that people

are naturally Innocent, yet fall naturally into the Practice of Vice; the greatest Instances of Virtue and Villainy are to be found in one and the same Person; and perhaps one and the same Motive produces both. The Observance or Non-observance of a few frivolous Customs, shall unite them in strict Friendship and Confederacy, or set them a cutting one another's Throats. (Letter 31, 27 May 1721; i 239)

The combination of virtue and villainy may also be found in Rivers and Mortimer, whose friendship indeed turns sour. Elsewhere, Cato writes 'Of the false Guises which Men put on, and their ill Effect':

The Affectation of Wisdom is a prevailing Folly in the World; Men fall naturally into the Practice of it ... when Men seek Credit this Way, in order to betray, and make use of their Grimaces as a Trap to deceive; when they turn their Admirers into Followers ... then appearing Wisdom becomes real Villainy, and these Pretenders grow dangerous Imposters. (Letter 46, 23 Sept. 1721; ii 92)

These remarks might well describe the behaviour of Rivers, as he persuades Mortimer to abandon Herbert on the heath.

For further discussion of Cato, see Robbins, *The Eighteenth-Century Commonwealthman* (Cambridge, Mass., 1959), pp. 115-25. C's interest in philosophy was aroused by a schoolboy reading of Cato (Orsini, *Coleridge and German Idealism* [Carbondale, 1969], p. 17).

247. Turgot, Anne Robert Jacques, *Réflexions sur la formation et la distribution des richesses*

Suggested date of reading: by spring 1794
References: EY 125

W was thinking of Turgot as he planned *The Philanthropist* in spring 1794, and probably encountered his work in France, where it was discussed among his Girondin friends. The

Réflexions were primarily an economic work, in which Turgot envisaged a moderation of taxation, so that landowners only would be taxed, and restrictions on commerce and industry abolished.

248. Vida, Marco Girolamo, *Poematum ... pars prima* ed. Thomas Tristram (Oxford, 1722)
Suggested date of reading: 1797
References: see note
The most important clue to this reading is the fact that there was a copy of Vida's *Poematum* in the Rydal Mount library which contained, according to the auction catalogue, 'Autographs of S. T. Coleridge and W.W.' (Park 70). This was probably the copy of Vida that C was reading in 1796: as H. J. Jackson observes, 'Coleridge refers familiarly to Vida (who is the same Marco Girolamo Vida mentioned by Kathleen Coburn in her note to *Notebooks* i 161) in 1796, if the review of *Musæ Etonenses* in *Critical Review* 18 (1796) 284-90 is his, as we believe it to be. (Charles Lamb thought so too.)' (letter to me). The reviewer of *Musæ Etonenses* (1795) points out that 'The works of Lucan, Statius, and Claudian, more frequently than those of Vida or Fracastorius, exhibit words, and combinations of words, unauthorised by the writers of the Augustan age' (*Critical Review* 18 [1796] 285). Jackson adds that there are poems by Vida in C's copy of *Carmina illustrium poetarum italorum* (Florence, 1719-26), referred to *Notebooks* ii 2590 (see also CC *Marginalia* ii 7-10).

Given C's evident interest in this writer in 1796, and the fact that he introduced W to Johannes Stobaeus in 1797 (see note 237), it is possible that he also introduced W to the works of Vida.

249. Virgilius Maro, Publius
(i) *Works*
Suggested date of reading: 1779-87; certainly by 1786
References: PW iv 422; Schneider 68
'My acquaintance with Virgil ... is intimate', wrote W in 1822 (*LY* i 125) - no idle boast. Virgil was one of the authors he read most while at Hawkshead, and numerous allusions to his works can be found in W's juvenilia. Here are a few examples.

On the inside front cover of *D.C.MS 2*, in use during 1786-7, a faint pencil inscription survives from *c.* 1786: 'Non hoc ista sibi tempus spectacula', from Virgil, *Aeneid* vi 37. In *The Death of the Starling* several pages later, we find the epigraph, 'Sunt lacrimae rerum' (*D.C.MS 2* 10r) from *Aeneid* i 462. *Death: A Dirge*, one of the drafts of *Dirge Sung by a Minstrel* composed in Jan. 1788 (*D.C.MS 2* 29v-31v), has two epigraphs from the *Aeneid*: 'In æternam clauduntur lumina noctem' (*Aeneid* x 746) and 'Nos flendo ducimus horas' (*Aeneid* vi 539).

The Hawkshead School Library in 1788 contained De La Cerda's edition of Virgil, as well as John Ogilby's translation (Wu *CWAAS* 276-9).

(ii) *Virgil's Aeneid* tr. Christopher Pitt (1736)
Suggested date of reading: 1784
References: see note
W's copy of this volume is now in the possession of Paul F. Betz. The verso of the first flyleaf bears the inscription, 'J Wordsworth 1784'; the recto of the second flyleaf bears the

inscriptions, 'Rd & Wm Wordsworth 1784' and, beneath it, 'John Wordsworth's Book 1787'. Pitt's translation may have been in W's mind in 1804 during work on the *Thirteen-Book Prelude*; see Trott and Wu, 'Three Sources for Wordsworth's *Prelude* Cave', *N&Q* NS 38 (1991) 298-9.

(iii) *Works* tr. John Dryden
Suggested date of reading: by 1787
References: see note
The central episode of *The Vale of Esthwaite* (1787), in which W is led beneath Helvellyn by a spectre-guide, parallels Aeneas' meeting in hell with his father, Anchises, in *Aeneid* VI, and contains an echo of Dryden's translation of Orpheus' underworld journey:

> Now as we wandered through the gloom
> In black Helvellyn's inmost *womb* (*D.C.MS 3* 20r; De Selincourt 350-1)

The powerful image of the mountain's 'womb' echoes Dryden's translation of the *Georgics*:

> Within a Mountain's hollow *Womb*, there lies
> A large Recess, conceal'd from Human Eyes ... (iv 603-4)

It is extremely likely that W read Dryden's Virgil before 1787.

(iv) *The Georgics*
Suggested date of reading: summer 1788-spring 1789
References: *N&Q* NS 37 (1990) 407-9; Schneider 165-6; Reed i 81
Scholars and critics have for some time been aware that, as a student at Cambridge, W made a number of translations from Virgil's *Georgics*. A full account of these is presented in my article, 'Three Translations of Virgil Read by Wordsworth in 1788', *N&Q* NS 37 (1990) 407-9. The surviving manuscripts indicate that the translations were made in summer 1788 and spring 1789.

(v) *The Georgics* tr. John Dryden
Suggested date of reading: summer 1788-spring 1789
References: *N&Q* NS 37 (1990) 407-9
For his translations of Virgil in summer 1788 and spring 1789, W drew on those by Dryden. Further details may be found in my article, 'Three Translations of Virgil Read by Wordsworth in 1788', *N&Q* NS 37 (1990) 407-9.

(vi) *The Georgics* tr. John Martyn
Suggested date of reading: summer 1788-spring 1789
References: *N&Q* NS 37 (1990) 407-9
For his translations of Virgil in summer 1788 and spring 1789, W drew on those by Martyn. Further details may be found in my article, 'Three Translations of Virgil Read by Wordsworth in 1788', *N&Q* NS 37 (1990) 407-9.

(vii) *The Georgics* tr. Joseph Warton
Suggested date of reading: summer 1788-spring 1789
References: *N&Q* NS 37 (1990) 407-9

For his translations of Virgil in summer 1788 and spring 1789, W drew on that by Warton. Further details may be found in my article, 'Three Translations of Virgil Read by Wordsworth in 1788', *N&Q* NS 37 (1990) 407-9.

(viii) *The Georgics*
Suggested date of reading: Dec. 1791-2
References: Cornell *DS* 100; Sheats 73
'Soon flies the little joy to man allow'd', *Descriptive Sketches* 636, is footnoted: 'Optima quæque dies, &c.' The reference is to Virgil, *Georgics* iii 66-8, which W translated in spring 1789 while working on *An Evening Walk*.

(ix) *The Aeneid*
Suggested date of reading: spring 1793
References: *Prose Works* i 64
Virgil was an influence on *A Letter to the Bishop of Llandaff*, composed spring 1793.

(x) works inc. *The Aeneid*
Suggested date of reading: 1796
References: Cornell *B* 86n

(xi) works inc. *The Aeneid*
Suggested date of reading: July 1798
References: Mason *LB* 212

250. Voltaire, François-Marie Arouet de, *Candide, ou l'optimisme* **[1759]**
Suggested date of reading: Dec. 1791-2
References: *Excursion* ii 484
In *The Excursion* W described *Candide* as 'this dull product of a scoffer's pen' (ii 484), and it is likely that he first encountered it during his time in France. Most English radicals were reading Voltaire during the early 1790s: in Dec. 1792 Southey refers to 'the witty impiety of Voltaire' (Curry i 13), and in April 1794 C boasts to his brother that 'I could not read without some degree of pleasure the levities of Voltaire' (Griggs i 78). Cornwell suggests that C read Voltaire's *Philosophical Dictionary* at Christ's Hospital: 'Presumably he had this work in mind when he claimed that he had read all the arguments for atheism by the age of fifteen' (*Coleridge: Poet and Revolutionary 1772-1804* [1973], p. 8).

251. Voss, Johann Heinrich, *Luise* **[Königsburg, 1795]**
Suggested date of reading: Feb. 1799
References: Parrish 179-80
Parrish writes that W 'evidently knew nothing of Voss until 1799, when Coleridge, who had translated parts of *Luise* some three years earlier ... mentioned Voss in one of the letters from Germany. The catalogues of homely pleasures in *Luise* may have left some mark on *Michael*, and there were doubtless other German strains in Wordsworth's pastorals' (Parrish 179-80). C's letter mentioning Voss has not survived, and Parrish infers its contents from W's reply of 27 Feb. 1799, which admits that 'of Voss I knew nothing' (*EY* 255). It is likely that W sought out Voss' *Luise* shortly after 27 Feb., for he confirmed his 'liking' of the poem to Henry Crabb Robinson in 1834 (Morley i 447), and encouraged his son, William, to read it in June 1830 (Shaver 307). He might have read the review of it in the *Critical Review* 17

(1795) 520-4, which contains generous quotations from the poem, and which was known to Southey and William Taylor of Norwich (Robberds i 215). W may also have seen C's literal prose translation of *Luise* in MS, copied in C's letter to Thelwall of 17 Dec. 1796 (Griggs i 283-4n); on 26 Aug. 1802 C told Sotheby of his intention to translate 'Voss's Idills in English Hexameters', the only surviving fragment of which is published Griggs ii 856-7.

252. Walker, John, *The Universal Gazetteer* (1795)
Suggested date of reading: 1795 onwards
References: see note
W's copy is now in the possession of Paul F. Betz, who purchased it from Pickering & Chatto, 1970. The volume is in its original boards and carries its original backlabel on the spine, reading 'UNIVERSAL GAZETTEER'. The second freestanding flyleaf bears the inscription, 'Wm Wordsworth'. Next to it, W has practised part of his signature: 'rd rd rd rds'. This is not the signature of William Wordsworth Jr. The inability of the Shavers to identify this volume (see Shaver 262) stems from the absence of a title-page. The fact that the inscription appears on the flyleaf suggests that the volume had no title-page when W purchased it - it was probably second-hand. This is consistent with the fact that the text contains numerous alterations not by W.

253. Walpole, Horace, 4th Earl of Orford, *The Castle of Otranto* [1765]
Suggested date of reading: by 1787
References: see note
The Vale of Esthwaite contains an episode in which W envisages a Baron surrounded by ancient portraits. It recalls Walpole's *The Castle of Otranto*, where Manfred, Prince of Otranto, sees a portrait 'quit its pannel' in the form of a ghost, and make 'a sign to follow him' (p. 24):

> So in his hall in times of yore
> Alone a Baron wandering oer
> At midnight hour with melting gaze
> The holy forms of other days
> Ere while the softning portrait's eyes
> With answering sympathy and love
> Has seen slow creeping round the wall
> A gloom as black as funeral pall
> And a tall Ghost of ashy hue
> On every canvass met his view (*D.C.MS 3* 19r; De Selincourt 311-18)

254. Warner, Richard, *A Walk Through Wales, in August 1797* (Bath, 1798)
Suggested date of reading: spring 1798
References: *N&Q* NS 18 (1971) 366-9
Jacobus, '*Tintern Abbey* and Topographical Prose', *N&Q* NS 18 (1971) 366-9, points out that

> One can be almost certain that Wordsworth read Richard Warner's *Walk Through Wales, in August 1797* (1798). When he and Dorothy were in Bath during July, just before setting off on their Wye tour, they ate several meals in Warner's company, and they are likely to have seen his recently published book. (p. 368)

143

Warner's *Walk through Wales* was on the shelves of the Bristol Library Society by early 1798 (*BLS* 119).

255. Warton, Joseph, *Odes on Various Subjects* [1746]
Suggested date of reading: during the 1780s
References: TWT 344
Thomas Bowman Jr reports that through his father W became acquainted with the poetry of 'the two Wartons' (TWT 344) - by which he probably means Joseph and Thomas the younger. Some of the poems in this volume were not by Joseph Warton; see Fairer, 'The Poems of Thomas Warton the Elder?', *RES* 26 (1975) 287-300, 395-406.

256. Warton, Thomas, the younger, *Poems*
Suggested date of reading: during the 1780s; by summer 1788
References: TWT 344
See previous note. A Hawkshead draft made by W in a notebook passed on to his brother Christopher reads: 'His crest nodded dreadful on his head like an oak ... shook by the wind upon the top of Teneriff' (Fink 80).[1] W alludes not to *Paradise Lost* iv 987 (though Milton's lines may be in his mind), but to Thomas Warton's portrayal of Contemplation, 'Whose mansion is *upon the topmost rock / Of cloud-capt Teneriff* (*Pleasures of Melancholy* 2-3).

257. Watson, Richard, Bishop of Llandaff, *A Sermon Preached before the Stewards of the Westminster Dispensary at the Anniversary Meeting, in Charlotte-Street Chapel, April 1785. With an Appendix.* (1793)
Suggested date of reading: early Feb. 1793
References: Reed i 142; *Prose Works* i 19-21
'In January 1793 Richard Watson, Bishop of Llandaff, unknowingly furnished Wordsworth, who was now living in London, with an occasion for speaking out in defence of republicanism' (*Prose Works* i 19). The *Sermon* and its *Appendix* were published on 30 Jan. 1793, and W probably read it soon after; the *Appendix* is reprinted Grosart i 24-30.

258. Webb, Daniel, *Inquiry into the Beauties of Painting* (2nd edn, 1761)
Suggested date of reading: 1787-90
References: Butler *WC* 59; Park 59; Shaver 270
W's copy is in the Wells Wordsworth Collection, Swarthmore College. Butler *WC* 59 reports that it is signed 'Wordsworth St. John's' on the flyleaf, indicating that it was in use during W's Cambridge years.

259. *Weekly Entertainer; or, Agreeable and Instructive Repository* (Sherborne) (i) 1795-6
Suggested date of reading: 23 July 1796 onwards
References: Pinney Papers, Account Book 1687

---

[1] I have dated W's entries in this notebook to summer 1788; see 'Tasso, Wordsworth, and the Fragmentary Drafts of 1788', *N&Q* NS 37 (1990) 409-11.

On 23 July 1796, Gill recorded that W read *The Weekly Entertainer* for the first time, from Gill's 'hoard': 'Lent Mr Wordsworth 4 Sheets of gilt edge paper - & the Entertainers from my Newspapers' (Pinney Papers, Account Book 1687). Perhaps these were of a similar vintage to Gill's copies of *Town and Country*, dating from Aug. 1795 if not before. By Sept. 1796, when W was writing to the *Entertainer*, he was buying his own copies.

(ii) 26 Sept. 1796
Suggested date of reading: late Sept. / early Oct. 1796
References: EY 171; Cornell *B* 228
W read 'Christian's own Account of the Mutiny on Board his Majesty's Ship Bounty, commanded by Captain Bligh, of which he was the Ringleader' in *The Weekly Entertainer* 28 (26 Sept. 1796) 255-6, some time in Sept. or Oct. 1796.

(iii) 7 Nov. 1796
Suggested date of reading: Nov. 1796
References: EY 171; Cornell *B* 228
W's response to the bogus account of the mutiny on the Bounty (see preceding note) appeared in the *Weekly Entertainer* 28 (7 Nov. 1796) 377: 'I have the best authority for saying that this publication is spurious' (*EY* 171). The 'authority' was probably Edward Christian, Fletcher's brother, an old friend of the Wordsworth family (*EY* 52-3), and Headmaster of Hawkshead Grammar School, July 1781-July 1782, during W's time there.

Sanborn suggests that Rivers' account of the abandonment of his ship's Captain at *Borderers* IV ii 22ff. 'borrowed extensively from Edward Christian's portrayal of the mutiny', as published in his letter to the *Cumberland Pacquet* (20 Nov. 1792), and in the Appendix to the *Minutes of the Court-martial held at Portsmouth, August 12, 1792 on Ten Persons Charged with Mutiny on Board His Majesty's Ship the Bounty* (1794); see 'The Madness of Mutiny: Wordsworth, the *Bounty* and *The Borderers*' (*WC* 23 [1992] 35-42, p. 38), and Wilkinson, *The Wake of the Bounty* (1953), pp. 72-4. Wilkinson notes that W and Christian were distantly related (p. 14).

(iv) 21 Nov. 1796
Suggested date of reading: late Nov. 1796
References: Reed i 26
W can be expected to have read this issue of the Entertainer, since it contains his *Address to the Ocean*.

(v) 6 March 1797
Suggested date of reading: March 1797
References: Reed i 327n
At the rear of *D.C.MS 16*, 59v, DW copied several extracts from a poem entitled *Address to Silence* which appeared in the *Weekly Entertainer* 29 (6 March 1797) 199-200 under the initials 'W.C.' This author has yet to be identified. I present the transcription here as it appears in the notebook. Line 16 is echoed in W's *Ode: Intimations of Immortality*: 'Our *noisy years seem moments* in the being / Of the eternal Silence' (lines 158-9); and in 1828, it was echoed in the first draft (and in the published version) of *On the Power of Sound*:

> Oh silence! are Man's *noisy years*
> No more than moments of thy life? (*D.C.MS 131*)

145

DW was probably working under W's direction, and copied selectively from the *Weekly Entertainer* text. To indicate the extent of her omissions, line numbers are supplied in square brackets.

Passages taken from an address to Silence
published in the Weekly Entertainer

Round Iceland's coast, the frozen Sea it's base,
Its top the sky, lit by the polar star
Thy throne is fixed ---------   [5] [lines 15-17]

[Far, far remote from noise thy presence dwells *deleted*]
The sleeping infant and his mother's eye;
The smiling picture, and the breathless bust;   [lines 39-41]
The lonely tower upon a desart rock;
The shining valley, with the full orb'd moon,   [10]
Are thy delights: with them thou art well pleased,
With thee 'tis peace: peace now; peace evermore!

Eternity of calmness is thy joy
Immensity of space is thine [domain *deleted*] abode
The rolling planets own thy sacred power   [15]
Our noisy years are moments of thy life
Our little world is lost amid thy spheres
The harmony serene of mind is thine;
And human thought that wings its boundless way
From earth to heaven is led through air by thee &c.   [20] [lines 44-55]

Hush winds! be still: Cease flood thy tedious voice   [line 57]
Or I must leave you & with silence stray
To the deep forest, or the deeper graves
Where neither winds nor waves disturb repose   [lines 59-61]

260. West, Thomas
(i) *A Guide to the Lakes*
Suggested date of reading: by 1787
References: Cornell *EW* 80; Fink 121
The *Vale of Esthwaite* contains an episode in which W is led by a spectre-guide into a Virgilian underworld beneath Helvellyn; there he is granted a strange, and so far unexplained vision:

I saw the Ghosts and heard the yell
Of every Briton [   ] who fell,
When Edmund deaf to horror's cries
Trod out the cruel Brother's eyes. (*D.C.MS 3* 20r; De Selincourt 369-72)

This is not a confused recollection of *King Lear*; its source is West's *Guide*, which offers an admirable account of the topographical and historical background to Grasmere. The vale, says West, is

> guarded at the upper end by Helme-Crag, a broken pyramidal mountain that exhibits an immense mass of antediluvian ruins. After this, the road ascends Dunmail-raise, where lie the historical stones, that perpetuate the name and fall of the last King of Cumberland, defeated there by the Saxon monarch Edmund, who put out the eyes of the two sons of his adversary ... (p. 81)

West's *Guide* was frequently revised and augmented; for full details, see Bicknell 13.1-14.2. As a Hawkshead schoolboy, Christopher Wordsworth owned the 1789 edition (Fink 121).

(ii) *A Guide to the Lakes*
Suggested date of reading: 1789-90
References: Cornell *EW* 62, 80
West was an important source for *An Evening Walk*.

(iii) *A Guide to the Lakes*
Suggested date of reading: 1796
References: Cornell *B* 19

261. White, Gilbert, *The Natural History and Antiquities of Selborne, in the County of Southampton* **(1789)**
Suggested date of reading: 1789-90
References: *MY* i 270
In Oct. 1808, W wrote to Wrangham: 'I remember reading White's *Natural History and Antiquities of Selborn[e]* with great pleasure when a Boy at school' (*MY* i 270). However, W was in his final year at Cambridge when it was published in Dec. 1789. Nevertheless, as late as 1833 he clearly recalled the first edition: 'The Book, as originally published was in Quarto entitled Natural History and Antiquities of Selborne, but the antiquities being of less general interest have not in many Editions been Reprinted' (*LY* ii 622). W's accuracy here proves that he did read the first edition, probably shortly after publication, though this reading cannot have taken place while he was a schoolboy. Perhaps he purchased his copy during his visit to London in Dec. 1789,[1] and read it on a subsequent visit to Hawkshead.

W would have paid at least one guinea for this handsome quarto, though it was available from bookseller Benjamin White in three styles of binding at 21 shillings, 24 shillings, and 29 shillings.[2] In March 1809, W told Wrangham to 'procure a sight' of White's *Natural History* (*MY* i 313); 20 years later he gave a copy to William Wordsworth Jr (Shaver 308).

262. Wieland, Christoph Martin, *Oberon*
Suggested date of reading: Nov. 1797-8; certainly by Sept. 1798
References: *Prose Works* i 98; *EY* 255; Shaver 273

---

[1] Reed i 95. Mabey points out that, then as now, booksellers were mindful of seasonal variations in trade, and copies of the first edition were 'delivered well in time for Christmas' (*Gilbert White* [1986], p. 206).
[2] Martin, *A Bibliography of Gilbert White of Selborne* (1934), pp. 90-7.

W's conversations with Klopstock show that he was well acquainted with *Oberon* by Sept. 1798, and it is likely that he first encountered it through C. 'I am translating the Oberon of Wieland', C told Poole, 20 Nov. 1797 (Griggs i 357). Beyer, 'Coleridge's *Oberon* translation and *The Wanderings of Cain*', *N&Q* NS 3 (1956) 82-4, argues that Wieland inspired much of C's 1798 poetry; see also Beyer's *The Enchanted Forest* (New York, 1963). Before sailing for Germany, W may have seen Sotheby's translation of *Oberon*, published 11 May 1798.

Among those books of C's which entered W's library was one catalogued as 'Aristipp an Lais' which, the Shavers suggest, was *Aristipp und einige seiner Zeitgenossen*, a compilation from Wieland's works (Shaver 314); a copy of *Oberon* (Reuttlingen, 1791) was also at Rydal Mount (Shaver 273). For W's opinions on *Oberon*, see the third of 'Satyrane's Letters' in *Biographia Literaria* (CC *Biographia* ii 202-3).

263. Wilkinson, Joshua Lucock, journals in MS
Suggested date of reading: Dec. 1792
References: see note
W met, and probably lodged with, Wilkinson in late 1792-early 1793, while preparing *Descriptive Sketches* for publication. The two men were born in Cockermouth at roughly the same time - in fact, Wilkinson's paternal grandfather built the house in Cockermouth in which the Wordsworth family lived. During the 1790s, as he pursued a legal career, Wilkinson shared lodgings with W's brother, Richard, and it was there that W headed on his return from France in late 1792. In Sept., he told Richard that

I look forward to the time of seeing you Wilkinson and my other friends with pleasure. I am very happy you have got into Chambers, as I shall perhaps be obliged to stay a few weeks in town about my publication you will I hope with Wilkinson's permission find me a place for a bed. Give Wilkinson my best Complts I have apologies to make for not having written to him, as also to almost all my other friends. (*EY* 81)

Wilkinson had returned from his own Continental tour in Nov. 1791, and since his itinerary had been similar to that followed by W in summer 1790, the two men would have compared notes. In particular, they would have discussed recent events at the place that 'made so great an impression on [W's] mind' (*LY* i 176): the Grande Chartreuse. In *Descriptive Sketches*, W describes the monastery at the onset of revolution:

The cloister startles at the gleam of arms,
And Blasphemy the shuddering fane alarms ... (lines 60-1)

It is doubtful that W saw soldiers at the Chartreuse in 1790; the couplet alludes to an event described in Wilkinson's account of his 1790 tour, *The Wanderer* (1795), based on his journals which W probably read in MS. Wilkinson says that 'a guard of a serjeant, and twelve men' had recently been called in to protect the monastery against 'some ungodly peasants, who seditiously presumed that men were equal':

On one side of the holy building, the monk was offering up his fervent, and incessant prayers to heaven, with many a pious and devout ejaculation against the obstinate perverseness and irreligion of the times; on the other side the soldiers were playing at cards, cursing and swearing, by *Sacré Dieu*! at the holy fathers, who, passing from their prayers, condescended to utter *comment vous en vat?* upon the reprobate copartners of the sacred mansion. (*Wanderer* i 154; his italics).

The contrast of manners seems to have impressed W as he completed work on *Descriptive Sketches* in Dec. 1792, and the observation was duly worked into his final draft. Wilkinson returned the compliment by alluding to *Descriptive Sketches* in his own published volume.[1]

It is likely that W also saw Wilkinson's *Political Facts, Collected in a Tour, in the Month of August, September, and October, 1793, Along the Frontiers of France; with Reflexions on the Same* (1793), and his translation, *State of France, in May, 1794 by Le Comte de Montgaillard* (1794). The two friends remained in touch: Wilkinson witnessed the bond drawn up by Richard Wordsworth in Oct. 1794 to protect, against JW Sr's creditors, the £600 intended by Raisley Calvert for W. And DW's journal entry for 28 Dec. 1801 records: 'After Tea message came from Wilkinson who had passed us on the road inviting Wm to sup at the Oak - he went' (*Grasmere Journals* 53). Pamela Woof notes this as a reference to Joshua Lucock, then visiting Lorton Hall near Cockermouth to settle the affairs of his recently deceased mother.

264. Williams, Helen Maria
(i) *Poems, in Two Volumes* (2 vols., 1786)
Suggested date of reading: 1786-7
References: Reed i 71; *BWS* 368
Williams' collected poems were published in June 1786, and W's first published poem, the *Sonnet, on Seeing Miss Helen Maria Williams Weep at a Tale of Distress* (1786), indicates that he read them soon after publication. Averill remarks: 'Wordsworth's poem evidences a sensitive reading of Williams' *Poems*, and, however misplaced the fervor, his response takes the form of imitation of language and dramatic structure' (Averill 35). However, I find only one clear echo of Williams in the *Sonnet* itself:

> She wept. - Life's purple tide began to flow
> In languid streams through *every thrilling vein* ... (lines 1-2)

The italicized phrase echoes Williams' *Part of an Irregular Fragment* first published in *Poems, in Two Volumes*, where the ghost of Sir Thomas Overbury is 'convuls'd with pain / That writhes in *every swelling vein*' (lines 113-14).

There are a number of borrowings from Williams in *The Vale of Esthwaite* (1787). At one point W describes the fleece of sheep 'seen / Between the Boughs of *sombrous* green' (*D.C.MS 3* 6v; De Selincourt 69-70). Williams used the same word to describe the shade of the Peruvian foliage:

> Thro' the lone vale, or forest's *sombrous* shade
> A dreary solitude, the mourner stray'd ... (*Peru* vi 55-6)

See also *Evening Walk* 72.

---

[1] For further discussion, see my article, 'The Grande Chartreuse and the Development of Wordsworth's *Recluse*', *CLB* NS 71 (July 1990) 235-46. See also Shaver, 'Wordsworth's Vaudracour and Wilkinson's *Wanderer*', *RES* 12 (1961) 55-7. *The Wanderer* was one of the most popular of the Bristol Library Society's holdings during the mid-1790s.

(ii) *A Farewell, for Two Years, to England* **(1791)**
Suggested date of reading: by Dec. 1791
References: *EY* 69
On 19 Dec. 1791, W told his brother, Richard, that 'Mrs [Charlotte] Smith who was so good as to give me Letters for Paris furnished me with one for Miss Williams, an English Lady who resided here lately, but was gone before I arrived' (*EY* 69). Prior to his intended visit to Williams in Orléans in early Dec. 1792, W probably read her recent publications. See *EY* 69.

(iii) *Letters Written in France, in the Summer 1790* **(1790)**
Suggested date of reading: by Dec. 1791
References: *EY* 69
See preceding note.

(iv) *Letters Containing a Sketch of the Politics of France from the thirty-first of May 1793, till the twenty-eighth of July 1794* **(2 vols., 1795)**
Suggested date of reading: Jan. 1796 onwards
References: *EY* 166; Reed i 177
'Miss Williams's Letters I will bring when I go to Race-down, as I propose giving them a second reading', wrote Azariah Pinney to W in Nov. 1795 (Pinney Papers, Family Letter Book 13). This was presumably one of the 'french things' DW read at Racedown in Jan.-Feb. 1796 (*EY* 166), and was drawn on by W shortly after. Landon, 'Wordsworth's Racedown Period: Some Uncertainties Resolved', *BNYPL* 68 (1964) 100-9, notes that it contaïns the French original of W's translation, *The Hour-Bell Sounds* (composed 1796). Gill adds that 'In its issues of 21, 28 Sept. and 5 Oct. 1795 the *Weekly Entertainer* carried long extracts from Williams's *Letters* under the heading "Affecting Incidents in the Revolutionary Prisons of France"' (Gill 444n66). The *Letters* were published 11 July 1795; W's copy entered the Rydal Mount library (Shaver 273).

265. Wither, George, *Juvenilia* **[1622]**
Suggested date of reading: Dec. 1797-June 1798
References: see note
Wither's *The Shepherd's Hunting* (1615) is a continuation of *The Shepherd's Pipe* (1614) by William Browne (1591-?1643); its influence can be detected in *The Tables Turned* (composed May-June 1798):

> One impulse from a vernal wood
> May teach you more of man;
> Of moral evil and of good,
> Than all the sages can. (*The Tables Turned* 21-4)

Stein points out that these lines are 'a bold re-turning of Wither's claim for his poetic muse, asserted in context by the fortune-oppressed Philarete':

> By the murmure of a spring,
> Or the least boughes rusteling.
> By a Dazie whose leaves spred,
> Shut when Tytan goes to bed;

Or a shady bush or tree,
She could more infuse in mee,
Then all Natures beauties can,
In some other wiser man. (iv 371-8)

This is, I think, a genuine allusion, and the first indication of W's reading of Wither.
C introduced Lamb to Wither's poetry in 1796 (Marrs i 34-5),[1] and probably introduced W to it too. His letter to the *Morning Post* 9 Jan. 1798 (CC *Essays* iii 8) suggests that he and W were reading Wither around Dec. 1797/Jan. 1798. Significantly, the lines from *Eclogue 4* to which W alluded in 1798, provide the epigraph of *To a Daisy* ('In youth from rock to rock') when it appeared in *Poems* (1815), and were included in the Album W compiled for Lady Mary Lowther in 1819 (*Album* 38-41). As late as 1843, Henry Reed recorded W's respect for Wither's poetry.[2] W may at some point have read Lamb's essay *On the Poetical Works of George Wither* (1818).

For Wither's possible influence on the *Immortality Ode* see Stein 189. C's copy of Wither's *Juvenilia* (1622), which contained *The Shepherd's Hunting*, found its way into the Rydal Mount Library (Shaver 361-2; Coffman W123). Although the Shavers indicate that it contained Coleridge marginalia, H. J. Jackson, present editor of the CC *Marginalia*, tells me that she has 'no record of marginal notes, nor even of its having been a "marked" book signed by Coleridge; its present whereabouts is unknown, and it isn't on George Whalley's "Lost List" of books once referred to as having marginalia by Coleridge, but since lost' (letter to me).

266. Wolcot, John ('Peter Pindar'), works

Suggested date of reading: Feb.-Aug. 1795, certainly by 21 March 1796
References: EY 169
Writing to Mathews, 21 March 1796, W comments:

> I attempt to write satires! and in all satires whatever the authors may say there will be found a spice of malignity. Neither Juvenal or Horace were without it, and what shall we say of Boileau and Pope or the more redoubted Peter. (*EY* 169)

W had probably read Boileau and Peter Pindar by 1795 when he came to prepare for the Juvenalian imitation to be composed with Wrangham. It seems likely that he had encountered 'the more redoubted Peter' before that, though there is no proving it.

Peter Pindar was the creation of Dr John Wolcot (1738-1819), whose political satires achieved considerable popularity in the mid-1790s, especially when 'Bottomless Pitt' (as he called the Prime Minister) raised taxes to pay for the war at a time when the country was enduring bad harvests and severe inflation. By 1798 the Bristol Library Society contained seven titles by him, including his *Works* (4 vols., 1794-6).

---

[1] W. C. Hazlitt describes Lamb's copy of Wither (present whereabouts unknown) as follows: 'Wither (George). Poems. The Bristol reprint. 3 vols. Interleaved and bound in 2 vols, 4to., and filled with MSS. notes and criticisms by Lamb. This passed into the hands of Mr. A. C. Swinburne' (*The Lambs* [1897], p. 64). This was probably a copy of the unfinished Bristol edition of 1820, published by J. M. Gutch.

[2] *Wordsworth and Reed: The Poet's Correspondence with his American Editor: 1836-1850* ed. L. N. Broughton (Ithaca, N.Y., 1933), pp. 85, 96.

267. Wollstonecraft, Mary
(i) *A Vindication of the Rights of Men* **[1790]**
Suggested date of reading: spring 1791
References: see note
Roe points out to me that the *Vindication* was probably one of the 'master Pamphlets of the day' that W remembered having read in the *Thirteen-Book Prelude* ix 97. Wollstonecraft was the first to respond to Burke's criticism of the French Revolution and British radicalism in his *Reflections* (pub. 1 Nov. 1790), with the *Vindication* (pub. 29 Nov.). However, the most likely date of W's reading is spring 1791; the *Vindication* was published by Joseph Johnson, who W probably knew by then.

(ii) *Letters Written During a Short Residence in Sweden, Norway, and Denmark* **(1796)**
Suggested date of reading: 1797-8; by 1797
References: see note
In his forthcoming article, 'Shelley, Spenser, Wordsworth, Wollstonecraft: The Instructed Imagination', Ian Reid suggests that 'the Wordsworth circle certainly knew' Wollstonecraft's *Letters Written During a Short Residence in Sweden, Norway, and Denmark* (1796). In Letter XVIII, Wollstonecraft recounts the story of Queen Matilda, sister of George III, who was married as a fifteen year-old to the cruel, unstable King Christian VII of Denmark. Matilda was outmanoeuvred by the Danish royal family, imprisoned, and died in her early twenties. Wollstonecraft saw the imbecilic puppet King Christian in 1795 and commented: 'What a farce is life! This effigy of majesty is allowed to *burn down to the socket*, whilst the hapless Matilda was hurried into an untimely grave' (p. 206). Reid suggests that W alluded to this story when, in *The Ruined Cottage* MS B, he wrote: 'Oh Sir! the good die first, / And they whose hearts are dry as summer dust / *Burn to the socket*' (lines 150-2).
The image in each case is of a candle burning down to the socket of a candlestick (the 'socket' being the hollow where the candle is placed); cf. Goldsmith's *Citizen of the World*, Letter xlvi: 'The candles were burnt to the socket, and the hour was five o'clock in the morning'.[1]
Wollstonecraft may have been in W's mind as he described the Sailor's ignominious end in *Adventures on Salisbury Plain*:

> They left him hung on high in iron case,
> And dissolute men, unthinking and untaught,
> Planted their festive booths beneath his face;
> And to that spot, which idle thousands sought,
> Women and children were by fathers brought ... (lines 820-4)

In Letter XIX Wollstonecraft describes her encounter with 'a crowd of people of every description', and being told that they have assembled to watch a man executed and his body burnt:

> I turned with disgust from the well-dressed women, who were returning with their children from this sight. What a spectacle for humanity! The seeing such a flock of idle gazers, plunged me into a train of reflections, on the pernicious effects produced by

---
[1] Goldsmith, *Collected Works* ed. Friedman (5 vols., Oxford, 1966), ii 196.

false notions of justice. And I am persuaded that till capital punishments be entirely abolished, executions ought to have every appearance of horrour given to them; instead of being, as they are now, a scene of amusement for the gaping crowd, where sympathy is quickly effaced by curiosity. (p. 207)

Like W, Wollstonecraft disapproves of the presence of women and children. Her distinctive phrase, 'idle gazers', is borrowed by W ('idle thousands', *Adventures* 823), and her attack on 'false notions of justice' is echoed in the penultimate stanza of *Adventures*, where W refers to 'Thou who of Justice bear'st the violated name!' (line 819).

Reid points out that there may be a dating problem, in that *Adventures* is work of 1795, and Wollstonecraft's book was published the following year. However, while W's poem was originally composed in 1795, the only extant draft, as Gill points out, was 'most likely made after April 1799 and before summer 1800, most probably after the beginning of May 1799' (Cornell *SP* 10). Given that there were moves to publish it, first in spring 1796 and then in spring 1798, it is likely that the poem was revised on at least two occasions before the copying of the draft that has come down to us. In fact, since Wollstonecraft's book was published by Feb. 1796,[1] it is possible that it influenced the fair copy W would have made with publication in mind in spring 1796.

It is significant that Wrangham owned a copy of the first edition of this title (see p. 172, below); C apparently read it, Sept.-Oct. 1796, and may have reviewed it (*Notebooks* i 261 and n). W later acquired a copy of the second edition of 1802 (Shaver 277); it is now in the Amherst Wordsworth Collection, and contains the inscription, 'Wm. Wordsworth, Rydal Mount' (Patton 259-60).

268. Wordsworth, Dorothy, Alfoxden Journal in MS
Suggested date of reading: 20 Jan.-17 May 1798
References: BWS 425-8; Moorman 355
Moorman 355 observes that Dorothy's 'Journal and William's fragmentary verse often record the same incident or the same view'. They seem frequently to have written together, and to have read each others' work.

269. Wordsworth, William, and Samuel Taylor Coleridge, *Lyrical Ballads* (Bristol, 1798)
Suggested date of reading: mid-Aug. 1798; mid-July 1799 onwards
References: see note
W presumably read this volume during and after the bulk of printing was completed in mid-Aug. 1798,[2] but he seems not to have acquired his own copy of the finished volume until much later. Not until 24 June 1799 did he write to Cottle requesting 'three copies of the Ballads' (*EY* 264), and on 27 July 1799 he thanked Cottle for the parcel sent earlier that month: 'We were much obliged to you for the Lyrical Ballads and Southey's second volume which we received safe' (Butler *JEGP* 149). This suggests that W first acquired a copy of the finished volume *c.* mid-July 1799.

[1] It was reviewed in the *Critical Review* 16 (1796) 209-12, for Feb., published *c.* 1 March.
[2] For dating see Foxon, 'The Printing of *Lyrical Ballads*, 1798', *The Library* 9 (1954) 221-41, pp. 240-1.

270. Wrangham, Francis, works, inc. poems in MS and *The Restoration of the Jews*
Suggested date of reading: summer 1794, probably by late July 1795
References: EY 159
'W and Wrangham very likely worked out an imitation of a large part of Juvenal VIII.1-86 while W was in London in 1795' (Reed i 340). It may have been in progress when W visited Wrangham's Cobham house in late July (Reed i 166), where he must have read Wrangham's *Poems* (dated 1795, but actually published 1802); that volume was

> a miscellaneous collection of poems, opening with a reprint of Wrangham's first Seatonian Poem *The Restoration of the Jews*; going on to a similar poem on *The Destruction of Babylon* (which competed for the Seaton Prize in 1795 but failed to obtain it); and concluding with a number of shorter poems, translations, imitations, and epigrams in various tongues. From the point of view of literary history the importance of the book lies in the fact that it contains (on pp. 79 and 81) a 28-line translation by Coleridge of a Latin poem of Wrangham's; on p. 83 a short three-stanza original poem by Coleridge adressed to the subject of the preceding verses; and on pp. 108, 109, and 111 a translation by Wordsworth (45 lines) of a French poem by Wrangham, *La Naissance de l'Amour*. (Sadleir 32)

Although the volume was not formally published until 1802, the watermarks in surviving copies show that some of it was in print by 1795 - making it likely that W (and, possibly, C) saw portions of it then. Sadleir 62-4 gives a thorough account of the edition.
By 1795, Wrangham had a number of publications under his belt which W may have seen:
1. Winning Greek and Latin epigrams submitted for Browne Gold medal (1787)[1]
2. *Reform: a farce modernised from Aristophanes* (1792)
3. *Prospectus soliciting pupils* (Cobham, 1794); no copy traceable
4. *The Restoration of the Jews* (Cambridge, 1795)
Wrangham was also in the habit of reading MS verses to his friends: C heard his 'Brutoniad' in Sept. 1794 (Griggs i 107 and n). For Wrangham's library, see pp. 171-2, below.

271. Xenophon, *Anabasis*
Suggested date of reading: 1786-7
References: Schneider 9; TWT 91
In her accounts for 'mr grenwod' - Robert Greenwood, the Hawkshead schoolboy who moved in with the Tysons in January 1786 - Ann Tyson recorded: 'Paid for Anabasis 7.0' (Ann Tyson's Account Book 34v). As Thompson points out, the entry has been crossed out, 'presumably when the 7s. was repaid' (TWT 91). W was studying Xenophon during 1787: Jared Curtis tells me that phrases from the *Anabasis* 'turn up in a Greek exercise (in Greek and Latin) in *D.C.MS 3*' (letter to me). Clancey and his colleague Don Poduska report on the exercise at p. 165, below.
W's copy of Xenophon, *De Cyri Expeditione Libri Septem* ed. Thomas Hutchinson (4th edn, Cambridge, 1785) is now in the Wordsworth Library (Shaver 285). The inside front cover bears the inscription: 'W Wordsworth / March 27 / 1789', indicating that it was in use

---

[1] Sadleir found 'no copy traceable', but both epigrams are in a MS collection of Prize Poems copied by J. J. Conybeare, in the Bodleian Library (MS Top.Oxon.c.216, 143v).

at Cambridge. 'Wm Wordsworth' appears on the flyleaf, and beneath it 'C Wordsworth' - suggesting that the volume was passed on to W's younger brother, Christopher, when he followed W up to Cambridge. The volume contains Greek and Latin texts of the *Anabasis*, with Latin footnotes.

272. Young, Edward
(i) *Night Thoughts*
Suggested date of reading: 1787-90
References: Cornell *EW* 72

In *An Evening Walk* (see Cornell *EW* 72), W footnotes an allusion to the thwarted marriage of Lysander and Aspasia in *Night Thoughts*:

> Fixt was the Nuptial Hour. Her stately Dome
> Rose on the sounding Beach. The glittering Spires
> Float in the Wave, and break against the Shore:
> So break those glittering Shadows, Human Joys. (v 1039-42)

W probably encountered Young's poem first during his Hawkshead years. In the *Fourteen-Book Prelude* W refers to Young as 'the Bard / Whose genius spangled o'er a gloomy theme / With fancies thick as his inspiring stars' (vii 564-6); see also the 1815 Preface (*Prose Works* iii 28).

(ii) *Night Thoughts*
Suggested date of reading: c. June 1797
References: Mason *LB* 114

(iii) *Night Thoughts*
Suggested date of reading: c. July 1798
References: see note

In *Tintern Abbey* W refers to 'all the mighty world / Of eye and ear, both what they half-create, / And what perceive' (lines 106-8). He notes that 'This line has a close resemblance to an admirable line of Young, the exact expression of which I cannot recollect' - indicating that he did not have a copy of Young to hand when the annotation was added prior to printing. However, the resemblance came to mind probably because W had recently reread *Night Thoughts*.

The *Tintern Abbey* lines allude to Young's celebration of the 'Senses, which inherit Earth, and Heavens', and which

> Take in, at once, the Landscape of the world,
> At a small Inlet, which a Grain might close,
> And half create the wonderous World, they see.
> Our Senses, as our Reason, are Divine. (*Night Thoughts* vi 425-8)

Stephen Cornford, Young's most recent editor, offers an interesting discussion of these lines, and traces Young's influence on the Romantics.[1]

---

[1] *Night Thoughts* ed. Stephen Cornford (Cambridge, 1989), pp. 10-12. See also my review, 'The death of Death', *TLS* (9-15 Feb. 1990) 150.

Appendix I

Possible readings

A list of possible readings could go on forever. I include such a list because, during the course of my researches, a number of scholars and critics have answered my requests for information on the subject of W's reading, some with extremely likely but thus far unproved titles. This list is appended to draw attention to some of those readings regarded by those in the field as likely, in the hope that evidence might one day be found for their inclusion in the above list. Each entry is followed by the name, in square brackets, of the person who suggested it. Where no attribution is given, the entry is mine.

[Roe] = suggested by Nicholas Roe
[Betz] = suggested by Paul F. Betz
[Chard] = suggested by Leslie F. Chard, II
[Clancey] = suggested by Richard Clancey
[Pittman] = suggested by Charles L. Pittman, 'An Introduction to a Study of Wordsworth's Reading in Science', *Furman Studies* 33 (1950) 27-60

A1. Aikin, John, especially poems
Suggested date of reading: 1787 onwards [Chard]

A2. Aristotle, *Poetics*
Suggested date of reading: probably not before 1800
References: see note
Aristotle tells us that poetry 'is a more philosophical and a higher thing than history' (*Poetics* ix 3 [1451b 5-7]; Butcher 35). With this in mind W commented, in the Preface to *Lyrical Ballads*: 'Aristotle, I have been told, has said, that Poetry is the most philosophic of all writing: it is so' (*Prose Works* i 139). Owen points out that 'Aristotle does not say what Wordsworth here attributes to him, but that poetry is more philosophical than history. Coleridge, presumably the source of Wordsworth's information, makes Aristotle say what Wordsworth here attributes to him' in *Biographia Literaria* (CC *Biographia* ii 126 and n). Owen concludes: 'It is improbable that Wordsworth had any first-hand knowledge of the *Poetics* at this date' (*Prose Works* i 179). W's claim in *The Prelude* that the work of poets is 'pregnant with more absolute truth' than that of historians (*Thirteen-Part Prelude* xi 92) is more faithful to Aristotle - suggesting that he was better acquainted with his source by 1804.

In response to my initial querying of this, Owen reiterated that, 'if Wordsworth read the *Poetics* at Cambridge, it is hard to know why he misquotes it in the Preface to *Lyrical Ballads*, and says "I have been told" what Aristotle said, unless Coleridge misinformed him' (letter to me). Clancey too assures me that W almost certainly had not read Aristotle prior to the writing of the 1800 Preface. He points to the fact that it was C who, as a Grecian at Christ's Hospital, would have read Aristotle, and that it is on him that W's comments on Aristotle in the Preface to *Lyrical Ballads* depend.

The Rydal Mount library contained René Rapin's *Reflections on Aristotle's Treatise of Poesie* tr. Thomas Rymer (1674) and *Aristotle's Treatise on Poetry* tr. Thomas Twining (2nd edn, 1812).

A3. Barbauld, Anna Laetitia, works
Suggested date of reading: 1787 onwards
On 18 Aug. 1795, DW was given a copy of Akenside's *The Pleasures of Imagination*, containing an introductory essay by Mrs Barbauld. In later years, W expressed disapproval of it. On 8 May 1812, Henry Crabb Robinson records that 'Wordsworth is not reconciled to Mrs Barbauld; his chief reproach against her now is her having published pretty editions of Akenside, Collins, etc., with critical prefaces which have the effect of utterly forestalling the natural feeling and judgment of young and ingenuous readers' (Morley i 74). This shows that W was following Barbauld's career, probably reading some of her works. He had no personal acquaintance with her prior to Dec. 1800 (Griggs vi 1013), but knew her well enough by 1812 to recall an encounter with her in the following terms: 'there unluckily I met the whole Gang among the rest the old Snake Letitia Barbauld' (*Love Letters* 158). [Chard]

A4. Barlow, Joel, poetry
See also note 18. [Chard]

A5. Beckford, William, *Dreams, Waking Thoughts, and Incidents* (1783)
Suggested date of reading: by Dec. 1792
References: *CLB* NS 71 (July 1990) 235–46
Beckford's *Dreams, Waking Thoughts, and Incidents* was never published. It was printed and ready for publication when, on 15 April 1783, Beckford instructed his solicitor, Thomas Wildman, to halt production, and send all copies to him. Its publisher would have been Joseph Johnson, to whom Beckford gave a copy of the work. I suspect that Johnson showed this copy to W, knowing that he would have been interested in Beckford's account of the Grande Chartreuse, also described in *Descriptive Sketches*. For more details, see my article, 'The Grande Chartreuse and the Development of Wordsworth's *Recluse*', *CLB* NS 71 (July 1990) 235–46.

A6. Coleridge, Samuel Taylor and Robert Southey, *The Fall of Robespierre* (1794)
Suggested date of reading: possibly Feb. 1795
References: Griggs i 101
Dyer agreed with C that he would distribute fifty copies of *The Fall of Robespierre*, shortly after publication (Griggs i 101). Perhaps, as Roe suggests to me, 'there may have been copies on the table when Wordsworth met Godwin in Dyer's company on 27 Feb. 1795. Evidence enough? Probably not. But Wordsworth certainly knew of Coleridge's (and Southey's) reputation *before* he went to Bristol in Aug. 1795; his letter to Mathews (*EY* 153) indicates that both were familiar with Coleridge's name and "talent"' (letter to me).

A7. Digby, Kenelm Henry, *Two treatises* (1665)
Suggested date of reading: 1787-91
This book was in the Rydal Mount library. Pittman states that 'There is no doubt' that W read this book at Cambridge (Pittman 55). I find no evidence for this, and the book goes unmentioned by Schneider. All we know is that it was in the Rydal Mount library by 1829. [Pittman]

A8. Edgeworth, Maria, works [Chard]

Appendix I

A9. Edgeworth, Richard Lovell and Maria Edgeworth, *Practical Education* **(2 vols., 1798)**
Suggested date of reading: 1797-8
References: Griggs i 418
'I pray you, my Love!' C wrote to his wife on 18 Sept. 1798,

> read Edgeworth's Essay on Education - read it heart & soul - & if you approve of the
> mode, teach Hartley his Letters - I am very desirous, that you should begin to teach him
> to read - & they point out some easy modes. - J. Wedgewood informed me that the
> Edgeworths were most miserable when Children, & yet the Father, *in his book*, is ever
> vapouring about their *Happiness*! - ! - However there are very good things in the work -
> & some nonsense! (Griggs i 418; his italics)

Practical Education was published by Joseph Johnson in early June 1798; Johnson probably
recommended it to C when they met in London in Aug. As former guardians of Basil
Caroline Montagu, W and DW would also have been interested in the book's contents.

A10. Gibbon, Edward, *The History of the Decline and Fall of the Roman Empire* **[6 vols.,
1776-88]**
Suggested date of reading: 1779-87
Owen observes that W's consideration of Mithradates as a subject at *Thirteen-Book Prelude*
i 186-202 was inspired not only by Percy's translation of Mallet (see note 167), but by
Gibbon (Cornell *14-Book Prelude* 33n; see also Cornell *13-Book Prelude* i 111n). If this is
correct, it is likely that W read the *Decline and Fall* at Hawkshead, since it was standard fare
for schoolchildren during the late eighteenth century. Southey, for instance, read it at
Westminster (Simmons 25). Gibbon is mentioned in one of C's earliest notebook entries,
dating from 1794 (*Notebooks* i 6f6). In an amusing letter to Godwin in 1800, C offered his
opinion of Gibbon's work: 'belonging to my Landlord, but in my possession, are almost all
the usual Trash of the Johnsons, Gibbons, Robertsons, &c with the Encyclopaedia Britannica,
&c &c' (Griggs i 619). W did not acquire his own set of Gibbon until 1836 (*LY* iii 201;
Shaver 102). [Betz]

A11. Hurdis, James, poetry [Chard]

A12. Ireland, Samuel William Henry, *Vortigern and Rowena* **(1799)**
Suggested date of reading: 20 Jan. 1798 onwards
References: CC *Essays* iii 162
In early 1798, Stuart wrote to C: 'As I suppose you have now returned from Shrewsbury I
send you Mrs Robinson's Novel... Inclosed in the Pamphlet you will also find two Vols: of
"Vortigern & Rowena", within one of which is Mrs Robinson's letter' (CC *Essays* iii 162).
In fact, C had not returned, and Poole forwarded Stuart's letter to C on 20 Jan. 1798.
Vortigern and Rowena was a forged Shakespearean tragedy by Samuel William Henry
Ireland, the published version of which is dated 1799; C refers to it in his letter to Stuart of
March 1798 (Griggs i 391), and there was a copy at the Bristol Library Society. If it was in
C's possession from late Jan. onwards, W may well have seen it.

A13. Knox, Vicesimus, *Essays Moral and Literary* **[1778]**
Suggested date of reading: 1779-87 [Betz]

A14. Lofft, Capel, *Remarks on the Letter of the Rt. Hon. Edmund Burke* [1790]
Suggested date of reading: spring 1791
Lofft's *Remarks* was probably one of the 'master Pamphlets of the day' that W remembered having read in the *Thirteen-Book Prelude* ix 97. It was published in Dec. 1790, but the most likely date of W's reading is spring 1791; Joseph Johnson, who W probably knew by then, was its publisher. [Roe]

A15. Montgomery, James, *Prison Amusements* (1797)
This volume was published by Joseph Johnson, 10 April 1797. Two other volumes by Montgomery, *The Loss of the Locks*, and *The Wanderer of Switzerland*, were in the Rydal Mount library by 1829 (Shaver 179). [Chard]

A16. Paine, Thomas, *A Letter to the Honourable T. Erskine on the Prosecution of T. Williams, for Publishing 'The Age of Reason'* (Paris, 1797)
Suggested date of reading: early 1798
References: CC *Essays* iii 162
In early 1798 Stuart wrote to C: 'You will also find a Pamphlet in the parcel, which I have sent as a rarity & a curiosity' (CC *Essays* iii 162). Erdman identifies this as Paine's *Letter to Erskine*. W already had an interest in Paine (see notes 194 [i]-[iii]) and, if C owned a copy of this scarce pamphlet, he is likely to have seen it.

A17. Pamphlets
Suggested date of reading: 1791-2
References: see note
It is not possible to identify all of the 'master Pamphlets' which W must have read during the early 1790s (*Thirteen-Book Prelude* ix 97). Owen points out that some might have been among the 'Pamphlets and ephemera - French, a bundle' (Shaver 194), retained in the Rydal Mount library: 'One might suppose that the "Residence in France" was the only time when W would have collected French pamphlets' (letter to me).

A18. Priestley, Joseph, works [Chard]

A19. Ray, John, *Observations, Topographical, Moral, and Physiological; made in a journey through part of the Low-countries, Germany, Italy, and France; with a catalogue of plants not native of England, found spontaneously growing in those parts, and their virtues* (1673)
Suggested date of reading: 1787-91
Pittman states that 'There is no doubt' that W read this book at Cambridge:

> Ray's classification of plants, which was in the poet's library, was in vogue in England until the latter part of the eighteenth century.... It is difficult to believe that Ray's classification of Cambridgeshire plants would have been neglected by the poet of Nature at Cambridge. (p. 55n)

I find no evidence that this book was owned during W's Cambridge years, let alone read at that time, although a copy was in the Rydal Mount library by 1829 (Shaver 212). It is not mentioned by Schneider. In 1844, W described Ray as 'one of the first men of his age' (*Prose Works* iii 341). [Pittman]

A20. Ridley, Mark, *A Short Treatise of Magneticall Bodies and Motions* **(1613)**
Suggested date of reading: 1787-91
This book was in the Rydal Mount library. Pittman states that 'There is no doubt' that W read this book at Cambridge (Pittman 55). I find no evidence for this, and the book goes unmentioned by Schneider. All we know is that it was in the Rydal Mount library by 1829 (Shaver 215). [Pittman]

A21. Robinson, Mary
(i) *Walsingham, or the pupil of nature* **(4 vols., 1797)**
Suggested date of reading: 20 Jan. 1798 onwards
References: CC *Essays* iii 162
Robinson contributed to the *Morning Post* as 'Tabitha Bramble', and was introduced to C by its editor, Daniel Stuart. In early 1798, Stuart wrote to C:

> As I suppose you have now returned from Shrewsbury I send you Mrs Robinson's Novel... Inclosed in the Pamphlet you will also find two Vols: of 'Vortigern & Rowena', within one of which is Mrs Robinson's letter ... (CC *Essays* iii 162)

In fact C had not returned, and Poole forwarded Stuart's letter to him on 20 Jan. 1798. Erdman identifies 'Mrs Robinson's Novel' as *Walsingham* (1797), published late Nov. 1797, of which C had already read extracts in the *Morning Post* (Griggs i 639). Some idea of the contents of Mrs Robinson's letter is given by Poole: 'Mrs R's letter to "Francini" is benevolent and flattering' (CC *Essays* iii 164). C already had a copy of *Hubert de Sevrac* (3 vols., 1796), which he had reviewed for the *Critical Review* some time in March 1797.[1] If *Walsingham* was in C's possession from 20 Jan. 1798, W may also have seen it.

(ii) periodical verse
Suggested date of reading: by Dec. 1799
By Dec. 1799, W had probably read verse produced by Mary Robinson and the Della Cruscan school, though there is little in the way of specific reference to confirm it. We do know that W read Robinson's poetry during 1800; see Landon, 'Wordsworth, Coleridge, and the *Morning Post*: An Early Version of *The Seven Sisters*', *RES* 11 (1960) 392-402. [Betz]

A22. Sappho
Suggested date of reading: 1779-87 [Betz]

A23. Sayers, Frank, poetry
Suggested date of reading: 1797-8
Coburn notes that C 'must have known Sayers's poems from 1795 onwards' (*Notebooks* i 32n), and it is possible that he introduced W to them. Sayers' *Disquisitions Metaphysical and Literary* (1793) was in the Rydal Mount library by 1829 (Shaver 226). [Chard]

A24. Volney, Constantine, Count of, *The Ruins, or A Survey of the Revolutions of Empires* **(1792)**
This volume was published in England by Joseph Johnson. [Chard]

---

[1] Reprinted by Raysor, *Coleridge's Miscellaneous Criticism* (1936), p. 382.

A25. Voss, Gerard John, *De arte grammatica, libri septem* **(Amsterdam, 1635)**
Suggested date of reading: 1779-87
References: see note
Voss' *De arte grammatica* (Amsterdam, 1685) was donated to the Hawkshead Grammar
School library in 1679, and appears in the library catalogue for 1788 (Wu *CWAAS* 281). W
may have used it during his time at Hawkshead. By 1829 W had acquired a copy of Voss'
Latina grammatica (Amsterdam, 1639); see Shaver 266. [Clancey]

A26. Watt, James, and Thomas Cooper, *Discours* **(Paris, 1792)**
Suggested date of reading: summer 1792
References: Chard 102
During his stay in France, W may have encountered James Watt,[1] who delivered a 'discours'
to the *Société des Amis de la Constitution* with another English radical, Thomas Cooper, on
13 April 1792. Chard writes that 'they expressed their sympathy with the Revolutionaries in
the face of "un concert des puissances despotiques de l'Europe" - the same sympathy that
Wordsworth showed in writing to Mathews in May, 1792... Possibly Watt led Wordsworth
to works the poet had missed during the summer; certainly he was to Wordsworth a kindred
spirit, one who helped him clarify his ideals' (p. 102). The *Discours* was published by the
Société in 1792, and W may have seen it.

A27. Williams, Edward, *Poems, Lyric and Pastoral* **(2 vols., 1794)**
Suggested date of reading: 1797-8
References: see note
A reference in a letter of 13 May 1796 (Griggs i 214) shows that C knew Williams by that
date, and it was probably at that time that Williams presented him with a copy of *Poems,
Lyric and Pastoral* (1794), now at the Victoria University Library (Dendurent 564; Coffman
W103). If C introduced W to Williams' work, he would have done so *c*. 1797-8. See also
Notebooks i 605 and n. [Chard]

---

[1] Reed i 125-6 debates the possibility of a meeting and concludes: 'James Watt, Jr., is possibly an associate
of W's' (Reed i 125). The closest W came to confirming this was in conversation with James Patrick Muirhead
(Watt's biographer), reported in a letter written by Muirhead to his mother, 1 Sept. 1841: 'W. was born, he says,
in 1770, and he thinks Mr Watt was two or three years his senior, for he went over to Paris at the time of the
Revolution in 1792 and 1793, and so was "pretty hot in it," but he found Mr Watt there before him, and quite
as hot in the same cause. They thus both began life as ardent (and he adds, thoughtless) radicals, but have both
become, in the course of their lives, as all sensible men he thinks have done, good, sober-minded *conservatives*'
(Muirhead 733; his italics). See also Roe 44-5, and Gill 437.

Appendix II

Wordsworth's Hawkshead and classical educations, and his College Examinations at Cambridge

Wordsworth's Hawkshead education

The subject of Wordsworth's education has been vexed since De Quincey wrote that,

> though Wordsworth finally became a very sufficient master of the Latin language, and read certain favourite authors, especially Horace, with a critical nicety, and with a feeling for the felicities of his composition, I have reason to think that little of this skill had been obtained at Hawkshead. As to Greek, that is a language which Wordsworth never had energy enough to cultivate with effect. (Masson ii 265)

Even the barest facts indicate that De Quincey is being unfair.

Hawkshead Grammar School was an exceptionally fine example of the English Free Grammar School. There were three headmasters during Wordsworth's time there. The first, James Peake, graduated from St John's College, Cambridge, 1763-4. When he took over the running of the school in 1766 it was in a sorry state - dilapidated, and badly-managed. He organized an effective system of rent collection for the School's land in Lancashire and reformed its teaching methods.[1] Like De Quincey, he enjoyed an excellent classical education at Manchester Grammar School, and was anxious that his charges be granted the same privilege. By the time he left in 1781 to become a priest, the Grammar School had established a fine reputation for classics and mathematics.

Edward Christian, Peake's successor, was an old friend of the Wordsworth family, having been their neighbour in Cockermouth; his brother, Fletcher (who was to become famous in the mutiny on the Bounty) had been at school with William there. This helps explain why Edward was engaged to fight the Lonsdale suit in a legal capacity on the Wordsworths' behalf, Dorothy recording that he 'is a friend of my Uncle, he knows my brother William very well' (*EY* 52-3).

William Taylor was headmaster from 1782-6. He had been educated at Hawkshead by Peake, who was also one of the executors of his will. He attended Emmanuel College, Cambridge, where he became Second Wrangler in 1778. George Dyer, one of his contemporaries, tells us more:

> William Taylor, fellow, took his A.B. degree in 1778, his A.M. in 1784. He afterwards became head master of Hawkshead school, in Lancashire, where he was first educated - a situation to which he was well fitted - for though his peculiar province was metaphysics and mathematics, yet he was no bad classical scholar, and he possessed a great stock of general reading. I can only speak of what he was while of Emmanuel College. Educated in a country school, accustomed to a Lancashire dialect, and bred up to books, he exhibited but little of an exterior polish. He was not a man of the world: he, so to speak, had never been in it: but a most piercing eye, a very fine physiognomy, a childlike modesty, and natural urbanity, commanded universal respect and esteem.

---

[1] He also opened up the old library, adding to it some of his own books. The library's copy of Stillingfleet's *Discourse Concerning the Doctrine of Christ's Satisfaction* (1696) contains, on its flyleaf, the inscription: 'James Peek - Hawkshead' (Wu *CWAAS* 253).

On leaving college, we took different courses; and having formed different connexions, lived in parts of the country very remote from each other: but let those who knew William Taylor, while a student in this college, bear testimony, that he was endowed with the most excellent qualities, both moral and intellectual. He died young, at Hawkshead, of a consumption, to which, by excess of study, he inclined, while in college.[1]

At Emmanuel, Taylor attended the lectures of William Bennett, later Bishop of Cloyne. Bennett lectured on classics, the Bible and 'logic' (which actually meant epistemology, theodicy, and logic). The texts of these lectures have survived in notes taken by Thomas Leman, Bennett's successor, and are now at Emmanuel. In them, Bennett commends the reading of contemporary poetry as essential to a full enjoyment of classical literature, praising Thomson's *Seasons* in particular. Taylor's great love of eighteenth-century poetry was due in great measure to Bennett, and he passed on this enthusiasm to Wordsworth.

When Taylor died in 1786 he was replaced by Thomas Bowman. Bowman encouraged Wordsworth's reading of old books in the School Library; according to Bowman's son, Wordsworth read Sandys' *Travels*, Sandys' *Ovid*, Foxe's *Book of Martyrs*, and Evelyn's *Forest Trees*. Bowman 'lent Wordsworth Cowper's "Task" when it first came out, and Burns' "Poems"' (TWT 344). He also introduced Wordsworth to Langhorne's *Poems*, Beattie's *Minstrel*, Percy's *Reliques*, Crabbe, Charlotte Smith and the poetry of the Wartons. In addition, Bowman 'used to get the latest books from Kendal every month'. Eileen Jay has suggested that this points to Bowman's use of the 'Kendal Newsroom' (or 'Coffee Room'), established in March 1779,[2] but I find that he did not become a member of the Newsroom until 30 January 1798.[3] Perhaps his son meant simply that he purchased the latest books in Kendal and lent them to Wordsworth, or perhaps he confused his dates.

Bowman must have had a good library of his own to which he gave Wordsworth access; when he expanded the School Library in 1789, he contributed from his own collection 'twenty volumes of the *Annual Register*, twenty-one volumes of the *Monthly Review*, and a copy of Hume's *History of England*, in eight volumes' (Christie 169) - some (or all) of which Wordsworth may have read. In addition, William and his brother Richard had access to the Boys' Book Club; their father's accounts for their education record:

1781 Gave Subscription to Books - 10.0 (John Wordsworth's Account Book 86v)

As Thompson points out, the subscription for each boy was five shillings (TWT 55).

The profusion of classical readings by Wordsworth at Hawkshead, ranging from Catullus to Xenophon, show that his studies in this area reached an advanced stage. Boys of sixteen were not generally expected to read Demosthenes, but a copy of the *Orations* was purchased for him on 8 August 1786.

---

[1] *A History of the University and Colleges of Cambridge* (2 vols., 1814), ii 392.

[2] *Wordsworth at Colthouse* (Kendal, 1981), p. 28.

[3] Wordsworth's uncle, William Cookson, became a member on 3 March 1795, and his best friend at Hawkshead, John Fleming of Rayrigg, in 1794. I find nothing to support Jay's claim that Wordsworth became a member in later life. See the records of the Kendal Newsroom, Cumbria Record Office, Kendal (WD/K/189). A list of subscribers' names appears at the back of another record book (WD/K/192).

Some further idea of what Wordsworth read at Hawkshead may be gleaned from a document among the Matson Papers at the Kendal Record Office, kindly brought to my attention by Dr Robert Woof. It is a receipt from James Ashburner, a bookbinder, for the binding of the school textbooks of Henry and Charles Morland, near contemporaries of Wordsworth's at Hawkshead.[1] The receipt was sent to Mrs Morland probably at the beginning of September 1786, and payment was received by Ashburner on the 18th.

			£.s.d
1785	July 9.th	First Principles of Religion, 2 vols	0.1.0
	Aug.t 10	2 Eton's Latin Gram.	0.3.0
1786	Jan.y 28	Ward's Greek Grammar bound	0.2.3
	Feb.y 8	Binding Ovid's Metamorphoses	0.1.4
	March 22	Salmon's Gazetteer	0.4.0
	May 15	1 Art of Speaking	0.5.0
		1 Greek Testament	0.2.6
	July 15	Ward's Greek Grammar, well bound	0.2.3
	Aug.t 3	½ quire broken quarto Post	0.0.2
	Aug.t 29	Willymotts Particles	0.3.6
		A small Common Prayer Book, gilt edges	0.1.9
			1.6.9

This receipt gives us an extremely good idea of the books used at Hawkshead, some of which were probably read (and owned) by Wordsworth.[2] I am reluctant to include them as entries in *Wordsworth's Reading* on the grounds that the Morland brothers, being younger than W, may have been taught by different masters with different techniques and slightly different textbook requirements. We know, for instance, that where Wordsworth learned Latin with Dyche (see below), his brother Christopher used John Mair's *Introduction to Latin Grammar*. And in 1818 Nicholas Carlisle recorded of the Hawkshead Grammar School that 'The ETON Grammars are now used here: and the system of Education is nearly the same as at all other public Schools'.[3] As Clancey has observed to me, the implication is that Taylor preferred teaching with some other textbook.

[1] The eldest of the Morland brothers, Henry, was two years W's junior; for more on them, see TWT 358.
[2] They can be identified as follows:
(i) 'First Principles of Religion, 2 vols'. I have been unable to identify this title.
(ii) 'Eton's Latin Gram.' *An Introduction to the Latin Tongue, for the use of youth* [Eton, 1769], frequently reprinted.
(iii) 'Ward's Greek Grammar'. Camden, William, *Institutio Graecae Grammatices compendiaria, In usum regiae scholae Westmonasteriensis* [1597]; ed. John Ward from 1769, frequently reprinted.
(iv) 'Salmon's Gazetteer'. Salmon, Thomas, *The Modern Gazetteer: or, a short view of the several nations of the world* [1746]. This had reached its 10th edition by 1782.
(v) 'Art of Speaking'. Burgh, James, *The Art of Speaking* [1761]. This had reached its 7th edition by 1787.
(vi) 'Willymotts Particles'. Willymott, William, *English Particles Exemplify'd in Sentences Design'd for Latin Exercises* [1703]. This had reached its 13th edition by 1789.
    Woof tells me that the Hawkshead Grammar School Library possesses a classical textbook containing Wordsworth's name, but I am unable to find it.
[3] *A Concise Description of the Endowed Grammar Schools in England and Wales* (2 vols., 1818), i 662.

Hawkshead and classical educations

Wordsworth's classical education

Wordsworth began his Latin education with Dyche's *Guide to the Latin Tongue*, before moving on to a more advanced grammar. During the early 1780s he went on to translate from Aesop and Cicero, and by 1786 was reading Catullus, Martial and Statius. For most of his translations he seems to have worked with a crib - a Latin text with a parallel English rendering. He would have needed it, because with this method of learning Latin, students did not always fully master Latin grammar. For this reason, as he admitted to Landor in 1822, he never mastered the art of Latin composition: 'I never practised Latin verse, not having been educated at one of the Public Schools. My acquaintance with Virgil, Horace, Lucretius, and Catullus is intimate; but as I never read them with a critical view to composition great faults in language might be committed which would escape my notice' (*LY* i 125). All the same, the constitution of Hawkshead Grammar School stipulated that scholars were required to speak only in Latin and Greek in the classroom.

Though a competent Latinist, Wordsworth was a less successful Grecian. Some indication of his skill can be gauged from a Greek exercise surviving in *D.C.MS 3* 3v-4r, in his hand, dating from *c.* 1787, the year he left Hawkshead. It consists of Greek sentences either dictated in English to be translated into Greek, or more likely copied from a Greek dictation to be rendered into Latin. Clancey and his colleague, Don Poduska, have analysed the exercise and find that Wordsworth is acquainted with the full range of Greek moods. The exercise contains a reference to Xenophon - the standard first Greek author studied in schools. References to the 'crown' suggest that Wordsworth is being prepared for Demosthenes, the standard major Greek author in the upper grammar school forms, and at university. The errors and blots on the MS suggest that the sentences come not from classical texts, but are hurriedly copied exercise sentences. They show Wordsworth on his way to fairly serious Greek study.

Clancey adds that the examination papers at Cambridge required a sophisticated ability to render Greek drama into English, as well as the ability to render Greek prose into really good Latin prose. Monk records examination questions and texts set for translation from 1810-23.[1] Requirements were stiffer for Greek translation then than they were in the late 1780s and 1790s, but on the basis of *D.C.MS 3* it is clear that Wordsworth could not have competed in those exams. Wordsworth had no Greek drama and in his last year at Hawkshead shows only a good beginning in the composition of Greek prose.

We do not know exactly what classical authors Wordsworth read at school, nor what editions he used. But Clancey has constructed a speculative list of authors that an able pupil at a good Grammar School like Hawkshead can be expected to have read, on the basis of what is known of the syllabus at other schools.

Greek: Alcaeus (lyrics, *Greek Anthology*); Anacreon (lyrics); Aristophanes (drama); Athenaeus, *Banquet of the Learned* (*Greek Anthology*); Callistratus; Demosthenes, *De Corona*; Herodotus; Homer; ?Longinus, *On the Sublime*; Lucian; ?Lysias;[2] Meleager (epigrams, *Greek*

---

[1] See Monk, *Cambridge Classical Examinations* (Cambridge, 1824).
[2] Butler taught Longinus to his pupils at Shrewsbury. Clancey observes that Wordsworth's education in this area anticipates many of the enriched features of a classical education in the nineteenth century.

165

Anthology); Moschus; Pindar; Plato, *Apology*; Sappho; Sophocles; Thucydides, esp. *History of the Peloponnesian Wars*; Xenophon, *Anabasis*.

Latin: Caesar, *Gallic Wars*, *Commentaries*; Catullus, *Carmina*; Cicero (oratory); Claudian; *Disticha Catonis* (sayings); Horace; Juvenal; Livy (history); Lucretius, *De rerum natura*; Martial; Cornelius Nepos; Ovid; Plautus; Pliny the Younger; Propertius; Quintilian, *Institutiones Oratoriae*; Sallust; Seneca; Statius, *Thebais* and *Silvae*; Suetonius Tranquillus, *Lives of the Caesars*; Tacitus, *Agricola*; Terence; Tibullus; Virgil.

Wordsworth's College examinations at Cambridge

In addition to the University's mathematics examinations,[1] Wordsworth was obliged at Cambridge to take a series of College examinations. This appendix provides a summary of the books on which he was examined by his College during his three years at St John's, and a summary of his results as recorded in the College Examination Book (C.15.6), now preserved at St John's College, Cambridge. He was as fortunate in his choice of College as in his choice of Grammar School. St John's was extremely successful in preparing candidates for University examinations; from 1780 to 1789, the College produced thirty-five Wranglers (as those who achieved first-class honours were called). With the exception of Trinity and Queens', no other college produced more than three during the same period.

Scott notes that Wordsworth was 'admitted sizar,[2] tutor Mr Frewen, 5 July 1787'.[3] Edward Frewen was born on 27 October 1744 at Rye and matriculated at St John's in 1765; he was a Fellow from 1769 to 1789.[4] Among the senior Fellows in 1787 were Sir Isaac Pennington, Professor of Chemistry; Thomas Gisborne, who became President of the Royal College of Physicians in 1791; William Craven, Professor of Arabic; John Mainwaring, Lady Margaret Professor in 1788; and William Pearce, Senior Tutor and Public Orator, who became Master of Jesus in 1789. Wordsworth's contemporaries included Castlereagh; a grandson of Lord Bute, who went into the service of the East India Company; Wellington's younger brother, Gerald, later a canon of St Paul's; Philip Francis, son of the author of the *Letters to Junius*; John Kelly, the Celtic scholar, and John Palmer of Cockermouth, later Professor of Arabic. Only Palmer (1769-1840) seems to have remained in contact with Wordsworth in later years. He visited Dove Cottage with Robert Jones on 13 September 1800 on his way to visit his widowed mother, Mrs Elizabeth Greenhow, and Dorothy bumped into him in August 1810 on the coach to Bury St Edmunds, though without apparently recalling the earlier meeting (*Grasmere Journals* 22, 168; *MY* i 421-2, 426).

Although the College's examination papers prior to 1808 are not extant, their content during Wordsworth's Cambridge years is suggested by the College Examination Book, which lists the books set and remarks on candidates' performance. With its help, I have listed some of the books Wordsworth read at St John's; those within square brackets were probably not read by him.

---

[1] Probably the most detailed account of these is given by Kipling, 'A Note on Wordsworth's Mathematical Education', *CLB* NS 59 (July 1987) 96-102.

[2] He shortly after became a scholar.

[3] *Admissions to the College of St John the Evangelist in the University of Cambridge. Part IV: July 1767-July 1802* ed. Robert Forsyth Scott (Cambridge, 1931), p. 56.

[4] For more on Frewen, see M. G. Underwood, 'A Tutor's Lot', *The Eagle* 69 (1984) 3-8.

December 1787
1. Xenophon, *Anabasis* (last book)
2. Horace, either *Ars Poetica* or *Epistles* I or II
3. Isaac de Beausobre, *Introduction to the Reading of the Holy Scriptures* [Cambridge, 1779]
4. Philip Doddridge, *Three Sermons on the Evidences of the Gospels; preached at Northampton*

Wordsworth can be presumed to have read all of these books, since the Examination Book reports that he came towards the bottom of the First Class in this examination. He knew *Anabasis* from his studies in Hawkshead, and probably had little preparation to do. It is interesting to see him classed at this early stage with Robert Jones (with whom he was to tour the continent in 1790) and John Myers, his cousin: 'In the 1st Class are Mr. Keane, Mr. Miller, Gawthrop, Stephenson, Baugh, Whitfield, Richards, Courthope, Wilde, R. Jones, Patterson, Walker, Winthrop, Moore, Myers, Babington, Wordsworth, Terrot, Forster, & Turner' (College Examination Book). Schneider 12-13 notes that 'The last book of the *Anabasis* reveals a Xenophon struggling mightily to hold his army together and get it home to Sparta by ceaselessly advocating order, honesty, and the long-run expediency against the disintegrating and diversionary opportunism of his soldiers, his allies, and his superiors'.

June 1788
1. Tacitus, *De Moribus Germanorum*
2. Euclid, *Elements* I-III

In the summer examinations at the end of his first year, Wordsworth dropped into the Second Class, as the Examination Book records: 'Winthrop, Patterson, Butcher & Wordsworth form the 2nd Class'. Schneider 15 summarizes the contents of *De Moribus Germanorum*, which Wordsworth can be assumed to have read.

December 1788
1. Sophocles, *Oedipus Coloneus*
2. Euclid, *Elements* I-VI
[3. Thomas Rutherforth, *Institutes of Natural Law*, Vol. 1 [1754]]

Wordsworth made a less auspicious start to his second year than he had to his first: 'Of those who did not go thro' the whole of the examination & yet had considerable merit, are Wordsworth, Johnson, Mr. Benyon, Mr. Rowley & Mr Pole.' Since he enjoyed classical literature and was already acquainted with Euclid, it is likely that the part of the examination that Wordsworth 'did not go thro'' was that dealing with Rutherforth.

June 1789
1. Livy, *History of Rome* XXI
2. John Locke, *An Essay Concerning Humane Understanding* [1690]

Again, the Examination Book classes Wordsworth with Jones: 'Gill distinguished himself at the Examination in Locke, & Jones & Wordsworth in the Classic'. The implication is that they failed to distinguish themselves in the examination on Locke. The report concludes with a warning from the examiners: 'The behaviour of those who have declared they had not attended to the subjects of the examination is considered by the Master and Examiners as highly improper and will in future render them liable to be degraded to the year before them.'

This was acted on in June 1791 when five men, 'having shown and avowed their ignorance of Mechanics', were degraded to the year below, and threatened that 'unless they pay attention to all the subjects, their terms will not be granted'.

December 1789
1. Demosthenes, *Demosthenis selectæ orationis. Ad codices MSS. recensuit, textum, scholiasten, & versionem plurimis in locis castigavit, notis insuper illustravit Ricardus Mounteney* [Cambridge, 1731]
2. Joseph Butler, *Analogy of Religion, Natural and Revealed, to the Constitution and Course of Nature*
3. Newton, *Opticks*

Wordsworth is not mentioned in the report for the first examination of his final year. After singling out those who distinguished themselves in each class, the report does mention that 'of all these tho'' the difference between those in the extremes was great yet the descent amongst them was so slow & gradual that it was not easy to distinguish them in the Classes.' Once again, it is far from certain that Wordsworth read all the books assigned.

June 1790
1. Juvenal, *Satires* III-XV[1]
[2. *A New Version of the Gospel According to Saint Matthew; with a Literal Commentary on all the Difficult Passages ... Written Originally in French by Messieurs De Beausobre and Lenfant* [Cambridge, 1779]]

In their final College examinations Wordsworth and Jones were unplaced, as the report reveals: 'Gawthrop, Stephenson, G. Courthope, Jones, Moore, Myers, Wordsworth, & Hughes are mentioned in the order in wch they stand on the boards & had considerable merit in the Subjects wch they undertook.' Undergraduates' names were written on boards in the order in which they were admitted to the College, and the order of those at the end of the report is indeed that in which they were admitted. The report implies that the candidates listed did not answer questions on all the subjects on the examination syllabus; since Wordsworth had probably known Juvenal since his schooldays (see note 142 [i]), it is likely that he answered on the *Satires* rather than on the *Gospel of St Matthew* (Schneider 172).

Wordsworth was not required to take a College exam in the Michaelmas Term of his fourth year, and spent the Long Vac of 1790 walking across France, returning to Cambridge late the following term. Jones, with whom Wordsworth was frequently classed in exams - and with whom he walked across the continent - did not take an Honours degree but was nevertheless elected to one of the Welsh Fellowships at St John's in 1791. He was ordained and subsequently presented to the living of Souldern in Oxfordshire. The two friends remained in contact until Jones' death in 1835 (see *LY* iii 34-7, 86-7).

---

[1] The reference in the examination book is read by Schneider as '3 10 15' (Schneider 263). My reading, with which Clancey agrees, is '3 to 15'.

Appendix III

Books purchased for Wordsworth, 1784-86

The accounts kept for the Wordsworth children by their guardians and Ann Tyson after the death of JW Sr in 1783 reveal that more books were purchased for Wordsworth while at Hawkshead than for any of his brothers. The guardians' accounts are now at the Wordsworth Library; those of Ann Tyson at the Hawkshead Grammar School. Since they provide the evidence for a number of entries on the reading list, I have summarized them below.

Ann Tyson's account book

Beatrix Potter's discovery of this ledger is described in TWT 7. Ann Tyson's accounts for 1785 include:

	£.s.d
A Greek Exercises	0.4.6
Paper	0.1.0
Ink and Quils	0.0.6
and A Euclid	0.4.6

(32r; see TWT 90)

On 27 July 1786, Ann Tyson entered against Wordsworth's name:

	£.s.d
Books	1.1.0
Book	1.1.0

(37v)

In the account for 'mr grenwod' - Robert Greenwood, the Hawkshead schoolboy who moved in with the Tysons in Jan. 1786 - Ann Tyson records:

	£.s.d
Paid for Anabasis	0.7.0

(34v; see TWT 91)

As Thompson points out, the entry has been crossed out, 'presumably when the 7s. was repaid'.

The accounts of Wordsworth's guardians

The accounts of Christopher Crackanthorpe Cookson and Richard Wordsworth of Whitehaven survive in the Wordsworth Library, Grasmere, among the Shepherd papers. As guardians of the orphaned Wordsworth children, they were required to keep records of what they spent. These mention a number of book purchases for William and his brother Christopher, which I have placed in chronological order, below.

Key
(C) accounts of Christopher Crackenthorpe Cookson (Shepherd MSS, Bundle 12 Item 7)
(R) accounts of Richard Wordsworth of Whitehaven (Shepherd MSS, Bundle 12 Item 25)

		£.s.d
1784	Febry 23ᵈ. By Cash paid for 2 Vol Homer & 1 Vol. Lucian for my Nephews	0.8.9 (R)
1784	Sept Paid for an Erasmus for Christopher	0.2.0 (C)
	Pd. for Mairs Introduction[1] for Christopher	0.2.0 (C)
1786	Jan 26th By my Nephew Wᵐ. for two Books	0.7.0 (R)
1786	March 13th Pᵈ. Anthony Soulby[2] for a Hedrick's Lexicon for William	1.0.0 (C)
1786	Aug 8th Pᵈ. Anthony Soulby a Demosthenes for William	0.4.0 (C)

---

[1] Mair, John, *An Introduction to Latin Syntax: or, An Exemplification of the Rules of Construction, as Delivered in Mr Ruddiman's Rudiments, without Anticipating Posterior Rules: Containing I. The Rules of Syntax, with a Brief Illustration II. Explanatory Notes III. Examples* [Edinburgh, 1750]. Mair's text was in widespread use throughout the late eighteenth and early nineteenth centuries. The fact that Christopher used this book at Hawkshead does not necessarily mean that it was used by Wordsworth.

[2] Anthony Soulby was a bookseller in Penrith whose services the Wordsworths continued to use in later years. He bound Wordsworth's Chaucer in February 1802 (*Grasmere Journals* 62, 176).

Appendix IV

Wrangham and his library

Wrangham was one of the few people to have known both Wordsworth and Coleridge before they knew each other. Coleridge met him during his last term in Cambridge and visited him in Cobham, Christmas 1794; Wordsworth met Wrangham in 1795 in London. It was probably after hearing Wordsworth read *Salisbury Plain* that Wrangham suggested they collaborate on a version of Juvenal's eighth satire.

Wordsworth visited Wrangham's house in Cobham for a few days in late July 1795, shortly before his departure for Racedown (Reed i 166). The ostensible reason must have been their collaboration, but Wrangham, who was already a book-collector, would have taken the opportunity to show his new friend his library. The catalogue of the English books in his library that he compiled, annotated, and printed privately in 1826, runs to 645 pages. As he states in his introduction: 'I went on accumulating them to the verification of the prophecy of a witty neighbour, who predicted that "they would creep over my walls like an erysipelas" ... My hall, dining-room, ante-room, dressing rooms, bed-rooms, garret, closets etc. ... all overflow' (Wrangham iii-iv). Something of his tenacity as a collector is implied by a letter of March 1813 to Sarah Priestley, a bookseller in London, requesting that she either sell him her books at the trade rate or pay their carriage to Yorkshire (BL Add.MS 28,654). Wrangham's bibliographer, Michael Sadleir, describes his collection as follows:

> Wrangham preferred an obscure book, which for one reason or another was (and must always remain) very hard even to find, to a notorious high-spot which - though also of great rarity - could be relied upon to head the bill in any auction or catalogue. He was the sort of bibliophile who loved to choose his own quarry and hunt it; and he measured the value of his library, not by the total of its current prices or by its place in competition with those of his book-collecting contemporaries, but by the number of ingenious discoveries and lucky captures which *he* knew that it contained. (Sadleir 43; his italics)

How extensive Wrangham's library was in 1795 we can only speculate, but he was already collecting at that date. Wordsworth's appreciation of this is implied by Wrangham's letter to him of February 1819:

> Does your Passion for old Books continue? Mine grows I think by increase of what it feeds on. What do you think of 14000 volumes, & about as many Tracts collected in about one tenth of the number of volumes - most of them scarce - and several (I doubt not) unique? I wish I had you here to enjoy and to appreciate them.
>
> (Wordsworth Library MS A/Wrangham/6)

I have extracted a number of entries from the 1826 catalogue, below. Wordsworth probably saw at least two of these in 1795: James I, *Demonology* (see note 140) and Marvell, *Works* (see note 172). The others are mentioned to give an idea of the kind of library Wrangham might have had in the mid-1790s. Entries are quoted from Wrangham's *The English Portion of the Library of the Ven. Francis Wrangham* (Malton, 1826), to which page numbers refer.

1. 'Aristotle's Poetic, by Pye, and Commentary 1792' (p. 35); see note A2
2. 'Beccaria on Crimes and Punishments 1767' (p. 127); see note 23
3. '(Beckford's) Vathek 1786' (p. 127); see note A5
4. 'Bell's (Joh.) Fugitive Poetry (Epistles) 5 in 2 [vols.] 1789' (p. 540); see note 25

5. 'Burke Revolution in France 1790' (p. 152); see note 41 (ii)
6. 'Colman's Iron Chest, with a Preface and Postscript 1796' (p. 191); see note 59
7. 'Dyer's Memoirs of Robinson 1796' (p. 221); see note 87 (ii)
8. Frend, William, *An Account of the Proceedings in the University of Cambridge, Against William Frend ... for publishing a pamphlet intitled Peace and Union, &c., containing the proceedings in Jesus College, the trial in the Vice-Chancellor's Court, and in the Court of Delegates. Published by the defendant* (Cambridge, 1793). I have not been able to place the 'Remarks on Tomline'.
   'Frend's Peace and Union, Trial, &c. Appendixes, and Remarks on Tomline, with Priestley's Two Replies to the Monthly Review 2 [vols.] 1783, 1784, 1793, &c.' (p. 240); see note 108
9. 'Godwin (W.) on Political Justice 1793' (p. 61); see note 118 (i)
10. 'Hartley (Dav.) on Man; his Frame, Duty, and Expectations 1749' (p. 265); see note 125
11. 'Helvetius on Man, by Hooper 1777' (p. 269)
12. 'James the First, on Dæmonologie 1603' (p. 68); see note 140
    Wrangham notes: 'Pronounced, by Dibdin, it's Royal Author's *"opus maximum"*'
13. 'Juvenal's Sixteen Satyrs, by Stapylton 1673' (p. 310); see note 142 (i)
14. 'Mackintosh's *Vindiciae Gallicae* 1791' (p. 337); see note 164
15. 'Marvell's Works, with his Life by Cooke 1772' (p. 346); see note 172
16. 'Moore's (J.) Views of Society &c. in France, Switzerland and Germany 1779' (p. 364); see note 180
17. 'Paine's Rights of Man in Two Parts 1791, &c.' (p. 383); see note 194 (ii)-(iii)
18. Priestley, Joseph, *Remarks on the Monthly Review of the Letters to Dr. Horsley, in which the rev. Mr. Samuel Badcock, the writer of that review, is called upon to defend what he has advanced in it* (Birmingham, 1784)
    For catalogue entry, see Frend.
19. Priestley, Joseph, *A Reply to the Animadversions on the History of the Corruptions of Christianity, in the Monthly Review for June 1783; with additional observations relating to the doctrine of the primitive church, concerning the person of Christ* (Birmingham, 1783)
    For catalogue entry, see Frend.
20. 'Schiller's Robbers 1792' (p. 406); see note 219 (i)
21. 'Cato's Humorous Letters in the London Journal, &c. 1721' (p. 174); see note 246
22. 'Cato's Letters 4 [vols.] 1733' (p. 550); see note 246
23. 'Godwin (Mrs. M. W.) Vindication of the Rights of Man (*v. Burke*) 1790' (p. 251); see note 267 (i)
24. 'Godwin (Mrs. M. W.) Vindication of the Rights of Woman 1792' (p. 251)
25. 'Godwin (Mrs. M. W.) History of the French Revolution 1794' (p. 251)
26. 'Godwin (Mrs. M. W.) Letters on Sweden, Norway, and Denmark 1796' (p. 251); see note 267 (ii)

Appendix V

Thomas Poole's library and The Stowey Book Society

Thomas Poole's library

Remarkably little is known of Poole's library. He seldom refers to his books in his letters, and only one or two are mentioned in the letters of his friends and acquaintances - as Whalley says, 'Poole's library as a whole has vanished almost without trace' (CC *Marginalia* i p. lxxvii). We know that Poole read widely in Latin and French; in a letter to Samuel Purkis, 23 August 1794, he declared: 'I, wishing to be perfectly familiar with French, and to increase my knowledge of Latin, seldom read a book out of one or other of those languages' (Sandford i 91). This was still the case in April 1796, when he remarked to Henrietta Warwick:

> L'Emile de Rousseau, for example - what a book is there! *'Comme il pense et comme il fait penser,'* as has been well said; but not only this book but many others which I could recommend you, if you read French. I have lately perused with much delight *La Citoyenne Roland.* Learn French, I pray, and you may make even your learning the language the vehicle of much solid instruction. (Sandford i 167; his italics)

I have attempted to identify some of the books owned by Poole in the year 1797-8:

1. *Philosophical Transactions of the Royal Society* 1792-1809

In the Introduction to the first volume of Coleridge's *Marginalia*, Whalley quotes a Sotheby sale catalogue of 1908 in which these volumes are described:

> *Philosophical Transactions of the Royal Society.* 18 vol. 1792-1809. This interesting copy was formerly in the library of Thos. Poole of Nether Stowey... Several of the volumes contain profuse pencil notes, in the margins, in the handwriting of Coleridge dating from 1796 onwards until his leaving the village.

Whalley postulates that, should these volumes ever come to light, 'what I think they will show is that there are notes in them in Coleridge's hand, that at least some of them are in pencil, that Poole may have attested the hand somewhere in the set, that Coleridge has not dated the notes himself, and that internal evidence would show that although a few notes may have been written as early as 1796, most, if not all, were written in 1807. If these notes were in fact written from 1796 to 1798, they precede by about five years all other evidence of copious annotation' (CC *Marginalia* i p. lxxvii).

2. Eden, Sir Frederick, *The State of the Poor; or, An History of the Labouring Classes in England, from the Conquest to the Present Period* (3 vols., 1797). See note 91.

3. Hortensius (pseudonym), *Deinology; or, The Union of Reason and Elegance, Instructions to a Young Barrister* (1789)

Writing to Azariah Pinney in March 1799, Basil Montagu commented:

> The book entitled 'Deinology' is the property of Thomas Poole of Stowey near Bridgwater: when you have done with it, take some opportunity of sending it to him. - Did you ever read Quintilian de Oratore? - If you attend to these subjects, perhaps you will derive more information from him, than from the Deinology: tho' it is a valuable little work. (Pinney Papers, Domestic Box R3)

Deinology offers instructions to young barristers on rhetoric.

Appendix V

4. The Encyclopædia Britannica
In July 1796, Sam Purkis billed Poole for several items including '29 Mar [1796] Enc. Brit. ‹ (2.Nos.) 0.17.0'. Purkis adds: 'When I get another number of·the Enc. Brit. I will send you the two I now have' (BL Add.MS 35,344). This is a reference to the third edition of the *Encyclopædia Britannica* (Edinburgh, 1797), to which Purkis contributed the article on Tanning. Poole wished to obtain a copy not just because he was a tanner himself, but because he had advised Purkis in its composition. We know this because on 10 May 1794 John Poole recorded in his Journal: 'T. Poole called before breakfast and bro't with him a paper, containing an account of the Art of Tanning, etc., written by M. Purkiss, and designed for the *Encyclopædia Britannica*' (Sandford i 95n). In view of the fact that the third edition of the *Britannica* could not have been in print as early as March 1796, it is probable that the bill submitted by Purkis was a subscription payment. The entry on Tanning can be found in Vol. 18, pp. 306-8.

The Stowey Book Society

Poole started the Stowey Book Society in 1793, which may have been used by Wordsworth and Coleridge in 1797-8. Coleridge must have been in the habit of using some of the Society's books, for he was annotating them as late as 1807.[1] In the absence of a catalogue our only clue to its holdings is the list published by Mrs Henry Sandford (Sandford i 45-6), the original of which is no longer to be found. I here present an expanded version of her list providing, where possible, full titles, dates and places of publication.
1. Downman, Hugh, *Tragedies* (Exeter, 1792)
'Dowman's *Tragedies*'
2. Fox, Charles James, *A Letter from the Right Honourable Charles James Fox, to the Worthy and Independent Electors of the City and Liberty of Westminster* (1793)
'Fox's *Letter to the Electors of Westminster*'
3. Gillies, John, *The History of Ancient Greece, its Colonies, and Conquests from the Earliest Accounts till the Division of the Macedonian Empire in the East* (2 vols., 1786)
'Gillies's *History of Greece*; and also his *Reign of Frederic the Second, with a parallel between that Prince and Philip of Macedon*. In all, 3 vols.'
4. Gillies, John, *A View of the Reign of Frederick II. of Prussia; with a Parallel between that Prince and Philip II. of Macedon* (1789)
5. Keate, George, *Sketches from Nature in a Journey to Margate* (2 vols., 1779)
'Keat's *Sketches from Nature*.'
6. Necker, Jacques, *An Essay on the True Principles of Executive Power in Great States. Translated from the French of M. Necker.* (2 vols., 1792)
'Neckar on Executive Government. 2 vols., tr. from the French.'
7. '*Pavis Lequel*'. I am unable to identify this title.
8. Radcliffe, Ann, *The Romance of the Forest* (1791)
'*The Romance of the Forest*.'

[1] Whalley, 'Coleridge Marginalia Lost', *The Book Collector* 17 (1968) 428-42, mentions 'an unidentified theological work, possibly on the subject of Miracles', which belonged to the Society, and which C annotated 'before Sept. 1807 thinking that it belonged to Thomas Poole' (p. 442); see Griggs iii 32.

9. Richards, George, *Songs of the Aboriginal Bards of Britain* (Oxford, 1792)
'Richard's *Songs of the Aboriginal Britons*.'[1]
10. Robertson, William, *An Historical Disquisition Concerning the Knowledge which the Ancients had of India; and the Progress of Trade with that Country prior to the Discovery of the Passage to it by the Cape of Good Hope* (Dublin, 1791)
'Robertson's *Disquisition on the Indies*.'
11. Watson, Robert, *The History of the Reign of Philip the Second, King of Spain* (2 vols., 1777)
'Watson's *History of the Reigns of Philip the Second and Third of Spain. In all, 3 vols*.'
12. Watson, Robert, *The History of the Reign of Philip the Third, King of Spain* (1783)
13. Wollstonecraft, Mary, *Vindication of the Rights of Woman* (1792)
'*Rights of Women*, by Mary Wolstoncraft.'

---

[1] Richards (1767-1837) was educated at Christ's Hospital and Cambridge, where he was known to Coleridge (see Griggs i 33 and n). Trott finds his influence in Wordsworth's early work, particularly *Salisbury Plain*.

Appendix VI

Coleridge's Bristol Library borrowings

There were a number of libraries at Wordsworth's disposal during the *annus mirabilis*: the Alfoxden House library, Coleridge's library (where he would have found a copy of Anderson's *British Poets*), Poole's library, and that of Thomas Beddoes in Bristol,[1] where Wordsworth might have found help with his efforts to learn German.

There was also the Bristol Library Society. Wordsworth was not a member of the Society and so nothing was borrowed in his name, but it is possible that Cottle, Azariah Pinney or Coleridge took him there to consult some of the volumes in the Society's King Street reading room.[2] This was mooted first by Beatty:

> We know that the record of books borrowed from the library is very imperfect evidence of books read; many must have been perused in the library building in King Street, at the table in comfortable proximity to the Grinling Gibbons fireplace.
> ('"The Borderers" and "The Ancient Mariner"', *TLS* [29 Feb. 1936] 184)

We can only speculate as to whether Wordsworth, as a guest, read the Society's holdings. On the other hand, we do know what Coleridge borrowed during 1797-8. Whalley's 'The Bristol Library Borrowings of Southey and Coleridge, 1793-8', *The Library* 4 (1949) 114-32, provides the most reliable account of these; a tantalizing but so far undiscussed sidelight is the possibility of Wordsworth having also read them.

I have attempted to discover the means by which each book was borrowed, whether it was possible for Wordsworth to have seen it, and to speculate on its value to him if he had. I have examined, as Whalley did, the registers of the Bristol Library Society, 1797-8.[3] Each page of the leather-bound, folio registers is divided into separate columns, indicating title and author of book borrowed, 'to whom delivered', date of loan, and date of return. Since some books were apparently delivered to the borrower, loan records are frequently made in the hand of the librarian, George Catcott. This cannot invariably be taken as evidence of the borrower's being out of Bristol, however. Like Whalley, I have inspected copies of books borrowed by Coleridge where they survive, and checked them against Johnes' *Catalogue of the Books Belonging to the Bristol Library Society* (Bristol, 1798).

As Whalley points out, many of the volumes borrowed by Southey and Coleridge now bear annotations, though none are unquestionably by either poet (Whalley 115n). In his amusing letter to the librarian of the Society, George Catcott, May 1797, Coleridge revealed that 'I read with a common place book' (Griggs i 323) - where, presumably, his marginalia was entered.

---

[1] This is now at the University of California, Los Angeles.

[2] Basil Cottle reports that 'The exterior of the handsome building, now housing civil servants and looking a little haggard, can still be seen in King St.; and the lovely panelled library room is incorporated in the new library on College Green' ('The Life [1770-1853], Writings, and Literary Relationships of Joseph Cottle of Bristol' [Ph.D. thesis, 1958], p. 49).

[3] These form a unique and fascinating record of reading trends during the late eighteenth century. Kaufman, *Borrowings from the Bristol Library 1773-1784: A Unique Record of Reading Vogues* (Charlottesville, 1960), deals with them in some detail. See also his helpful article, 'The Community Library: A Chapter in English Social History', *Transactions of the American Philosophical Society* 57 (1967) 7.

18-28 August 1797 (10 days)
Massinger, Philip, *Dramatick Works* ed. J. M. Mason (4 vols., 1779)
Coleridge borrowed Vols. 1 and 2 only.

Coleridge visited Bristol, *c.* 14 July, to see Mrs Barbauld (Reed i 204). On the last day of his stay, Friday 18 August, he signed for the books in the Library register, and the next day walked back to Stowey, via Bridgwater (Griggs i 340-1). During the next two weeks he worked on *Osorio*, for which his reading of Massinger may have been undertaken. He probably discussed Massinger with Wordsworth at this time, though Wordsworth did not obtain his own set of the *Works* until April 1798, when Cottle sent him one (*EY* 217-18). It is likely that Coleridge was in Bristol when he borrowed Nash's *Antiquities of Worcestershire* on 25 August, and when the Massinger was returned 28 August. He may have attended the Bristol Fair on 1 September (Griggs i 345).[1]

The contents of the *Dramatick Works* would have interested Wordsworth, and he probably read them in 1798. This is supported by the fact that he was sent his own set of the *Works* by Cottle (see note 174). Besides the plays, Wordsworth would have been interested in Colman's introductory remarks on the nature of language (especially pp. xxviii-xxxii).

The set survives at the Central Library in Bristol, rebound probably some time in the nineteenth century. It contains no marginalia.

25 August-13 October 1797 (49 days)
Nash, Treadway Russell, *Collections for the History and Antiquities of Worcestershire* (2 vols., 1781-2)
Coleridge borrowed both volumes.

Although Coleridge was in Stowey working on *Osorio* in late August, he seems to have visited the Bristol Fair at the end of the month (see his note to Poole of 30 August, Griggs i 345) and, despite the fact that Nash was signed out on his behalf by the librarian, George Catcott, was probably in Bristol when the loan was made. Three days later he returned the volumes of Massinger.

He returned to Stowey and departed for Shaftesbury to meet Bowles, *c.* 6 September. The size and weight of Nash's *Worcestershire* makes it unlikely that he took the volumes with him; possibly he left them with Poole. On his way back from Shaftesbury, *c.* 13-14 September, Coleridge passed through Bath and met Southey, telling him about *Osorio* and *The Borderers* (Curry i 148-9, 152). He returned to Nether Stowey by Friday 15 September, where Wordsworth visited him two days later on Sunday (Reed i 207). Wordsworth apparently went for a short visit to Bristol on 21 Sept (*EY* 192; Reed i 207), perhaps with the expectation of meeting Southey, then passing through on his way to London. On 4 October, Coleridge sent a letter to the Bristol Library Society, requesting an extension of the loan, as recorded in the Register. Other meetings between Wordsworth and Coleridge must have taken place during the loan period, the last of which may have been on 9 October at Poole's. Reed notes that on 11-13 October 'STC is absent for a day or two from Nether Stowey; his whereabouts are unknown' (Reed i 208). The Bristol Library register would suggest that he

[1] It is difficult to say. Coleridge's note to Poole of 30 August is now in the British Library, BL Add.MS 35,343, and bears only Poole's name. It was probably delivered by hand, and written in Stowey.

was in Bristol, returning Nash. On Saturday 14 October, the day after his return, he wrote to Thelwall (Griggs i 349).

I strongly doubt that Wordsworth saw this book. Its influence on Coleridge is discussed Nethercot 175-7; see also *Notebooks* i 806 and n. These volumes survive in the Central Library, Bristol, and were rebound some time in the twentieth century. They contain no marginalia.

25 October-9 November 1797 (15 days)

Burney, Charles, *General History of Music* (4 vols., 1776-89)
Coleridge borrowed only Vol. 2 (1782).

The handwriting in the Library Register on 25 October is not Coleridge's, suggesting that this book may have been borrowed by post. The size and weight of this quarto volume would have made it an unwelcome companion on the walking tour to Lynton, via the coast, in early November 1797, on which Coleridge accompanied the Wordsworths - although the tour would have given them ample opportunity to discuss its contents. Besides the tour, Coleridge's movements in early November are excessively difficult to trace.

The contents of this book would have been of considerable interest to Wordsworth, particularly Burney's comments on language and song; see ii 220, 231-2, 319. The Library copy has not, unfortunately, survived.

1-15 December 1797 (15 days)

Benyovszky, Móric Agost, Gróf, *The Memoirs and Travels of Mauritius Augustus Count de Benyowsky ... Written by Himself. Translated from the Original Manuscript in Two Volumes. [by William Nicholson]* (2 vols., 1789-90)
Coleridge borrowed only Vol. 1 (1789).

The Wordsworths travelled to London in late November, and remained there for 3-4 weeks (Reed i 211-12). They cannot, therefore, have seen this volume. On 1 December, Coleridge visited the Library and signed for it. He was in Bristol on 7 December, and, in view of the flurry of loans which took place during the next week, must have remained in Bristol for the whole of the loan period, if not longer.

Even if the Wordsworths had seen the book, one would expect it to have been of interest primarily to Coleridge. Having completed *Osorio*, he was searching for a subject to dramatize, and evidently believed that Benyovszky's adventures would be appropriate. He discovered in the New Year that they had already been put on the stage; on 23 January 1798, he told Wordsworth:

> I met a young man, a Cambridge undergraduate - talking of plays &c, he told that an acquaintance of his was printing a translation of one of Kotzebu's Tragedies, entitled, Beniowski - The name startled me, and upon examination I found that the story of my 'Siberian Exiles' has been already dramatized. (Griggs i 378)

According to the *Morning Chronicle*, William Render's translation of Kotzebue's *Count Benyowsky; or the Conspiracy of Kamschatka* was published 24 March 1798.

Both quarto volumes survive in the Central Library, Bristol, in their original leather bindings. Inside the covers of each can be found the bookplates of the Society and the press-marks. A label in the front of the first volume suggests that Coleridge wrote some pencilled marginalia on p. 263; these are not, however, in his hand.

11 December 1797-26 February 1798 (46 days)
Edda Sæmundar hinns Fróda (Hafniæ, 1787)
This volume was signed out on Coleridge's behalf by Catcott, though Coleridge was almost certainly in Bristol. He was still there on 13-14 December when he borrowed Rousseau; on 16 December when the Wordsworths arrived back from London; and on 21 December when, sitting in Estlin's study on St Michael's Hill, he copied a passage from Steuart's *Political Œconomy* into his notebook (*Notebooks* i 308n). He had returned to Stowey by Christmas Day, when he received Wedgwood's draft for £100 (Griggs i 360). The Wordsworths remained in Bristol until 3 January 1798, when they returned to Alfoxden.

On 11 January, Coleridge left for Shrewsbury to take up his post as Unitarian minister. A note above the entry in the register records that on 17 January Coleridge wrote (from Shrewsbury) to extend the loan. He returned to Stowey on 9 February. Dorothy Wordsworth's *Journal* shows that Coleridge was not in Bristol on 26 February when the volume was returned, and it seems likely that the book was posted back to the library. Wordsworth and Coleridge met many times during the loan period, mainly during February; most of these meetings are noted by Dorothy.

Coleridge's borrowing of the *Edda* in the original Icelandic coincides with the publication of Amos Cottle's translation. The original impetus for Amos' translation had come from Southey, who borrowed *Edda Sæmundar hinns Fróda*, with its facing Icelandic and Latin texts, in 1795.[1] Explaining the inaccuracy of Amos' work to William Taylor in April 1799 he recalled that

> He was in a hurry, and wanted northern learning, but seemed to have no idea of knowing how or where to look for it. The 'Edda' fell into his hands and delighted him. His brother, who knows no language but English, wanted to read it, and he had begun a prose translation, when I advised him to versify it: in the course of six weeks he had the book half printed. All this was not as it should have been. (Robberds i 246)

In fact, Amos did not translate the Icelandic text; he merely translated into English the Latin version also in the volume. All the same, he made numerous errors, for Wordsworth too writes of the 'many inaccuracies which ought to have been avoided' (*EY* 196). Coleridge's aim in borrowing the Latin text was to compare it with Amos' translation, published in the first week of November by his brother, Joseph. Coleridge's interest in Amos dated back at least to May 1797, when he read his Latin poem, *Italia, vastata* (Griggs i 324), and he clearly wished to take some care in assessing Amos' most ambitious project to date. Joseph also checked his brother's translation since he borrowed these volumes from the Society, 11 September-16 November 1797. Coburn has gone so far as to suggest that Coleridge was not only checking, but revising Amos' work, and adds that the translation may have more bearing on *Christabel* and *The Ancient Mariner* than has been formerly recognized. See also Lowes 204, 466. It is unlikely that Wordsworth took the same care as Coleridge in assessing Amos' work.

---

[1] This 724-page volume contains parallel Icelandic and Latin texts, an Icelandic-Latin glossary, and an index of proper names and things. It is the first volume of a three-volume edition. Vol. 2 was published in 1818, Vol. 3 in 1823.

Appendix VI

13-14 December 1797 (1 day)
Rousseau, Jean Jacques, *Collection complete des œuvres de J. J. Rousseau, citoyen de Geneve* (15 vols., Geneva, 1782)
Coleridge borrowed only Vol. 7.
Coleridge was in Bristol on the Wednesday and Thursday on which he borrowed this book; he signed for it in the Library register himself. The Wordsworths were in London.
The contents of Vol. 7 are as follows:
1. *Discours sur Cette Question: Quelle est la Vertu la plus nécessaire aux Héros; & quels sont les Héros à qui cette Vertu a manqué?*
2. *Discours qui a remporté le prix a l'academie de Dijon, en l'année 1750. Sur cette Question proposée par la même Académie: Si le rétablissement de Sciences & des Arts a contribué à épurer les moeurs.*
3. *Lettre a M. L'Abbé Raynal*
4. *Lettre de Jean-Jaques Rousseau, Sur la réfutation de son Discours, Par M. Gautier*
5. *Reponse au Roi de Pologne Duc de Lorraine, sur Observations de Jean-Jaques Rousseau, sur la Réponse qui a été faite à son Discours*
6. *Derniere reponse de Jean-Jaques Rousseau*
7. *Lettre de Jean-Jaques Rousseau, Sur une nouvelle Réfutation de son Discours, par un Académicien de Dijon*
8. *Le Lévite D'Ephraïm*
9. *Lettres a Sara*
10. *La Reine Fantastique, Conte*
11. *Le Persifleur*
12. *Traduction du Premier Livre de l'Histoire de Tacite*
13. *Traduction de l'Apocolokintosis de Seneque, Sur la mort de l'Empereur Claude*
14. *Olinde et Sophronie, Tiré du Tasse (Traduction du Commencement du Second Chant de la Jerusalem Délivrée)*
15. *Fragmens pour un Dictionnaire des Termes d'Usage en Botanique*
16. *Lettres Élémentaires sur la Botanique, a Madame de Lxxx.*
The unusually short loan period suggests that Coleridge knew exactly what he wanted from the volume. A clue to this appears in Southey's letter from Bristol to his friend, Wynn, a few months earlier, on 22 September 1797: 'Do you know Rousseaus *Levite of Ephraim*? If not, you will find a poem that has not a word too much' (Curry i 148). Only a week before writing this, Southey had encountered Coleridge in Bath (as the latter returned from meeting Bowles in Shaftesbury), and might well have enthused to him about *Le Lévite d'Ephraïm*, the eighth item in the volume Coleridge borrowed. Southey was still recommending it over six months later when, on 6 April 1798, he told John May to 'Read the "Levite of Ephraim;" with the exception of two similes, it is, in my judgment, a perfect poem. And read his letter to Voltaire - the most beautiful defence of optimism that has ever yet appeared'.[1]
Given his liking for the poetry of Gessner (see note 113), Coleridge would have had a particular interest in *Le Lévite d'Ephraïm*. He would have understood that Rousseau was influenced by Gessner's idylls, especially *Der Tod Abels*; Hibberd explains:

[1] *Selections from the Letters of Robert Southey, &c. &c. &c.* ed. John Wood Warter (4 vols., 1856), i 54.

In *Le Lévite d'Éphraïm* ... [Rousseau] told a story of atrocity culminating in the final triumph of virtue. In his *Confessions*, Rousseau relates that he attempted to treat the biblical story in the manner of Gessner... The idyllic and sentimental episodes, the references to the simple ways of the Israelites, and above all Rousseau's poetic prose in this minor work do, indeed, recall Gessner's idylls. The epic pretensions of *Le Lévite d'Éphraïm*, its division into cantos, derive from *Der Tod Abels*.

(Salomon Gessner [Cambridge, 1976], p. 132)

The Society's copy is now at the Central Library, Bristol, and contains no marginalia.

8-15 January 1798 (7 days)
Middleton, Conyers, *History of the Life of Marcus Tullius Cicero* (8th edn, 3 vols., 1767)
Coleridge borrowed only Vol. 1.
The Wordsworths returned to Alfoxden from Bristol on 3 January (Reed i 213), and would have seen Coleridge shortly after, when they would also have heard of the draft sent by the Wedgwoods. Meanwhile, Coleridge was seeking to borrow the means with which to pay off his debts before leaving for Shrewsbury. On 6 January Coleridge wrote to Josiah Wade requesting £5, hoping to 'hear from you immediately'; this is his last surviving word from Stowey that month. Although Reed has suggested that Coleridge left Stowey on 11 January (Reed i 213), it is possible that he was in Bristol by 8 January, when this book was borrowed. He had much business to sort out - money owed and money owing (Griggs i 367-9) - and would have needed the three days prior to his departure for Shrewsbury on Friday 12 January. (Coleridge's signature, it should be added, does not appear under this entry in the Library register.) We know that he arrived at Shrewsbury on the evening of Saturday 13 January (Griggs i 369-70). Before leaving Bristol, he probably left the book with Joseph Cottle, who returned it to the Library the following Monday. In fact, it is apparent that Cottle not only returned the book but read it as well, for he borrowed Vol. 2 of the set on his own behalf the same day, retaining it until 19 February.

Perhaps Coleridge thought it would contain material he could use in his sermons. I doubt whether it was seen by Wordsworth. The copy, now in the Central Library, Bristol, contains some markings, most notably a cross, in ink, on the margin of page 122.

29 January-26 February 1798 (29 days)
Blair, Hugh, *Lectures on Rhetoric and Belles Lettres* (2 vols., 1783)
Coleridge borrowed only Vol. 2.
Coleridge left Shrewsbury on the morning of Monday 29 January and arrived in Bristol the following day (Griggs i 383). Someone else - probably Cottle - must have borrowed the volume in readiness for his arrival, since it was not signed by out by him (nor could it have been). Coleridge returned to Stowey on 9 February, meeting the Wordsworths frequently thereafter. I presume that he posted the book back to the Library for 26 February.

Coleridge's borrowing of the second volume suggests that he was already familiar with the first. The loan is of particular interest because Vol. 2 contains the famous Lecture 38, 'Nature of Poetry - Its Origin and Progress - Versification', in which Blair makes a number of statements that had a strong influence on the author of the Preface to *Lyrical Ballads*. At one point, he discusses poetry 'in its ancient original condition', when it spoke 'the language of passion, and no other; for to passion, it owed its birth. Prompted and inspired by objects, which to him seemed great, by events which interested his country or his friends, the early Bard arose and sung' (ii 322). Wordsworth may have been thinking of these words when he discussed how 'the passions of men are incorporated with the beautiful and permanent forms of nature', and how men in a state of nature 'hourly communicate with the best objects from which the best part of language is originally derived' (*Prose Works* i 124). For more on Blair's influence on the Preface, see especially Abrams, *The Mirror and the Lamp* (1953), and Little, 'A Note on Wordsworth and Blair', *N&Q* NS 7 (1960) 254-5.

There is something on nearly every page of Blair's *Lectures* that would have interested Wordsworth and Coleridge, and which ties in with various statements they made subsequently. This was the most important single borrowing during the period, and was one of a succession of books (including Massinger's *Dramatick Works* and Burney's *General History of Music*) that helped establish the thinking behind the Lyrical Ballads.

The copy survives today in the Central Library, Bristol, and contains some pencil markings on pp. 51 and 111. See also Owen's annotations and introduction to the Preface to *Lyrical Ballads* (*Prose Works* i 113, 173, 175-8).

20 April-22 May 1798 (32 days)
Memoirs of the Literary and Philosophical Society of Manchester (4 vols., 1785, 1790, 1793, 1796)
The Register indicates that Coleridge borrowed 'Vol 2nd', which may mean that Coleridge borrowed either the volume for 1785 (the second volume in the series), or - as I suspect - that for 1790 (the second volume owned by the Society).
Coleridge returned to Stowey from a visit to his brother at Ottery St Mary in Devon, on 18 April. Whether he then departed for Bristol is difficult to say. The loan of this book on 20 April, and of the following entry on 23 April, would suggest that he was in Bristol for at least a few days at this time, though in neither case does his signature appear in the library register. If he indeed went to Bristol, he had returned to Stowey by 24 April (*DWJ* i 16). During the following month, Wordsworth and Coleridge met frequently. Wordsworth went to Bristol on 18 May, and either he or Cottle returned it (along with the next entry) on Coleridge's behalf. Wordsworth returned to Alfoxden, 22 May, probably without Cottle, who followed c. 25 May.
Vol. 3 of the *Manchester Memoirs* (1790) contains, among other things, John Ferriar's *Essay on the Dramatic Writings of Massinger*; the same author's *Observations Concerning the Vital Principle*; and Thomas Cooper's *Propositions Respecting the Foundation of Civil Government*. Lowes 546, 470-1, 565, and Nethercot 59-62, examine Coleridge's use of it, which he refers to in his *Notebooks* (i 258 and n). It might have been of interest to Wordsworth, but no hard evidence points to a reading. Thomas Beddoes borrowed 'Vol 5th' of the *Manchester Memoirs* from the Library, 13-17 July, perhaps after Coleridge had recommended them. Unfortunately, none of the Society's copies have survived.

23 April-22 May 1798 (29 days)
Philosophical Transactions of the Royal Society of London
Coleridge borrowed only Vol. 75 (1785).
See above entry for the likelihood of Coleridge having borrowed this book and of Wordsworth (or Cottle) having returned it. Coleridge had been familiar with these volumes for some time. He was reading Vol. 77 (1787) in 1795 (see *Notebooks* i 32 and n) and had

access to Poole's copies (see p. 173, above). Volume 75 (1785) contains, among other things: Erasmus Darwin, *An Account of an Artificial Spring of Water*; William Herschel, *Catalogue of Double Stars* and *On the Construction of the Heavens*; Joseph Priestley, *Experiments and Observations Relating to Air and Water*; Everard Home, *Description of a New Marine Animal*. Lowes explores the influence of the *Transactions* on *The Ancient Mariner*, pp. 14, 40-1, 80-3, 67-71, 180-1, 289-91 (though he apparently had access only to an abridged edition of the *Transactions*). Unfortunately, the Society's copies have not survived.

25 May-1 June 1798 (7 days)
Letters and Papers on Agriculture, Planting, etc., Selected from the Correspondence of the Bath and West of England Society for the Encouragement of Agriculture, Arts, Manufactures and Commerce
The Register records that Coleridge borrowed 'Vol 10 & 11'; at about the same time, someone added the dates '1792 & 1793' above each volume number in pencil. Unfortunately Vols. 10 and 11 were published in 1805 and 1807; there is no volume for 1793, and Vol. 6 was published in 1792. The Society Catalogue (1798) quite correctly enters 'Bath Society's Letters and Papers on Agriculture, Planting, &c. 7 Vol. *Bath* 1783-95 8vo.': the first seven volumes of the series indeed run between these dates. Unfortunately the copies themselves have not survived, or they may have helped to explain the strange disjunction between the catalogue and the Register. The Register must be in error, and in my discussion I have assumed that Coleridge probably borrowed Vols. 6 (1792), and, possibly, 7 (1795).
The fact that Coleridge's signature does not appear under this entry in the Library register would suggest that Cottle borrowed these volumes on his behalf on the day he left Bristol to visit Wordsworth and Coleridge at Alfoxden. He had returned to Bristol by 27 May, making it almost certain that he borrowed and returned the volumes on Coleridge's behalf.
The *Letters of the Bath and West of England Society* were primarily of agricultural interest, and contain articles on growing cabbages, planting trees, and cultivating mangelwurzels. Oddly enough, this was probably their main attraction to Coleridge. His interest in agricultural matters is revealed by the fact that while in Germany, in a letter now lost, he requested Poole to send him some 'agricultural queries'; Poole replied on 22 November 1798:

> You desired me to send you the agricultural queries and I send you those proposed by the Board to the Surveyors of the different committees. You will see where they are and where they are not applicable - *I shall admire to read your answers to those queries* - remember and don't be *sparing and modest of your agricultural knowledge.*
> (BL Add.MS 35,343; his italics)

At this point Thomas Ward takes over, and copies out a page of 'queries'. Molly Lefebure assures me that Coleridge had a great interest in agriculture - though on a theoretical, rather than a practical level.
In Vol. 6 (1792) of the *Letters of the Bath and West of England Society*, there are a number of articles that might have interested Wordsworth: one is by the Secretary to the Society, William Matthews, *On the Best Method of Providing for the Poor*, followed by Richard Pew, *Twenty Minutes Observations on a Better Mode of Providing for the Poor* and William Matthews, *Remarks on the Same, and Collateral Subjects Continued*. Vol. 7 (1795) continues the discussion with Sir Mordaunt Martin, *On the Poor Rates, Outlines of a Scheme to*

Alleviate the Very Unequal Burthen of Poor Rates, Remarks on Mr Pew's Observations on the Poor Laws and *A Plan for the Prevention of Poverty*. No hard evidence exists to confirm a reading of either volume by Wordsworth. Unfortunately, the Society's copies of these volumes have not survived.

31 May-13 July 1798 (44 days)

Benyovszky, Móric Agost, Gróf, *The Memoirs and Travels of Mauritius Augustus Count de Benyowsky ... Written by Himself. Translated from the Original Manuscript in Two Volumes. [by William Nicholson] (2 vols., 1789-90)*
Coleridge borrowed both volumes.

It is likely that Cottle borrowed these volumes on Coleridge's behalf, and sent them to him at Stowey. Wordsworth departed for Shirehampton 4-12 June, and Coleridge went to Bristol on 10 June, where he spent the rest of the loan period. Given the circumstances of the loan and the reasons for Coleridge first wanting to borrow it, it is unlikely that Wordsworth would have seen this book.

8-14 June 1798 (6 days)

Massinger, Philip, *Dramatick Works* ed. J. M. Mason with introductions by T. Davies and George Colman (4 vols., 1779)
Coleridge borrowed Vols. 3 and 4.

Coleridge was in Bristol during the loan period, and did not meet Wordsworth there. This and the previous borrowing were concurrent, suggesting that Coleridge was at the time thinking seriously about writing another play. In neither case does his signature appear in the library register. Beddoes borrowed Vol. 2 of the set from 4-9 July, perhaps at Coleridge's urging.

Conclusion

These books were in the first instance loans undertaken by Coleridge, and in no case does positive evidence exist for any of them having been read by Wordsworth at the same time. However, Coleridge may have discussed them with him, and the contents of at least five of them would have appealed to Wordsworth:

1. Massinger, Philip, *Dramatick Works* ed. J. M. Mason (4 vols., 1779)
2. Burney, Charles, *General History of Music* (4 vols., 1776-89)
3. Blair, Hugh, *Lectures on Rhetoric and Belles Lettres* (2 vols., 1783)
4. *Memoirs of the Literary and Philosophical Society of Manchester*
5. *Letters and Papers on Agriculture, Planting, etc., Selected from the Correspondence of the Bath and West of England Society for the Encouragement of Agriculture, Arts, Manufactures and Commerce*

Since the evidence presented above is largely circumstantial, none of these titles has been entered in *Wordsworth's Reading* solely on that basis. Only two of them appear in the general list, above: (i) Massinger's *Works* (sent to Wordsworth by Cottle - note 174); (ii), Blair's *Lectures* (note 29).

Appendix VII

Joseph Cottle's Bristol Library borrowings

By 1798 Coleridge had long been in the habit of borrowing Society books through intermediaries; in 1794, for instance, John Frederick Pinney borrowed the Society copy of Bruce's *Travels* on his behalf during composition of *Religious Musings*. Coleridge's most frequent emissary to the Society was Joseph Cottle; in his letter of *c.* 6 May 1797 to the librarian, George Catcott, he gives his address as 'S. T. Coleridge / Mr Cottle's / Bookseller, / High Street / Bristol' (Griggs i 323). Since some or all of Cottle's 1798 borrowings may have been dispatched to Coleridge - and may thus have been seen also by Wordsworth - they deserve mention here.

12 January-2 February
Rousseau, J. J., *The Confessions of J. J. Rousseau; with the Reveries of the Solitary Walker* tr. Anon. (2 vols., 1783)
Cottle borrowed only Vol. 1.

15 January-19 February
Middleton, Conyers, *The History of the Life of Marcus Tullius Cicero* (8th edn, 3 vols., 1767)
Cottle borrowed only Vol. 2.

2-26 February
Rousseau, J. J., *The Confessions of J. J. Rousseau; with the Reveries of the Solitary Walker* tr. Anon. (2 vols., 1783)
Cottle borrowed only Vol. 2.

21 February-9 March
Middleton, Conyers, *The History of the Life of Marcus Tullius Cicero* (8th edn, 3 vols., 1767)
Cottle borrowed only Vol. 3.

20-27 March
Philosophical Transactions of the Royal Society
Cottle borrowed Vol. 86, Parts 1 and 2.

27-29 March
Goguet, A. Y., *Origin of Laws, Arts, and Sciences*, Tr. Anon. (3 vols., Edinburgh, 1761)
Cottle borrowed only Vol. 1.

30 March-3 April
Philosophical Transactions of the Royal Society
Cottle borrowed 'Pt. 1'; no vol. number given.

11-18 May
Blair, Hugh, *Lectures on Rhetoric and Belles Lettres* (2 vols., 1783)
Cottle borrowed only Vol. 2.

1-5 June

Strutt, Joseph, *horda Anjel-cynnan: or A Compleat View of the Manners, Customs, Arms, Habits, &c. of the Inhabitants of England, from the Arrival of the Saxons, till the Reign of Henry the Eighth* (3 vols., 1775-6)
Cottle borrowed both vols.

6-14 June

Strutt, Joseph, *horda Anjel-cynnan: or A Compleat View of the Manners, Customs, Arms, Habits, &c. of the Inhabitants of England, from the Arrival of the Saxons, till the Reign of Henry the Eighth* (3 vols., 1775-6)
Cottle borrowed only Vol. 1.

Strutt, Joseph, *The Chronicle of England* (2 vols., 1777-8, of which the Library owned only Vol. 1 [1777])
Cottle borrowed Vol. 1

Since Coleridge borrowed Middleton's *Life of Cicero* Vol. 1 on 8-15 January 1798, it is possible that Cottle borrowed Vol. 2, 15 January-19 February, on his behalf. Coleridge's reading of the *Philosophical Transactions of the Royal Society* Vol. 75, 23 April-22 May 1798, gives rise to the suspicion that Cottle's borrowings of Vol. 86, 20-27 March, and another unknown volume, 30 March-3 April, were also meant for Coleridge. Cottle's borrowing of Blair's *Lectures* Vol. 2, 11-18 May, looks like a follow-up to his friend's reading of the same book, 29 January-26 February. This argument is supported by the abrupt end to Cottle's 1798 borrowings shortly before Coleridge's departure for Germany in September.

Bibliography

The bibliography lists works referred to in the annotations under the following headings:
1. Manuscripts and ephemera
2. Texts of William and Dorothy Wordsworth
3. Works cited or quoted
4. Bibliographies, catalogues, etc.

1. Manuscripts and ephemera

Bodleian Library, Oxford
John Farish's notebook (MS Eng.misc.d.586)
Gilpin and Farish papers (MS Eng.misc.d.585)
Bristol Central Library
The Registers of the Bristol Library Society, 1796-9
Bristol Record Office
Playbills for the Theatre Royal, Bath, and the Theatre Royal, Bristol (8982 [46] and 8982 [3])
British Library
Poole papers (Add.MS 35,343; Add.MS 34,046)
Cumbria Record Office, Kendal
Records of the Kendal Newsroom (WD/K/189; WD/K/192)
Catalogue of 115 books given to the Hawkshead School Library by Daniel Rawlinson and others (WD/TE/Bound Vol. 8, 127-9)
Hawkshead Grammar School
Ann Tyson's account book
St John's College, Cambridge
The College Examination Book (C.15.6.)
University of Bristol Archives
Pinney Papers (Family Letter Book 13; Account Book 1687; Account Book 1685; Letter Box R3; Box 34; Volume 1791)
Wordsworth Library
Literary MSS (D.C.MS 2; D.C.MS 3; D.C.MS 4; D.C.MS 11; D.C.MS 14; D.C.MS 16)
Mary Wordsworth's memoranda of the Hutchinson and Monkhouse families (D.C.MS 167)
Basil Montagu's narrative of the birth and upbringing of his son (MS A/Montagu,B/26)
Letter: Francis Wrangham to William Wordsworth, 15 Feb. 1819
John Wordsworth's account book
The accounts of Christopher Crakanthorpe Cookson (Shepherd MSS, bundle 12, item 7)
The accounts of Richard Wordsworth of Whitehaven (Shepherd MSS, bundle 12, item 25)

2. Texts of William and Dorothy Wordsworth

Butler, James A. 'Wordsworth, Cottle, and the *Lyrical Ballads*: Five Letters, 1797-1800'. *JEGP* 75 (1976) 139-53
The Cornell Wordsworth. General Ed. Stephen M. Parrish. Ithaca, N.Y.: Cornell University Press.
  The Borderers. Ed. Robert Osborn. 1982
  Descriptive Sketches. Ed. Eric Birdsall. 1984
  An Evening Walk. Ed. James Averill. 1984

The Fourteen-Book Prelude. Ed. W. J. B. Owen. 1985
Home at Grasmere. Ed. Beth Darlington. 1977
Peter Bell. Ed. John Jordan. 1985
Poems in Two Volumes, and Other Poems, 1800-1807. Ed. Jared Curtis. 1985
The Prelude, 1798-1799. Ed. Stephen Parrish. 1977
The Ruined Cottage and The Pedlar. Ed. James Butler. 1979
Shorter Poems, 1807-1820. Ed. Carl H. Ketcham. 1989
The Thirteen-Book Prelude. Ed. Mark L. Reed. 2 vols. 1991
The White Doe of Rylstone. Ed. Kristine Dugas. 1988
Journals of Dorothy Wordsworth. Ed. Ernest De Selincourt. 2 vols. London: Macmillan & Co. Ltd., 1941
Dorothy Wordsworth: The Grasmere Journals. Ed. Pamela Woof. Oxford: Clarendon Press, 1991
The Letters of William and Dorothy Wordsworth: The Early Years 1787-1805. Ed. Ernest De Selincourt. Rev. Chester L. Shaver. Oxford: Clarendon Press, 1967
The Letters of William and Dorothy Wordsworth: The Middle Years 1806-1820. Ed. Ernest De Selincourt. Rev. Mary Moorman and Alan G. Hill. 2 vols. Oxford: Clarendon Press, 1969-70
The Letters of William and Dorothy Wordsworth: The Later Years 1821-1853. Ed. Ernest De Selincourt. Rev. Alan G. Hill. 4 vols. Oxford: Clarendon Press, 1978-88
The Love Letters of William and Mary Wordsworth. Ed. Beth Darlington. Ithaca, N.Y.: Cornell University Press, 1981
Poems and Extracts Chosen by William Wordsworth for an Album Presented to Lady Mary Lowther, Christmas, 1819. London: Henry Frowde, 1915
The Poetical Works of William Wordsworth. Ed. Ernest De Selincourt and Helen Darbishire. 5 vols. Oxford: Clarendon Press, 1940-9
The Prose Works of William Wordsworth. Ed. Revd. Alexander B. Grosart. 3 vols. London: Edward Moxon, Son, and Co., 1876
The Prose Works of William Wordsworth. Ed. W. J. B. Owen and Jane Worthington Smyser. 3 vols. Oxford: Clarendon Press, 1974
William Wordsworth. Ed. Stephen Gill. The Oxford Authors. Oxford: Oxford University Press, 1984
William Wordsworth: Poems, Volume I. Ed. John O. Hayden. Harmondsworth: Penguin Books, 1977
William Wordsworth: The Prelude, or Growth of a Poet's Mind. Ed. E. De Selincourt. Rev. Helen Darbishire. 2nd edn. Oxford: Clarendon Press, 1959
Wordsworth & Coleridge: Lyrical Ballads 1798. Ed. W. J. B. Owen. 2nd edn. Oxford: Oxford University Press, 1969
Wordsworth and Coleridge: Lyrical Ballads. Ed. R. L. Brett and A. R. Jones. 2nd edn. London: Routledge, 1991
Wordsworth, William, and Samuel Taylor Coleridge. *Lyrical Ballads*. Ed. Michael Mason. Longman Annotated Texts. London and New York: Longman, 1992
Wordsworth and Reed: The Poet's Correspondence with his American Editor: 1836-1850. Ed. Leslie Nathan Broughton. Ithaca, N.Y.: Cornell University Press, 1933

Bibliography

3. Works cited or quoted

Abrams, M. H. *The Mirror and the Lamp: Romantic Theory and the Critical Tradition.* London: Oxford University Press, 1953.

Aikin, John and Anna Laetitia Aikin. *Miscellaneous Pieces in Prose.* London, 1773

Akenside, Mark. *The Pleasures of Imagination.* London, 1744
The Poems of Mark Akenside. London, 1772

Allen, B. Sprague. 'William Godwin's Influence upon John Thelwall'. *PMLA* 37 (1922) 662-82

Allott, Robert. *England's Parnassus.* London, 1600

Anacreon. *The Works.* Trans. John Addison. London, 1735

Anon. 'Memoir of William Wordsworth, Esq.' *New Monthly Magazine* 11 (1819) 48-50

Appleyard, J. A. *Coleridge's Philosophy of Literature.* Cambridge, Mass.: Harvard University Press, 1965

Aristotle. *The Poetics of Aristotle.* Ed. S. H. Butcher. 4th edn. London: Macmillan and Co., Ltd.: 1911

Averill, James H. 'Another Early Coleridge Reference to *An Evening Walk'. ELN* 13 (1976) 270-3
'Wordsworth and "Natural Science": The Poetry of 1798'. *JEGP* 77 (1978) 232-46
Wordsworth and the Poetry of Human Suffering. Ithaca, N.Y.: Cornell University Press, 1980

Ball, W. W. Rouse. *A History of the Study of Mathematics at Cambridge.* Cambridge: Cambridge University Press, 1889

Bartlett, Phyllis. 'A Critical and Textual Study of Wordsworth's An Evening Walk and Descriptive Sketches'. B.Litt. thesis, University of Oxford, 1928

Bate, Jonathan. *Shakespeare and the English Romantic Imagination.* Oxford: Clarendon Press, 1986

Beattie, James. *Dissertations Moral and Critical.* London, 1783
'An Extract from *Illustrations on Sublimity*; in the same Work'. *Annual Register* 26 (1783) ii 130-6
The Minstrel, in Two Books: with some other poems. London, 1779
Original Poems and Translations. London, 1760

Beatty, Arthur. 'Joseph Fawcett: The Art of War'. *University of Wisconsin Studies in Language and Literature* 2 (1918) 224-69
'"The Borderers" and "The Ancient Mariner"'. *TLS* (29 Feb. 1936) 184
William Wordsworth: His Doctrine and Art in Their Historical Relations. Madison: University of Wisconsin, 1922

Beccaria Bonesara, Cesare. *An Essay on Crimes and Punishments.* Trans. Anon. London, 1767

Bement, Peter. 'Simon Lee and Ivor Hall: A Possible Source'. *WC* 13 (1982) 35-6

Berkeley, George. *Alciphron: or, the Minute Philosopher. In Seven Dialogues.* 2 vols. London, 1732

Betz, Paul Frederick. 'The Elegiac Mode in the Poetry of William Wordsworth: A Commentary on Selected Verse, 1786-1805, with a critical edition'. Ph.D. thesis, Cornell University, 1965

Bewell, Alan. *Wordsworth and the Enlightenment: Nature, Man, and Society in the Experimental Poetry.* New Haven and London: Yale University Press, 1989

Beyer, Werner W. 'Coleridge's *Oberon* translation and *The Wanderings of Cain*'. *N&Q* NS 3 (1956) 82-4

    The Enchanted Forest. New York: Barnes & Noble, 1963

Bicentenary Wordsworth Studies. Ed. Jonathan Wordsworth. Ithaca, N.Y.: Cornell University Press, 1970

Blair, Hugh. *Lectures on Rhetoric and Belles Lettres.* 2 vols. London, 1783

Boswell, James. *Boswell's Life of Johnson.* Ed. George Birkbeck Hill, rev. L. F. Powell. 6 vols. Oxford: Clarendon Press, 1934-50

Bowles, William Lisle. *Fourteen Sonnets, Elegiac and Descriptive.* Bath, 1789

    Sonnets Written Chiefly on Picturesque Spots During a Tour. Bath, 1789

Brooke, Henry. *Gustavus Vasa, the Deliverer of his Country.* London, 1739

Broughton, Leslie Nathan. *The Theocritean Element in the Works of William Wordsworth.* Halle: Max Niemeyer, 1920

Brown, John. *A Description of the Lake at Keswick, (And the Adjacent Country) in Cumberland. Communicated in a Letter to a Friend. By a Late Popular Writer.* Kendal, 1770

Brydone, Patrick. *A Tour through Sicily and Malta in a Series of Letters to William Beckford, Esq. of Somerly in Suffolk.* 2 vols. Dublin, 1773

Burke, Edmund. *A Philosophical Enquiry into the Origin of our Ideas of the Sublime and Beautiful.* Ed. James T. Boulton. 2nd edn. Oxford: Basil Blackwell, 1987

    A Letter from Mr. Burke, to a Member of the National Assembly. Paris and London, 1791

Burney, Charles. *General History of Music.* 4 vols. London, 1776-89

Burns, Robert. *The Kilmarnock Poems.* Ed. Donald A. Low. London: Dent, 1985

Butler, James A. Review of Chester L. and Alice C. Shaver, *Wordsworth's Library* (1979). *ELN* 18 (1981) 301-4

Callistratus. *Ode From the Greek of Callistratus.* Trans. John Baynes. *European Magazine* 12 (1787) 142

Carlisle, Nicholas. *A Concise Description of the Endowed Grammar Schools in England and Wales.* 2 vols. London, 1818

Carter, Elizabeth. *Poems on Several Occasions.* 3rd edn. London, 1776

Casson, Edmund. 'Wordsworth and Theocritus'. *TLS* (11 Sept. 1937) 656

Catullus. *Catullus, Tibullus, Per Vigilium Veneris.* Trans. F. W. Cornish, J. P. Postgate, J. W. Mackail, rev. G. P. Goold. Loeb Classical Library. 2nd edn. Cambridge, Mass.: Harvard University Press, 1988

    The Poems. Trans. John Nott. 2 vols. London, 1795

Celoria, Frances. 'Chatterton, Wordsworth and Stonehenge'. *N&Q* NS 23 (1976) 103-4

Cestre, Charles. *John Thelwall.* London: Sonnenschein, 1906

Chandler, James. *Wordsworth's Second Nature: A Study of the Poetry and Politics.* Chicago: University of Chicago Press, 1984

Chard, Leslie F., II. *Dissenting Republican: Wordsworth's Early Life and Thought in their Political Context.* The Hague: Mouton, 1972

    'Joseph Johnson: Father of the Book Trade'. *BNYPL* 79 (1975-6) 51-82

Chatterton, Thomas. *Poems, Supposed to Have Been Written at Bristol, by Thomas Rowley, and Others, in the Fifteenth Century.* London, 1777

Christensen, Francis. 'The Date of Wordsworth's *The Birth of Love'. MLN* 53 (1938) 280-2

Christie, Ian R. *Stress and Stability in Late Eighteenth-Century Britain: Reflections on the British Avoidance of Revolution.* Oxford: Clarendon Press, 1984

Clark, M. L. *Greek Studies in England 1700-1830.* Cambridge: Cambridge University Press, 1945

Clayden, P. W. *The Early Life of Samuel Rogers.* London, 1887

Coe, Charles Norton. 'A Source for Wordsworth's *Effusion in the Pleasure-Ground'. N&Q* 196 (1951) 80-1

    'Did Wordsworth read Coxe's *Travels in Switzerland* before making the Tour of 1790?' *N&Q* 195 (1950) 144-5

Wordsworth and the Literature of Travel. New Haven: Yale University Press, 1953

Coleridge, Samuel Taylor. *The Collected Works of Samuel Taylor Coleridge.* General Ed. Kathleen Coburn. Bollingen Series 75. Princeton, N.J.: Princeton University Press

    I. *Lectures 1795 on Politics and Religion.* Ed. Lewis Patton and Peter Mann. 1971

    II. *The Watchman.* Ed. Lewis Patton. 1970

    III. *Essays on His Times.* Ed. David V. Erdman. 3 vols. 1978

    IV. *The Friend.* Ed. Barbara Rooke. 2 vols. 1969

    V. *Lectures 1808-1819 On Literature.* Ed. R. A. Foakes. 2 vols. 1987

    VI. *Lay Sermons.* Ed R. J. White. 1972

    VII. *Biographia Literaria.* Ed. James Engell and W. Jackson Bate. 2 vols. 1983

    X. *On the Constitution of the Church and State.* Ed. John Colmer. 1976

    XII. *Marginalia.* Ed. George Whalley and H. J. Jackson. 5 vols. 1980-

    XIII. *Logic.* Ed. J. R. de J. Jackson. 1981

    XIV. *Table Talk.* Ed. Carl Woodring. 2 vols. 1990

Fears in Solitude, France an Ode, and Frost at Midnight. London, 1798

Letters. Ed. E. L. Griggs. 6 vols. Oxford: Clarendon Press, 1956-71

Coleridge's Miscellaneous Criticism. Ed. Thomas Middleton Raysor. Cambridge, Mass.: Harvard University Press, 1936

Notebooks. Bollingen Series 50. 5 vols. Ed. Kathleen Coburn et al. New York: Pantheon Books, 1957 -

The Philosophical Lectures of Samuel Taylor Coleridge. Ed. Kathleen Coburn. London: Pilot Press, 1949

Poetical Works. Ed. E. H. Coleridge. 2 vols. Oxford: Clarendon Press, 1912

Collins, William. *Thomas Gray and William Collins: Poetical Works.* Ed. Roger Lonsdale. Oxford: Oxford University Press, 1977

The Poems of Gray, Collins and Goldsmith. Ed. Roger Lonsdale. Longman Annotated English Poets Series. London: Longman, 1969

Constant, Benjamin. *Observations on the Strength of the Present Government of France, and upon the Necessity of Rallying Round It.* Trans. James Losh. Bath, 1797

Cooper, Anthony Ashley, 3rd Earl of Shaftesbury. *Characteristicks of Men, Manners, Opinions, Times.* 3 vols. London, 1711

Cornwell, John. *Coleridge, Poet and Revolutionary 1772-1804: A Critical Biography.* London: Allen Lane, 1973

Cottle, Basil. 'The Life (1770-1853), Writings, and Literary Relationships of Joseph Cottle of Bristol'. Ph.D. thesis, University of Bristol, 1958

Cottle, Joseph. *Alfred*. London, 1800
Early Recollections, Chiefly Relating to the Late Samuel Taylor Coleridge, During his Long Residence in Bristol. 2 vols. London, 1837
Malvern Hills: A Poem. London, 1798

Cowley, Abraham. *The Works of Mr Abraham Cowley*. London, 1669

Cowper, Henry Swainson. *Hawkshead*. London and Derby, 1899

Cowper, William. *The Poems of William Cowper*. Volume 1: 1748-1782. Ed. John D. Baird and Charles Ryskamp. Oxford: Clarendon Press, 1980
Poetical Works. Ed. H. S. Milford. 3rd edn. London: Oxford University Press, 1926

Coxe, William. *Travels in Switzerland. In a Series of Letters to William Melmoth, Esq., From William Coxe, M.A., F.R.S., F.A.S.* 3 vols. London, 1789

Crabbe, George. *The Poetical Works of the Revd. George Crabbe*. Ed. George Crabbe Jr. 8 vols. London, 1834
'An Extract from THE VILLAGE, a Poem by the Rev. G. CRABBE, Chaplain to his Grace the Duke of Rutland, &c.' *Annual Register* 26 (1783) ii 183-9

Crowe, William. *Lewesdon Hill*. Oxford, 1788

Crum, M. C. 'The Life of Basil Montagu'. B.Litt. thesis, University of Oxford, 1950

Curtis, Jared. 'Wordsworth and Earlier English Poetry'. *Cornell Library Journal* 1 (1966) 28-39
'Wordsworth, Coleridge, and *Lines, left upon a Seat in a Yew-tree*'. *Bulletin of Research in the Humanities* 87 (1986-7) 482-8

Daniel, Samuel. *The Poetical Works of Mr. Samuel Daniel*. 2 vols. London, 1718

Dante Alighieri. *The Divine Comedy*. Trans. Charles S. Singleton. Bollingen Series 80. Princeton: Princeton University Press
I. *Inferno*. 1970
II. *Purgatorio*. 1973

Darbishire, Helen. 'Milton and Wordsworth'. *TLS* (4 Oct. 1947) 507

Darwin, Erasmus. *The Botanic Garden: A Poem, in Two Parts*. Part I, *The Economy of Vegetation*. London, 1791. Part II, *The Loves of the Plants*. London, 1789

Davila, Enrico Caterina. *The History of the Civil Wars of France*. Trans. Ellis Farnesworth. 2 vols. London, 1758

De Quincey, Thomas. *Collected Writings*. Ed. David Masson. 14 vols. Edinburgh: A.& C. Black, 1889-90

Dodsley, Robert, Ed. *Select Collection of Old Plays*. 2nd edn. 12 vols. London, 1780

Drummond, William. *The Most Elegant, and Elabourate Poems of That Great Court-Wit, Mr. William Drummond*. London, 1659

Dryden, John. *Poems*. Ed. James Kinsley. 4 vols. Oxford: Clarendon Press, 1958

Duffy, Edward. *Rousseau in England*. London: University of California Press, 1979

Dunn, John J. 'Coleridge's Debt to Macpherson's Ossian'. *Studies in Scottish Literature* 7 (1969) 76-89

Dyer, George. *A History of the University and Colleges of Cambridge*. 2 vols. London, 1814
Poems. London, 1792

Dyer, John. *Poems*. London, 1761

Emerson, Ralph Waldo. *English Traits*. Boston, 1856

Erdman, David V. 'Coleridge, Wordsworth, and the Wedgwood Fund'. *BNYPL* 60 (1956) 425-3, 487-507

    Commerce des Lumières: John Oswald and the British in Paris, 1790-1793. Columbia: University of Missouri Press, 1986

    'Immoral Acts of a Library Cormorant: the Extent of Coleridge's Contributions to the *Critical Review*'. *BNYPL* 63 (1959) 433-54, 515-30, 575-87

Estlin, John Prior. *The Nature and the Causes of Atheism, Pointed out in a Discourse, Delivered at the Chapel in Lewin's-Mead, Bristol*. Bristol, 1797

Evans, Bergen, and Hester Pinney. 'Racedown and the Wordsworths'. *RES* 8 (1932) 1-18

Fagin, N. Bryllion. *William Bartram: Interpreter of the American Landscape*. Baltimore: Johns Hopkins Press, 1933

Fairer, David. 'The Poems of Thomas Warton the Elder?' *RES* 26 (1975) 287-300, 395-406

Fawcett, Joseph. *The Art of War. A Poem*. London, 1795

Fawkes, Francis. *Original Poems and Translations*. London, 1761

    The Works of Anacreon, Sappho, Bion, Moschus and Musæus. London, 1760

Finch, Anne, Countess of Winchelsea. *Miscellany Poems, on Several Occasions*. London, 1713

Finch, John Alban. 'Wordsworth, Coleridge, and The Recluse, 1798-1814'. Ph.D. thesis, Cornell University, 1964

Fink, Z. S. *The Early Wordsworthian Milieu*. Oxford: Clarendon Press, 1958

    'Wordsworth and the English Republican Tradition'. *JEGP* 47 (1948) 107-26

Foxon, D. F. 'The Printing of *Lyrical Ballads*, 1798'. *The Library* 9 (1954) 221-41

Gibson, Warren E. 'An Unpublished Letter from John Thelwall to S. T. Coleridge'. *MLR* 25 (1930) 85-90

Gilbert, William. *The Hurricane: A Theosophical and Western Eclogue*. Bristol, 1796

Gilchrist, J., and W. J. Murray. *The Press in the French Revolution*. Melbourne and London: Cheshire & Ginn, 1971

Gill, Stephen. *William Wordsworth: A Life*. Oxford: Clarendon Press, 1989

Gilpin, William. *Observations, Relative Chiefly to Picturesque Beauty, Made in the Year 1772, in Several Parts of England; Particularly the Mountains and Lakes of Cumberland and Westmoreland*. 2 vols. London, 1786

    Observations, Relative Chiefly to Picturesque Beauty, Made in the Year 1776, on Several Parts of Great Britain; Particularly the High-Lands of Scotland. 2 vols. London, 1789

Gittings, Robert, and Jo Manton. *Dorothy Wordsworth*. Oxford: Clarendon Press, 1985

Godwin, William. *Caleb Williams*. Ed. David McCracken. London: Oxford University Press, 1970

Goldsmith, Oliver. *Collected Works of Oliver Goldsmith*. Ed. Arthur Friedman. 5 vols. Oxford: Clarendon Press, 1966

Graver, Bruce Edward. 'Wordsworth's Translations from Latin Poetry'. Ph.D. thesis, University of North Carolina, 1983

    'Wordsworth and the Romantic art of Translation'. *WC* 17 (1986) 169-74

Gray, Thomas. *The Poems of Mr Gray*. Ed. William Mason. 2 vols. York, 1775

Hayley, William. *A Poetical Epistle to an Eminent Painter*. London, 1778

Bibliography

The Poetical Works of William Hayley, Esq. 3 vols. Dublin, 1785

Hazlitt, William. *The Spirit of the Age.* London, 1825

Works. Ed. P. P. Howe. 21 vols. London: Dent, 1930-4

Hazlitt, W. C. *The Lambs: Their Lives, Friends and Correspondence.* London and New York, 1897

Hearn, Ronald B. *The Road to Rydal Mount: A Survey of William Wordsworth's Reading.* Salzburg: Universität Salzburg, 1973

Hentzner, Paul. *A Journey into England by Paul Hentzner.* Trans. Horace Walpole. Strawberry Hill, 1757

Paul Hentzner's Travels in England. Trans. Horace Walpole. London, 1797

Hibberd, John. *Salomon Gessner: His Creative Achievement and Influence.* Anglica Germanica Series 2. Cambridge: Cambridge University Press, 1976

Hill, Alan G. 'Wordsworth and the Two Faces of Machiavelli'. *RES* 31 (1980) 285-304

Horace. *The Odes and Epodes.* Trans. C. E. Bennett. Loeb Classical Library. Cambridge, Mass.: Harvard University Press. 1936

Christopher Smart's Verse Translation of Horaces' Odes: Text and Introduction. Ed. Arthur Sherbo. English Literary Studies Monograph Series No. 17. Victoria, B.C.: University of Victoria, 1979

The Odes, Epodes, and Carmen Seculare of Horace. Trans. Philip Watson. 2 vols. London, 1741

Hunt, Bishop C., Jr. 'Wordsworth and Charlotte Smith'. *WC* 1 (1970) 85-103

'Wordsworth's Marginalia in Dove Cottage, to 1800: A Study of his Relationship to Charlotte Smith and Milton'. B.Litt. thesis, University of Oxford, 1965

'Wordsworth's Marginalia on *Paradise Lost*'. *BNYPL* 73 (1969) 167-83

Isola, Agostino. *Pieces Selected From the Italian Poets.* 2nd edn. Cambridge, 1784

Jacobus, Mary. *Tradition and Experiment in Lyrical Ballads, 1798.* Oxford: Clarendon Press, 1976

'"Tintern Abbey" and Topographical Prose'. *N&Q* NS 18 (1971) 366-9

Jay, Eileen. *Wordsworth at Colthouse.* Kendal: Westmorland Gazette, 1981

Jaye, Michael C., 'William Wordsworth's Alfoxden Notebook: 1798', *The Evidence of the Imagination: Studies of Interactions between Life and Art in English Romantic Literature.* Ed. Donald H. Reiman, Michael C. Jaye, and Betty T. Bennett, with the assistance of Doucet Devin Fischer and Ricki B. Herzfeld. New York: New York University Press, 1978, pp. 42-85

Johnson, Samuel. *The Yale Edition of the Works of Samuel Johnson.* New Haven and London: Yale University Press

III-V. *The Rambler.* Ed. W. J. Bate and Albrecht B. Strauss. 3 vols. 1969

VI. *Poems.* Ed. E. L. McAdam Jr with George Milne. 1964

VII-VIII. *Johnson on Shakespeare.* Ed. Arthur Sherbo. 2 vols. 1968

Johnston, Kenneth R. 'Philanthropy or Treason? Wordsworth as "Active Partisan"'. *SIR* 25 (1986) 371-409

'The Politics of *Tintern Abbey*'. *WC* 14 (1983) 6-14

Jump, Harriet. '"That Other Eye": Wordsworth's 1794 Revisions of *An Evening Walk*'. *WC* 17 (1986) 156-63

194

Kaufman, Paul. *Borrowings from the Bristol Library 1773-1784: A Unique Record of Reading Vogues*. Charlottesville: Bibliographical Society of the University of Virginia, 1960

'The Community Library: A Chapter in English Social History'. *Transactions of the American Philosophical Society* 57 (1967) 7

'*The Hurricane* and the Romantic Poets'. *English Miscellany* 21 (1970) 99-115

Kelley, Paul. 'Charlotte Smith and *An Evening Walk*'. *N&Q* NS 29 (1982) 220

'Rousseau's *Discourse on the Origins of Inequality* and Wordsworth's *Salisbury Plain*'. *N&Q* NS 24 (1977) 323

'Wordsworth and Lucretius' *De Rerum Natura*'. *N&Q* NS 30 (1983) 219-22

'Wordsworth and Pope's *Epistle to Cobham*'. *N&Q* NS 28 (1981) 314-15

Kennedy, Michael L. *The Jacobin Clubs in the French Revolution: The First Years*. Princeton, N.J.: Princeton University Press, 1982

The Jacobin Clubs in the French Revolution: The Middle Years. Princeton, N.J.: Princeton University Press, 1988

Kinsley, James. 'Historical Allusions in *Absalom and Achitophel*'. *RES* 6 (1955) 291-7

Kipling, Charlotte. 'A Note on Wordsworth's Mathematical Education'. *CLB* NS 59 (July 1987) 96-102

Kitson, Peter. 'Coleridge's *The Plot Discovered*: A New Date'. *N&Q* NS 31 (1984) 57-8

Knight, Frida. *University Rebel*. London: Victor Gollancz, 1971

Lamb, Charles. *The Letters of Charles and Mary Anne Lamb 1796-1817*. Ed. Edwin J. Marrs, Jr. 3 vols. Ithaca, N.Y.: Cornell University Press, 1975-8

The Letters of Charles and Mary Lamb 1796-1843. Ed. E. V. Lucas. London: Dent & Methuen, 1935

Landon, Carol D. 'A Survey of an Early Manuscript of Wordsworth, Dove Cottage, MS 4, Dating from his School Days, and of Other Related Manuscripts, Together with an Edition of Selected Pieces'. Ph.D. thesis, University of London, 1962

'Some Sidelights on *The Prelude*'. *Bicentenary Wordsworth Studies*. Ed. Jonathan Wordsworth. Ithaca, N.Y.: Cornell University Press, 1970. Pp. 359-76

'Wordsworth, Coleridge, and the *Morning Post*: An Early Version of *The Seven Sisters*'. *RES* 11 (1960) 392-402

'Wordsworth's Racedown Period: Some Uncertainties Resolved'. *BNYPL* 68 (1964) 100-9

Langhorne, John. *The Country Justice*. London, 1774-7

Owen of Carron. London, 1778

Poetical Works. 2 vols. London, 1766

Lawrence, Berta. *Coleridge and Wordsworth in Somerset*. Newton Abbot: David & Charles, 1970

Legouis, Emile. *The Early Life of William Wordsworth: 1770-1798*. Trans. J. W. Matthews. London: J. M. Dent & Co., 1921

Letters and Papers on Agriculture, Planting, etc., Selected from the Correspondence of the Bath and West of England Society for the Encouragement of Agriculture, Arts, Manufactures and Commerce 6 (1792); 7 (1795)

Leyburn, Ellen D. 'Berkeleian Elements in Wordsworth's Thought'. *JEGP* 47 (1948) 14-28

Lienemann, Kurt. *Die Belesenheit von William Wordsworth*. Berlin: Mayer & Müller, 1908

Lindenberger, Herbert. *On Wordsworth's Prelude.* Princeton, N.J.: Princeton University Press, 1963

Little, Geoffrey L. 'A Note on Wordsworth and Blair'. *N&Q* NS 7 (1960) 245-5

Locke, Don. *A Fantasy of Reason: The Life & Thought of William Godwin.* London: Routledge & Kegan Paul, 1980

Locke, John. *An Essay Concerning Human Understanding.* Ed. Peter H. Nidditch. Oxford: Clarendon Press, 1975

Lockhart, John Gibson. *Memoirs of the Life of Sir Walter Scott.* 2nd edn. Edinburgh, 1842

Louvet de Couvray, Jean-Baptiste. *Narrative of the Dangers to Which I have been Exposed, since the 31st of May, 1793.* Trans. Anon. London, 1795

Lowes, John Livingstone. *The Road to Xanadu.* 2nd edn. London: Constable and Company Ltd., 1930

Lowth, Robert. *Lectures on the Sacred Poetry of the Hebrews.* Trans. George Gregory. London, 1787

Lyon, Judson Stanley. *The Excursion: A Study.* New Haven: Yale University Press, 1950

Lyttelton, George, Baron Lyttelton. *The Works of George Lord Lyttelton.* London, 1774

Mabey, Richard. *Gilbert White.* London: Century Hutchinson, 1986

MacGillivray, J. R. 'Wordsworth and J.-P. Brissot'. *TLS* (29 Jan. 1931) 79

Machiavelli, Niccolò. *Machiavel's Discourses upon the First Decade of T. Livius.* Trans. Edward Dacres. 2nd edn. London, 1674

Mackintosh, James. *Vindiciæ Gallicæ.* London, 1791

Maclean, C. M. 'Lewesdon Hill and Its Poet'. *Essays and Studies* 27 (1941) 30-40

Macpherson, James. *Fingal: An Ancient Epic Poem.* London, 1762

  Temora: An Ancient Epic Poem. London, 1763

Mallet, David. *The Works of Mr. Mallet: Consisting of Plays and Poems.* London, 1743

Mallet, Paul-Henri. *Northern Antiquities: or, a Description of the Manners, Customs, Religion and Laws of the Ancient Danes, and other Northern Nations; Including those of Our own Saxon Ancestors.* Trans. Thomas Percy. 2 vols. London, 1770

Marlowe, Christopher. *The Poems.* Ed. Millar Maclure. The Revels Plays. London: Methuen, 1968

Martin, C. G. 'Coleridge and William Crowe's *Lewesdon Hill'.* *Modern Language Review* 62 (1967) 400-6

Marvell, Andrew. *The Poems and Letters of Andrew Marvell.* Ed. H. M. Margoliouth, revised by Pierre Legouis with the collaboration of E. E. Duncan-Jones. 3rd edn. 2 vols. Oxford: Clarendon Press, 1971

  The Works of Andrew Marvell, Esq. Ed. Thomas Cooke. 2 vols. London, 1772

Mason, William. *Poems.* 4th edn. York, 1774

Massinger, Philip. *The Dramatic Works of Mr. Philip Massinger, Revised by Mr Coxeter.* 4 vols., London, 1759

  The Dramatick Works of Philip Massinger ... with Notes Critical and Explanatory by John Monck Mason. 4 vols., London, 1779

Matlak, Richard. 'Wordsworth's Reading of *Zoonomia* in Early Spring'. *WC* 21 (1990) 76-81

Mayo, Robert. 'Two Early Coleridge Poems'. *Bodleian Library Record* 5 (1956) 311-18

Mays, J. C. C. 'Coleridge's Borrowings From Jesus College Library, 1791-94'. *Transactions of the Cambridge Bibliographical Society* 8 (1981-5) 557-81

Memoirs of the Literary and Philosophical society of Manchester. 4 vols. Manchester, 1785, 1790

Mendilow, A. A. 'Robert Heron and Wordsworth's Critical Essays'. *MLR* 52 (1957) 329-38

Milton, John. *The Poetical Works of John Milton.* Ed. Helen Darbishire. 2 vols. Oxford: Clarendon Press, 1952-5

Paradise Lost. A Poem in Twelve Books. Ed. Thomas Newton. London, 1763

Monk, James Henry, Ed. *Cambridge Classical Examinations.* Cambridge: Cambridge University Press, 1824

Moore, John Robert. 'Wordsworth's Unacknowledged Debt to Macpherson's *Ossian*'. *PMLA* 40 (1925) 362-78

Moore, Thomas. *Memoirs, Journal, and Correspondence of Thomas Moore.* Ed. Rt. Hon. Lord John Russell, MP. 8 vols. London, 1853-6

Moorman, Mary. 'Ann Tyson's Ledger: An Eighteenth-Century Account Book'. *Transactions of the Cumberland and Westmorland Antiquarian and Archaeological Society* 50 (1950) 152-63

William Wordsworth: A Biography. 2 vols. Oxford: Clarendon Press, 1957-67

'Wordsworth's Commonplace Book'. *N&Q* NS 4 (1957) 400-5

Moschus. *The Idyllia, Epigrams, and Fragments, of Theocritus, Bion, and Moschus, with the Elegies of Tyrtæus.* Trans. Revd. Richard Polwhele. Exeter, 1786

Muirhead, James Patrick. 'A Day with Wordsworth'. *Blackwood's Magazine* 221 (1927) 728-43

Nabholtz, John R. 'Wordsworth and William Mason'. *RES* 15 (1964) 297-302

Nash, Treadway Russell. *Collections for the History and Antiquities of Worcestershire.* 2 vols. London, 1781-2

Nethercot, Arthur H. *The Road to Tryermaine: A Study of the History, Background, and Purposes of Coleridge's 'Christabel'.* Chicago: University of Chicago Press, 1939

Newlyn, Lucy. *Coleridge, Wordsworth, and the Language of Allusion.* Oxford: Clarendon Press, 1986

[Newton, John]. *An Authentic Narrative of Some Remarkable and Interesting Particulars in the Life of [the Revd. J. Newton] Communicated in a Series of Letters to The Revd. T. Haweis.* 3rd edn. London, 1765; 6th edn. London, 1786; 7th edn. London, 1790

Orsini, G. N. G. *Coleridge and German Idealism: A Study in the History of Philosophy with Unpublished Materials from Coleridge's Manuscripts.* Carbondale and Edwardsville, Illinois: Southern Illinois University Press, 1969

Owen, W. J. B. 'Literary Echoes in *The Prelude*'. *WC* 3 (1972) 3-16

'Two Addenda'. *WC* 13 (1982) 98

'Understanding *The Prelude*'. *WC* 22 (1991) 100-9

Wordsworth as Critic. London: Oxford University Press, 1969

Wordsworth's Preface to Lyrical Ballads. Copenhagen: Rosenkilde and Bagger, 1957

Ovid. *Ovid's Metamorphosis Englished.* Trans. George Sandys. Oxford, 1632

Pares, Richard. *A West-India Fortune.* London: Longmans, Green & Co., 1950

Parrish, Stephen. *The Art of the Lyrical Ballads.* Cambridge, Mass.: Harvard University Press, 1973

Percy, Thomas. *Reliques of Ancient English Poetry.* 3 vols. London, 1765

Philosophical Transactions of the Royal Society of London 75 (1785)

Pittman, Charles L. 'An Introduction to a Study of Wordsworth's Reading in Science'. *Furman Studies* 33 (1950) 27-60

Pollin, Burton R. 'Permutations of Names in *The Borderers*, or Hints of Godwin, Charles Lloyd, and a Real Renegade'. *WC* 4 (1973) 31-5

Pope, Alexander. *The Twickenham Edition of the Works of Alexander Pope.* General Ed. John Butt. London: Methuen and Co. Ltd

    I. *Pastoral Poetry and An Essay on Criticism.* Ed. E. Audra and Aubrey Williams. 1961

    II. *The Rape of the Lock.* Ed. Geoffrey Tillotson. 3rd edn. 1962

    III i. *An Essay on Man.* Ed. Maynard Mack. 1950

    III ii. *Epistles to Several Persons.* Ed. F. W. Bateson. 2nd edn. 1961

    IV. *Imitations of Horace.* Ed. John Butt. 2nd edn. 1953

    VII-VIII. *The Iliad.* Ed. Maynard Mack. 1967

    IX-X. *The Odyssey.* Ed. Maynard Mack. 1967

Popkin, Jeremy D. 'Journals: The New Face of News'. *Revolution in Print: The Press in France 1775-1800.* Ed. Robert Darnton and Daniel Roche. Berkeley, Calif.: University of California Press in collaboration with The New York Public Library, 1989. Pp. 141-64

Potts, Abbie Findlay. *Wordsworth's Prelude: A Study of Its Literary Form.* Ithaca, N.Y.: Cornell University Press, 1953

Radcliffe, Ann. *The Romance of the Forest.* 3 vols. London, 1791

Ramond de Carbonnières, Louis François Elizabeth. *Lettres de M. William Coxe à M. W. Melmoth sur l'état politique, civil, et naturel de la Suisse; traduits de l'Anglais, et augmentées des observations faites dans le même pays par le traducteur.* 2nd edn. 2 vols. 2nd edn. Paris, 1782

Reed, Mark L. *Wordsworth: The Chronology of the Early Years: 1770-1799.* Cambridge, Mass.: Harvard University Press, 1967

    Wordsworth: The Chronology of the Middle Years: 1800-1815. Cambridge, Mass.: Harvard University Press, 1974

    'Wordsworth on Wordsworth and Much Else: New Conversational Memoranda'. *Papers of the Bibliographical Society of America* 81 (1987) 451-8

Richardson, David Lester. *Literary Leaves or Prose and Verse.* London, 1840

Robberds, J. W., Ed. *A Memoir of the Life and Writings of the Late William Taylor of Norwich.* 2 vols. London, 1843

Robbins, Caroline. *The Eighteenth-Century Commonwealthman.* Cambridge, Mass.: Harvard University Press, 1959

Robinson, Henry Crabb. *Henry Crabb Robinson on Books and Their Writers.* Ed. Edith J. Morley. 3 vols. London: Dent, 1938

    Diary, Reminiscences, and Correspondence of Henry Crabb Robinson. Ed. Thomas Sadler. 3 vols. London, 1869

Roe, Nicholas. 'Citizen Wordsworth'. *WC* 14 (1983) 21-30

    The Politics of Nature. Macmillan Studies in Romanticism. London: Macmillan, 1992

    'Radical George: Dyer in the 1790s'. *CLB* NS 49 (Jan. 1985) 17-26

Wordsworth and Coleridge: The Radical Years. Oxford English Monograph Series. Oxford: Clarendon Press, 1988

'Wordsworth's Account of Beaupuy's Death'. *N&Q* NS 32 (1985) 337

Rogers, Samuel. *Recollections of the Table-Talk of Samuel Rogers. To Which is Added Porsoniana.* Ed. Revd. Alexander Dyce. London, 1856

The Pleasures of Memory. London, 1792

Rosset, Pierre Fulcrand de. *L'Agriculture. Poëme.* Paris, 1774-82

Rousseau, Jean Jacques. *Collection complete des œuvres de J. J. Rousseau, citoyen de Geneve.* 15 vols. Geneva, 1782

Russell, Thomas. *Sonnets and Miscellaneous Poems.* Ed. W. Howley. Oxford, 1789

Sanborn, Geoffrey. 'The Madness of Mutiny: Wordsworth, the *Bounty* and *The Borderers*'. *WC* 23 (1992) 35-42

Sandford, Mrs Henry. *Thomas Poole and his Friends.* 2 vols. London, 1888

Schiller, Johann Christoph Friedrich von. *The Robbers.* Trans. Alexander Fraser Tytler. London, 1792

Schneider, Ben Ross. *Wordsworth's Cambridge Education.* Cambridge: Cambridge University Press, 1957

Scott, John. *Critical Essays on Some of the Poems of Several English Poets.* London, 1785

The Poetical Works of John Scott Esq.. London, 1782

Scott, Robert Forsyth, Ed. *Admissions to the College of St John the Evangelist in the University of Cambridge. Part IV: July 1767-July 1802.* Cambridge: Cambridge University Press, 1931

Shakespeare, William. *The Riverside Shakespeare.* Ed. G. Blakemore Evans. Boston: Houghton Mifflin Company, 1974

Sharrock, Roger. 'Wordsworth and John Langhorne's *The Country Justice*'. *N&Q* NS 1 (1954) 302-4

Shaver, Chester L. 'Wordsworth's Debt to Thomas Newton'. *MLN* 62 (1947) 344

'Wordsworth's Vaudracour and Wilkinson's Wanderer'. *RES* 12 (1961) 55-7

Shaw, Cuthbert. *Monody to the Memory of a Young Lady who Died in Child-bed.* London, 1768

Sheats, Paul D. *The Making of Wordsworth's Poetry, 1785-1798.* Cambridge, Mass.: Harvard University Press, 1973

Sidney, Algernon. *Discourses Concerning Government, by Algernon Sidney, Son to Robert Earl of Leicester, and Ambassador from the Commonwealth of England to Charles Gustavus King of Sweden. Published from an Original Manuscript of the Author.* London, 1698

Sidney, Sir Philip. *The Poems of Sir Philip Sidney.* Ed. William A. Ringler, Jr. Oxford: Clarendon Press, 1962

Simmons, Jack. *Southey.* London: Collins, 1945

Smith, Charlotte. *Elegiac Sonnets.* 3rd edn. London, 1786

Smith, H. Rossiter. 'Wordsworth and his Italian Studies'. *N&Q* 198 (1953) 248-50

Smollett, Tobias. *The Expedition of Humphry Clinker.* Ed. Lewis M. Knapp. London: Oxford University Press, 1966

Plays and Poems. London, 1784

Southey, Robert. *New Letters of Robert Southey 1792-1838.* Ed. Kenneth Curry. 2 vols. New York and London: Columbia University Press, 1965
The Life and Correspondence of the Late Robert Southey. Ed. Revd. Charles Cuthbert Southey. 6 vols. London, 1850
Metrical Tales and Other Poems. London, 1805
Poems. Bristol, 1797
The Poetical Works of Robert Southey. Paris: A. & W. Galignani, 1829
Review of Francis Wrangham, *Poems* (1795). *Annual Review* 1 (1803) 655-7
Selections from the Letters of Robert Southey, &c. &c. &c. ed. John Wood Warter. 4 vols. London, 1856
Spenser, Edmund. *The Works of Edmund Spenser: A Variorum Edition.* Ed. Edwin Greenlaw, Charles Grosvenor Osgood, Frederick Morgan Padelford, Ray Heffner. 2 vols. Baltimore: Johns Hopkins Press, 1943-7
Stallknecht, Newton P. *Strange Seas of Thought: Studies in William Wordsworth's Philosophy of Man and Nature.* Bloomington, Ind.: Indiana University Press, 1958
Stein, Edwin. *Wordsworth's Art of Allusion.* University Park, Penn.: The Pennsylvania State University Press, 1988
Stewart, Lawrence D. *John Scott of Amwell.* Berkeley and Los Angeles: University of California Press, 1956
Stock, John Edmonds. *Memoirs of the Life of Thomas Beddoes.* London, 1811
Stockwell, A. W. 'Wordsworth's Politics'. B.Litt. thesis, University of Oxford, 1950
Sturrock, June. 'Wordsworth's Italian Teacher'. *Bulletin of the John Rylands University Library of Manchester* 67 (1985) 797-812
'Wordsworth: An Early Borrowing from Dante'. *N&Q* NS 27 (1980) 204-5
Sultana, Donald. *Samuel Taylor Coleridge in Malta and Italy.* New York: Barnes and Noble, 1969
Swift, Jonathan. *The Correspondence of Jonathan Swift.* Ed. Harold Williams. 5 vols. Oxford: Clarendon Press, 1963-5
Letters, Written by the Late Jonathan Swift, D.D. Dean of St Patrick's, Dublin, and Several of his Friends. From the Year 1703 to 1740. Published from the Originals; with Notes Explanatory and Historical, by John Hawkesworth, L.L.D. 3 vols. London, 1766
Tanner, J. R., Ed. *The Historical Register of the University of Cambridge.* Cambridge: Cambridge University Press, 1917
Tasso, Torquato. *Jerusalem Delivered; An Heroick Poem: Translated from the Italian of Torquato Tasso.* Trans. John Hoole. 2 vols. London, 1763
The Gerusalemme Liberata of Tasso. Ed. Agostino Isola. 2 vols. Cambridge, 1786
Theocritus. *Theocritus, Edited with a Translation and Commentary.* Trans. A. S. F. Gow. 2 vols. 2nd edn. Cambridge: Cambridge University Press, 1952
Thomas, W. K., and Warren U. Ober. *A Mind For Ever Voyaging: Wordsworth at Work Portraying Newton and Science.* Edmonton, Alta.: The University of Alberta Press, 1989
Thompson, E. P. 'Disenchantment or Default? A Lay Sermon'. *Power and Consciousness.* Ed. Conor Cruise O'Brien and William Dean Vanech. London: University of London Press, 1969. Pp. 149-81

'Wordsworth's Crisis'. *London Review of Books* 10 (8 Dec. 1988) 3-6

Thompson, T. W. *Wordsworth's Hawkshead.* Ed. Robert Woof. London: Oxford University Press, 1970

Thomson, James. *Liberty, The Castle of Indolence, and Other Poems.* Ed. James Sambrook. Oxford: Clarendon Press, 1986

The Seasons. Ed. James Sambrook. Oxford: Clarendon Press, 1981

Tickell, Thomas. *The Poetical Works of Thomas Tickell.* Edinburgh, 1781

Trenchard, John, and Thomas Gordon. *Cato's Letters; or, Essays on Liberty, Civil and Religious.* 3rd edn. 4 vols. London, 1733

Trott, Nicola. '*The Old Cumberland Beggar*: The Poor Law and the Law of Nature'. Lecture, Wordsworth Winter School 1989

'Wordsworth and the Picturesque: A Strong Infection of the Age'. *WC* 18 (1987) 114-21

'Wordsworth's Revisionary Reading'. D.Phil. thesis, University of Oxford, 1990

Trott, Nicola, and Duncan Wu. 'Three Sources for Wordsworth's *Prelude* Cave'. *N&Q* NS 38 (1991) 298-9

Tyson, Gerald P. *Joseph Johnson: A Liberal Publisher.* Iowa City: University of Iowa Press, 1979

Underwood, M. G. 'A Tutor's Lot'. *The Eagle* 69 (1984) 3-8

Virgil. *Eclogues, Georgics, Aeneid, 1-6.* Trans. H. Rushton Fairclough. Loeb Classical Library. 2nd edn. Cambridge, Mass.: Harvard University Press. 1986

Aeneid 7-12, The Minor Poems. Trans. H. Rushton Fairclough. Loeb Classical Library. 2nd edn. Cambridge, Mass.: Harvard University Press. 1986

The Bucolicks of Virgil, with an English Translation and Notes. Trans. John Martyn. 2nd edn. London, 1749

The Georgicks of Virgil, with an English Translation and Notes. Trans. John Martyn. 3rd edn. London, 1750

Georgics Books I-IV. Ed. Richard F. Thomas. Cambridge Greek and Latin Classics. 2 vols. Cambridge: Cambridge University Press. 1988

The Works of Virgil. In English Verse. The Aeneid Translated By the Rev. Mr. Christopher Pitt, The Eclogues and Georgics, with Notes on the Whole, By the Rev. Mr Joseph Warton. Trans. Joseph Warton. 4 vols. London, 1758

Walpole, Horace, 4th Earl of Orford. *The Castle of Otranto.* Ed. W. S. Lewis. The World's Classics Series. Oxford: Oxford University Press, 1982

Warner, Richard. *A Walk Through Wales, in August 1797.* Bath, 1798

Warton, Joseph. *Odes on Various Subjects.* London, 1746

Warton, Thomas. *The Pleasures of Melancholy.* London, 1747

West, Thomas. *A Guide to the Lakes.* 3rd edn. London, 1784

Whalley, George. 'The Bristol Library Borrowings of Southey and Coleridge, 1793-8'. *The Library* 4 (1949) 114-32

'Coleridge Marginalia Lost'. *The Book Collector* 17 (1968) 428-42

Wilkinson, C. S. *The Wake of the Bounty.* Cassell & Co. Ltd.: London, 1953.

Wilkinson, Joshua Lucock. *Political Facts, Collected in a Tour, in the Month of August, September, and October, 1793, Along the Frontiers of France; with Reflexions on the Same.* London, 1793

The Wanderer. London, 1795

trans. *State of France, in May, 1794, by Le Comte de Montgaillard.* London, 1794
Williams, Helen Maria. *Poems.* 2 vols. London, 1786
Williams, John. *Wordsworth: Romantic Poetry and Revolution Politics.* Manchester: Manchester University Press, 1989
Wither, George. *Juvenilia.* London, 1622
Wollstonecraft, Mary. *Letters Written During a Short Residence in Sweden, Norway and Denmark.* London, 1796
Woof, Robert Samuel. 'The Literary Relations of Wordsworth and Coleridge, 1795-1803: Five Studies'. Ph.D. thesis, University of Toronto, 1959
'Wordsworth's Poetry and Stuart's Newspapers: 1797-1803'. *SIB* 15 (1962) 149-89
'Peter Bell'. Lecture, Wordsworth Winter School 1991. Tape recording published by The Wordsworth Trust, 1991
Wordsworth, Christopher, Jr. *Memoirs of William Wordsworth.* 2 vols. London, 1851
Wordsworth, Jonathan. *Ancestral Voices: Fifty Books from the Romantic Period.* Spelsbury: Woodstock Books, 1991
The Music of Humanity. New York: J.& J. Harper, 1969
William Wordsworth: The Borders of Vision. Oxford: Clarendon Press, 1982
Worthington, Jane. *Wordsworth's Reading of Roman Prose.* Yales Studies in English 102. New Haven: Yale University Press, 1946
[Wrangham, Francis.] *Poems.* London, 1795 [actually 1802]
Wu, Duncan. 'The Ancient Mariner: A Wordsworthian Source'. *N&Q* NS 38 (1991) 301
'A Chronological Annotated Edition of Wordsworth's Poetry and Prose: 1785-1790'. D.Phil. thesis, University of Oxford, 1990
'Chronology 1770-1850', *William Wordsworth and the Age of British Romanticism*, Jonathan Wordsworth, Michael C. Jaye, and Robert Woof, with the assistance of Peter Funnell. New Brunswick and London: Rutgers University Press, 1987. Pp. 239-49
'Cottle's *Alfred*: Another Coleridge-Inspired Epic'. *CLB* NS 73 (Jan. 1991) 19-21
'The Death of Death'. Review of Edward Young, *Night Thoughts*. *TLS* (9-15 Feb. 1990) 150
'The Grande Chartreuse and the Development of Wordsworth's *Recluse*'. *CLB* NS 71 (July 1990) 235-46
'*Lyrical Ballads* (1798): The Beddoes Copy'. *The Library* (forthcoming 1993)
'The Original Peter Bell'. *N&Q* NS 37 (1990) 411-12
'Tasso, Wordsworth, and the fragmentary drafts of 1788'. *N&Q* NS 37 (1990) 409-11
'Three translations of Virgil read by Wordsworth in 1788'. *N&Q* NS 37 (1990) 407-9
'William Wordsworth and the Farish Brothers'. *Bodleian Library Record* 14 (1991) 99-101
'Wordsworth/Lamb/Elton: A New Literary Connection'. *CLB* NS 68 (Oct. 1989) 129-31
'Wordsworth's Copy of Smart's Horace'. *N&Q* NS 38 (1991) 303-5
'Wordsworth's *Orpheus and Eurydice*: The Unpublished Final Line'. *N&Q* NS 38 (1991) 301-2
'Wordsworth's Poetry of Grief'. *WC* 21 (1990) 115-17
'Wordsworth's Reading of Ahmad Ardabîlî'. *N&Q* NS 37 (1990) 412
'Wordsworth's Reading of Bowles'. *N&Q* NS 36 (1989) 166-7
'Wordsworth's Reading of Marvell'. *N&Q* (forthcoming)

Bibliography

'Wordsworth's Reading of Swift's Letters', *N&Q* NS 39 (1992) 161-2
'Wordsworth's Translation of Callistratus: A Possible Redating'. *N&Q* NS 38 (1991) 302-3
'Wordsworth and *The Morning Chronicle*'. *N&Q* (forthcoming, March 1993)
Yarnall, Ellis. *Wordsworth and the Coleridges*. London and New York: Macmillan, 1899
Young, Edward. *Night Thoughts*. Ed. Stephen Cornford. Cambridge: Cambridge University Press, 1989
Zall, Paul M. 'The Cool World of Samuel Taylor Coleridge: Vicesimus Knox, Elegant Activist'. *WC* 10 (1979) 345-7
ed. *Coleridge's Sonnets from Various Authors bound with Revd. W. L. Bowles' Sonnets*. Glendale, California: La Siesta Press, 1968

4. Bibliographies, catalogues, etc.

Berrecloth, B. 'Archbishop Sandys' Endowed School, Hawkshead: The Complete Library Catalogue'. Unpublished. Not dated
Bicknell, Peter. *The Picturesque Scenery of the Lake District 1752-1855: A Bibliographical Study*. Winchester: St Paul's Bibliographies, 1990
Broughton, Leslie Nathan. *The Wordsworth Collection Formed by Cynthia Morgan St John and Given to Cornell University by Victor Emanuel*. Ithaca, N.Y.: Cornell University Press, 1931
Butler, James A. 'Wordsworth in Philadelphia Area Libraries, 1787-1850'. *WC* 4 (1973) 41-64
Coffman, Ralph J. *Coleridge's Library: A Bibliography of Books Owned or Read by Samuel Taylor Coleridge*. Boston, Mass.: G. K. Hall & Co., 1987
Cole, John. *A Bibliographical and Descriptive Tour from Scarborough to the Library of a Philobiblist, in it's Neighbourhood*. Scarborough, 1824
Dendurent, H. O. 'The Coleridge Collection in Victoria University Library, Toronto'. *WC* 5 (1974) 225-86
Eddy, Donald D. *A Bibliography of John Brown*. New York: Bibliographical Society of America, 1971
Healey, George A. *The Cornell Wordsworth Collection*. Ithaca, N.Y.: Cornell University Press, 1957
[Johnes, Revd. Thomas]. *A Catalogue of the Books Belonging to the Bristol Library Society; to which are prefixed The Rules of the Institution, and A List of the Subscribers*. Bristol, 1798
Martin, André, and Gérard Walter. *Catalogue de L'histoire de la Révolution Française*. Vol. 5: *Ecrits de la période révolutionnaire: journaux et almanachs*. Paris: Bibliothèque Nationale, 1943
Martin, Edward A. *A Bibliography of Gilbert White*. London: Halton & Co., Ltd., 1934
Martin, John. *Bibliographical Catalogue of Privately Printed Books*. 2nd edn. London, 1854
Noyes, Russell. *The Indiana Wordsworth Collection: A Catalogue*. Boston, Mass.: G. K. Hall & Co., 1978

Park, Roy, Ed. *Sales Catalogues of Libraries of Eminent Persons: Poets and Men of Letters* Vol. 9: *Wordsworth, Southey, Moore, Barton, Haydon.* London: Mansell with Sotheby Parke Bernet Publications, 1974

Patton, Cornelius Howard. *The Amherst Wordsworth Collection.* Hartford, Conn.: The Trustees of Amherst College, 1936

Sadleir, Michael. *Archdeacon Francis Wrangham 1769-1842. The Library,* Supplement 12. Oxford: The Bibliographical Society, 1937

Shaver, Chester L., and Alice C. Shaver. *Wordsworth's Library: A Catalogue.* New York, N.Y.: Garland Publishing, Inc., 1979

Sotheby, S. Leigh. *Catalogue of the First Portion of the Extensive and Valuable Library of the Late Venerable Archdeacon Wrangham, F.R.S.* London, 1843

Catalogue of the Second Portion of the Extensive and Valuable Library of the Late Venerable Archdeacon Wrangham, F.R.S. London, 1843

[Soulby, Anthony]. *A Catalogue of the Circulating Library, of Anthony Soulby, Printer & Bookseller, Penrith.* Penrith, 1808. (Cumbria Record Office, Carlisle: D/Hud/17/132/2)

Wrangham, Francis. *The English Portion of The Library of the Ven. Francis Wrangham, M.A., F.R.S., Archdeacon of Cleveland.* Malton: privately published by the author in an edition of seventy copies, 1826

Wu, Duncan. 'Basil Montagu's Manuscripts'. *Bodleian Library Record* 14 (1992) 246-51

'The Hawkshead School Library in 1788: A Catalogue'. *Transactions of the Cumberland and Westmorland Antiquarian and Archaeological Society* 91 (1991) 173-97

'The Wordsworth Family Library at Cockermouth: Towards a Reconstruction'. *The Library* 14 (1992) 127-35

Index

Hearne, Samuel, *A Journey from Prince of Wales's Fort*, 52, 72-3
Hederich, Benjamin, *Graecum lexicon manuale*, 73, 170
Helvellyn, 141
Helm Crag, 147
Helvetius, 172
Hentzner, Paul, *A Journey into England* tr. Horace Walpole, 73-4
Herd, David, ed. *Ancient and Modern Scottish Songs*, 74; *The Cruel Mother*, 74
Herodotus, 165
Heron, Robert, *Observations in Scotland*, 74
Herschel, William, 183
Hibberd, John, 63 and n, 180-1
Hill, Alan G., 91
Hipparchus, 24
Holbach, Paul Heinrich Dietrich, Baron d', *Système de la Nature*, 74-5
Holcroft, Thomas, 60, 103, 139; *The Man of Ten Thousand*, 75
Home, Everard, 183
Home, John, *Douglas*, 75
Homer, 122, 165; '2 Vol Homer', 75, 170; *Iliad*, 75; *Odyssey*, 75; *Iliad* and *Odyssey* tr. Alexander Pope, 75-6
Hondeschoote, Battle of, 89
Hoole, John, *see* Tasso
Horace, 11, 17, 162, 165, 166; Horatian style, 51, 122; *Ars Poetica* and *Epistles* I or II, 76, 167; *Ode to Apollo*, 76; *Odes* tr. Philip Watson, 76 and n; *Works*, 76-7; *Works* tr. Christopher Smart, 76-7; ode to the Bandusian fountain, 76
Hortensius, *Deinology*, 173
Howley, W., *see* Russell, Thomas
Hume, David, *History of England*, 163; *see also* Barlow, Joel, *Hume's History of England*
Hunt, Bishop, 100, 120, 126, 128
Hurdis, James, poetry, 158
Hutchinson family, 103
Hutchinson, Mary, *see* Wordsworth, Mary (W's wife)
Hutchinson, Sara, 9; copy of Newton's edition of *Paradise Lost*, 99-100
Hutchinson, William, *Excursion to the Lakes*, 77

Ianson, Mr William, 41
Ilam, near Ashbourne, 36 and n; W visits, 36
Inscriptions, 80, 126; presentation, 2, 5, 53, 104 and n, 109, 118; ownership, 7, 9, 15, 28, 43, 48, 50, 52, 61, 76, 87, 99-100, 109, 111-12, 120, 128, 140, 141, 143, 144, 153, 154
Ireland, Samuel William Henry, *Vortigern and Rowena*, 158

Irton, Edmund, 27
Isola, Agostino, 7, 91, 94, 111, 131, 134; editor of Tasso and Ariosto, 134; *Pieces Selected from the Italian Poets*, 77
Italian books, 45; 'Italian Gram.', 77-8

Jackson, H. J., 140, 151
Jacobus, Mary, 2, 9, 20, 21, 53, 58, 66, 73n, 74, 93, 101, 107, 137, 143-4
James I, *Demonology*, 78, 97, 171, 172
Jay, Eileen, 163 and n
Jaye, Michael C., 81 and n
Jeffrey, Edward, 73
Johnes, Revd. Thomas, *Catalogue of ... the Bristol Library Society*, 176
Johnson, Joseph, 35, 62n, 68, 77, 81, 89, 94, 110, 118, 122, 127, 152, 157, 158, 159, 160; introduced to W, 3 and n; meets W in 1798, 4, 26, 94, 101-2, 138; publishes C's *Fears in Solitude*, 33
Johnson, Samuel, 82, 122, 158; poetry, especially *The Vanity of Human Wishes* and *London*, 79; prose, 78; *Rasselas*, 78; *The Vanity of Human Wishes* (and other poems), 78-9; *see also* Juvenal
Johnston, Kenneth, 112
Jones, Robert, 56, 166, 167-8
Jones, William, *Institutes of Hindu Law*, 42
Jonson, Ben, 2
Journal du département de Loir-et-Cher, 5
Jump, Harriet, 1
Juvenal, 17, 166; *Mores Hominum* tr. Sir Robert Stapylton, 79-80, 172; *Satire* VIII tr. W and Wrangham, 78, 79, 171; *Satires* III-XV, 79, 80, 168; *Satires*, 80; *Satyrae*, 80

Kant, Immanuel, 108; *Project for a Perpetual Peace*, 81; works including *The Critique of Judgement*, 80-1; *see also* Nitsch, F. A., *and* Willich, A. F. M.
Kaufman, Paul, 63, 176n
Keate, George, *Sketches from Nature*, 174
Kelley, Paul, 90, 113, 119
Kelly, John, 166
Kelly, Michael, 87
Kendal Newsroom, 163 and n
Kendal Record Office, 164
Kennedy, Michael, 5 and n, 62n
Kerrigan, John, 8
Keswick, 19
King's School, The, Canterbury, 23
King's Theatre, Haymarket, 57
Kipling, Charlotte, 166n
Kitson, Peter, 31
Klopstock, Friedrich Gottlieb, 4, 53, 54, 66, 67, 69 80, 81, 86, 102, 108, 119, 121-2, 148; gives book

Index

216

217

Index

144

Wedgwood, John, 45

Wedgwood, Josiah, 86, 158, 179, 181

Weekly Entertainer, The, 53, 120, 144-6; *Address to Silence*, 145-6; 'Christian's own Account', 145; extracts from Helen Maria Williams' *Letters*, 150

West, Thomas, *A Guide to the Lakes*, 19, 70, 146-7

Westminster School, 67, 158

Whalley, George, 14, 38, 173, 174n, 176; 'Lost List', 151

Whig Party, 104

White, Benjamin, 147

White, Gilbert, *Natural History of Selborne*, 147

Wieland, Christoph Martin, 68; *Oberon*, 102, 147-8; tr. William Sotheby, 148

Wiener, Leo, 21

Wildman, Thomas, 157

Wilkinson, C. S., 85, 145

Wilkinson, Joshua Lucock, 104; journals in MS, 148-9; *Political Facts*, 104, 149; *State of France*, 149; *The Wanderer*, 148

Williams, Edward, *Poems*, 161

Williams, Helen Maria, *American Tale, An*, 127; *Farewell, for Two Years, to England, A*, 150; *Letters Containing a Sketch of the Politics of France*, 150; *Letters Written in France*, 135, 150; *Part of an Irregular Fragment*, 149; *Peru*, 127; *Poems, in Two Volumes*, 54, 149; *see also* St Pierre, Jacques Henri Bernardin de

Williams, John, 19, 42, 84 and n

Willich, A. F. M., 102 and n; *Elements of the Critical Philosophy*, 81 and n

Willymott, William, *English Particles*, 164 and n

Wilson, Christopher, 79

Windermere, Lake, 1

Windy Brow, Keswick, 16, 71, 77, 104, 111, 120, 128

Wither, George, Lamb's copy of, 151n; *Eclogue 4*, 151; *Juvenilia*, 150-1; *The Shepherd's Hunting*, 150-1

Wolcot, John ('Peter Pindar'), 17; works, 151

Wollstonecraft, Mary, *Letters Written During a Short Residence*, 152-3, 172; *Vindication of the Rights of Men*, 152, 172; *Vindication of the Rights of Woman*, 139, 172, 175

Wood, James, 60

Woof, Pamela, 2, 26, 118, 149

Woof, Robert, 7, 12, 24, 25, 30n, 63, 65, 67, 71, 74, 81, 106, 110, 111, 114, 115, 117, 164 and n

Wordsworth children, 8

Wordsworth, Christopher (W's brother), 55, 85n, 88, 147, 164, 169-70; W uses his book, 82-3; uses W's book, 155

Wordsworth, Christopher Jr (son of Christopher Wordsworth), 99, 117, 123, 132

Wordsworth, Dora (W's daughter), 121, 128

Wordsworth, Dora (W's grand-daughter), 15

Wordsworth, Dorothy (W's sister), 2, 7, 8, 11, 15, 18, 20, 21, 23, 31, 32, 40, 45, 64, 67, 70, 89, 103, 117, 118, 133, 150, 166, 179; learns Italian, 16, 45-6, 111, 135; buys books, 21, 23, 111; journal, 52, 86, 149; inherits JW Sr's books, 58, 72, 85-6; involved in Norwich literary society, 68; transcriptions by, 74, 94-5, 98, 107, 145; given books by W, 64, 75; translates Lessing, 86; Alfoxden Journal in MS, 153; prudishness of, 138n

Wordsworth, John Sr (W's father), 15, 61, 149; ownership inscription of, 141; Library, 26, 28, 58, 74, 105, 133; accounts of, 85, 163

Wordsworth, John (W's brother), gives W Anderson's *British Poets*, 5; sends W copies of *Morning Chronicle*, 104; ownership inscription of, 141

Wordsworth, John (W's son), 15, 47

Wordsworth, Jonathan, 8, 48, 62-3, 68, 70, 99-100, 120 and n, 130

Wordsworth Library, Grasmere, 2, 5, 9, 17, 21, 28, 29, 30, 47, 51, 73, 75, 85, 100, 114, 129

Wordsworth, Mary (W's wife), 15, 31, 120; reads Daniel, 43; Memoranda of the Hutchinson and Monkhouse Families, 131

Wordsworth, Miss (*Albert Herring*), 60

Wordsworth, Richard (W's brother), 75, 148, 149, 150, 163; W leaves books with, 7, 77, 103, 134; asks W to return books, 16; ownership inscription of, 50, 61, 141; leaves Hawkshead, 90; forwards books to W, 77-8, 120

Wordsworth, Richard of Branthwaite (W's cousin), 15, 28, 58-9, 75, 85-6, 90

Wordsworth, Richard of Whitehaven, accounts of, 75, 89-90, 169-70

Wordsworth, William, copies of books formerly owned or used by, 5, 7, 9, 15, 17, 21, 28, 29, 42-3, 49-50, 51-2, 61, 76, 77-8, 80, 99-100, 109, 111-12, 114, 118, 128, 129, 140-1, 143, 144, 154-5; visits France in 1802, 17, 114; visits Wrangham in 1800, 18; Album for Lady Mary Lowther, 14, 99, 151; reads C's books, 43, 86, 116; transcription by, 81-2; takes possession of C's books, 86, 136, 148, 151; Italian studies at Cambridge, 45, 77-8; visits North Wales, 56; Commonplace Book, 74; inherits father's books, 74; classical education, 165-6; books purchased for, 169-70; visits C, 177; visits Southey, 177

POETRY

Address to the Ocean, 30, 145

Adventures on Salisbury Plain, 57, 58, 84, 92, 106, 152-3

218

Index

Index